Kung Fu (I)

功夫(一)

只要功夫深，铁杵磨成针。

Zhǐyào gōngfu shēn, tiěchǔ móchéng zhēn.

With perseverance an iron pestle can be ground into a needle.
("Little strokes fell great oaks.")

Related Titles Published by The Chinese University Press

Gateway to Chinese Language (I & II)
《汉语入门》(上、下册)
By Jing-Heng Sheng Ma 马盛静恒 著 (2006)

Gateway to Chinese Character Writing
《汉字入门》
By Jing-Heng Sheng Ma 马盛静恒 著 (2006)

Business Chinese
《商业汉语》
By Jiaying Howard and Tsengtseng Chang
庄稼婴、张增增 合著 (2005)

Zhongda Chinese-English Dictionary
《中大汉英词典》
By Liang Derun and Zheng Jiande
梁德润、郑建德 主编 (2003)

Business Chinese: An Advanced Reader
《商贸汉语高级读本》
By Songren Cui 崔颂人 著 (2003)

Talk Mandarin Today
By Hong Xiao (2003)

Chinese Language and Culture: An Intermediate Reader
《汉语与文化读本》
By Weijia Huang and Qun Ao 黄伟嘉、敖群 合著 (2002)

A Student Handbook for Chinese Function Words
《汉语虚词学习手册》
By Jiaying Howard 庄稼婴 著 (2002)

A Learners' Handbook of Modern Chinese Written Expression
《现代汉语书面语学习手册》
By Yu Feng 冯禹 著 (2000)

A Guide to Proper Usage of Spoken Chinese
《汉语口语指引》
By Tian Shou-he 田寿和 著 (2005 simplified Chinese edition)

Chinese-English Dictionary
《汉英小字典》
Edited by Chik Hon Man and Ng Lam Sim Yuk
植汉民、吴林婵玉 合编
(1994 second edition)

A Practical Chinese Grammar
By Hung-nin Samuel Cheung
in collaboration with
Sze-yun Liu and Li-lin Shih (1994)

Fifty Patterns of Modern Chinese
By Dezhi Han (1993)

English-Cantonese Dictionary
《英粤字典》
Edited by New Asia–Yale-in-China Chinese Language Center,
The Chinese University of Hong Kong (1991)

Kung Fu (I)

功夫 (一)

An Elementary Chinese Text

By John C. Jamieson and Lin Tao

with the special collaboration of Zhao Shuhua

The Chinese University Press

Kung Fu (I): An Elementary Chinese Text
By John C. Jamieson and Lin Tao,
with the special collaboration of Zhao Shuhua

ISBN: 978-962-201-867-9

First edition 2002
Second printing 2006
Third printing 2009
Fourth printing 2013
Fifth printing 2016

The Chinese University Press
The Chinese University of Hong Kong
Sha Tin, N.T., Hong Kong
Fax: +852 2603 7355
E-mail: cup@cuhk.edu.hk
Website: www.chineseupress.com

Printed in Hong Kong

Contents
目 录

Lesson Text 课 文

Introduction
简介

The *Kung Fu* series began as a concept at a conference at the University of California, Berkeley about a decade ago. The authors agreed then to combine the resources at both their universities, Peking University and Berkeley, to produce a set of texts that would have fresh and accurate language, communicate effectively with an international audience, have clear and orderly structural explanations, and contain a good number of contextual, task-based exercises for stimulating students to higher levels of fluency. For the convenience of instructors, structural and exercise explanations would be in Chinese as well as English. Later, when the Berkeley portion was shifted to The Chinese University of Hong Kong, work started in earnest. Teams at both institutions whose members' names have been listed in our "Acknowledgments" assisted the authors. They were then joined by Professor Zhao Shuhua of the Beijing Language and Culture University, a leading grammarian and richly experienced Chinese teaching and testing specialist.

The Chinese Language

Prior to describing *Kung Fu*'s content and strategies, users of our text will benefit from a sketch of the language they are to study, its contours as a spoken medium and its script. Chinese is the most widely spoken language in the world, the number of native speakers approximating 1 billion. It is segmented into seven regional forms or dialects: Mandarin, Wu (Yangtze Delta region), Xiang (Hunan), Kejia (widespread, with concentrations in Guangdong, Fujian and Jiangxi and Sichuan), Gan (Hubei, Jiangxi), Min (Fujian) and Yue (Guangdong, Hong Kong). Mandarin is the most widely distributed, and is spoken throughout China, with a population of speakers of over 700 million. The other six dialects, as noted, are concentrated in the southeastern part of the country. There are major pronunciation differences between the dialects (which, for the most part, are not mutually intelligible), but sound structure, word formation and sentence structure are basically uniform. Putonghua, "Common Speech", is also referred to as Guoyu "National Language", Guanhua "Mandarin", or Huayu "Chinese". It is based on standard Beijing pronunciation and is the common language of communication throughout China. It is the language of this text's concern.

Chinese is a tonal language, where the same syllable is pronounced with fixed high, low, rising or falling pitches to distinguish meaning. For example, ma means "mother" when pronounced with a high, level tone, and "scold, curse" if the tone falls to a low pitch. Dialects have different numbers of tones, Cantonese (i.e. Yue) with nine, Shanghai with seven and Putonghua with only four. We distinguish the four tones in Putonghua with diacritics, or symbols above the main vowel as follows: mā 妈 "mother", má 麻 "hemp", mǎ 马 "horse", mà 骂 "scold, curse".

The Chinese syllable is both simple in structure and clearly demarked. Most syllables must have a vowel, and consonants are predominantly at the front. In Putonghua, consonants that can close a syllable are rare and limited to the two nasal sounds "-n" and "-ng". Consonant clusters such as "sk", "fl", and "str" do not exist.

Chinese syllables are traditionally divided into two parts, initials and finals. The initial is the opening consonant, while the final is all that follows the initial. It can be a single vowel, a vowel cluster or a vowel or vowels with an ending consonant. For example, in the syllables ta 他, gāo 高, bān 班, liàng 亮 and suān 酸, the opening consonants "t", "g", "b", "l" and "s" are initials. What follows them, "a", "ao", "an", "ang", and "uan" are the finals. A syllable that lacks a beginning consonant is said to have "zero" initial, such as ài 爱 "love, care for" or ǒu 藕 "lotus root".

There are twenty-one initials in Putonghua and thirty-five finals, and their combinations have a very high degree of regularity. As an example, the initials "g", "k" and "h" cannot combine with the final "i" or finals that begin with "i". Syllables such as "gi", "kia", or "hin" do not exist.

Words in Chinese are primarily monosyllabic or disyllabic. They are constructed of morphemes, and Chinese morphemes are in large measure monosyllabic. Some morphemes are words themselves, such as dà 大 "big", rén 人 "man" or tīng 听 "to listen". Others must be part of combinations of morphemes, even though they may have meanings. Yǔ 语 "speech" is an example that cannot stand alone in modern Chinese, but must be linked with other morphemes such as yǔyán 语言 "language", yǔfǎ 语法 "grammar", yǔdiào 语调 "intonation", Yīngyǔ 英语 "English", kǒuyǔ 口语 "spoken language", or chéngyǔ 成语 "idiom". Morphemes that are themselves words may also combine with other morphemes to form compound words. An example is the high frequency word rén 人 which is part of dozens of compounds including rénmín 人民 "people", réngé 人格 "personality", rénkǒu 人口 "population", rénshēng 人生 "life", nánrén 男人 "man, men", gōngrén 工人 "laborer", shīrén 诗人 "poet", chāorén 超人 "superman", etc. Most disyllabic compounds in modern Chinese are constructed in this manner, and predominate in the vocabulary.

A prominent feature of the grammar of Chinese is the lack of morphological change. Wǒ dǎ tā 我打他 "I hit him" and tā dǎ wǒ 他打我 "he hits me" are opposite in meaning, but in Chinese only require a change in word order, shifting the positions of wǒ 我 and tā 他. Not one of the three words changes morphologically, unlike in other widely used languages such as English. Grammatical significance through morphological change in English is expressed in numerous other ways in Chinese. For example, in the English sentence "He is hitting me", verb change expresses the progressive tense. That condition would translate in Chinese as Tā zhèngzài dǎ wǒ 他正在打我, using the adverb zhèngzài 正在 "in the process of" to express the ongoing nature of the action.

Verbs and adjectives as subjects, objects or adverbs in English characteristically undergo change. The verb "walk", for example, becomes "walking" as a subject, and the adjective "quick" as an adverb is "quickly". Chinese is without such change. Zǒu 走 "walk" and kuài 快 "quick" remain as they are irrespective of their position in a sentence. In contrast to English, Chinese nouns, verbs and adjectives are multifunctional in a sentence.

Chinese characters form the script for recording the Chinese language. One character basically represents one morpheme. For example, the three words bùrú 不如 "not as good as", bùwèi 部位 "location" and sànbù 散步

"stroll" all have homophonic morphemes bù as part of them. But the meaning of each bù is different, "not", "part" and "step", and the character for each is also different, 不, 部, and 步. The Chinese script can thus be said to be a morphophonemic writing system.

Characters are constructed of one or more strokes, and are square in form, or conceived of as filling a square shape. The stroke is the minimal written unit of the character. There are seven basic strokes, and they are written in a definite order. However, since these basic strokes are in different locations in different characters, their shape and size will vary somewhat. For example, in writing the character xiao 小 "small", the middle stroke 亅 is written first, then the left "dot" ' and finally the right "dot" 丶 ("dot" dian 点 being the name of that stroke). Since the two "dots" are in different positions, their shape and manner of writing are also slightly different.

Characters can be divided into single component and compound component forms. Single component characters have only one structural unit, examples being rén 人 "man", rì 日 "sun" and dà 大 "big". Compound forms are made up of two or more structural units. Examples are míng 明 "bright", formed of rì 日 "sun" and yuè 月 "moon"; quán 全 "complete", formed of rén 人 and wáng 王 "king"; guó 国 "country", composed of wéi 囗 "surround" (archaic) and yù 玉 "jade"; xiè 谢 "thanks", composed of yán 讠 "word", shēn 身 "body", and cùn 寸 "inch". Simple component characters are limited in number, with compound forms in the overwhelming majority.

Chinese script is patently more difficult to write and commit to memory than alphabetic or syllabic writing. Still, it is not without its system and order. Most compound characters are made up of one structural unit representing meaning and another sound. For example, mā 妈 "mother" is composed of nǚ 女 "female" and mǎ 马 representing the sound. Similarly, qīng 清 "clear" is composed of "water" and the right side element 青 indicating the sound. That being said, the Chinese script is one of the oldest in continuous use, where most characters in the modern inventory have been part of the writing system for well over a millennium. During that time, both sound and form have undergone significant change, making it difficult to analyze the structure of many characters to determine their phonetic and semantic values. Rote memorization is thus an unavoidable task.

The most commonly used Chinese characters total roughly 3,000. Control of that number and their combinations into words makes it possible to read a range of ordinary material, such as daily newspapers. In 1956, the People's Republic of China announced the Plan for Simplification of the Chinese Script that reduced the number of strokes in many characters. Examples are shū 書 "book" where the strokes in the traditional form are reduced to four 书; xué 學 "to study", reducing sixteen original strokes to eight 学; guān 关 "to close", reducing an original eighteen stroke total to six 关. This reduction simplified learning and writing, at the same time it logically conformed to a pattern of evolution from complicated to simplified forms that had been proceeding gradually for centuries. The approved simplified forms have been in use for decades now on the China mainland, as well as in Singapore and by Chinese communities in Malaysia and Indonesia. For the convenience of those students who either have background in traditional forms or will be working in areas where they are still used (Hong Kong, Taiwan), we include them after each new entry in our separate *Student Exercise* manual.

Kung Fu Content

We have set our text narrative in a city in China, at a university where Chinese is taught to foreign students. Seven of those students interact as friends:

Shānběn (Yamamoto), male, from Japan
Jīn Zhōngyī (Kim Chung-il), male, from Korea
Fāng Xiǎoyīng, female, French of Chinese ancestry
Mǎ Dīng (Martin), male, a German
Ānnà (Anna), female, from the UK
Dàwèi (David), male, an American
Zhāng Lǎoshī (Ms. Zhang), an instructor of Chinese

Their lives grow close, and intertwined in unanticipated ways.

Material in each of the twenty-two lessons in *Kung Fu* (I) is arranged in the following order:

- Lesson text in Chinese characters.
- Vocabulary, with contextual examples for selected entries.
- Supplementary vocabulary. A few additional items needed in the lesson narrative, but of secondary importance at that particular point for memorization, are added, as are proper names.
- Grammar notes. Points of structure are explained fully, with adequate contextual examples as reinforcement. A good grammar foundation is established in *Kung Fu* (I), with most fundamental points covered and analyzed.
- Phrases and sentences, a series of phrases and complete declarative, imperative, interrogative, or exclamatory sentences for drill reinforcement of new material.
- Lesson text in *pinyin* romanization.
- Lesson text in English translation.
- Classroom activities. These are task-based activities meant to be handled by groups of three or four students. The instructor may use them as models for expanding their number when required.
- Reading comprehension. These are review readings in unromanized Chinese, weaving the grammar and vocabulary used in previous lessons into new narratives. There are eight in total and they follow lessons 2, 5, 7, 10, 12, 15, 18 and 20.

These twenty-two lessons are preceded by eight that systematically cover the sound structure of Putonghua and introduce expressions routinely used in class, such as "Please say it again" or "Are there any questions?". Audio tapes are available for all thirty lessons.

The main body of lesson texts is grouped into units of five lessons, each followed by a review summary of the grammar and vocabulary introduced in that unit. On average, three grammar points are introduced in each lesson, along with twenty-eight vocabulary items, five common nouns or supplementary words, and twenty-five Chinese characters. The ideal approach for more rapid and secure spoken proficiency is to leave the written language until a spoken-listening base has been established. However, demands of most college courses are rigorous, requiring that students remain in lock step for reading as well as spoken skills through each level. Should that not be the case, it is a simple matter for the instructor to segment, and then stagger spoken and written materials in the text. However, while learners struggle initially with Chinese writing, experience has proven that the burden lightens as knowledge builds, with characters less and less painful to organize and commit to memory.

Kung Fu (I) is meant to satisfy a two semester, five to seven session per week elementary program. Semesters are effectively fourteen weeks long. The material would be presented for that twenty-eight week block of time as follows: two weeks of phonetic drilling, twenty-two weeks of one lesson per week, and one week for each of the four review lessons.

Our grammatical analysis follows the system laid down in the late 1950s by the Chinese Ministry of Education, then used in Chinese as a second language texts at such programs as those at Peking University and the Beijing Language and Culture University, and elsewhere internationally. It has recently (2002) been restated in the "Grammatical Outline" section of the work *Gāoděng xuéxiào wàiguó liúxuéshēng Hànyŭ zhuānyè jiàoxué dàgāng* 《高等学校外国留学生汉语专业教学大纲》("Outline for the Teaching of Chinese to Overseas Students Major at Tertiary Institutions"), published by the Ministry of Education's National Teaching of Chinese to Foreigners Leading Group. We have attempted to keep our analysis simple and user-friendly, and periodically revisit and summarize conceptually more difficult aspects. There should be something in each explanation for all, from students with a high degree of interest in grammar to those with practically none. *Pinyin* and word grouping conventions are those used in the Language Reform Commission's publication *Hànyŭ pīnyīn zhèngcífă jīběn guīzé* 《汉语拼音正词法基本规则》("Basic rules of Chinese Pinyin Orthography") and followed in the various editions of the standard dictionary *Xiàndài Hànyŭ cídiăn* 《现代汉语词典》("A Dictionary of Modern Chinese").

At the risk of having it shelved with martial arts titles, we have named our text series *Kung Fu*. "Kung fu" is the spelling that has entered English via Cantonese for a secondary meaning, "unarmed martial art", but the word itself has a place in many lexicons. It is written variously 功夫 or 工夫, and its core sense is the "effort" or "discipline" that is put into perfecting an art form or acquiring a skill. It has migrated into Korean, pronounced *kongbu*, as the common verb "to study", and to Japanese, pronounced kufū, meaning "ingenuity" or an "idea". Thus, it is a familiar concept to a large portion of the students who will be using our series. It embodies what the study of Chinese should be, and the satisfaction derived from doing it well. Our hope is that *Kung Fu* will serve as an effective guide along the way.

The Authors
Hong Kong and Beijing
February, 2002

Acknowledgments
鸣 谢

These texts have been seven or so years in the making, from initial concept to construction through experimental use in draft form on to formal printing. It has been a long process in which many have contributed. Perhaps if their role was at an early stage they may even have forgotten it and what value it has been to us. We haven't, and now offer sincere thanks to all.

First, to the two university teams, members of which critiqued the initial plan, contributed textual and exercise material, and experimented with the results in classes.

Peking University's Center for the Teaching of Chinese to Foreigners colleagues:

Ms. Zhao Yanjiao 赵燕皎
Mr. Yang Defeng 杨德峰
Ms. Li Xiaoqi 李晓琪

The Chinese University of Hong Kong Yale-in-China Chinese Language Center (CLC) team:

Mr. Wong Ho-put 王浩勃
Ms. Chu Hsiao-mi 朱小密
Ms. Li Hung 李红
Mr. Yeung Siu Kai 杨绍箕
Ms. Dolfin Hsi-ching 周西京
Ms. Han Chiang-ning 韩江宁
Ms. Chou Li-ru 周丽如

Mr. Wong and Ms. Li Hung were especially helpful in their crafting of task-oriented classroom activities, while Ms. Chu Hsiao-mi has shared her sound judgment at each step. Other CLC staff who made suggestions or assisted in valued ways in the course of our work include Ms. Ginny Chan

King Ying 陈京英 of the Center's Cantonese Division and Mr. Ho Cheuk Sang 何焯生, Ms. Christina Fong Yin Tsang 曾芳燕, Mr. Andrew Kwok Chi Poon 潘国智, Ms. Angela Hing Kwan Ho 何庆群 and Ms. Doris Mei Yin Wong 黄美贤 of the Administrative Office. Ms. Ho and Ms. Wong endured the taxing drudgery of creating and juggling fonts, and typing numerous drafts from scrawl in two or three languages. They have retained their sanity remarkably well and remain on speaking terms with us in spite of it.

Thanks, as well, to Professor James E. Bosson — now (2002) Visiting Professor of East Asian Languages and Cultures at Harvard University — and his students at Umea University in Sweden who used *Kung Fu* (I) in draft form over two terms and shared their fresh perspectives with us.

The unique background of our Chinese University Press editor, Ms. Esther Chung Sze Tsang 曾诵诗, who is not only fluent in Putonghua but understands its syntax, has been immensely valuable in the vexing last stages of the project. We thank her warmly. So, too, we thank two of The Chinese University of Hong Kong's leaders. Pro-Vice-Chancellor Ambrose King 金耀基, serving as chairman of the Yale-in-China Chinese Language Center's oversight committee, supported our project from its inception, and former Vice-Chancellor Charles K. Kao 高锟 provided funding at a very critical juncture.

Our students cap this list. Their reasoned dissatisfaction with what went before the *Kung Fu* series was an important initial stimulus to beginning the project. Through its preparation, they worked without complaint with awkwardly unfinished material, and supplied us with thoughtful suggestions for making the final product clearer and more useful. We are grateful, and hope that we've inspired them toward fuller understanding of China.

The Organs of Speech
发音器官图
Fāyīn Qìguān Tú

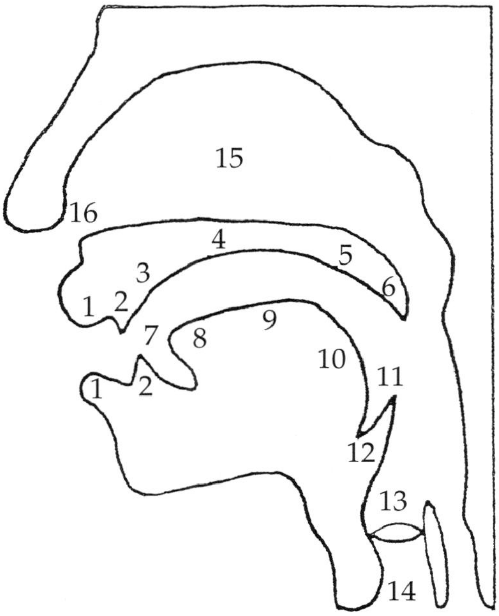

1. 上下唇 shàng xià chún
   Upper lip & Lower lip
2. 上下齿 shàng xià chǐ
   Upper teeth & Lower teeth
3. 齿龈 chǐyín
   Alveolar ridge
4. 硬腭 yìng'è
   Hard palate
5. 软腭 ruǎn'è
   Soft palate (velum)
6. 小舌 xiǎoshé
   Uvula
7. 舌尖 shéjiān
   Tip of tongue
8. 舌面（前）shémiàn (qián)
   Front of tongue
9. 舌面（后）shémiàn (hòu)
   Back of tongue
10. 舌根 shégēn
    Root of tongue
11. 咽头 yāntóu
    Pharyngeal cavity
12. 会厌 huìyàn
    Epiglottis
13. 声带 shēngdài
    Vocal cords
14. 气管 qìguǎn
    Trachea
15. 鼻腔 bíqiāng
    Nasal cavity
16. 鼻孔 bíkǒng
    Nostril

Abbreviations
略语表

i	interjection
adj	adjective
adv	adverb
Attr	attributive
CD	complement of degree
CDI	directional complement
CM	V-measure word complement
CP	potential complement
CQ	quantity complement
CR	resultative complement
CT	time complement
imit	imitiative sound, onomatope
m	measure word
n	noun
n-pw	localizer, place word
nu	numeral
O	object
o.v	optative verb
P	predicate
prep	preposition
part	particle
pro	pronoun
S	subject
v	verb
c	conjunction

Linguistic Terminology
语言学术语

Phonetic Terms 语音术语

fǔyīn	辅音	consonant
yuányīn	元音	vowel
qīngyīn	清音	voiceless
zhuóyīn	浊音	voiced
cāyīn	擦音	fricative
sèyīn	塞音	plosive
sècāyīn	塞擦音	plosive affricate
biānyīn	边音	lateral
bíyīn	鼻音	nasal
shēngmǔ	声母	initial
yùnmǔ	韵母	final
dānyùnmǔ	单韵母	simple final
fùyùnmǔ	复韵母	compound final
bíyīnyùnmǔ	鼻音韵母	nasal final
shēngdiào	声调	tone
biàndiào	变调	tone sandhi
qīngshēng	轻声	neutral tone
érhuàyùn	儿化韵	retroflex final
yīnjié	音节	syllable

Grammar Terms 语法术语

1. Parts of speech 词类

míngcí	名词	noun (n)
fāngwèicí	方位词	localizer, place word (n-pw)
dàicí	代词	pronoun (pro)
rénchēng dàicí	人称代词	personal pronoun
zhǐshì dàicí	指示代词	demonstrative pronoun
yíwèndàicí	疑问代词	interrogative pronoun
shùcí	数词	numeral (nu)
liàngcí	量词	measure word (m)
dòngcí	动词	verb (v)
néngyuàn dòngcí	能愿动词	optative verb (o.v)
xíngróngcí	形容词	adjective (adj)
fùcí	副词	adverb (adv)
jiècí	介词	preposition (prep)
liáncí	连词	conjunction (c)
zhùcí	助词	particle (part)
dòngtài zhùcí	动态助词	aspect particle
jiégòu zhùcí	结构助词	structural particle
yǔqìzhùcí	语气助词	modal particle
tàncí	叹词	interjection (i)
xiàngshēngcí	象声词	imitative sound, onomatope (imit)

2. Phrases 词组

zhǔwèi jiégòu	主谓结构	S-P construction
dòngbīn jiégòu	动宾结构	V-O construction

dòngbǔ jiégòu	动补结构	V-complement construction
xíngróngcí jiégòu	形容词结构	adjectival construction
jiècíjiégòu	介词结构	prepositional phrase
“de”zì jiégòu	“的”字结构	de construction

3. Sentence elements 句子成分

zhǔyǔ	主语	subject (S)
wèiyǔ	谓语	predicate (P)
bīnyǔ	宾语	object (O)
dìngyǔ	定语	attributive (Attr)
zhuàngyǔ	状语	adverbial adjunct
bǔyǔ	补语	complement
zhōngxīnyǔ	中心语	central word/modified word
chéngdùbǔyǔ	程度补语	complement of degree (CD)
jiéguǒbǔyǔ	结果补语	resultative complement (CR)
qūxiàngbǔyǔ	趋向补语	directional complement (CDI)
kěnéngbǔyǔ	可能补语	potential complement (CP)
dòngliàngbǔyǔ	动量补语	V-measure word complement (CM)
shíliàngbǔyǔ	时量补语	time complement (CT)
shùliàngbǔyǔ	数量补语	quantity complement (CQ)

4. Sentences 句子

dānjù	单句	simple sentence
fùjù	复句	compound sentence
zhǔwèijù	主谓句	S-P sentence
wúzhǔjù	无主句	sentence without a subject
dúcíjù	独词句	one word sentence

dòngcí wèiyǔjù	动词谓语句	verbal predicate sentence
xíngróngcí wèiyǔjù	形容词谓语句	adjectival predicate sentence
míngcí wèiyǔjù	名词谓语句	nominal predicate
zhǔwèi wèiyǔjù	主谓谓语句	S-P predicate sentence
chénshùjù	陈述句	declarative sentence
yíwènjù	疑问句	interrogative sentence
qǐshǐjù	祈使句	imperative sentence
gǎntànjù	感叹句	exclamatory sentence
liándòngjù	连动句	sentence with verbal constructions in series
jiānyǔjù	兼语句	pivotal sentence
bèidòngjù	被动句	passive verb sentence
"bǎ"zìjù	"把"字句	ba sentence
"shì … de"jù	"是……的"句	shi … de sentence
cúnxiànjù	存现句	sentence showing existence, emergence or disappearance

Abbreviation Key
词类名称

n	=	noun 名词
v	=	verb 动词
o.v	=	optative verb 助动词
adj	=	adjective 形容词
nu	=	numeral 数词
m	=	measure word 量词
pro	=	pronoun 代词 (包括人称、指示、疑问)
adv	=	adverb 副词
prep	=	preposition 介词
c	=	conjunction 连词
part	=	particle 助词 (包括结构、动态、语气)
i	=	interjection 叹词
on	=	onomatope 象声词
i.e	=	idiomatic expression 惯用词
n suff	=	noun suffix 名词词尾
nu pref	=	numeral prefix 数词词头

Radicals
部首

The following are forty of the highest frequency "radicals", basic structural parts of Chinese Characters that are broad semantic indicators. Radicals are used as organizing units in character dictionaries.

	English Meaning
1. 亻，人	man, human being
2. 刂，刀	knife
3. 讠，言	speech
4. 氵，水	water
5. 忄，心	heart
6. 宀	roof
7. 门	door
8. 辶	walking
9. 艹	grass
10. 土	earth
11. 扌，手	hand
12. 口	mouth
13. 山	mountain
14. 彳	"double man"
15. 饣，食	food
16. 女	woman, female
17. 子	child

18. 阝(left) mound
19. 阝(right) city
20. 纟 silk
21. 马 horse
22. 火，灬 fire
23. 礻，示 omen
24. 玉，（王） jade, popularly referred to as the "king" radical
25. 木 wood
26. 车 vehicle
27. 日 sun
28. 月 moon
29. 月（肉） flesh
30. 疒 sick
31. 衤，衣 clothing
32. 石 stone
33. 田 field
34. 钅，金 metal
35. 禾 grain
36. 羊 sheep
37. 米 rice
38. ⺮，竹 bamboo
39. ⻊，足 foot
40. 雨，⻗ rain

Initials and Simple Finals
声母和单韵母

The syllable is generally regarded as the major phonetic unit in Chinese. It is made up of an initial, a final and a tone.

汉语的语音单位是音节，音节由声母、韵母、声调组成。

1. Initial 声母

   The consonant that begins a syllable is called an initial. There are 21 in all. (International Phonetic Alphabet (IPA) equivalents are in parentheses.)

   一个音节开头的辅音叫做声母。声母一共有21个(方括号内是国际音标)：

b〔p〕	p〔p'〕	m〔m〕	f〔f〕
d〔t〕	t〔t'〕	n〔n〕	l〔l〕
z〔ts〕	c〔ts'〕	s〔s〕	
zh〔tʂ〕	ch〔tʂ'〕	sh〔ʂ〕	r〔ʐ〕
j〔tɕ〕	q〔tɕ'〕	x〔ɕ〕	
g〔k〕	k〔k'〕	h〔x〕	

   Syllables without beginning consonants are called zero initial consonants. E.g., a, ou, en, ê.

   开头没有辅音的音节叫零声母音节。例如：a, ou, en, ê.

2. Single vowel finals 单韵母

   What follows the initial is called the final. Finals with but one vowel are called simple finals, and there are seven of them:

一个音节中声母后边的部分是韵母。只有一个元音的韵母叫单韵母。单韵母一共有七个：

a〔a〕 o〔o〕 e〔ə〕 ê〔ɛ〕 i〔I〕 u〔u〕 ü〔y〕

3. Spelling conventions (1)

拼写规则 (1)

The standard spelling (romanization) of Putonghua is called *pinyin*. (See complete table at pronunciation lesson 8.)

(1) When i, u or ü stand alone as syllables, they are written yi, wu and yu:

i、u、ü 自成音节时，要写成 yi、wu、yu，即：

i → yi

u → wu

ü → yu

Note additional examples in this category in pronunciation Lesson 2 at 3.2.

(2) When ü appears after j, q or x, the umlaut or double dot diacritic over the ü is not written.

ü 出现在 j、q、x 后面时，要略去上面的两点，如：

jü → ju

qü → qu

xü → xu

练习

1. Read these initials. Note that your instructor or the tape will add vowels in each case. This is the standard manner in which these initials are read in China.

读下面的声母：

b(o)	p	m	f
d(e)	t	n	l
z(i)	c	s	
zh(i)	ch	sh	r
j(i)	q	x	
g(e)	k	h	

2. Read the following finals:

读下面的韵母：

(1)	a	e,	e	a
(2)	a	o,	o	a
(3)	e	o,	o	e
(4)	e	ê,	ê	e
(5)	i	u,	u	i
(6)	i	ü,	ü	i
(7)	u	ü,	ü	u

3. Read the following syllables:

读下面的音节：

bo	po	mo	fo
de	te	ne	le
ge	ke	he	
ji	qi	xi	
yi	wu	yu	

4. Distinguish between the following consonants:

分辨下面各组声母的发音：

z / j	c / q	s / x
z / zh	c / ch	s / sh
j / zh	q / ch	x / sh

5. Read and practice spelling the items below:

拼读下表：

	a	o	e	i	u	ü
b	ba	bo		bi	bu	
p	pa	po		pi	pu	
m	ma	mo		mi	mu	
f	fa	fo			fu	
d	da		de	di	du	
t	ta		te	ti	tu	
n	na		ne	ni	nu	nü
l	la		le	li	lu	lü
z	za		ze		zu	
c	ca		ce		cu	
s	sa		se		su	
zh	zha		zhe		zhu	
ch	cha		che		chu	
sh	sha		she		shu	
r			re		ru	
j				ji		ju
q				qi		qu
x				xi		xu
g	ga		ge		gu	
k	ka		ke		ku	
h	ha		he		hu	

Compound Finals and Finals with Nasal Endings 复韵母和鼻音韵母

1. Compound finals

   复韵母

   Finals composed of two or three vowels are called compound finals, of which there are thirteen:

   由两个或三个元音构成的韵母叫做复韵母，复韵母一共有13个：

   ai〔ai〕 ao〔au〕

   ou〔ou〕

   ei〔ei〕

   ia〔ia〕 ie〔iɛ〕 iao〔iau〕 iou〔iou〕

   ua〔ua〕 uo〔uo〕 uai〔uai〕 uei〔uei〕

   üe〔yɛ〕

2. Finals with nasal endings

   鼻音韵母

   There are sixteen finals where vowels are followed by -n or -ng.

   元音后面带上鼻音韵尾 -n〔n〕或 -ng〔ŋ〕构成的韵母叫做鼻音韵母。鼻音韵母一共有16个：

   an〔an〕 ang〔aŋ〕

   ong〔uŋ〕

   en〔ən〕 eng〔əŋ〕

   in〔in〕 ing〔iŋ〕 ian〔iɛn〕 iang〔iaŋ〕 iong〔yuŋ〕

uen〔uən〕 ueng〔uəŋ〕 uan〔uan〕 uang〔uaŋ〕

ün〔yn〕 üan〔yɛn〕

3. Spelling conventions (2)

拼写规则 (2)

(1) ê stands alone as a syllable, always as an exclamatory word ("ah?" "what?"). Then it is written with the caret or inverted v diacritic. When the vowel follows i or ü, the diacritic is omitted:

ê 除可单独成为音节外，只出现在 i 和 ü 的后面，这时上面的 ∧ 要略去：

iê → ie, üê → üe。

(2) Finals beginning with i, u and ü that stand alone as syllables, that is, when no consonant precedes them, are written as follows:

以 i、u、ü开头的韵母自成音节时，其书写形式如下：

i	ia → ya	ie → ye
	iao → yao	iou → you
	ian → yan	in → yin
	iang → yang	ing → ying
	iong → yong	
u	ua → wa	uo → wo
	uai → wai	uei → wei
	uan → wan	uen → wen
	uang → wang	ueng → weng
ü	üe → yue	üan → yuan
	ün → yun	

Similar to with i, u or ü standing alone as introduced in the preceding lesson, y and w are used as conventions to indicate their independant syllabic status.

(3) When the finals iou, uei and uen are preceded by consonant initials, the o and e are omitted.

韵母 iou、uei、uen 和声母相拼，书写时略去 o、e，例如：

d + iou → diu　　　t + uei → tui

ch + uen → chun

练习

1. Read the following aloud.

练习拼读：

(1)

	ai	ei	ao	ou	ia	ie	iao	iou	ua	uo	uai	uei	üe
j					jia	jie	jiao	jiu					jue
q					qia	qie	qiao	qiu					que
x					xia	xie	xiao	xiu					xue
z	zai	zei	zao	zou						zuo		zui	
c	cai		cao	cou						cuo		cui	
s	sai		sao	sou						suo		sui	
zh	zhai	zhei	zhao	zhou					zhua	zhuo	zhuai	zhui	
ch	chai		chao	chou					chua	chuo	chuai	chui	
sh	shai	shei	shao	shou					shua	shuo	shuai	shui	
r			rao	rou						ruo		rui	

(2)

韵母 声母	an	en	ang	eng	ong	ian	in	iang	ing	iong	uan	uen	uang	ueng	üan	ün
b	ban	ben	bang	beng		bian	bin		bing							
p	pan	pen	pang	peng		pian	pin		ping							
m	man	men	mang	meng		mian	min		ming							
f	fan	fen	fang	feng												
d	dan	den	dang	deng	dong	dian			ding		duan	dun				
t	tan		tang	teng	tong	tian			ting		tuan	tun				
n	nan	nen	nang	neng	nong	nian	nin	niang	ning		nuan					
l	lan		lang	leng	long	lian	lin	liang	ling		luan	lun				
g	gan	gen	gang	geng	gong						guan	gun	guang			
k	kan	ken	kang	keng	kong						kuan	kun	kuang			
h	han	hen	hang	heng	hong						huan	hun	huang			

2. Distinguish between these final pairs.

   分辨下面各组韵母的发音：

   (1) Compound finals

   复韵母

   ai — ei　　ao — ou　　ie — üe　　uo — ou

   ei — uei　　ao — iao　　ou — iou　　ai — uai

   (2) Nasal finals

   鼻韵母

   an — ang　　en — eng　　in — ing　　ün — iong

   an — en　　en — in　　in — ün　　ün — üan

   ang — eng　　ing — eng

3. Read these syllables, noting the pronunciation of rounded vowels in each.

   读下面的音节，注意每组音节中圆唇元音的发音：

   (1) zuo　cuo　suo　zhuo　chuo　shuo　ruo

   (2) zou　cou　sou　zhou　chou　shou　rou

(3) jue que xue

(4) long tong song hong

(5) zhuang kuang shuang guang

(6) duan guan huan kuan

4. Read the following syllables, paying attention to spelling rules.

读下面的音节，注意拼写规则：

(1) ju qu xu jue que xue

juan quan xuan jun qun xun

(2) you wei wen

jiu hui zun

liu zhui dun

(3) yi ya ye yao

wu wa wo wai

yu yue

(4) yan yang yin ying yong

wan wang wen weng

yuan yun

Tones
声 调

1. Tones

声 调

Along with initials and finals, tone is an integral component of the syllable in Chinese. Tone refers to the variation in pitch of a syllable. We illustrate this variation as below using five points on the vertical line to indicate relative height of pitch: high (5), middle high (4), middle (3), middle low (2) and low (1). The four tones of Putonghua contour as follows:

汉语一个音节的组成成分，除了声母和韵母外，还有声调。声调是指一个音节中音高的高低升降。如果用一条直线代表一个音节的音高变动范围，把直线分成四格五点，由下向上的1、2、3、4、5就表示低、半低、中、半高、高。汉语的声调一共有四个，见下图：

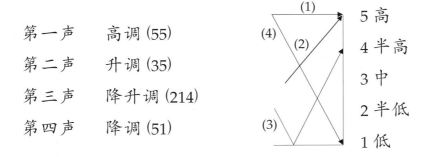

第一声	高调 (55)
第二声	升调 (35)
第三声	降升调 (214)
第四声	降调 (51)

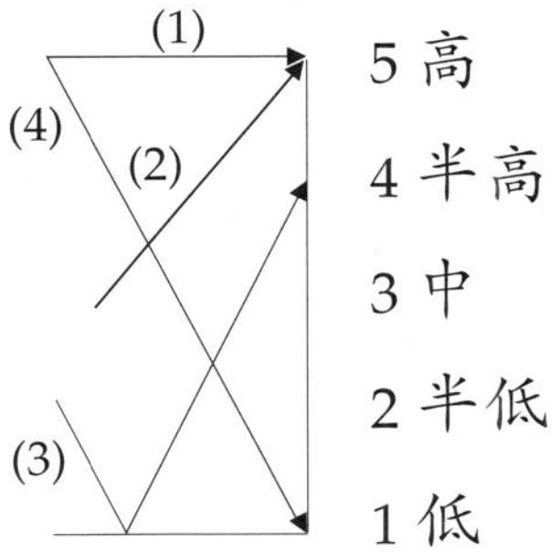

In the romanized syllables, these four tones are indicated by diacritics: level (¯), rising (´), dipping (ˇ) and falling (`). The tone mark is placed over the main vowel, the one pronounced loudest and with the mouth open widest (other vowels are "on-glides" or "off-glides").

书写时分别用 ˉˊˇˋ 四种声调符号标在音节上，如果韵母中不只一个元音，标在开口度大的元音上，即：有a标在a上，没有a标在o、e上。iu、ui标在后面的u、i上。例如：

	mother, hemp, horse, to curse
mā má mǎ mà	(妈 麻 马 骂)
	to guess, talent, to pick, vegetable
cāi cái cǎi cài	(猜 才 采 菜)
	wok, country, fruit, to pass by
guō guó guǒ guò	(锅 国 果 过)
	street, festival, older sister, to borrow
jiē jié jiě jiè	(街 节 姐 借)
	thousand, money, shallow, to owe
qiān qián qiǎn qiàn	(千 钱 浅 欠)
	to slide, to flow, willow, six
liū liú liǔ liù	(溜 流 柳 六)
	ash, to return, to regret, to know how
huī huí huǐ huì	(灰 回 悔 会)

As can be seen, tone changes the meaning of a syllable.

一个音节的声母、韵母相同，声调不同，意思就不一样。

2. Half-third tone

半三声

In actual speech, the full 214 contour of the third tone is only pronounced when the syllable is at the end of a word, at the end of a sentence or by itself, in particular when it is stressed. It is a "half-third" when it comes before syllables in the 1st, 2nd and 4th tones, and before most neutral tone (see next lesson) syllables. The contour is the first half of this of a whole third tone (21), or it could be considered a low level tone.

在实际语言中，只有在词尾、句尾或单念(特别是强调)时，才读完全的第三声(214)，如果在一、二、四声音节和大部分轻声音节前，要读成半三声。半三声就是只读原来第三声的前一半降调(211)，甚至可以读成低调(11)，见下图。

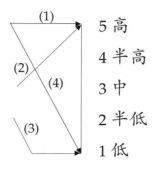

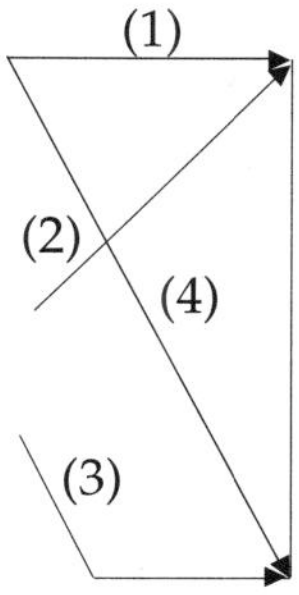

Example:

例如：

(1)	pŭtōng	(普通)	ordinary
	jiănchá	(检查)	to examine
	tĭyù	(体育)	sports
	huŏchē	(火车)	train
	gănqíng	(感情)	emotion
	zhŭnbèi	(准备)	to prepare
(2)	nĭ	(你)	you
	hăo	(好)	to be good, fine
	píngguŏ	(苹果)	apple
	qiānbĭ	(铅笔)	pencil
	shēntĭ	(身体)	body
	Xiànzài sān diăn.	(现在三点。)	It is 3:00 now.
	Tiānqì zhēn lĕng.	(天气真冷。)	It is really cold weather.

Thus, the half third is much more common than the full third.

因此，我们读半三声的机会很多，读全三声的机会是很少的。

3. Spelling conventions (3)

拼写规则 (3)

When syllables beginning with the vowels a, e and o follow other syllables, an apostrophe separates the syllables to avoid confusion. E.g., hǎi'àn (海岸) sea coast, nǚ'ér (女儿) daughter, pèi'ǒu (配偶) spouse.

a、e、o开头的音节连接在其他音节后面时，为了避免音节的界限发生混淆，用隔音符号（'）隔开。例如：hǎi'àn（海岸）、nǚ'ér（女儿）、pèi'ǒu（配偶）。

练习

1. Read the following syllables.

读下面的音节：

(1)	jī	jí	jǐ	jì
(2)	niū	niú	niǔ	niù
(3)	shēn	shén	shěn	shèn
(4)	quān	quán	quǎn	quàn
(5)	chōng	chóng	chǒng	chòng

2. Tonal practice:

练习声调：

(1) First tone

第一声

gōngkāi	公开	open
gōngsī	公司	company
gōng'ān	公安	public security

kāifā	开发	to develop
kāixīn	开心	to be happy
kāizhī	开支	expenses
tiānkōng	天空	midair
tiānchuāng	天窗	skylight
tiānzhēn	天真	to be innocent
qiūtiān	秋天	autumn
qiūqiān	秋千	swing (ridden on)
qiūfēng	秋风	autumn breeze

(2) Second tone

第二声

cáihuá	才华	artistic talent
cáinéng	才能	ability
cáijué	裁决	make a verdict
míngcí	名词	noun
míngnián	明年	tomorrow
míngrén	名人	famous person
xuéxí	学习	to study
xuéshí	学时	teaching period
xuénián	学年	academic year
réncái	人才	talented person
rénmín	人民	the people
rényuán	人员	staff (people)

(3) Fourth tone

第四声

bànlù	半路	half way
bànpiào	半票	half price ticket
bànjià	半价	half price
dàgài	大概	probably
dàbàn	大半	greater half
dàlù	大路	main road
jìhuà	计划	plan
jìlǜ	纪律	discipline
jìxù	继续	continue
zhìxiè	致谢	offer thanks
zhìyuàn	志愿	ambition
zhìzào	制造	manufacture

(4) Half third tone

半三声

hǎotīng	好听	pleasant (to hear)
hǎorén	好人	good person
hǎokàn	好看	attractive
fǎnguāng	反光	reflected light
fǎncháng	反常	abnormal
fǎnduì	反对	oppose
guǒzhī	果汁	fruit juice
guǒyuán	果园	orchard
guǒjiàng	果酱	jam, jelly
xiǎoxīn	小心	to be careful
xiǎoshí	小时	hour
xiǎofèi	小费	tip ($)

3. Read these bisyllables

读下面的双音节词：

(1) Zhōngwén　Chinese

tīngxiě　dictation

gōngzuò　work

(2) míngtiān　tomorrow

niúnǎi　milk

qíngkuàng　condition

(3) rènzhēn　conscientious

wèntí　question

kèbiǎo　schedule

4. Distinguish the tones in the following.

分辨下面各组的声调：

{ xiā　shrimp
{ xià　next

{ shōu　to receive
{ shòu　to suffer

{ tóng　same
{ tòng　ache

{ tiáo　to mix
{ tiào　to jump

{ liànxí　exercise
{ liánxì　contact

{ jiè shū　to borrow books
{ jiéshù　to end

5. 读下面各组词，注意隔音符号的作用：

{ jī'áng　roused
{ jiāng　river

{ pí'ǎo　fur-lined jacket
{ piāo　to float

{ yīn'àn　dark
{ yínán　thorny (as a problem)

míng'é	quota of people
míngē	folk song

Classroom Expressions 课堂用语

1.	Gēn wǒ niàn.	(跟我念。)	Read after me.
2.	Tīng wǒ niàn.	(听我念。)	Listen while I read.
3.	dì-yī shēng	(第一声)	First tone
4.	dì-èr shēng	(第二声)	Second tone
5.	dì-sān shēng	(第三声)	Third tone
6.	dì-sì shēng	(第四声)	Fourth tone

Neutral Tone and Tone Sandhi
轻声和变调

1. Neutral tone

   轻 声

   Some syllables are pronounced quickly and lightly when following another syllable, losing their normal tonal value. They are tagged "neutral" and are so indicated by the absence of a tone diacritic.

   有些音节在别的音节后面读得又轻又短，失去了原有的调值，这就是轻声。轻声不标声调符号。例如：

tā de	his	xiānsheng	sir
biéren	other people	shénme	what
wǒmen	we, us	xǐhuan	to like
tàiyang	the sun	yuèliang	the moon

2. Tone sandhi

   变 调

   Tones in context change in regular, and fortunately limited, ways. The phenomenon is called "sandhi", a linguistic term from the Sanskrit meaning "joining together". One of the two major sandhis is when two third tones come together. The first third changes to the second tone contour: ˇ + ˇ → ˊ + ˇ :

   几个音节连续读的时候，声调有时发生变化，这种现象叫做变调。例如：两个第三声连续读时，前一个音节要读成第二声。即 ˇ + ˇ → ˊ + ˇ 。例如：

shǒubiǎo → shóubiǎo	wrist watch
yǒngyuǎn → yóngyuǎn	forever
Nǐ hǎo → Ní hǎo	How do you do?
hěn lěng → hén lěng	very cold
Wǒ hěn hǎo → Wó hén hǎo	I am very well./I am fine.

NOTE that (1) when there are two or more thirds together, all those before the final third become second, and (2) we do not change the tone diacritics.

需要变调的第三声音节拼写时声调符号不改变。例如 shǒubiǎo 不改写成 shóubiǎo。

Tone sandhi also includes the "half third" tone (see previous lesson).

半三声也是变调的一种。

练习

1. Neutral tone:

轻声练习：

(1)	māma	妈妈	mother	gēge	哥哥	older brother
	tāmen	他们	them, they	yīfu	衣服	clothing
	bēizi	杯子	cup	zhuōzi	桌子	table
	dōngxi	东西	thing	xiāngzi	箱子	box
	shōushi	收拾	to tidy up	gānjing	干净	clean
	qīngchu	清楚	clear	xiūxi	休息	to rest
	shūfu	舒服	comfortable	shēngri	生日	birthday
	cōngming	聪明	smart	zhīdao	知道	to know

(2)	yéye	爷爷	grandfather	míngzi	名字	name
	xuésheng	学生	student	péngyou	朋友	friend
	shíhou	时候	time	liángkuai	凉快	cool
	máfan	麻烦	trouble	juéde	觉得	to feel that
	háizi	孩子	child	piányi	便宜	inexpensive
	róngyi	容易	easy	shénme	什么	what
	tóufa	头发	hair	bízi	鼻子	nose
	méimao	眉毛	eyebrow	qiánmian	前面	front
(3)	jiějie	姐姐	older sister	nǎinai	奶奶	grandmother
	nǐmen	你们	you (pl.)	wǒmen	我们	us
	yǐzi	椅子	chair	běnzi	本子	notebook
	mǔqin	母亲	mother	dǎting	打听	to inquire
	xǐhuan	喜欢	to like	wǎnshang	晚上	evening
	zǎoshang	早上	morning	zěnme	怎么	how
	yǎnjing	眼睛	eyes	ěrduo	耳朵	ear
	nuǎnhuo	暖和	warm	jiǎozi	饺子	dumpling
(4)	bàba	爸爸	dad	dìdi	弟弟	younger brother
	mèimei	妹妹	younger sister	rènshi	认识	to recognize
	tàitai	太太	Mrs./lady	wàimian	外面	outside
	hòumian	后面	in back	piàoliang	漂亮	attractive
	gàosu	告诉	to tell	gùshi	故事	story
	kànjian	看见	to see	yìsi	意思	meaning
	dìfang	地方	place (n.)	fùqin	父亲	father
	nàme	那么	in that case	shìqing	事情	matter (n.)

2. Tone sandhi:

变调练习：

(1) ˘ + ˘ → ˊ + ˘

shuĭguŏ	水果	fruit	biăoyăn	表演	to perform
kĕyĭ	可以	can	xiăozŭ	小组	group
yŭsăn	雨伞	umbrella	zhănlăn	展览	exhibit
xuănjŭ	选举	elect	lŭguăn	旅馆	inn
shŏubiăo	手表	wrist watch	lăohŭ	老虎	tiger
chăngzhăng	厂长	factory manager	mĕihăo	美好	excellent
guănlĭ	管理	to manage	zhĭdăo	指导	to guide
gŭdiăn	古典	classics	xĭ zăo	洗澡	to bathe

(2) ˘ ˘ + ˘ → ˊ ˊ + ˘

lĕngshuĭ zăo	冷水澡	cold bath
shŏubiăo chăng	手表厂	wrist watch factory
xiăozŭ zhăng	小组长	group leader

(3) ˘ + ˘ ˘ → ˋ⋰ + ˊ ˘ (ˊ + ˊ ˘)

xiăo lăohŭ	小老虎	tiger pup
lăo chăngzhăng	老厂长	the old factory manager
xuăn zŭzhăng	选组长	select a team leader

(4) ˘ + ˉ (ˊ ˋ) → ˋ⋰ + ˉ (ˊ + ˋ)

jĭnzhāng	紧张	tense	hăotīng	好听	beautiful (to hear)
huŏchē	火车	train	lăoshī	老师	teacher
wăngqiú	网球	tennis	kĕnéng	可能	possible
yĭwéi	以为	assume	xiăoshí	小时	hour
shuĭpíng	水平	standard	xuănzé	选择	choice

zhǔrén	主人	host (n.)	lǚtú	旅途	journey
kěshì	可是	but	bǐjiào	比较	compare
hǎokàn	好看	beautiful	gǎnmào	感冒	catch cold
kǎoshì	考试	examination	yǐhòu	以后	later
wǎnhuì	晚会	evening event	mǎnyì	满意	satisfied
yǐnliào	饮料	beverage	kěpà	可怕	frightening
xiě zì	写字	to write	qǐng jià	请假	request leave

3. Distinguish these initials:

分辨声母：

nǔlì	努力	hard	dà nù	大怒	angry
lǚlì	履历	biodata	dàlù	大陆	continent
zhúbù	逐步	step by step	mínzú	民族	nation
chūbù	初步	preliminary	mínzhǔ	民主	democracy
shùmù	数目	amount	yánsè	颜色	colour
xùmù	序幕	prologue	yánrè	炎热	burning hot

4. Distinguish these tones:

分辨声调：

Shānxī	山西	(name of a province)
Shǎnxī	陕西	(name of a province)
tiāndì	天地	scope (of activities)
tiándì	田地	farm lands
tóngbān	同班	in the same class
tóngbàn	同伴	companion
sōngshù	松树	pine tree
sōngshǔ	松鼠	squirrel
diàndēng	电灯	electric lamp
diǎn dēng	点灯	light a lamp

huīzhāng	徽章	badge
huìzhǎng	会长	the president of an association or society

zhēn xiān	真鲜	really fresh
zhēn xián	真咸	really salty
zhēn xiǎn	真险	really dangerous
zhēnxiàn	针线	needlework

Classroom Expressions 课堂用语

1.	Fāndào dì-sì yè.	(翻到第四页。)	Turn to page four.
2.	Tīng wǒ shuō.	(听我说。)	Listen while I say it.
3.	Qǐng nǐ niàn.	(请你念。)	Please read it aloud.
4.	Dà shēng niàn.	(大声念。)	Read it louder.
5.	Zài niàn yí biàn.	(再念一遍。)	Read it aloud once more.
6.	Xiànzài tīngxiě.	(现在听写。)	Take dictation now.
7.	Xiànzài xiūxi.	(现在休息。)	Rest/take a break now.

Retroflex er and Retroflexed Syllable
er 和儿化韵

1. The retroflex final

   卷舌韵母 er

   While pronouncing e〔ə〕, move the tip of the tongue up to the palatal ridge and you'll have the retroflex final. With a bit of practice!

   发er 时，舌头的位置接近于e〔ə〕，只是翘起舌尖，对着硬颚，形成一个带有卷舌作用的e。er不能直接和声母相拼，只能自成音节，如：

   ér（儿）son　　ěr（耳）ear　　èr（二）two

   NOTE that the retroflex final does not take initials. It is as an independent syllable.

2. Retroflexed final

   儿化韵

   These are finals modified by a retroflex ending. Such retroflexing is a common feature of the speech of Beijing, and of northern Putonghua generally. It is indicated by adding an "r" to the final in *pinyin*, and the character 儿 in Chinese script.

   韵母后边可以加上er，形成儿化韵母，书写时在原韵母后面加r，写成汉字时要在汉字后加"儿"。如：

   gēr（歌儿）song　　huār（花儿）flower

   shìr（事儿）thing　　niǎor（鸟儿）bird

   NOTE that when a final ending with -i or -n is retroflexed, the -i or -n are absorbed and not pronounced.

如果韵母的收尾是 -i、-n，在形成儿化韵音节时，-i、-n 不再读出来。如：

wèir	（味儿）	taste	wánr	（玩儿）	to play
xiǎoháir	（小孩儿）	child	pángbiānr	（旁边儿）	beside

练习

1. Read the following retroflex vowel words.

读下列词语，注意er的发音：

ēr			ér		
ěr			èr		
értóng	儿童	child	érqiě	而且	furthermore
érnǚ	儿女	sons and daughters	érzi	儿子	son
ěrjī	耳机	earphone	ěrhuán	耳环	earring
ěrshú	耳熟	familiar (to the ear)	ěrduo	耳朵	ear
èr bān	二班	section two	èr lóu	二楼	second floor
èrbǎi	二百	two hundred	èryuè	二月	February

2. Read the following retroflexed words.

读下列带儿化韵的词语：

zhèr	这儿	here	nàr	那儿	there
wánr	玩儿	to play	xiǎoháir	小孩儿	child
qìshuǐr	汽水儿	soda (soft drink)	méi shìr	没事儿	"Don't mention it"
hàomǎr	号码儿	number	xiàohuàr	笑话儿	joke (n.)
yíxiàr	一下儿	once, a bit	fànguǎnr	饭馆儿	restaurant
liáo tiānr	聊天儿	chat	yìdiǎnr	一点儿	a little

hǎowánr	好玩儿	fun	zhōngjiānr	中间儿	middle
bīnggùnr	冰棍儿	popsicle	chàng gēr	唱歌儿	to sing
miàntiáor	面条儿	noodles	huāyàngr	花样儿	variety

3. Distinguish between these words, noting the effect on meaning of retroflexion.

辨析下列各组词，注意儿化与不儿化的不同含义：

huà	画	to draw
huàr	画儿	picture
jiān	尖	sharp
jiānr	尖儿	point
yí kuài	一块	a piece of
yíkuàir	一块儿	together

4. Read the following polysyllabic words.

多音节连读：

(1)	xīngqītiān	星期天	Sunday
	pǔtōnghuà	普通话	Putonghua
	jiǎngxuéjīn	奖学金	scholarship
	zhàoxiàngjī	照相机	camera
	fúwùyuán	服务员	service attendant
	diànyǐngyuàn	电影院	cinema
	túshūguǎn	图书馆	library
	chàbuduō	差不多	almost
	wèishénme	为什么	Why?
	zěnmeyàng	怎么样	How (as a predicate)
(2)	Hànyǔ cídiǎn	汉语词典	Chinese dictionary
	Zhōngguó dìtú	中国地图	map of China

nǔlì xuéxí	努力学习	study diligently
zūnshǒu jìlǜ	遵守纪律	observe discipline
kètáng huódòng	课堂活动	classroom activity
kèwài liànxí	课外练习	extracurricular practice
bìyè diǎnlǐ	毕业典礼	graduation ceremony
lǚxíng yúkuài	旅行愉快	have a pleasant journey

5. Commit the following words and sentences to memory.

熟记下列词语：

wánr	(玩儿)	to play
yìdiǎnr	(一点儿)	a little
wǒmen	(我们)	we, us
nǐmen	(你们)	you
tāmen	(他们)	they, them
Nǐmen zài zuǒbianr.	(你们在左边儿。)	You are on the left.
Tāmen zài yòubianr.	(他们在右边儿。)	They are on the right.

Classroom Expressions 课堂用语

1.	Yǒu wèntí ma?	(有问题吗？)	Are there questions?
2.	Méi yǒu wèntí.	(没有问题。)	No questions; No problem (it's alright).
3.	Kuài bu kuài?	(快不快？)	Is it fast?
4.	Bú kuài.	(不快。)	It's not fast.
5.	Qǐng shuō de màn yìdiǎnr.	(请说得慢一点儿。)	Please speak slower.
6.	Qǐng děng yi děng.	(请等一等。)	Please wait a bit.

Aspirated and Unaspirated Initials and the Initials j, q and x
送气不送气声母及声母 j 、q 、x

1. Aspirated and unaspirated initials

   送气不送气声母

   There are six pairs of initials among the total of 21 that are distinguished by aspiration or the degree of breath release. All other aspects of mouth shape and tongue position are the same within each pair. They are:

   在21个声母中有六对对立的声母，每对发音部位相同，但是发音方法不同，有送气和不送气的区别。这六对声母是：

(1)	b	p
(2)	d	t
(3)	g	k
(4)	j	q
(5)	zh	ch
(6)	z	c

   Those on the left, the unaspirates, are characterized by a weak release of breath. The pronounciation of b, d and g, for example, is similar to the English "p", "t" and "k" in the words "spool", "stool" and "sky".

   左边一行b、d、g、j、zh、z，发这些声母时口腔中送出的气流较弱，称为不送气声母。其中b、d、g与英语spool、stool、sky中的p、t、k、的发音相似。

   Those on the right, the aspirates, are characterized by a stronger release of breath. The pronounciation of p, t and k is similar to the English "p", "t" and "c" in "pool", "tool" and "cool".

右边一行p、t、k、q、ch、c，发这些声母时口腔中送出的气流较强。称为送气声母。其中p、t、k与英语pool、tool、cool中p、t、c的发音相似。

2. The initials j, q and x

   声母j、q、x

   These three are palatals, produced with the front of the tongue on the palate, as if a "y" sound followed them. The j and q are an aspirated/unaspirated pair (see above). x is a fricative, sounding something like "sy-".

   The three initials only appear in *pinyin* followed by i or ü. NOTE that in spelling convention, the umlaut dots above the ü are not written in this context. Examples are:

   这三个声母都是舌面音。发j和q时，前舌面贴着硬腭，气流从舌面和硬腭之间冲出去，产生爆发摩擦的声音。j是不送气音，气流较弱；q是送气音，气流较强。x是擦音，前舌面和硬腭接近，气流从中间挤出。j、q、x都是清音，发音时声带不振动。

   j、q、x只跟i、ü和以i、ü开头的韵母相拼。如：

jī	qī	xī
jiā	qiā	xiā
jiǔ	qiǔ	xiǔ
jiǎng	qiǎng	xiǎng
jù	qù	xù
jué	qué	xué
jún	qún	xún

练习

1. Practice these aspirates and nonaspirates.

练习送气与不送气音：

b	p	d	t	g	k
bō	pō	dì	tì	gē	kē
bù	pù	dāi	tāi	gǔ	kǔ
bǎo	pǎo	duō	tuō	gǒu	kǒu
bān	pān	dǒng	tǒng	guāng	kuāng

zh	ch	j	q	z	c
zhā	chā	jiā	qiā	zū	cū
zhù	chù	jiǎn	qiǎn	zòu	còu
zhāi	chāi	jīng	qīng	zāng	cāng
zhōng	chōng	jué	qué	zǎn	cǎn

2. Distinguish between these groups.

分辨下面各组音：

(1) b　p

bái	white	báishuǐ	plain boiled water
pái	drain away	pái shuǐ	drain off water

(2) d　t

dǐ	bottom	dǐxì	ins and outs
tǐ	body	tǐxì	system

(3) g　k

gàn	to do	nénggàn	competent
kàn	to read	néng kàn	can read

(4) zh　ch

zhù	to live	zhùsuǒ	dwelling place
chù	place	chùsuǒ	location

(5) j q

jiān	a measure word	sān jiān	three rooms
qiān	thousand	sānqiān	three thousand

(6) z c

zuò	to do	bú zuò	not to do
cuò	wrong	búcuò	pretty good

3. Practice writing and reading the palatal initial series j, q and x.

练习j、q、x的拼读：

(1)

jī	qī	xī
jiáo	qiáo	xiáo
jiě	qiě	xiě
jìn	qìn	xìn
jīng	qīng	xīng
jióng	qióng	xióng
jiǎn	qiǎn	xiǎn
jū	qū	xū
juàn	quàn	xuàn

(2)

xuéxiào	学校	school	xuéqī	学期	term (semester)
jiějué	解决	solve	jiānqiáng	坚强	staunch
qiūjì	秋季	autumn season	xiàjì	夏季	summer season
jiūjìng	究竟	after all	xìjūn	细菌	germ
jiānjù	艰巨	extremely difficult	jìxù	继续	continue
xīngqī	星期	week	qǔxiāo	取消	cancel

jiěquàn	解劝	mollify	xiāngxìn	相信	believe
xìngqù	兴趣	interest	xióngxīn	雄心	grand ambition
jīqi	机器	machine	xiūxi	休息	to rest
jiāju	家具	furniture	jìxing	记性	memory

4. Fill in the initials as dictated.

听写声母：

(1) a. _____ēn_____ǎo (奔跑) to run

b. _____iān_____ào (鞭炮) firecrackers

c. _____áng_____iān (旁边) beside

d. _____ǎo_____ù (跑步) to run

e. _____iàn_____ái (电台) radio station

f. _____ì_____ǎn (地毯) carpet

g. _____uǒ_____àng (妥当) appropriate

h. _____ì_____ài (替代) to replace

i. _____ù_____è (顾客) customer

j. _____ǎn_____uài (赶快) quickly

k. _____āi_____uān (开关) switch

l. _____uān_____uǎng (宽广) broad

m. _____ī_____íng (批评) criticism

n. _____áo_____ài (淘汰) to sift out

(2) a. _____ū (虚) empty

b. _____ū (区) district

c. _____uǎn (选) choose

d. _____uè (确) firmly

e. _____ián (前) front

f. _____iǎo (巧) skilful

g. _____iǎng (讲) speak

h. _____iǎo (脚) foot

i. _____iáng (强) strong

j. _____īn_____íng (心情) frame of mind

k. _____iān_____uè (鲜血) blood

l. _____iāo_____iǎn (消遣) divert oneself

m. _____ián_____ī (前期) early days

n. _____ū_____īn (虚心) modest

o. _____īng_____iàng (倾向) tendency

p. _____iàn_____iàng (现象) appearance

5. Fluency practice. Read the words and sentences below.
熟读下列词语：

(1) Qǐng jìn. (请进。) Come in, please.

(2) Qǐng zuò. (请坐。) Sit down, please.

(3) xuéxí (学习) study

(4) Hànyǔ (汉语) the Han language (Chinese)

(5) Wǒmen xuéxí Hànyǔ. (我们学习汉语。) We are studying Chinese.

Classroom Expressions 课堂用语

1. Xiànzài shàng kè. (现在上课。) We'll start class now.
2. Xiànzài xià kè. (现在下课。) We'll end class now.
3. Qǐng dǎkāi shū. (请打开书。) Please open your books.
4. Qǐng héshang shū. (请合上书。) Please close your books.

5. Qǐng kàn hēibǎn.	（请看黑板。）	Please look at the blackboard.
6. Jīntian xuéxí dì-liù kè.	（今天学习第六课。）	Today we'll study lesson 6.

z, c, s and the Final -i; zh, ch, sh, r and the Final -i
z、c、s 和韵母 -i 及 zh、ch、sh、r 和韵母 -i

1. Initials z, c and s

   声母 z、c、s

   These three voiceless sounds are called blade-alveolars. The z and c are an aspirated/unaspirated pair, produced by putting the tip of the tongue against the back of the upper teeth or at the alveolar ridge. Hence, their name. s is a fricative, produced by pushing the breath out when the tip of the tongue is near the front teeth.

   这三个声母都是舌尖前音。发z和c时，舌尖顶住上齿背面，气流从舌尖和齿背间爆发摩擦而出，但c送气，z不送气。s是擦音，舌尖接近上齿背面，气流从中间挤出去。z、c、s也都是清音。如：

zài	cài	sài
zāng	cāng	sāng
zū	cū	sū
zuì	cuì	suì

   The z sound approximates the “ds” in English “cads”, and the c is like the “ts” in “cats”.

   z的发音与英语cads中的ds相近，但声带不振动。c的发音与英语cats中的ts相近，只是气流比ts更强一些。

2. The final -i

韵母 -i〔ɿ〕

After z, c and s, this can be considered a zero vowel, just a prolonging of the consonant sound. The PALATAL i vowel (as in biāo, yāo) does not appear after these consonants.

韵母-i出现在z、c、s后面，听起来就象前面声母z、c、s摩擦成分的延长，只是同时声带要颤动，由清音变成浊音。写作-i，是因为读成〔i〕的i不会出现在z、c、s的后面。例如：

zī	cī	sī
zì	cì	sì

3. Initials zh, ch, sh, r

声母 zh、ch、sh、r

There are blade-palatals and take a bit of practice curling the tongue tip up behind the alveolar ridge. zh and ch are an unaspirated/aspirated pair.

这四个声母都是舌尖后音，发zh和ch时，翘起舌尖，顶住硬腭，气流从舌尖和硬腭之间冲出去，产生爆发摩擦的声音。zh是不送气音，气流较弱；ch是送气音，气流较强。发sh和r时舌尖翘起接近硬腭，气流从舌尖和硬腭之间挤出。sh和r都是擦音，二者不同在于sh是清音，r是浊音。如：

zhè	chè	shè	rè
zhú	chú	shú	rú
zhuō	chuō	shuō	ruō
zhăng	chăng	shăng	răng

The sounds of the set can be compared to the sounds in "judge" (dg), "chair" (ch), "shirt" (sh) and "royal" (r) in English. But don't round the lips. Keep them spread, exaggerating it at first and gradually relaxing the more accurate you get.

英语中没有舌尖后音。英语judge、chair、show、right中的dg、ch、sh、r与zh、ch、sh、r虽然相似，但并不相同。英语发这几个音时舌尖不翘起，唇要突出呈圆形；发汉语zh、ch、sh、r时舌尖要翘起，唇是扁平的。

4. The final -i

韵母 -i〔ʅ〕

As with the z, c, s set, the vowel following zh, ch, sh, r can be considered a zero value entity, simply indicating a prolongation of the consonant sound. The PALATAL -i vowel does not combine with these sounds.

韵母i出现在zh、ch、sh、r后面，听起来就象zh、ch、sh、r摩擦成分的延长，只是同时声带要颤动，读成浊音。写作-i，也是因为读成〔i〕的i不会出现在zh、ch、sh、r的后面。例如：

zhī	chī	shī	rī
zhì	chì	shì	rì

练 习

1. Practice pronouncing the following.

练习z、c、s的拼读：

(1)

zì	cì	sì
zǎo	cǎo	sǎo
zài	cài	sài
zōng	cōng	sōng
zuān	cuān	suān

(2)

míngzi	名字	name	zàijiàn	再见	goodbye
zǎoshang	早上	morning	zǒu lù	走路	to walk
zuótian	昨天	yesterday	gānzào	干燥	dry, parched

	zìjǐ	自己	oneself	zǒngjié	总结	summarize
	zuìhòu	最后	the last	zěnme	怎么	how
	zuòyè	作业	homework	zìxíngchē	自行车	bicycle
(3)	cídiǎn	词典	dictionary	cǎisè	彩色	color
	cāochǎng	操场	sports ground	búcuò	不错	not bad
	cōngming	聪明	intelligent	cóngqián	从前	formerly
	qīngcài	青菜	green vegetables	xīcān	西餐	western food
	zhōngcān	中餐	Chinese food			
(4)	gōngsī	公司	company	zàisān	再三	repeatedly
	qīngsōng	轻松	light, relaxed	sùshè	宿舍	dormitory
	suíbiàn	随便	as you wish, casual	suǒyǐ	所以	so
	dǎsuàn	打算	calculate, plan	gàosu	告诉	to tell
	sìshí	四十	forty	yǔsǎn	雨伞	umbrella
	yìsi	意思	meaning	suīrán	虽然	although

2. Practice pronouncing the following.

练习zh、ch、sh、r的拼读：

(1)	zhà — zhè	炸 — 这	to explode — this
	zhān — Zhāng	粘 — 张	to stick — (a surname)
	chóu — chú	稠 — 除	thick — except
	ròu — rù	肉 — 入	meat — to enter
	zhū — chū	猪 — 出	pig — to go out
	shù — chù	树 — 处	tree — place

zhuā — shuā	抓 — 刷	to catch — to brush
chūn — chōng	春 — 冲	spring — to rush
zhuàng — chuàng	撞 — 创	to run into — to achieve
zhuō — shuō	桌 — 说	table — to say
zhī — chī	知 — 吃	to know — to eat
shì — rì	是 — 日	to be — the sun

(2)	zhàopiàn	照片	photo	zhùyì	注意	take note of
	dìzhǐ	地址	address	zhōngwǔ	中午	noon
	jǐnzhāng	紧张	tense	chuánzhēn	传真	fax
	zhǔnbèi	准备	prepare	zhuōzi	桌子	table
	zhēnde	真的	really	zhīdao	知道	to know
(3)	cháyè	茶叶	tea leaves	fēicháng	非常	unusually
	cháoshī	潮湿	damp (humid)	chènshān	衬衫	shirt
	chī fàn	吃饭	to eat	chúfáng	厨房	kitchen
	hǎochī	好吃	tasty	huǒchē	火车	train
	jīchǎng	机场	airport	chéngji	成绩	grades (performance)
(4)	shāngchǎng	商场	mall	xuésheng	学生	student
	shūfu	舒服	comfortable	shēngdiào	声调	tone (of Chinese)
	shōushi	收拾	tidy up	duōshao	多少	how much
	jièshào	介绍	introduce	kǎoshì	考试	examination
	shuì jiào	睡觉	to sleep	diànshì	电视	television
(5)	rènao	热闹	bustling	rènshi	认识	to recognize
	rúguǒ	如果	if	róngyi	容易	easy

ránhòu	然后	after that	rénmín	人民	the people
dāngrán	当然	of course	shēngri	生日	birthday
ruòxiǎo	弱小	small and weak	réngjiù	仍旧	as before

3. Distinguish these pairs.

辨音练习：

(1) zh、ch、sh与z、c、s

zhǐ — zǐ	chí — cí	shì — sì
shǎn — sǎn	zhāng — zāng	chūn — cūn
chuī — cuī	shēn — sēn	chóng — cóng
zhuǎn — zuǎn	zhòu — zòu	chuò — cuò

(2) zh、ch、sh与j、q、x

zhēnjiǔ	针灸	acupuncture	shǒuxù	手续	procedure
chéngqiáng	城墙	city wall	zhǐjiào	指教	instruct (polite)
shùxué	数学	mathematics	chángqī	长期	long term
zhōngjiān	中间	middle	shēnxīn	身心	in body and mind
chūqí	出奇	exceptional			

4. Fill in the dictated initials.

听写声母：

_____ī	（织）	_____ǎ	（傻）	_____á	（茶）
_____ǎo	（早）	_____uì	（岁）	_____ān	（三）
_____ōu	（抽）	_____ù	（住）	_____ī	（吃）
_____uáng	（床）	_____ōu	（周）	_____ú	（熟）
_____óng	（从）	_____ì	（字）	_____āi	（猜）

5. Write the dictated words.

听写词语：

早操	车站	出色	正在	日程
数字	衬衫	著作	专长	宿舍
装饰	尊重	手指	生词	如此

6. Familiarize yourself with these words and sentences.

熟记下列词语：

(1) lǎoshī	(老师)	teacher
xuésheng	(学生)	student
qù	(去)	to go
jiàoshì	(教室)	classroom
túshūguǎn	(图书馆)	library
Lǎoshī qù jiàoshì.	(老师去教室。)	The teacher goes to the classroom.
Xuésheng qù túshūguǎn.	(学生去图书馆。)	The students go to the library.

Classroom Expressions 课堂用语

1. Fùxí dì-qī kè.	(复习第七课。)	Review lesson 7.
2. Yùxí dì-bā kè.	(预习第八课。)	Prepare lesson 8.
3. Jīntian de zuòyè shi …	(今天的作业是…)	Today's homework is …
4. Míngtian kǎoshì.	(明天考试。)	Tomorrow we have a test.
5. Dǒng le ma?	(懂了吗？)	Do you understand?
6. Dǒng le.	(懂了。)	Yes, I do.
7. Bù dǒng.	(不懂。)	No, I don't.
8. Qǐng zài shuō yí biàn.	(请再说一遍。)	Please say it once more.

General Review
总复习

1. Read the initials from the chart, paying attention to the shape of the mouth and position of the tongue and teeth.

读声母表，分析声母的发音部位及发音方法：

manner of pronunciation 发音方法 / 发音部位 point of articulation	不送气 清塞音和 塞擦音 unaspirated voiceless plosives and affricates	送气 清塞音和 塞擦音 aspirated voiceless plosives and affricates	浊鼻音 voiced nasals	清擦音 voiceless fricatives	浊边音、 浊擦音 voiced lateral, voiced fricative
唇音 labial	b	p	m	f	
舌尖音 alveolar	d	t	n		l
舌尖前音 blade - alveolar	z	c		s	
舌尖后音 blade - palatal	zh	ch		sh	r
舌面音 palatal	j	q		x	
舌根音 velar	g	k		h	

2. Read the finals from the chart.

读韵母表：

		i	u	ü
单韵母 simple finals	a	ia	ua	
	o		uo	
	e (r)			
	ê	ie		üe
复韵母 compound finals	ai		uai	
	ei		uei (ui)	
	ao	iao		
	ou	iou (iu)		
鼻音韵母 finals with nasal endings	an	ian	uan	üan
	en	in	uen (un)	ün
	ang	iang	uang	
	eng	ing	ueng	
	ong	iong		

3. Practice distinguishing these sounds.

辨音练习：

(1) Initials

分辨声母

bǎole	（饱了）	filled (satisfied)
pǎole	（跑了）	ran
dúshū	（读书）	to read a book
túshū	（图书）	books
qíngle	（晴了）	It's clearing up.
xíngle	（行了）	All right
méi zuò	（没做）	Didn't do it.
méi cuò	（没错）	I'm quite sure

niánjié	(年节)	New Year's and other holidays
liánjié	(廉洁)	pure (incorrupt), honest
zhōnghé	(中和)	combination
zōnghé	(综合)	synthesize
gèrén	(个人)	individual
kèren	(客人)	guest
shīshì	(失事)	accident (plane, etc.)
sīshì	(私事)	personal matter
jīngzhuāng	(精装)	fine edition
qīngzhāung	(轻装)	travel light (little baggage)
jījīn	(基金)	foundation (philanthropic)
zījīn	(资金)	capital
zhùsuǒ	(住所)	residence
chùsuǒ	(处所)	place

(2) Finals

分辨韵母

guānxīn	(关心)	to be concerned about
gānxīn	(甘心)	to be willing, willingly
fùzá	(复杂)	difficult, complicated
fù zé	(负责)	to be responsible for
yuánzhuō	(圆桌)	round table
yuánzhōu	(圆周)	circumference
hòuchē	(候车)	wait for a train
huòchē	(货车)	baggage car
dōngfēng	(东风)	east wind
dōngfāng	(东方)	east, orient

xìngfú	（幸福）	happiness, to be happy
xìnfú	（信服）	be convinced
Jiāngnán	（江南）	South of the (Yangtze) River
jiānnán	（艰难）	difficult, hard (hardship)
sànshī	（散失）	scattered and disappeared
sàngshī	（丧失）	forfeit

4. Practice distinguishing these words.

辨调练习：

(1)

shìshí	（事实）	fact
shíshì	（实事）	real matters
tiáolǐ	（条理）	orderliness
tiáolì	（条例）	regulation
zhīyuán	（支援）	aid
zhìyuàn	（志愿）	aspiration
niánjí	（年级）	year (of college, etc.)
niánjì	（年纪）	age
bù mǎi	（不买）	don't buy
bú mài	（不卖）	don't sell
dǎdǎo	（打倒）	knock down
dádào	（达到）	reach (a destination, goal)
dà dào	（大道）	main road
zhèngzhì	（政治）	politics
zhēngzhí	（争执）	be at odds with
zhèngzhí	（正直）	upright, honest
zhěngzhì	（整治）	renovate
zhěngzhī	（整枝）	pruning

jiēshì	（街市）	street market
jiěshì	（解释）	to explain
jièshí	（届时）	at the appointed time
jié shí	（节食）	to diet
jiēshi	（结实）	sturdy, durable

(2)

bēizi	（杯子）	cup
bèizi	（被子）	quilt

shōushi	（收拾）	tidy up, organize
shǒushi	（首饰）	ornament, jewelry

dǒng le	（懂了）	understood
dòng le	（冻了）	frozen

xiǎo le	（小了）	to become small
xiào le	（笑了）	smiled

5. Read the following aloud, taking note of tone sandhi.

读下列词语，注意变调：

xiǎozǔ	（小组）	group
yǔsǎn	（雨伞）	umbrella
biǎoyǎn	（表演）	perform

jiǎndān	（简单）	simple
hǎotīng	（好听）	pleasant (to hear)
jǐnzhāng	（紧张）	tense

yǐqián	（以前）	before
kěnéng	（可能）	possibly
měinián	（每年）	each year

gǎnmào	（感冒）	catch cold
hǎokàn	（好看）	pleasant (to look at)
yǐnliào	（饮料）	beverages

wǎnshang	(晚上)	evening
nǎinai	(奶奶)	grandma
nuǎnhuo	(暖和)	warm, cozy

6. Practice these tones in context.

练习四声连读：

(1)	diànhuà	电话	telephone
(2)	jìnbù	进步	progress
(3)	fùyìn	复印	photocopy
(4)	zhàopiàn	照片	photo
(5)	duànliàn	锻练	exercise (physical)
(6)	shùnbiàn	顺便	as is convenient
(7)	zàijiàn	再见	goodbye
(8)	huàjù	话剧	a play
(9)	shàng kè	上课	attend class
(10)	xià kè	下课	finish class
(11)	sàn bù	散步	stroll
(12)	zhào xiàng	照相	to photograph
(13)	Hànzì	汉字	Chinese characters
(14)	sùshè	宿舍	dormitory
(15)	fùshù	复述	retell
(16)	jiàn miàn	见面	to meet

7. Practice with polysyllabic expressions.

练习多音节连读：

(1) jiǎng xiàohuar （讲笑话儿） to tell jokes
lái chàng gēr （来唱歌儿） come to sing
ài xiǎoháir （爱小孩儿） to like children
hěn hǎowánr （很好玩儿） very amusing

(2) Tiānqì búcuò. （天气不错。） The weather is pretty good.
Shēntǐ hěn hǎo. （身体很好。） (His) health is good.
jièshào jīngyàn （介绍经验） to pass on one's experiences
wénhuà jiāoliú （文化交流） cultural exchange
chūn xià qiū dōng （春夏秋冬） Spring, summer, autumn and winter
nán nǚ lǎo shào （男女老少） male, female, old and young
dōng nán xī běi （东南西北） east, south, west and north
qián hòu zuǒ yòu （前后左右） front, back, left and right

8. Memorize these words and sentences.

熟记下列词语：

(1) yī （一） one　èr （二） two　sān （三） three
sì （四） four　wǔ （五） five　liù （六） six
qī （七） seven　bā （八） eight　jiǔ （九） nine
shí （十） ten

(2) rén （人） people
shi （是） to be (to equal)
Zhōngguó （中国） China
Tā shi Zhōngguó rén. （他是中国人。） He is a Chinese.

Classroom Expressions 课堂用语

1.	Xuéxí shēngcí.	(学习生词。)	We'll learn the vocabulary.
2.	Xiě Hànzì.	(写汉字。)	We'll write the Chinese characters.
3.	Niàn kèwén.	(念课文。)	Read the text.
4.	Zhùyì fāyīn.	(注意发音。)	Watch the pronunciation.
5.	Huídá wèntí.	(回答问题。)	Answer the questions.
6.	"… " zěnme shuō?	("…"怎么说？)	How do you say …?

附：声韵拼合总表

普通话声韵拼合总表

Table of Combinations of Initials and Finals in Common Speech

韵母 / 声母	a	o	e	ê	-i	er	ai	ei	ao	ou	an	en	ang	eng	ong
	a	o	e	ê		er	ai	ei	ao	ou	an	en	ang	eng	
b	ba	bo					bai	bei	bao		ban	ben	bang	beng	
p	pa	po					pai	pei	pao	pou	pan	pen	pang	peng	
m	ma	mo	me				mai	mei	mao	mou	man	men	mang	meng	
f	fa	fo						fei		fou	fan	fen	fang	feng	
d	da		de				dai	dei	dao	dou	dan	den	dang	deng	dong
t	ta		te				tai		tao	tou	tan		tang	teng	tong
n	na		ne				nai	nei	nao	nou	nan	nen	nang	neng	nong
l	la		le				lai	lei	lao	lou	lan		lang	leng	long
z	za		ze		zi		zai	zei	zao	zou	zan	zen	zang	zeng	zong
c	ca		ce		ci		cai		cao	cou	can	cen	cang	ceng	cong
s	sa		se		si		sai		sao	sou	san	sen	sang	seng	song
zh	zha		zhe		zhi		zhai	zhei	zhao	zhou	zhan	zhen	zhang	zheng	zhong
ch	cha		che		chi		chai		chao	chou	chan	chen	chang	cheng	chong
sh	sha		she		shi		shai	shei	shao	shou	shan	shen	shang	sheng	
r			re		ri				rao	rou	ran	ren	rang	reng	rong
j															
q															
x															
g	ga		ge				gai	gei	gao	gou	gan	gen	gang	geng	gong
k	ka		ke				kai	kei	kao	kou	kan	ken	kang	keng	kong
h	ha		he				hai	hei	hao	hou	han	hen	hang	heng	hong

韵母 / 声母	i	ia	iao	ie	iu	ian	in	iang	ing	iong	u	ua	uo	uai	ui	uan	un	uang	ueng	ü	üe	üan	ün
	yi	ya	yao	ye	you	yan	jin	yang	ying	yong	wu	wa	wo	wai	wei	wan	wen	wang	weng	yu	yue	yuan	yun
b	bi		biao	bie		bian	bin		bing		bu												
p	pi		piao	pie		pian	pin		ping		pu												
m	mi		miao	mie	miu	mian	min		ming		mu												
f											fu												
d	di		diao	die	diu	dian			ding		du		duo		dui	duan	dun						
t	ti		tiao	tie		tian			ting		tu		tuo		tui	tuan	tun						
n	ni		niao	nie	niu	nian	nin	niang	ning		nu		nuo			nuan				nü	nüe		
l	li	lia	liao	lie	liu	lian	lin	liang	ling		lu		luo			luan	lun			lü	lüe		
z											zu		zuo		zui	zuan	zun						
c											cu		cuo		cui	cuan	cun						
s											su		suo		sui	suan	sun						
zh											zhu	zhua	zhuo	zhuai	zhui	zhuan	zhun	zhuang					
ch											chu	chua	chuo	chuai	chui	chuan	chun	chuang					
sh											shu	shua	shuo	shuai	shui	shuan	shun	shuang					
r											ru	rua	ruo		rui	ruan	run						
j	ji	jia	jiao	jie	jiu	jian	jin	jiang	jing	jiong										ju	jue	juan	jun
q	qi	qia	qiao	qie	qiu	qian	qin	qiang	qing	qiong										qu	que	quan	qun
x	xi	xia	xiao	xie	xiu	xian	xin	xiang	xing	xiong										xu	xue	xuan	xun
g											gu	gua	guo	guai	gui	guan	gun	guang					
k											ku	kua	kuo	kuai	kui	kuan	kun	kuang					
h											hu	hua	huo	huai	hui	huan	hun	huang					

Personalities in the Text
课文主要人物

张老师 Mrs. Zhang

山本 Yamamoto

大卫 David

安娜 Anna

金中一 Kim Chung-il

方小英 Fang Xiaoying

马丁 Martin

第一课

你是哪国人？

汉字课文

（一）

大　卫：你好！

山　本：你好！

大　卫：你是山本吗？

山　本：是，我是山本。

大　卫：他们是谁？

山　本：他是金中一，她是方小英。

（二）

大　卫：方小英是日本人吗？

金中一：不是，她是中国人。

大　卫：你也是中国人吗？

金中一：我不是中国人，我是韩国人。你是不是英国人？

大　卫：我不是英国人。

金中一：你是哪国人？

大　卫：我是美国人。

生词语

1.	你	nǐ	(pro)	you
2.	是	shì	(v)	(equational verb) equals, is

3.	哪	něi; nǎ	(pro)		which
4.	国	guó	(n)		country
5.	人	rén	(n)	[个 gè]	man (male or female), person, people
6.	好	hǎo	(adj)		to be good
		a. 你好！			
		b. 你们好！			
7.	吗	ma	(part)		(interrogative particle)
8.	我	wǒ	(pro)		I, me
9.	他	tā	(pro)		he, him
10.	们	men	(n suff)		(pluralizing suffix for pronouns and some personal nouns)
11.	他们	tāmen	(pro)		they, them
12.	谁	shéi; shuí	(pro)		who, whom
13.	不	bù	(adv)		(negates verbs, including adjectival and optative verbs)
		a. 他不是金中一。			
		b. 他们不是韩国人。			
14.	她	tā	(pro)		she, her
15.	也	yě	(adv)		also, too
		a. 我是美国人，她也是美国人。			
		b. 大卫不是中国人，山本也不是中国人。			
		c. 方小英不是英国人，也不是日本人。			

专有名词

1.	大卫	Dàwèi	David
2.	山本	Shānběn	Yamamoto

3.	金中一	Jīn Zhōngyī	Kim Chung-il
4.	方小英	Fāng Xiǎoyīng	Fang Xiaoying
5.	日本	Rìběn	Japan
6.	中国	Zhōngguó	China
7.	韩国	Hánguó	Korea (Southern)
8.	英国	Yīngguó	England
9.	美国	Měiguó	America

语 法 点

1. The equational shì, 是

“是”字句

Generally speaking, there is an A = B symmetry to a shì sentence, with the object defining what the subject is.

一般来说，“是”字句形式是“A是B ”。宾语B说明主语A是什么。

S + 是 + O

a. Wǒ shi Shānběn.

我是山本。

I am Yamamoto.

b. Tā shi Zhōngguorén.

他是中国人。

He is (a) Chinese.

Shì is negated by bù 不

“是”的否定形式是在“是”前加“不”。

S + 不 + 是 + O

c. Tā bú shi Fāng Xiǎoyīng.

她不是方小英。

She isn't Fang Xiaoying.

d. Wǒ bú shi Měiguorén.

我不是美国人。

I'm not an American.

* Verbs in Chinese do not change under any condition. They are not influenced by person (I, me, he, him), time, etc.

汉语动词本身在任何情况下都没有变化，不受人称、时间等的影响。

2. The interrogative particle <u>ma</u> 吗

表示疑问的语气助词"吗"

A declarative sentence can be made into a question by adding the modal particle <u>ma</u> 吗.

在陈述句句尾加上语气助词"吗"，就构成疑问句。

a. Nǐ shi Rìběnrén ma?

你是日本人吗？

Are you Japanese?

b. Tā shi Dàwèi ma?

他是大卫吗？

Is he David?

3. Interrogative pronoun questions

用疑问代词的疑问句

Converting a declarative sentence into a question requires no change of order when an interrogative pronoun is used. Just put the interrogative word where the answer is expected.

用疑问代词的疑问句不需要改变词序，只需要把疑问代词放在要求答案的位置上。

a. Shéi shi Dàwèi?

谁是大卫？

Who is David?

b. Tā shi shéi?

他是谁？

Who is he? (lit. He is who?)

c. Tā shi nă guó rén?

她是哪国人？

Which country is she from?

4. Affirmative-negative question

正反疑问句

The equational can be made interrogative by putting affirmative and negative side by side.

把谓语的肯定形式和否定形式并列在一起，就构成正反疑问句。

S + V 不 V + O?

a. Nĭ shì bu shì Hánguorén?

你是不是韩国人？

Are you Korean?

b. Tā shì bu shì Jīn Zhōngyī?

他是不是金中一？

Is he Kim Chung-il?

The predicate object may also divide the affirmative and negative forms.

谓语中的宾语也可以插在肯定式与否定式之间。

S + V + O + 不 V?

c. Nǐ shi Hánguorén bú shì?

你是韩国人不是？

Are you Korean?

d. Tā shi Jīn Zhōngyī bú shì?

他是金中一不是？

Is he Kim Chung-il?

* This last usage, at least with shì, might be habit among certain speakers. Foreign learners can live quite comfortably understanding it, but not using it.

宾语插在肯定式与否定式之间的用法是某些中国人的习惯用法，初学汉语的外国人只是了解有这种句式而不一定去使用，照样不会影响他的生活。

NOTE 注释

1. Pronounciation of bù 不

“不”的声调

4th tone	when it is by itself, e.g. bù 不 “no”. when it is followed by words in the 1st, 2nd or 3rd tones, or 1st, 2nd or 3rd tones that have been neutralized; e.g., bù duō 不多 bù nán 不难 bù mǎi 不买
第四声	“不”字单念时，如“bu 不”。“不”字后面有一、二、三声字(或有由一、二、三声变来的轻声字)时，如“bù duō 不多”、“bù nán 不难”、“bù mǎi 不买”。
2nd tone	when it is followed by words in the 4th tone, or neutralized 4th tone; e.g., bú shì 不是, bú qù 不去.
第二声	“不”字后面是四声字(或有由四声变来的轻声字)时，如“bú shì 不是”、“bú qù 不去”。

词组和句子

1. 中国人　美国人　日本人　韩国人　英国人　哪国人
2. 我是大卫，他是山本。
3. 我是日本人，他是英国人，她也是英国人。
4. 我们是美国人，不是英国人。
5. 他不是中国人，也不是日本人。
6. 你是金中一吗？
7. 你们是美国人吗？
8. 你们是韩国人，他们也是韩国人吗？
9. 谁是方小英？
10. 谁是英国人？
11. 他是谁？
12. 她们是哪国人？
13. 金中一是哪国人？
14. 他们是不是中国人？
15. 你们是韩国人不是？
16. 你是不是山本？
17. 他是大卫不是？

参考资料

拼音课文

Nǐ shi něi guó rén?

(I)

Dàwèi:　　Nǐ hǎo!

Shānběn:	Nǐ hǎo!
Dàwèi:	Nǐ shi Shānběn ma?
Shānběn:	Shì, wǒ shi Shānběn.
Dàwèi:	Tāmen shi shéi?
Shānběn:	Tā shi Jīn Zhōngyī, tā shi Fāng Xiǎoyīng.

(II)

Dàwèi:	Fāng Xiǎoyīng shi Rìbenrén ma?
Jīn Zhōngyī:	Bú shì, tā shi Zhōngguorén.
Dàwèi:	Nǐ yě shi Zhōngguorén ma?
Jīn Zhōngyī:	Wǒ bú shi Zhōngguorén, wǒ shi Hánguorén. Nǐ shì bu shì Yīngguorén?
Dàwèi:	Wǒ bú shi Yīngguorén.
Jīn Zhōngyī:	Nǐ shi něi guó rén?
Dàwèi:	Wǒ shi Měiguorén.

英译课文

Where are you from?

(I)

David:	Hello!
Yamamoto:	Hello!
David:	Are you Yamamoto?
Yamamoto:	Right, I'm Yamamoto.
David:	Who are they?
Yamamoto:	He is Kim Chung-il and she is Fang Xiaoying.

(II)

David:	Is Fang Xiaoying Japanese?
Kim Chung-il:	No, she's Chinese.

David:	Are you Chinese, too?
Kim Chung-il:	I'm not Chinese, I'm a Korean.
	Are you an Englishman?
David:	I'm not an Englishman.
Kim Chung-il:	What are you?
David:	I'm an American.

课堂活动

I. shi sentences

“是”字句

Students form pairs. Student A is given chart A, student B chart B. ✗ on the chart indicates that the answer should be negative. Student A asks B the nationality and name of the characters at 1 and 2 on the chart in accordance with the question patterns heading the columns. B answers on the basis of the B chart, A then writes the answered nationality and name in the blank spaces. B asks about the characters at 3 and 4 on the B chart, and A answers according to the A chart, with B filling the blanks as above.

老师分组，二人一组，学生A持表A，学生B持表B。先由A就表中第1、2两个人物的国籍、姓名分别按表A上的指示提问，B按表B上的指示回答，A听后将答案填在空格中。第3、4两个人物由B提问，A回答，做法同前。表格中的“✗”代表答案是否定的。

The sequence would be as with this example:

问答过程举例如下：

A: Tā shì Zhōngguorén ma?

他是中国人吗？

B: Tā bú shì Zhōngguorén.

他不是中国人。

A: Tā shì bú shì Rìbenrén? (or) Tā shì Rìbenrén bú shì?

他是不是日本人？(或者)他是日本人不是？

B: Tā yě bú shì Rìbenrén.

他也不是日本人。

A: Tā shì nĕi guo rén?

他是哪国人？

B: Tā shì Hánguorén.

他是韩国人。

A: Tā shì shéi?

他是谁？

B: Tā shì Jīn Zhōngyī.

他是金中一。

A	他／她	是……吗？	是不是？ 是……不是？	哪国人？	谁？
1		韩国人？	英国人？		
2		日本人？	中国人？		
3		✗	✗	日本人	山本
4		✗	✗	中国人	方小英

B	他／她	是……吗？	是不是？ 是……不是？	哪国人？	谁？
1		✗	✗	美国人？	大卫
2		✗	✗	韩本人？	金中一
3		美国人？	英国人？		
4		韩国人？	日本人？		

II. shì..., yě shì...　　bú shì..., yě bú shì...

"是……，也是……"　　"不是……，也不是……"

Students form pairs. Student A is given chart A, student B chart B. Student A asks about the nationality of the characters on lines 1, 2 and 3 on the basis of chart A, B answers with the information on chart B and A puts a check or cross after the question mark. B follows the same pattern with lines 4, 5 and 6 on the B chart, with A answering. Note that the question mark indicates that a question form should be used. The check equals affirmative, the cross negative.

老师分组，二人一组。学生A持表A，学生B持表B。先由A就表中第1、2、3行人物的国籍按表A上的指示提问，B按表B上的指示回答，A听后将答案划在问号后面。第4、5、6行的人物由B提问，A回答，做法同前。表格中，"✓"代表答案是肯定的，"✗"代表答案是否定的。方格中带问号的就是问句。

A

	他／她	是？	他／她	也是？ 也不是？
1		美国人？		美国人？
2		中国人？		中国人？
3		日本人？		日本人？
4		韩国人 ✓		韩国人 ✓
5		英国人 ✗		英国人 ✗
6		日本人 ✗		日本人 ✓

B	他／她	是？	他／她	也是？ 也不是？
1		美国人 ✗		美国人 ✗
2		中国人 ✓		中国人 ✓
3		日本人 ✓		日本人 ✗
4		韩国人？		韩国人？
5		英国人？		英国人？
6		日本人？		日本人？

III. shéi shì…?

“谁是……？”

Students form pairs. In the first round, student A takes slip A1 and student B takes B1. A questions and B answers, with A writing the answers on the slip. In the second round, A takes A2, B takes B2 and B asks the questions following the same pattern.

老师分组，二人一组。第一轮，学生A持表A1，学生B持表B1。A提问，B回答。第二轮，A持表A2，B持表B2， B提问，A回答。把答案填在图中。

A1 谁是英国人？韩国人？日本人？

日中	大卫	本中	大山	小美

B1

韩国人	英国人	日本人	英国人	日本人
日中	大卫	本中	大山	小美

A2

美国人	日本人	美国人	中国人	中国人
小方	小金	小英	小韩	小山

B2 谁是美国人？中国人？日本人？

小方	小金	小英	小韩	小山

第二课

我是六班的学生

汉字课文

(一)

安　娜：一、二、三、四、五、六、七、八、九、十，这个班有十个学生。

方小英：你是哪班的学生？

安　娜：我是六班的学生。

方小英：我也是六班的学生。你叫什么名字？

安　娜：我叫安娜。你叫什么名字？

方小英：我叫方小英。你是哪国人？

安　娜：我是英国人。你是韩国人吗？

方小英：我不是韩国人，我是中国人。那个同学是韩国人。

安　娜：我们班有没有日本人？

方小英：有，有两个。

(二)

山　本：你好！

张老师：你好！

山　本：您是六班的老师吗？

张老师：是，我姓张。

山　本：张老师，我是六班的学生。

张老师：你是山本吗？

山　本：是。老师，我们班的同学多不多？

张老师：不很多。我们班有十个人：七个男同学，三个女同学。男同学多，女同学少。

生词语

1.	六	liù	(nu)		six
2.	班	bān	(n)	[个]	section, class
3.	的	de	(part)		(structural particle)
4.	学生	xuésheng	(n)	[个]	student
5.	一	yī	(nu)		one
6.	二	èr	(nu)		two
7.	三	sān	(nu)		three
8.	四	sì	(nu)		four
9.	五	wǔ	(nu)		five
10.	七	qī	(nu)		seven
11.	八	bā	(nu)		eight
12.	九	jiǔ	(nu)		nine
13.	十	shí	(nu)		ten
14.	这	zhèi; zhè	(pro)		this
15.	个	gè	(m)		(general measure word)
16.	有	yǒu	(v)		to have, to exist
17.	叫	jiào	(v)		to be called
18.	什么	shénme	(pro)		what
19.	名字	míngzi	(n)	[个]	name
20.	那	nèi; nà	(pro)		that

21. 我们	wǒmen	(pro)		we, us
22. 没	méi	(adv, v)		negative for yǒu ("to have, to exist")
23. 两	liǎng	(nu)		two of something (must be followed by m)
24. 您	nín	(pro)		you (polite)
25. 老师	lǎoshī	(n)	[位wèi，个]	teacher
26. 姓	xìng	(v, n)	[个]	to be surnamed

a. 你们的老师姓什么？

b. 他姓方，不姓张。

c. "方"是她的姓，"小英"是她的名字。

27. 多	duō	(adj)		to be many
28. 很	hěn	(adv)		very (somewhat lighter than the English "very")
29. 男	nán	(adj)		male (must be followed by another nominal)

a. 我们班有一个男老师，一个女老师。

b. 你们班有男同学，也有女同学。他们班没有女同学。

30. 同学	tóngxué	(n)	[个，位]	classmate
31. 女	nǚ	(adj)		female (must be followed by another nominal)
32. 少	shǎo	(adj)		to be few

专有名词

1. 安娜	Ānnà	Anna
2. 张	Zhāng	(a surname)

补充生词

1.	先生	xiānsheng	(n)	[位]	Mr. (usually with a pronoun), husband
2.	太太	tàitai	(n)	[位]	Mrs. (usually with a pronoun), wife
3.	小姐	xiǎojie	(n)	[位]	Miss

语法点

1. Yǒu 有 sentences

“有”字句

Yǒu denotes possession or existence. When it expresses existence, the noun subject is usually a place or institution, and the object the person or thing existing there.

“有”表示领有或存在。表示存在时，“有”字句中的主语通常是处所或表示机构的词语，宾语是存在的人或事物。

S + 有 + O

a. Zhāng lǎoshī yǒu hěn duō xuésheng.

张老师有很多学生。

Mr. Zhang has a lot of students.

b. Wǒmen bān yǒu shí ge xuésheng.

我们班有十个学生。

There are ten students in our section.

c. Qībān yǒu yí ge Rìběnrén.

七班有一个日本人。

There is a Japanese in Section Seven.

<u>Yǒu</u> is negated by <u>méi</u>, the order of the structure remaining unchanged.
"有"的否定形式是在"有"前加"没"，句子的词序不变。

S + 没 + 有 + O

d. Tāmen bān méiyǒu Zhōngguo xuésheng.
他们班没有中国学生。
There are no Chinese students in their section.

e. Sìbān méiyǒu Yīngguorén.
四班没有英国人。
There are no Englishmen in Section Four.

Affirmative-negative question:
正反疑问句的形式：

S + 有 + 没有 + O ?
S + 有 + O + 没有 ?

f. Nǐmen bān yǒu méiyǒu Měiguo tóngxué?
你们班有没有美国同学？
Are there American classmates in your section?

g. Tāmen bān yǒu nán lǎoshī méiyǒu?
他们班有男老师没有？
Does their section have male teachers?

* The <u>ma</u> interrogative particle introduced in Lesson One can be used to form a question with <u>yǒu</u> sentences.
第一课介绍的语气助词"吗"在"有"字句中也可以使用。

2. The structural particle <u>de</u> 的
结构助词"的"

The de particle is used after a noun or pronoun that is meant to express possession of something, e.g. Fāng Xiǎoyīng de lǎoshī 方小英的老师 (Fang Xiaoying's teacher), wǒde míngzi 我的名字 (my name). De may be omitted in the case of a pronoun modifier when a close relationship exists between the modifier and the modified, for example in the case of family, friends or a social unit: wǒ māma 我妈妈 (my mother), wǒ tóngxué 我同学 (my classmate), nǐmen xuéxiào 你们学校 (your school), tāmen bān 他们班 (their section).

结构助词"的"用在名词或代词充任的定语后，表示领属关系。如"方小英的老师""我的名字"。当定语和中心语之间表示的关系较为密切时，如家庭关系、朋友关系或社会关系等，"的"字可以省略。如"我妈妈""我同学""你们学校""他们班"。

3. Measure words

量词

Most nouns in Chinese carry special measure words. It is as if the practice in English of assigning "head" as a measure word for "cattle", for example, "a head of cattle" rather than "a cattle", were applied to the universe of nouns. When a noun is preceded by a numeral or a demonstrative pronoun, there should be an intervening measure word.

汉语的名词大都有自己特定的量词，这和英语里一些名词的用法相似。在英语里，名词"牛"要和"头"一起用，要说"a head of cattle"，不说"a cattle"。在汉语里，这种用法是普遍存在的。当名词前有数词或指示代词时，中间应该用量词。

a. Zhèige bān yǒu bā ge xuésheng, liù ge nán tóngxué, liǎng ge nǚ tóngxué.

   这个班有八个学生，六个男同学，两个女同学。

   There are eight students in this section, six male and two female.

b. Nèi ge Yīngguorén shi shéi?

   那个英国人是谁？

   Who is that English gentleman/lady?

4. Sentences with adjectival predicates

形容词谓语句

When an adjective as predicate immediately follows the subject, <u>shì</u> is not used to join the two! Note, also, that the adjective is frequently preceded by <u>hěn</u> 很 in affirmative sentences (NOT in negative or interrogative sentences). Its degree, "very", sense is quite weak in this context. Without it, comparison or contrast is often implied.

形容词作为谓语直接出现在主语后面时，主语和谓语之间不用"是"。注意：在肯定句里（而不是在否定句或疑问句中），形容词前往往加"很"，"很"在这里已经弱化，并不真正表示程度。如果不用"很"字，往往含有对比或比较的意思。

S + 很 + Adj

a. Wǒmen bān de tóngxué hěn duō.

我们班的同学很多。

There are a lot of students in our section.

b. Nán tóngxué duō, nǚ tóngxué shǎo.

男同学多，女同学少。

There are many male students and few female students.

The negative form of such sentences is:

这种句子的否定形式是：

S + 不 + Adj

c. Nǚ tóngxué bù duō, nán tóngxué yě hěn shǎo.

女同学不多，男同学也很少。

There aren't many female students and there are also very few male students.

The affirmative-negative question form of this type sentence is:

这种句子的正反疑问形式是：

S + Adj 不 Adj ?

d. Nǐmen bān de xuésheng duō bu duō?

你们班的学生多不多？

Are there many students in your section?

NOTE 注释

1. Èr 二 and liǎng 两

“二”和“两”

When the concept “two” precedes a noun as a measure, it changes to liǎng, e.g., liǎng ge tóngxué 两个同学 (two classmates). It does not change if it describes the order in a series, e.g., èr bān 二班 (section number two).

“二”在量词前时，要用“两”，如“两个同学”。表示序数时，仍用“二”，如“二班”。

词组和句子

1. 二班的老师　她的名字　安娜的同学　张老师的学生
2. 我们班　他们老师　我同学
3. 美国人　日本同学　中国老师
4. 九个班　十个韩国学生　这个人　那个班
   这个名字　那个女同学
5. 女老师　男老师　女同学　男同学　男人　女人
6. 很多　不多　多吗　多不多　不很多
7. 那个同学叫什么名字？
8. 我们班的老师姓什么？
9. 安娜是她的名字，不是她的姓。

10. 你有中国名字吗？
11. 我有两个名字：一个英国名字，一个中国名字。
12. 他有没有中国名字？
13. 谁没有中国名字？
14. 我们班有四个女同学，三个男同学。
15. 哪个班没有英国同学？
16. 七班的学生多吗？
17. 这个班的学生不很多。
18. 五班的同学多不多？
19. 那个班的女同学很少。
20. 那个班的男学生多，这个班的男学生少。
21. 女老师多，男老师少。

参考资料

拼音课文

Wǒ shi liùbān de xuésheng

(I)

Ānnà: Yī, èr, sān, sì, wǔ, liù, qī, bā, jiǔ, shí, zhèige bān yǒu shí ge xuésheng.

Fāng Xiǎoyīng: Nǐ shi něi bān de xuésheng?

Ānnà: Wǒ shi liùbān de xuésheng.

Fāng Xiǎoyīng: Wǒ yě shi liùbān de xuésheng. Nǐ jiào shénme míngzi?

Ānnà: Wǒ jiào Ānnà. Nǐ jiào shénme míngzi?

Fāng Xiǎoyīng: Wǒ jiào Fāng Xiǎoyīng. Nǐ shi něi guó rén?

Ānnà: Wǒ shi Yīngguorén. Nǐ shi Hánguorén ma?

Fāng Xiǎoyīng: Wǒ bú shi Hánguorén. Wǒ shi Zhōngguorén. Nèi ge tóngxué shi Hánguorén.

Ānnà: Wǒmen bān yǒu méiyǒu Rìbenrén?

Fāng Xiǎoyīng: Yǒu, yǒu liǎng ge.

(II)

Shānběn: Nǐ hǎo.

Zhāng lǎoshī: Nǐ hǎo.

Shānběn: Nín shi liùbān de lǎoshi ma?

Zhāng lǎoshī: Shì, wǒ xìng Zhāng.

Shānběn: Zhāng lǎoshī, wǒ shi liùbān de xuésheng.

Zhāng lǎoshī: Nǐ shi Shānběn ma?

Shānběn: Shì. Lǎoshī, wǒmen bān de tóngxué duō bu duō?

Zhāng lǎoshī: Bù hěn duō. Wǒmen bān yǒu shí ge rén: qī ge nán tóngxué, sān ge nǚ tóngxué. Nán tóngxué duō, nǚ tóngxué shǎo.

英译课文

I'm in Section VI

(I)

Anna: One … ten, there are ten students in this section.

Fang Xiaoying: Which section are you in?

Anna: I'm in Section 6.

Fang Xiaoying: I'm in Section 6, too. What's your name?

Anna: Anna, and you?

Fang Xiaoying: Fang Xiaoying. Where are you from?

Anna: I'm English. Are you Korean?

Fang Xiaoying: I'm not Korean, I'm Chinese. That student is Korean.

Anna: Are there any Japanese in our section?

Fang Xiaoying: Yes, two.

(II)

Yamamoto:	Hello!
Mrs. Zhang:	Hello!
Yamamoto:	Are you the Section VI instructor?
Mrs. Zhang:	Yes, my name is Zhang.
Yamamoto:	Mrs. Zhang, I'm a Section VI student.
Mrs. Zhang:	Are you Yamamoto?
Yamamoto:	Yes. Mrs. Zhang, are there a lot of students in our section?
Mrs. Zhang:	Not very many. There are ten in our section, seven male and three female. There are more males than females.

课堂活动

I. yǒu sentences / "有"字句 — adjectival predicate sentences / 形容词谓语句

Students form pairs, with A following chart A and B following chart B, asking and answering questions as indicated. A should write B's answers in the blanks. The first four questions (excluding the example) are asked of B by A, the last four of A by B. A check ✓ indicates an affirmative answer and a cross ✗ a negative answer. Note the following correspondences.

△	hěn shǎo	很少	△	hěn shǎo	很少
△△△	bù duō	不多	△△△	bù duō	不多
△△△△△	hěn duō	很多	△△△△△	hěn duō	很多

老师分组，二人一组。A持表A，B持表B。先由A就表中前四个班的情况按表A上的指示提问，B按表B上的指示回答，A听后将答案填在空格中。后四个班的情况由B提问，A回答，作法同前。表格中，"✓"代表答案是肯定的，"✗"代表答案是否定的。

Example:

A: Èrbān yǒu meiyǒu Méiguo tóngxué? (or)

二班有没有美国同学？(或者)

Èrbān yǒu Méiguo tóngxué ma?

二班有美国同学吗？

B: Yǒu, èrbān yǒu Měiguo tóngxué.

有，二班有美国同学。

A: Èrbān de Měiguo tóngxué duō bù duō?

二班的美国同学多不多？

B: Èrbān de Měiguo tóngxué hěn shǎo.

二班的美国同学很少。

A

(例)

	有？	多？少？
二班	美国同学？	
五班	英国同学？	
三班	韩国同学？	
十班	美国同学？	
七班	日本女同学？	
一班	✗	
八班	✓	△
四班	✓	△△△
六班	✓	△△△△△

B

(例)

	有？	多？少？
二班	✓	△
五班	✓	△△△△△
三班	✓	△△△
十班	✗	
七班	✓	△
一班	中国同学？	
八班	英国同学？	
四班	韩国男同学？	
六班	美国女同学？	

II. Questions with interrogative pronouns

用疑问代词的疑问句

"… last name is what?" "… is called what?" "… is from what country?" "… is a student in which section?"

"…… 姓什么？" "…… 叫什么名字？" "…… 是哪国人？" 和 "……是哪班的学生？"

Students form pairs, with A following chart A and B following chart B. A first asks the nationality of the first three people (blanks on his chart), B answers, with A writing in those answers. A continues asking about the remaining information, then B follows the same pattern with chart B (the last three blank lines).

老师分组，二人一组。学生A持表A，学生B持表B。先由A就表中前三个人物的国籍按表A上的指示提问，B按表B上的指示回答，A听后将答案填在空格中。后三个人物由B提问，A回答，作法同前。

A

他／她	姓？	名字？	哪国？	哪班？

	韩	韩学人	美国人	六
	安	安英	韩国人	二
	张	张国生	中国人	九

B

他／她	姓？	名字？	哪国？	哪班？
	方	方娜	英国人	五
	中山	中山英男	日本人	七
	张	张大中	韩国人	四

III. MW & de

量词和"的"

Students form pairs to interview each other. The instructor gives each student a card and a form. Information on the card is about the one being interviewed. Interviewers ask questions on the basis of the form, then fill in those answers on the form. Do this until all forms are filled in. Students will then recap the interview from the completed forms.

老师分组，二人一组，互相采访。

老师给每个同学一张卡片和一张表格。卡片上的资料代表被采访者的情况。采访时填好表格，采访后把采访到的资料复述一遍。

卡片 (1)

方大卫		美国人
4班 (bān)	:	3个韩国人 2个美国人 1个日本人 4个英国人
男 (nán)	:	5个人
老师 (lǎoshī)	:	张英 (Zhāng Yīng)

卡片 (2)

金小美		韩国人
8班 (bān)	:	4个日本人 2个韩国人 2个英国人 1个中国人
男 (nán)	:	7个人
老师 (lǎoshī)	:	方娜 (Fāng Nà)

卡片 (3)

安英		中国人
6班 (bān)	：	2个美国人 5个韩国人 1个英国人 2个中国人
男 (nán)	：	3个人
老师 (lǎoshī)	：	韩学中 (Hán Xuézhōng)

表格

名　字：__________

哪国人：__________

哪　班：__________

韩国人：__________

英国人：__________

美国人：__________

日本人：__________

中国人：__________

女同学：__________

男同学：__________

老　师：__________

表格

名　字：__________

哪国人：__________

哪　班：__________

韩国人：__________

英国人：__________

美国人：__________

日本人：__________

中国人：__________

女同学：__________

男同学：__________

老　师：__________

阅读练习

我叫韩学英，是四班的学生。我们班有七个人：三个男同学，四个女同学。五个同学有中国名字，两个同学没有中国名字。我们班有两个英国人，一个日本人，三个韩国人。我是美国人。

我们的老师姓方，叫方国中。方老师是我们班的老师，也是二班的老师。二班有两个老师，一个是他，一个是金老师。方老师是男老师，金老师是女老师。我们的女老师多，男老师少。我们有很多男同学，也有不少女同学。

第三课

一个星期有几天？

汉字课文

大　卫：明天我们学年、月、日、星期吗？

山　本：不，明天不学，后天学。

大　卫：你现在预习吗？

山　本：预习。

大　卫：我们一起预习好不好？

山　本：好。我问，你回答；你问，我回答。好吗？

大　卫：好，我问一个问题：今年是二〇〇几年？

山　本：今年是二〇〇一年。明年是二〇〇几年？

大　卫：明年是二〇〇二年。去年呢？

山　本：去年是二〇〇〇年。今天是几月几号星期几？

大　卫：今天是九月十八号星期二。昨天呢？

山　本：昨天是九月十七号星期一。一个星期有几天？

大　卫：一个星期有七天。这七天是星期一、星期二、星期三……星期日。星期日也叫星期天，对不对？

山　本：对。

大　卫：一年有多少个月？

山　本：有十二个月。这个月是几月？

大　卫：这个月是九月。上个月和下个月呢？

山　本：上个月是八月，下个月是十月。一个月有多少天？

大卫：有的三十天，有的三十一天。

山本：不对。

大卫：为什么不对？

山本：二月是二十八天。

大卫：也不对，二月有的时候是二十八天，有的时候是二十九天。

生词语

1.	星期	xīngqī	(n)	[个]	week
2.	几	jǐ	(pro)		how many of something (must be followed by m)
3.	天	tiān	(n)		day of the week; sky heaven
4.	明天	míngtiān	(n)		tomorrow
5.	学	xué	(v)		to study
6.	年	nián	(n)		year (a bound word, i.e., it cannot be used alone)
7.	月	yuè	(n)	[个]	month (a bound word); moon
8.	日	rì	(n)		day (a bound word); sun
9.	后天	hòutiān	(n)		the day after tomorrow
10.	现在	xiànzài	(n)		now
11.	预习	yùxí	(v)		to prepare for a lesson
12.	一起	yìqǐ	(adv, n)		together
13.	问	wèn	(v)		to ask
14.	回答	huídá	(v)		to answer, reply
15.	问题	wèntí	(n)	[个]	a question
16.	今年	jīnnián	(n)		this year

17.	明年	míngnián	(n)		next year
18.	去年	qùnián	(n)		last year
19.	呢	ne	(part)		(particle for questions in context)

a. 你叫安娜，她呢？

b. 我们今天学"一个星期有几天"，明天呢？

c. 六班有八个学生，二班呢？

20.	今天	jīntiān	(n)		today
21.	号	hào	(n)		day of the month; number (a bound word)
22.	昨天	zuótiān	(n)		yesterday
23.	星期日	xīngqīrì	(n)	[个]	Sunday
24.	对	duì	(adj)		towards
25.	多少	duōshao	(pro)		how much, how many
26.	上	shàng	(n-pw)		on top of (a bound word); last (of month, week, time, etc.)
27.	和	hé	(c)		and (connects nominals)
28.	下	xià	(n-pw)		below (a bound word); next (of month, time, etc.)
29.	有的	yǒude	(pro)		some
30.	为什么	wèishénme	(pro)		why

a. 你为什么不预习？

b. 为什么这班的学生很少？

31.	时候	shíhou	(n)		time (note its different shapes in different contexts)

a. 你什么时候预习？

b. 老师有的时候问问题，有的时候不问问题。

补充生词

1.	前天	qiántiān	(n)	the day before yesterday
2.	前年	qiánnián	(n)	the year before last
3.	后年	hòunián	(n)	the year after next

语 法 点

1. Sentences with verbal predicates
   动词谓语句

These are constructed pretty much as in English.
汉语中动词谓语句的结构与英语一样。

S + V	S + V + O

a. Wǒmen yùxí.
   我们预习。
   We prepare for class.

b. Lǎoshī wèn wèntí.
   老师问问题。
   The teacher asks questions.

To negate such sentences, a <u>bù</u> 不 precedes the verb.
否定形式是在动词前面加上“不”。

c. Wǒmen bān jīntian bù xué nián, yuè, rì, xīngqī.
   我们班今天不学年、月、日、星期。
   Our section is not studying years, months, days and days of the week today.

d. Wǒ xiànzài bú yùxí

我现在不预习。

I won't prepare now.

And the affirmative-negative question type:

正反疑问句有如下两种形式：

S + V 不 V + O?　　S + V + O + 不 V?

e. Wǒmen jīntian xué bu xué nián, yuè, rì, xīngqī?

我们今天学不学年、月、日、星期？

Are we studying years, months, days and days of the week today?

f. Lǎoshī wèn wèntí bú wèn?

老师问问题不问？

Does/Will the teacher ask questions?

2. Adverbial adjuncts

状语

Note that the modifier-modified order prevails, and that adverbials, adjectives and time words are among those items that modify verbs.

副词、形容词和时间词语都可以做状语。状语修饰中心语（动词或形容词）时，状语在前，中心语在后。

S + Adv + V + O　　S + Adv + Adj

a. Tā shi liùbān de xuésheng. Tā <u>yě</u> shi liùbān de xuésheng. Wǒ <u>bú</u> shi liùbān de xuésheng.

她是六班的学生，他也是六班的学生。我不是六班的学生。

She is in section six, and he's in section six, too. I'm not in section six.

b. Wǒmen yìqǐ yùxí, hǎo bu hǎo?

我们一起预习，好不好？

Let's prepare for class together, shall we?

c. Wǒmen bān de nán tóngxué hěn duō, tāmen bān de nán tóngxué yě hěn duō.

我们班的男同学很多，他们班的男同学也很多。

There are many male students in our section, and there are many male students in their section, too.

Time words as adverbs: *NOTE* that time words as adverbs can come before the subject or before the verb.

时间词做状语：要注意，时间词做状语时，可以在主语前，也可以在动词前。

d. Jīntiān wǒmen xué nián, yuè, rì, xīngqī.

今天我们学年、月、日、星期。

Today we'll study the years, months, days and days of the week.

e. Lǎoshī jīntiān bú wèn wèntí.

老师今天不问问题。

The teacher won't ask questions today.

3. Numbers under 100

一百以下称数法

Numbers in Chinese build up on the decimal system straightforwardly and unvaryingly. Memorize one to ten and you've got it, constructing "eleven" as "ten one" (shíyī 十一), "twenty" as "two ten" (èrshí 二十), "twenty-one" as "two ten one" (èrshi yī 二十一) and so forth.

汉语是用十进法来称数的。我们已经学了"一"到"十"这十个数，由它们可以构成"十"以上的数目。如"十一(10 + 1)""二十(2 × 10)""二十一(2 × 10 + 1)等等。

4. Years, months, days and days of the week

年、月、日和星期

Years are expressed by stringing the number before nián (year): yī jiǔ yī jiǔ nián (1919).

年：年的说法是把数词放在"年"之前，如"一九一九年"。

Months of the year are simply number + yuè (moon, month) from one to twelve.

月：月份的说法是把数词放在"月"（月亮）前，如"一月、二月……十二月"。

Days of the month are number + rì (sun, day) or hào (number). In the case of days, rì (sān rì 三日, the third) is commonly written or has a slightly more formal ring when spoken, while hào (sān hào 三号, the third) is the usual spoken form.

日：日的说法是把数词放在"日"（太阳）或者"号"前，如"三日"或"三号"。"日"多用于书面语，"号"多用于口语。

Days of the week are numbered, as well, the number added to the noun xīngqī or "week". Monday through Saturday are xīngqīyī through xīngqīliù, and Sunday is easily remembered as xīngqīrì (rì = "sun").

星期：它的说法是把数词放在"星期"之后，如"星期一，星期二……星期六"。"星期日"很容易记，"日"就是"太阳"的意思。

A slight complication is that the noun lǐbài is used in the same manner and perfectly parallel with xīngqī (lǐbàiyī, etc.). Zhōu 周 "circuit" is also becoming more commonly used (zhōuyī 周一……, zhōurì 周日). Early learners are wise to use one set consistently from this unusual profusion.

"星期"也可以说成"礼拜(lǐbài)"，如"礼拜一、礼拜二……礼拜日"。"星期"还可以说成"周"（zhōu，圈子），如"周一、周二……周日"。初学者选用一种说法即可。

Expressing a date that includes year, month, day and day of the week is done in that order, from the largest to the smallest unit, e.g., Yī jiǔ yī jiǔ nián wǔyuè sì rì xīngqīrì 一九一九年五月四日星期日, "Sunday, May 4, 1919".

年、月、日、星期等连在一起时，顺序是：年、月、日、星期，如"一九一九年五月四号星期日"。

5. Jǐ 几 and duōshao 多少

"几"和"多少"

When the number inquired about is less than ten, the interrogative jǐ is used. A measure word must be added to it when it modifies a noun, e.g., Nǐmen bān yǒu jǐ ge nǚ tóngxué? 你们班有几个女同学？(How many female classmates are there in your section?). Duōshao is generally used for numbers over ten. The measure word can be eliminated when modifying a noun, e.g., Sānbān yǒu duōshao xuésheng? 三班有多少学生？(How many students are there in Section Three?)

"几"用于询问十以下的数目。当它修饰名词时，后面一定要带上量词，如"你们班有几个同学？""多少"一般代表大于十的数目，它可以直接修饰名词，后面的量词可以省略，如"三班有多少学生？"

6. Questions with ne 呢

用"呢"的疑问句

Míngtian ne? 明天呢？"How about tomorrow?" The modal particle ne forms questions of fragment statements. These questions are part of (a) an explicit context or (b) a presupposed context. All participants in the situation are presumed to know what is going on. Ne is generally added to nouns or pronouns, as in our text sentence.

语气助词"呢"可以直接加在名词、代词等后面，构成用"呢"的省略式疑问句。如果(a)有上下文，就可以根据上下文来判断疑问所在。如果(b)没有明确的上下文，往往由共识的语境来决定疑问所在。

a. Tā jiào Jīn Zhōngyī, nǐ ne? (Nǐ jiào shénme?)

他叫金中一，你呢？(你叫什么？)

His name is Kim Chung-il. And you? (What's your name?)

b. Zhāng lǎoshī ne?

张老师呢？

Where is Mrs. Zhang?

NOTE 注释

Nián 年 "year" and tiān 天 "day" are among the unusual nouns that do not need measure words. *yí ge tiān 一个天 or *liǎng ge nián 两个年 are NOT CORRECT. Rather, one must say yì tiān 一天 or liǎng nián 两年.

"年"和"天"是不需要用量词的名词，我们不能说"一个天""两个年"，只能说"一天""两年"。

词组和句子

1. 十月六号(日)　　九月二十四号(日)星期二

   一九九五年十二月十八号(日)星期一

   一九九几年几月几号(日)星期几

2. 上个月　　下个月　　这个月

   上个星期　　下个星期　　这个星期

   上星期一　　下星期日　　这个星期三

3. 几个人　　几个班　　几个老师　　几个同学　　几个韩国人

   几年　　几个月　　几个星期　　几天

   多少天　　多少(个)月　　多少(个)人　　多少(个)班

4. 有的老师　　有的学生　　有的人　　有的班　　有的时候

5. 今天我和他们一起预习。
6. 你现在预习不预习？
7. 我现在不预习，明天预习。
8. 这个星期五我们学什么？
9. 我们下星期几学年、月、日、星期？
10. 七月是三十一天，八月也是三十一天。
11. 为什么一九九六年的二月是二十九天？
12. 一年有多少个星期？
13. 你们班有多少个学生？几个男同学？几个女同学？
14. 有的班学生多，有的班学生少。
15. 你们有的时候预习，有的时候不预习，对不对？
16. 老师问问题，我们回答。
17. 你有两个问题，他呢？
18. 上个星期我们学“几”和“多少”，这个星期呢？

参考资料

拼音课文

Yí ge xīngqī yǒu jǐ tiān?

Dàwèi: Míngtian wǒmen xué “nián”, “yuè”, “rì”, “xīngqī” ma?

Shānběn: Bù, míngtian bù xué, hòutian xué.

Dàwèi: Nǐ xiànzài yùxí ma?

Shānběn: Yùxí.

Dàwèi: Wǒwen yìqǐ yùxí hǎo bu hǎo?

Shānběn: Hǎo. Wǒ wèn, nǐ huídá, nǐ wèn, wǒ huídá, hǎo ma?

Dàwèi: Hǎo, wǒ wèn yí ge wèntí: jīnnián shi èr líng líng jǐ nián?

Shānběn: Jīnnián shi èr líng líng yī nián. Míngnián shi èr líng líng jǐ nián?

Dàwèi: Míngnián shi èr líng líng èr nián. Qùnián ne?

Shānběn: Qùnián shi èr líng líng líng nián. Jīntian shí jǐ yuè jǐ hào xīngqī jǐ?

Dàwèi: Jīntian shi jiǔ yuè shíbā hào xīngqī'èr. Zuótian ne?

Shānběn: Zuótian shi jiǔ yuè shíqī hào xīngqīyī. Yí ge xīngqī yǒu jǐ tiān?

Dàwèi: Yí ge xīngqī yǒu qī tián. Zhè qī tiān shi xīngqīyī, xīngqī'èr, xīngqīsān … xīngqīrì. Xīngqīrì yě jiào xīngqītiān, duì bu duì?

Shānběn: Duì.

Dàwèi: Yì nián yǒu duōshao ge yuè?

Shānběn: Yǒu shí'èr ge yuè. Zhège yuè shi jǐ yuè?

Dàwèi: Zhège yuè shi jiǔyuè. Shàng ge yuè hé xià ge yuè ne?

Shānběn: Shàng ge yuè shi báyuè, xià ge yuè shi shíyuè. Yí ge yuè yǒu duōshao tiān?

Dàwèi: Yǒude sānshí tiān, yǒude sānshiyī tiān.

Shānběn: Bú duì.

Dàwèi: Wèishénme bú duì?

Shānběn: Èryuè shi èrshibā tiān.

Dàwèi: Yě bú duì, èryuè yǒude shíhou shi èrshibā tiān, yǒude shíhou shi èrshijiǔ tiān.

英译课文

How many days are there in a week?

David: Are we going to study the year, month, day and week tomorrow?

Yamamoto: No, not tomorrow, the day after tomorrow.

David: Are you preparing the lesson now?

Yamamoto: Yes.

David: Let's prepare together, all right?

Yamamoto:	All right. I'll ask and you answer, then you ask and I'll answer, how's that?
David:	Fine. I'll ask a question… This year is two thousand what?
Yamamoto:	This year is 2001. Next year is two thousand what?
David:	Next year is 2002. How about last year?
Yamamoto:	Last year was 2000. What month, day of the month and day of the week is today? (or, What's today's date and day of the week?)
David:	Today is Tuesday, September 18th. How about yesterday?
Yamamoto:	Yesterday was Monday, September 17th. How many days are there in a week?
David:	There are seven days in a week. They are Monday, Tuesday, Wednesday … Sunday. Sunday (xīngqīrì) is also called Sunday (xīngqītiān), isn't it?
Yamamoto:	Yes.
David:	How many months are there in a year?
Yamamoto:	There are twelve. What is this month?
David:	This is September. How about last month and next month?
Yamamoto:	Last month was August and next month is October. How many days are there in a month?
David:	Some thirty and some thirty-one.
Yamamoto:	Wrong.
David:	Why is it wrong?
Yamamoto:	February is twenty-eight days.
David:	That's wrong, too. Sometimes February is twenty-eight days and sometimes it is twenty-nine days.

课堂活动

I. Numbers under 100

一百以下称数法

A. Instructor picks students randomly, asking them to say the numbers from X to X.

不按座位次序，老师点学生报数。

B. Instructor asks students to each say an odd number in sequence (student A "one", student B "three", etc.), then even numbers.

逢奇数报或逢偶数报。

C. Ask students to say numbers over 10, or over 82, etc.

让学生从10以后报或从82以后报。

II. Year, month, day of the month, day of the week

年、月、日、星期

Instructor holds up a calendar and asks students the date (year, month, day of the month and week)

老师出示日历让学生说出是几月几号星期几。

III. jǐ and duōshao

"几"和"多少"

Use the following types of questions:

用下列问题提问并回答：

1. X bān yǒu X guó tóngxué ma? (or)

"X班有X国同学吗？"(或者)

X bān yǒu méiyǒu X guó tóngxué?

"X班有没有X国同学？"

2. X bān yǒu jǐ ge X guó tóngxué? (or)

"X 班有几个 X 国同学？"(或者)

X bān yǒu duōshao ge X guó tóngxué?

"X 班有多少个 X 国同学？"

Students form pairs. Student A asks questions according to the suggestions on chart A. B answers with the information on chart B, with A filling in the answers. Then it is B's turn.

老师分组，二人一组。学生A持表A，学生B持表B。先由A就表中前两个班的情况按表A上的指示提问，B按表B上的指示回答，A听后将答案填空格中。后两个班的情况由B提问，A回答，作法同前。

A.

班号	美国	韩国	日本	英国	多少？	男？	女？
二							
五							
六	4	8	2	／	14	5	9
九	5	6	5	／	16	7	9

B.

班号	美国	韩国	日本	英国	多少？	男？	女？
二	3	9	4	1	17	11	6
五	5	4	7	3	19	7	12
六							
九							

IV. Numbers

数字

Photocopy a batch of these number cards and pass out one to each student. The instructor selects any one card, reads out the numbers, then students check to see which of their cards matches the instructor's. The student holding the matching card raises his/her hand and says "duì le", then reads out the numbers on that card. Rotate a few times in this manner.

四张卡片复制若干份，发给班上同学，每人一张。老师选择四张卡片中的任何一张，读出数字，让学生分辨老师读的与自己卡片上的数字是否完全一致，认为一致的同学举手说"对了"并读出他卡片上的数字，进行核对。

卡片一	卡片二	卡片三	卡片四
10 44 35	4 14 45	10 40 15	4 40 45
47 83 29	41 38 92	71 48 62	77 18 26

V. Month and day of the month

月、日

As above.

作法同练习IV。

卡片一	卡片二	卡片三	卡片四
10月25号	12月15号	12月25号	10月15号
6月29号	6月19号	9月16号	9月26号
10月10号	10月 4号	4月 4号	4月10号
7月17号	1月11号	1月17号	7月11号

第四课

你去哪儿？

汉字课文

(一)

金中一：方小英，你去哪儿？

方小英：我去图书馆，你去哪儿？

金中一：我回宿舍。

方小英：你回宿舍做什么？

金中一：我回宿舍看书。

方小英：你跟我一起去图书馆做作业吧！

金中一：我的作业本子在宿舍。

方小英：你去拿，我在这儿等你。

金中一：好，我马上来。

(二)

安　娜：金中一，你去哪儿？

金中一：我回宿舍。

安　娜：你回宿舍做什么？

金中一：我回宿舍拿本子。你呢？你现在去哪儿？

安　娜：我去朋友家吃饭，晚上跟她去看电影。

金中一：看什么电影？

安　娜：看一个中国电影。

金中一：去哪个电影院看？

安　娜：去天星电影院。

生词语

1.	去	qù	(v)		to go
2.	哪儿	nǎr	(pro)		where
3.	图书馆	túshūguǎn	(n)	[个]	library
4.	回	huí	(v)		to return
5.	宿舍	sùshè	(n)	[个，间jiān]	hostel, dormitory, dormitory room
6.	做	zuò	(v)		to do
7.	看	kàn	(v)		to look, look at, watch (film, TV), to read
8.	书	shū	(n)	[本běn，部bù]	book
9.	跟	gēn	(prep)		together with, and (connecting nouns and nominals)

a. 他跟我们去看电影。

b. 我跟她一起回家。

10.	作业	zuòyè	(n)		homework
11.	吧	ba	(part)		(modal particle indicating doubt or seeking confirmation)
12.	本子	běnzi	(n)	[个]	notebook
13.	在	zài	(v, prep)		to be in, on, at
14.	拿	ná	(v)		to take, get hold

a. 他回宿舍拿什么？

b. 她去拿书和本子。

15.	这儿	zhèr	(pro)		here
16.	等	děng	(v)		to wait
17.	马上	mǎshàng	(adv)		immediately

a. 他们在图书馆等你，你马上去吧！

b. 我们现在马上吃饭。

18.	来	lái	(v)		to come
19.	朋友	péngyou	(n)	[个，位]	friend
20.	家	jiā	(n)	[个]	home, family
21.	吃饭	chī fàn	(vo)		to eat
	吃	chī	(v)		to eat
	饭	fàn	(n)	[顿 dùn]	cooked rice, meal
22.	晚上	wǎnshang	(n)	[个]	evening
23.	电影	diànyǐng	(n)	[个，部]	film, movie
24.	电影院	diànyǐngyuàn	(n)	[个，家 jiā]	cinema, theater

专有名词

天星电影院	Tiānxīng Diànyǐngyuàn	Star Theater

补充生词

剧场	jùchǎng	(n)	[个，家]	theater (for drama)

语法点

1. Sentences with verbal expressions in series (1)

   连动句 (1)

When the predicate contains more than one main verb, and these verbs are actions of the same subject, the pattern is

在动词谓语句中，谓语里如果有两个或两个以上的主要动词，而且这些动词共一个主语，这种句子就叫连动句。格式是：

$$S + V_1 (+ O_1) + V_2 (+ O_2)$$

In this construction, one goes, comes, returns, etc. to some place to do something. The first verb/verb construction contains lái 来, qù 去, huí 回, etc. and the second verb/verb construction describes what is to be done there.

在连动句 (1) 中，前一动词表示某人到 (回) 某地去 (来)，后一个动词说明前一个动作的目的，即到某地做什么。

a. Shānběn qù túshūgǔan kàn shū.

山本去图书馆看书。

Yamamoto is going to the library to read books.

b. Wǒ lái péngyou jiā chī fàn.

我来朋友家吃饭。

I am coming/came to my friend's house to eat.

c. Shānběn qù kàn shū.

山本去看书。

Yamamoto is going to read books.

d. Wǒ lái chī fàn.

我来吃饭。

I am coming/came to eat.

e. Wǒ qù ná.

我去拿。

I'll go pick it up.

2. The verb <u>zài</u> 在 and the preposition <u>zài</u> 在

动词"在"和介词"在"

The verb <u>zài</u> denotes existence, and sentences with <u>zài</u> are patterned thusly:

动词"在"表示存在。用动词"在"的句子，格式是：

S (person or thing) + 在 + O (place)

a. Fāng Xiǎoyīng zài túshūguǎn.

方小英在图书馆。

Fang Xiaoying is at the library.

b. Shānběn zài nǎr?

山本在哪儿？

Where is Yamamoto?

c. Wǒ de běnzi zài sùshè.

我的本子在宿舍。

My notebook is in the dormitory.

The preposition <u>zài</u> and its object (a noun or noun expression denoting place) form a prepositional phrase describing the place where an action occurs. It is most often used adverbially.

介词"在"和它的宾语（表示处所的名词或名词词组）组成介词词组，多做状语，说明动作发生的处所，格式是：

S + 在 + PO (place) + V + O

d. Tā zài túshūguǎn kàn shū.

她在图书馆看书。

She's reading at the library.

e. Shānběn zài nǎr zuò zuòyè?

山本在哪儿做作业？

Where is Yamamoto doing his homework?

* Remember that modifier precedes modified. Do not make the error of reversing these!

牢记：修饰语在被修饰语之前，不要颠倒它们的位置。

3. The modal particle

语气助词

Modal particles are a peculiar feature of Chinese, syllables that are neutral in tone and added to expressions, quite often to the end of sentences. They indicate the speaker's attitude (questioning, suggesting, etc.) or feeling (change, affirmation, etc.) toward a given action or condition. We have already encountered ma 吗, the neutral question modal (Lesson 1) and ne 呢, the contextual question modal (Lesson 3).

语气助词是汉语中很有特色的一个词类，它用在句子或词组的末尾，读轻声，表示说话人对一种行为或情况的态度或感情(疑问、建议、变化、肯定等)。我们已经遇到过表示无倾向性疑问的语气助词“吗”(第一课)和按照上下文判断疑问所在的语气助词“呢”(第三课)。

The modal particle ba 吧 (1)

语气助词“吧”(1)

Ba 吧 is used at the end of a sentence to express suggestion. As we progress, we will encounter additional contexts where ba changes the tone or emphasis of an utterance in other ways.

“吧”用在句尾，表示商量、建议的语气。以后我们还会学到“吧”表示的其他意义。

a. Wǒmen yìqǐ yùxí ba.

我们一起预习吧。

Let's do our preparation together.

b. Míngtian wǎnshang qù kàn diànyǐng ba.
明天晚上去看电影吧。
Let's go see a film tomorrow night.

词组和句子

1. 在家　在图书馆　在宿舍　在电影院　在这儿　在哪儿
在家等他　在图书馆看书　在宿舍预习　在电影院看电影
在这儿做作业　在哪儿吃饭
2. 他现在去做作业。
3. 今天晚上我朋友来吃饭。
4. 他现在去图书馆做作业。
5. 今天晚上我朋友来我家吃饭。
6. 她晚上来我的宿舍跟我一起预习。
7. 我跟她一起去电影院看电影。
8. 我马上回家去拿作业本子。
9. 谁去老师家？他们去老师家做什么？
10. 大卫和山本去老师家，他们去老师家问问题。
11. 张老师在不在家？
12. 我的书不在这儿，也不在宿舍。我的书呢？
13. 星期日晚上我不去图书馆看书，我去朋友家吃饭。
14. 我和他在哪儿等你？
15. 你们在这儿等我吧！
16. 星期六我不回家，我在天星电影院等你，我们一起去看电影吧！

参考资料

拼音课文

Nǐ qù nǎr?

(I)

Jīn Zhōngyī: Fāng Xiǎoyīng, nǐ qù nǎr?
Fāng Xiǎoyīng: Wǒ qù túshūguǎn, nǐ qù nǎr?
Jīn Zhōngyī: Wǒ huí sùshè.
Fāng Xiǎoyīng: Nǐ huí sùshè zuò shénme?
Jīn Zhōngyī: Wǒ huí sùshè kàn shū.
Fāng Xiǎoyīng: Nǐ gēn wǒ yìqǐ qù túshūguǎn zuò zuòyè ba!
Jīn Zhōngyī: Wǒ de zuòyè běnzi zài sùshè.
Fāng Xiǎoyīng: Nǐ qù ná, wǒ zài zhèr děng ni.
Jīn Zhōngyī: Hǎo, wǒ mǎshàng lái.

(II)

Ānnà: Jīn Zhōngyī, nǐ qù nǎr?
Jīn Zhōngyī: Wǒ huí sùshè.
Ānnà: Nǐ huí sùshè zuò shénme?
Jīn Zhōngyī: Wǒ huí sùshè ná běnzi. Nǐ ne? Nǐ xiànzài qù nǎr?
Ānnà: Wǒ qù péngyou jiā chī fàn, wǎnshang gēn tā qù kàn dìanyǐng.
Jīn Zhōngyī: Kàn shénme diànyǐng?
Ānnà: Kàn yí ge Zhōngguo diànyǐng.
Jīn Zhōngyī: Qù něige diànyǐngyuàn kàn?
Ānnà: Qù Tiānxīng Diànyǐngyuàn.

英译课文

Where are you going?

(I)

Kim Chung-il:	Where are your going, Fang Xiaoying?
Fang Xiaoying:	I'm going to the library, where are you going?
Kim Chung-il:	I'm going back to the dorm.
Fang Xiaoying:	What are you going to do back at the dorm?
Kim Chung-il:	I'm going to read back at the dorm.
Fang Xiaoying:	Why don't you go to the library with me to do the homework?
Kim Chung-il:	My homework notebook is at the dorm.
Fang Xiaoying:	Go get it and I'll wait for you here.
Kim Chung-il:	All right, I'll be right back.

(II)

Anna:	Kim Chung-il, where are you going?
Kim Chung-il:	I'm going back to the dorm.
Anna:	What are you going to do back at the dorm?
Kim Chung-il:	I'm going back to the dorm to get my notebook. And you? Where are you going now?
Anna:	I'm going to a friend's house to eat, then going to see a film with her in the evening.
Kim Chung-il:	What film are you seeing?
Anna:	We're seeing a Chinese film.
Kim Chung-il:	At which theater will you see it?
Anna:	The Star Theater.

课堂活动

I. Sentences with verbal constructions in series (1)

连动句 (1)

A. Q/A

用下列问题提问并回答：

1. Xīngqī X nǐ qù … ma? (or)

   "星期X你去……吗？"(或者)

   Xīngqī X nǐ qù búqù …?

   "星期X你去不去……？"

2. Xīngqī X wǒ yě qù … wǒmen yìqǐ qù ba.

   "星期X我也去……我们一起去吧。"

Students form groups of four, with each student in a group taking a different chart (A, B, C & D). The first line on a chart is that student's plan. One student then asks the other three when they intend to go to the library to do their homework, go to the theater to see a film, etc. Answers (day of the week) and that student's name are written on the chart. If a student answers with the same day that the questioner will be going, the questioner then says "I'm also going to … or X. Let's go together."

老师分组，四人一组，学生A持表A，学生B持表B，学生C持表C，学生D持表D。表中第一行为持表人自己的计划。走访组内其他三位同学，看看他们打算星期几去图书馆做作业、去电影院看电影、去金中一家吃饭、去图书馆看书，把同学的姓名和答案(时间)填在表上。如果同学的时间与你的时间一样，你就说"星期X我也去……我们一起去吧。"

A

你	星期一	星期五	星期天	星期四
你的同学B				
你的同学C				
你的同学D				

B

你	星期三	星期五	星期六	星期二
你的同学A				
你的同学C				
你的同学D				

C

你	星期五	星期六	星期天	星期二
你的同学A				
你的同学B				
你的同学D				

D

你	星期五	星期天	星期六	星期四
你的同学A				
你的同学B				
你的同学C				

B. Q/A

用下列问题提问并回答：

1. Xiànzài nǐ qù nǎr?

   "现在你去哪儿？"

2. Nǐ ... zuò shénme?

   "你……做什么？"

Same pattern as above.

做法同练习I.A。

A

	哪儿？	做什么？
你	去小美家	做作业
你的同学B		
你的同学C		
你的同学D		

B

	哪儿？	做什么？
你	回家	拿书
你的同学A		
你的同学C		
你的同学D		

C

	哪儿？	做什么？
你	回宿舍	拿本子
你的同学A		
你的同学B		
你的同学D		

D

	哪儿？	做什么？
你	去同学家	吃饭
你的同学A		
你的同学B		
你的同学C		

C. Q/A using verbal constructions in series.

用连动结构提问并回答：

Míngtian nǐ qù ... ma?

明天你去……吗？

Students form groups of four, with each student taking a card (A, B, C & D) and asking the questions written there. The object is to find the student whose plans (answers) are the same as yours. ✗ equals negative. ✓ equals affirmative.

准备四种卡片，各若干张(视班上人数而定)，每个学生持一卡与同学互相问答，找出答案与自己完全一致的同学。卡片上的“✓”“✗”是自己的答案。“✓”代表答案是肯定的，“✗”代表答案是否定的。

卡片A

图书馆	做作业	✗
老师家	吃饭	✗
金星电影院	看电影	✓
大卫宿舍	预习	✓

卡片B

图书馆	做作业	✗
老师家	吃饭	✗
金星电影院	看电影	✓
大卫宿舍	预习	✗

卡片C

图书馆	做作业	✗
老师家	吃饭	✗
金星电影院	看电影	✗
大卫宿舍	预习	✓

卡片D

图书馆	做作业	✗
老师家	吃饭	✗
金星电影院	看电影	✗
大卫宿舍	预习	✗

II. The verb zài and the preposition zài

动词"在"和介词"在"

Q/A

用下列问题提问并回答：

1. Jīntian wǎnshang nǐ zài … ma? (or)

   "今天晚上你在……吗？"(或者)

   Jīntian wǎnshang nǐ zài bú zài …? (or)

   "今天晚上你在不在……？"(或者)

   Jīntian wǎnshang nǐ zài nǎr?

   "今天晚上你在哪儿？"

2. Nǐ zài … zuò shénme?

   "你在……做什么？"

Students form pairs, with student A holding chart A and student B holding chart B. A asks a question first to see where B will be tonight, tomorrow night, the day after tomorrow night and Friday night, and what he/she will be doing wherever that may be. A writes down B's answers. Then B goes through the same sequence.

老师分组，二人一组。学生A持表A，学生B持表B。先由A提问，看看B今天晚上、明天晚上、后天晚上、星期五晚上都在哪儿，在那儿做什么，把B的答案填在表上。然后由B提问，作法同前。

A

	B		A（我）	
	在……吗？ 在不在……？ 在哪儿？	做什么？	在……	做……
今天晚上			宿舍	预习
明天晚上			朋友家	吃饭
后天晚上			图书馆	看书
星期五晚上			宿舍	等同学

B

	B（我）		A	
	在……	做……	在……吗？ 在不在……？ 在哪儿？	做什么？
今天晚上	图书馆	做作业		
明天晚上	山本宿舍	跟山本一起预习		
后天晚上	同学家	看电影		
星期五晚上	宿舍	看书		

第五课

这本词典是你的吗？

汉字课文

(晚上，大卫、金中一和一个四班的同学，在宿舍复习生词和课文)

大　卫：你有这本词典吗？

金中一：没有，这本词典好吗？

大　卫：很好。这本词典是最新的。

同　学：什么词典？

大　卫：《汉语小词典》。

同　学：我也有一本。不过，我那本是旧的。

金中一：大卫，这本词典是你的吗？

大　卫：不是我的，是安娜的。我明天去书店买一本。

金中一：我也去买一本。

同　学：明天你们什么时候去？我跟你们一起去。

大　卫：明天下午你有课吗？

同　学：有，上午和下午都有。

大　卫：我们中午去好不好？

金中一：几点去？

同　学：我十二点下课，下午两点半上课。你们呢？

大　卫：我们也十二点下课。十二点零五分去，好吗？

同　学：十二点一刻吧。

大卫和金中一：好。

生词语

1.	本	běn	(m)		(measure word for books)
2.	词典	cídiǎn	(n)	[本，部]	dictionary
3.	复习	fùxí	(v)		to review (a lesson)
4.	生词	shēngcí	(n)	[个]	vocabulary, new words
5.	课文	kèwén	(n)	[课]	lesson text
6.	最	zuì	(adv)		most

a. 这是一本最新的《汉语小词典》。

b. 那两本书都不很好，这本最好。

7.	新	xīn	(adj)		to be new
8.	小	xiǎo	(adj)		to be small; to be young

a. 那个图书馆很小。

b. 这是一个小问题。

9.	不过	búguò	(c)		but

a. 我有一本汉语词典，不过，那本词典不很好。

b. 那个书店有很多词典，不过，没有《汉语小词典》。

10.	旧	jiù	(adj)		to be old (in the outdated or second-hand sense)
11.	书店	shūdiàn	(n)	[个，家]	bookshop
12.	买	mǎi	(v)		to buy
13.	你们	nǐmen	(pro)		you (plural)
14.	下午	xiàwǔ	(n)	[个]	afternoon, p.m.
15.	课	kè	(n)	[节 jié]	class, lesson
16.	上午	shàngwǔ	(n)	[个]	forenoon, a.m.
17.	都	dōu	(adv)		all (sums up two or more preceding nominals)

a. 他们都去，我们都不去。

b. 晚上，我们不都去图书馆，有的人在宿舍看书。

18. 中午	zhōngwǔ	(n)	[个]	noon
19. 点	diǎn	(m)		(an hour point on the clock e.g., yìdiǎn 1:00)
20. 下课	xià kè	(vo)		to end class, finish a lesson
下	xià	(v)		to finish (class, work)
课	kè	(n)	[节]	class
21. 半	bàn	(nu)		half
22. 上课	shàng kè	(vo)		to attend, go to (class, work)
上	shàng	(v)		to attend
课	kè	(n)	[节]	class
23. 零	líng	(nu)		zero
24. 分	fēn	(m)		a minute of time
25. 刻	kè	(m)		a quarter of the hour

a. 现在是两点一刻。

b. 十点三刻是十点四十五分，对不对？

专有名词

1. 汉语	Hànyǔ	the Han language, Chinese
2. 《汉语小词典》	Hànyǔ Xiǎo Cídiǎn	A Concise Chinese Dictionary

补充生词

1. 大	dà	(adj)		to be big
2. 早饭	zǎofàn	(n)	[顿 dùn]	breakfast

3.	午饭	wǔfàn	(n)	[顿]	lunch
4.	晚饭	wǎnfàn	(n)	[顿]	dinner, supper

语法点

1. De 的 as a nominalizer

   "的"字结构

De is joined with nouns, pronouns, adjectives and verbs or verb phrases to form a nominal, with the word modified ("central word") omitted. The resultant noun is often used as subject or object.

"的"字可以出现在名词、代词、形容词、动词和动词结构的后面，形成名词性结构，后面不再出现被修饰的名词(中心语)。"的"字结构在句中经常做主语或宾语。

a. Zhège běnzi shi Ānnà de.

   这个本子是安娜的。

   This notebook is Anna's.

b. Nèi běn shū shi xīn de, bú shi wǒ de, wǒ de shi jiù de.

   那本书是新的，不是我的，我的是旧的。

   That book is new. It isn't mine. Mine is old.

2. Expressing time of the day in Chinese is according to the construction HOUR diǎn (dot, point) + FRACTION OF THE HOUR. The following examples cover the range of possibilities:

   钟点表示法：汉语的钟点表示法是，先说"点"，再说其他的。具体如下：

8:00	bā diǎn	八点
9:05	jiǔ diǎn líng wǔ fēn	九点零五分
9:15	jiǔ diǎn shíwǔ (fēn)	九点十五(分)
	jiǔ diǎn yí kè	九点一刻

10:30	shí diǎn sānshí (fēn)	十点三十（分）
	shí diǎn bàn	十点半
11:45	shíyī diǎn sìshí wǔ (fēn)	十一点四十五（分）
	shíyī diǎn sān kè	十一点三刻

3. The adverb dōu 都

副词"都"

> The adverb dou 都 sums up the elements that precede it.
> 副词"都"表示总括，所总括的部份一般在"都"前。

a. Dàwèi hé Ānnà dōu lái.

(Sums up the doers of the action)

大卫和安娜都来。

David and Anna will both come.

b. Xīngqīliù hé xīngqīrì nǐ dōu kàn diànyǐng ma?

(Sums up a time adverbial)

星期六和星期日你都看电影吗？

Do you see films on (both) Saturday and Sunday?

c. Tāmen bù dōu qù, yǒude rén qù, yǒude rén bú qù.

他们不都去，有的人去，有的人不去。

They're not all going; some are and some aren't.

4. The adverb yě 也

副词"也"

> The adverb yě 也 "too, also, as well" indicates that the two elements on either side of the yě have a symmetry in nature or an equality in weight. These elements can be the subject or the predicate.
> 副词"也"表示两件事情相同或相仿。进行对比的可以是主语，也可以是谓语。

a. Tā shi Rìběnrén, wǒ yě shi Rìběnrén.

她是日本人，我也是日本人。

She's Japanese and I'm Japanese, too.

b. Wǒ kàn Zhōngguo diànyǐng, yě kàn Měiguo diànyǐng.

我看中国电影，也看美国电影。

I watch Chinese films, and American films, as well.

c. Zhèi bān de nǚ tóngxué hěn duō, nèi bān de nǚ tóngxué yě hěn duō.

这班的女同学很多，那班的女同学也很多。

There are many female students in this section, and many in that section, too.

* Yě is not a conjunction, but an ADVERB. It is placed before the VERB and not before the SUBJECT.
"也"是副词，不是连词，必须放在动词前，不能放在主语前。

Dōu 都 and yě 也 both come before the predicate verb and cannot be placed in front of the subject. When they are both used in the same sentence, yě comes first, dōu second.

"都"和"也"一样，也必须出现在动词前，不能在主语前。当"都"和"也"在同一个句子里出现时，"也"在"都"前。

d. Tāmen qù, wǒmen yě dōu qù.

他们去，我们也都去。

They are going, and all of us are going, too.

NOTE 注释

When monosyllabic adjectives are used as attributives (= adjectival modifiers), we do not use the structural particle de 的, e.g.,

单音节形容词修饰名词时，不用结构助词"的"，例如：

hǎo diànyǐng	好电影	a good film
xīn sùshè	新宿舍	a new dormitory
hǎo xuésheng	好学生	a good student
jiù shū	旧书	a used book

However, if the adjective itself is modified, do use de, e.g.,
如果单音节形容词本身又被其他词语修饰时，形容词后面就要用"的"。例如：

zuì xīn de cídiǎn	最新的词典	the newest dictionary
hěn xiǎo de shūdiàn	很小的书店	a very small bookstore
hěn hǎo de túshūguǎn	很好的图书馆	a fine library

词组和句子

1.
一点二十（分）	(1:20)	两点半	(2:30)
三点十五（分）	(3:15)	四点一刻	(4:15)
五点四十五（分）	(5:45)	六点三刻	(6:45)
七点零七分	(7:07)	十二点五十五（分）	(12:55)

2. 那本词典是老师的，不是大卫的。
3. 这个本子是不是你的？
4. 这个作业本子是谁的？
5. 那个本子不是安娜的，安娜的本子是小的。
6. 这本书很新，不是我的，我的是旧的。
7. 现在是几点？
8. 你上午九点半上课吗？
9. 今天晚上你几点去图书馆，我跟你一起去。
10. 我两点零五分在宿舍等你。

11. 你们下午几点上课？什么时候下课？
12. 今天晚上的电影是几点的？是七点一刻的吗？
13. 今天他们都去看电影，我们也都去。
14. 那个书店不很小，新书也很多。
15. 为什么那个书店的书，都是旧的？
16. 那是一个旧书店，不过，有的时候也有新书。
17. 星期日我们不都去买书，安娜和金中一去，我们都不去。

参考资料

拼音课文

Zhèi běn cídiǎn shi nǐ de ma?

(Wǎnshang, Dàwèi, Jīn Zhōngyī hé yí ge sìbān de tóngxué, zài sùshè fùxí shēngcí hé kèwén)

Dàwèi:	Nǐ yǒu zhèi běn cídiǎn ma?
Jīn Zhōngyī:	Méiyǒu, zhèi běn cídiǎn hǎo ma?
Dàwèi:	Hěn hǎo. Zhèi běn cídiǎn shi zuì xīn de.
Tóngxué:	Shénme cídiǎn?
Dàwèi:	*Hànyǔ Xiǎo Cídiǎn.*
Tóngxué:	Wǒ yě yǒu yì běn. Búguò, wǒ nèi běn shi jiù de.
Jīn Zhōngyī:	Dàwèi, zhèi běn cídiǎn shi nǐ de ma?
Dàwèi:	Bú shi wǒ de, shi Ānnà de. Wǒ míngtian qù shūdiàn mǎi yì běn.
Jīn Zhōngyī:	Wǒ yě qù mǎi yì běn.
Tóngxué:	Míngtian nǐmen shénme shíhou qù? Wǒ gēn nǐmen yìqǐ qù.
Dàwèi:	Míngtian xiàwǔ nǐ yǒu kè ma?
Tóngxué:	Yǒu, shàngwǔ hé xiàwǔ dōu yǒu.

Dàwèi: Wǒmen zhōngwǔ qù hǎo bu hǎo?

Jīn Zhōngyī: Jǐ diǎn qù?

Tóngxué: Wǒ shí'èr diǎn xià kè, xiàwǔ liǎng diǎn bàn shàng kè. Nǐmen ne?

Dàwèi: Wǒmen yě shí'èr diǎn xià kè. Shí'èr diǎn líng wǔ fēn qù, hǎo ma?

Tóngxué: Shí'èr diǎn yí kè ba.

Dàwèi hé Jīn Zhōngyī: Hǎo.

英译课文

Is this dictionary yours?

(It is evening and David, Kim Chung-il and a Section 4 student are reviewing the vocabulary and text in the dormitory.)

David: Do you have this dictionary?

Kim Chung-il: No, is this a good dictionary?

David: Very good. This dictionary is the newest one.

Classmate: Which dictionary?

David: The *Concise Chinese Dictionary*.

Classmate: I have one, too, but mine is an old one.

Kim Chung-il: David, is this dictionary yours?

David: No, it's not mine. It's Anna's. I'm going to the book shop tomorrow to buy one.

Kim Chung-il: I'm going too to buy one.

Classmate: What time are you going tomorrow? I'll go along with you.

David: Do you have a class tomorrow afternoon?

Classmate: Yes, both morning and afternoon.

David: Let's go at noon.

Kim Chung-il: What time?

Classmate: I finish class at 12:00 and go to class in the afternoon at 2:30. How about you?

David: We finish class at 12:00, too. Let's go at 12:05, all right?

Classmate: How about quarter past twelve?

David and Kim Chung-il: All right.

课堂活动

I. shi ... de

"是"+"的"字结构

A. Students form pairs, each student taking one chart. Student A asks student B the first five questions on the chart. B answers with material from his/her chart and A writes down those answers, then it is B's turn. ✓ = affirmative, ✗ = negative.
老师分组，二人一组。学生A持表A，学生B持表B。先由A就表中前五行提问，B按表B上的提示回答。A将听到的答案填在自己表上的空格中。后五行由B提问，A回答，作法同前。表格中"✓"代表答案是肯定的，"✗"代表答案是否定的。

Example:

1. Zhè běn cídiǎn shì bú shì Zhāng lǎoshī de?
这本词典是不是张老师的？

(or) Zhè běn cídiǎn shì Zhāng lǎoshī de ma?
(或者) 这本词典是张老师的吗？

2. Shì, zhè běn cídiǎn shì Zhāng lǎoshī de.
是，这本词典是张老师的。

(or) Zhè běn cídiǎn bú shì Zhāng lǎoshī de, shì Ānnà de.
(或者) 这本词典不是张老师的，是安娜的。

A

	{…是不是…的？ …是…的吗？	{是，…是…的。 …不是…的，是…的。
这本词典	张老师	
那个电影	中国	
这个本子	你	
那个宿舍	男同学	
这个作业	昨天	
这本书		✗他
这个电影院		✓
那本《学生词典》		✗旧
那个女同学		✗五班
你们班的老师		✗男

B

	{…是不是…的？ …是…的吗？	{是，…是…的。 …不是…的，是…的。
这本词典		✗安娜
那个电影		✗日本
这个本子		✓
那个宿舍		✗女同学
这个作业		✗今天
这本书	你	
这个电影院	新	
那本《学生词典》	新	
那个女同学	四班	
你们班的老师	女	

When the exercise is finished, the instructor requests various students to read out each question and response.

问答练习做完后，老师再指定学生读出每行的问题和答案。

B. Students form pairs, each student with one chart. A begins, asking the first four questions as suggested by the chart. B answers according to his/her chart and A fills in those answers. Then it is B's turn.

老师分组，二人一组。学生A持表A，学生B持表B。先由A就表中前四项按指示提问，B按表B上的指示回答，A听后将答案填在空格中。后四项由B提问，A回答，做法同前。表格中"✓"代表答案是肯定的，"✗"代表答案是否定的。

A

	是谁的？	是新的吗？	是不是旧的？	好不好？
那本词典				
这本书				
那个本子				
那个宿舍				
这个小本子	她	✗	✓	不好
这本《汉语词典》	方小英	✓	✗	很好
那本书	我朋友	✓	✗	很好
那个图书馆	学生	✗	✓	很小，书不多

B

	是谁的？	是新的吗？	是不是旧的？	好不好？
那本词典	我	✗	✓	不很好
这本书	老师	✓	✗	很好
那个本子	大卫	✗	✓	不好
那个宿舍	新同学	✓	✗	很小，不很好
这个小本子				
这本《汉语词典》				
那本书				
那个图书馆				

When the exercise is finished, the instructor selects students to describe any one item. Example: Nàge túshūguǎn shì xuésheng de, bú shì xīn de, shì jiù de. Nàge túshūguǎn hěn xiǎo, shū bù duō.
做完问答以后，老师可指定学生介绍其中任何一项，如：那个图书馆是学生的，不是新的，是旧的。那个图书馆很小，书不多。

II. Telling time

钟点表示法

A. The instructor asks students to tell the time, using a sample clock.
老师用教具时钟拨出不同时间，让学生读出。

B. Students write out times of the clock that the instructor gives them orally.
老师说时间，同学听写。

III. Time words as adverbial adjuncts

时间状语

A. Students form pairs, each student with one chart. Each student asks about Xiǎoměi's schedule for tomorrow. A starts asking about the first four time slots, B answers, and A fills in those answers. Then it is B's turn.

老师分组，二个人一组。学生A持表A，学生B持表B。通过问答写出小美明天的活动时间表。A先就前四个时间提问，B回答，A听后将答案填在表上。B就另外四个时间提问，A回答，作法同前。

Example:

A: Míngtian shàngwǔ shí diǎn Xiǎoměi zài nǎr?
明天上午十点小美在哪儿？

B: Míngtian shàngwǔ shí diǎn tā zài sùshè.
明天上午十点她在宿舍。

A: Tā zài sùshè zuò shénme?
她在宿舍做什么？

B: Tā zài sùshè kàn shū.
她在宿舍看书。

A

上午8:15	
上午10:30	
中午12:20	
中午12:45	
下午2:50	图书馆/复习
下午6:30	朋友家/吃饭
晚上7:15	小金家/看电影
晚上9:00	宿舍/预习

B

上午8:15	图书馆/做作业
上午10:30	老师家/上课
中午12:20	宿舍/吃饭
中午12:45	书店/买词典
下午2:50	
下午6:30	
晚上7:15	
晚上9:00	

B. Students form pairs, each student holding one chart. Students ask back and forth to determine a time that they can go to the theater together. A blank indicates that there is no schedule at that time, i.e. the slot is free.

老师分组，二人一组。学生A持表A，学生B持表B，通过问答，找出一个共同时间，可以一起去看电影。格内空白表示自己没有活动安排。

Example:

A: Wǒmen yìqǐ qù kàn diànyǐng, hǎo bù hǎo?

我们一起去看电影，好不好？

B: Hǎo, wǒmen shénme shíhou qù?

好，我们什么时候去？

A: Nǐ xīngqīyī wǎnshang zuò shénme?

你星期一晚上做什么？

B: Wǒ xīngqīyī wǎnshang qī diǎn yí kè shàng kè. Nǐ xīngqī'èr wǎnshang zuò shénme?

我星期一晚上七点一刻上课。你星期二晚上做什么？

Etc.

A

星期一 晚上	星期二 晚上	星期三 晚上	星期四 晚上	星期五 晚上	星期六 下午1:00	星期日 上午
	复习生词 和课文		去图书馆		回家	

B

星期一 晚上7:15	星期二 晚上	星期三 晚上7:40	星期四 晚上	星期五 晚上6:30	星期六 下午	星期日 上午
上课		做作业		去朋友家		

IV. dōu and yě

“都”和“也”

The instructor writes the material from the cards below on the blackboard, then has students compare Fang Ying and Fang Na using dōu and yě in their sentences.

For example:

“Fang Ying is Chinese. Fang Na is also (yě) Chinese. They are both (dōu) Chinese.” or “Fang Ying isn’t Japanese. Fang Na isn’t Japanese either (yě). Neither of them (dōu) is Japanese.”

老师把下面两张卡片复制在黑板上，让学生用“也”“都”比较方英和方娜的情况，例如：“方英是中国人，方娜也是中国人，她们都是中国人。”或者“方英不是日本人，方娜也不是日本人，她们都不是日本人。”

中国人
姓方
老师
有男朋友
有二十五个学生

方英

中国人
姓方
老师
有男朋友
有二十五个学生

方娜

阅读练习

今天是九月十二号，星期五。上午我们有课，九点半上(课)，十二点二十下(课)。中午我跟我们班的同学一起吃饭。下午，(我们)没有课。有的同学回宿舍复习，有的同学回家，有的同学去图书馆看书，我去书店买词典。我有一本汉语词典，不过，那本词典是旧的，今天下午我去买一本新的。四点我回宿舍做作业，跟我的同学一起预习新课的生词和课文。我问问题，他回答；他问问题，我回答。晚上七点一刻，我和我的中国朋友去天星电影院看电影。

第一单元复习

1. Sentences with verbal predicates

   动词谓词句

   I. general

      一般的动词谓语句

      a. We are going today; they're not.

         今天我们去，他们不去。

      b. I'm reviewing the vocabulary and lesson text now.

         我现在复习生词和课文。

   II. with specific features(1)

      特殊的动词谓语句(1)

      A. shi sentences

         "是"字句

         a. He is our teacher, and our friend too.

            他是我们的老师，也是我们的朋友。

         b. This dictionary is his, not David's.

            这本词典是他的，不是大卫的。

         c. This is my friend's house.

            这是我朋友家。

         d. It is now 12:05.

            现在是十二点零五分。

      B. yǒu sentences

         "有"字句

a. She has two copies of the *New Chinese-English Dictionary*.

她有两本《汉语小词典》。

b. I have a question; may I ask you now?

我有一个问题，现在可以问您吗？

c. There are ten students in Section Two.

二班有十个学生。

d. There are twelve months in a year.

一年有十二个月。

e. We have a class on Saturday morning, but not in the afternoon.

星期六上午我们有课，下午没有。

C. verbal expressions in series

连动句

a. He is going back to the dormitory to review.

他回宿舍复习。

b. My friend is coming to my home on Sunday to eat.

星期日我朋友来我家吃饭。

c. I'm going with friends to see a movie day after tomorrow.

后天晚上我和朋友去看电影。

2. Sentences with adjectival predicates

形容词谓语句

a. That library is not small, and there are a lot of books.

那个图书馆不小，书也很多。

b. Her book is new; mine is old.

她的书新，我的书旧。

3. Interrogative sentences

疑问句

I. with ma

用“吗”的疑问句

a. Is Kim Chung-il your classmate?

金中一是你的同学吗？

b. Do you have American friends?

你有美国朋友吗？

c. Are you going to prepare the new lesson in the library this afternoon?

今天下午你在图书馆预习新课吗？

d. Is that film good?

那个电影好吗？

II. with interrogative pronouns

用疑问代词的疑问句

a. Which section are you in? What is your teacher's last name?

你是哪个班的？你们的老师姓什么？

b. Whose notebook is this? Why doesn't it have a name on it?

这是谁的本子？为什么没有名字？

c. How many students are there in this section? How many female? How many male?

这个班有多少同学？几个女同学？几个男同学？

d. When do you attend class? Where?

你们什么时候上课？在哪儿上？

e. How is that film?

那个电影怎么样？

III. affirmative-negative questions

正反疑问句

a. Is this exercise book yours?

这个作业本子是不是你的？

b. Do you have class tomorrow afternoon?

你们明天下午有课没有？

c. Are you going to the bookstore to buy books this noon?

今天中午你去不去书店买书？

d. Do you have many Chinese friends?

你的中国朋友多不多？

IV. with ne

用“呢”的疑问句

a. It's thirty-one days for July, how about August?

七月是三十一天，八月呢？

b. Mr. Zhang has class in the morning. How about the afternoon?

张老师上午有课，下午呢？

c. There are a lot of new words in this lesson. How about that one?

这课的生词很多，那课呢？

d. What about Yamamoto?

山本呢？

4. Attributives

定语

a. She is a new student. What is her name?

她是新同学，她叫什么名字？

b. That Japanese student studies with their section.

那个日本学生在他们班上课。

c. That is a copy of the very latest Chinese dictionary.

那是一本最新的汉语词典。

d. Where is my book?

我的书在哪儿？

5. Adverbial adjuncts

状语

a. In 1990, I studied Chinese in China.

一九九零年我在中国学汉语。

b. His homework was all correct last week. This week, his homework is good, too.

上（个）星期他的作业都对，这（个）星期他的作业也很好。

c. He'll be here right away. Let's wait for him here.

他马上来，我们在这儿等他吧。

阅读

我有一个朋友，她跟我都在六班。我们上午八点半上课，中午十二点二十下课。下午我有的时候去图书馆做作业，有的时候在宿舍复习生词和课文；她有的时候去图书馆，有的时候回家。上课的时候，我有问题，都问她；她有问题，也问我。不过，我的问题少，她的问题多。有的时候，她问我很多问题。这个星期六下午，我和我的同学跟她一起去天星电影院看电影，晚上，我们去她家吃饭。

有（的）人问我："她是谁？"

“她是张老师。”

“张老师？张老师是你的朋友？”

“是，张老师是我们的老师，也是我们的朋友。”

第六课

我想约你去听音乐

汉字课文

安　娜：方小英，昨天下课以后，你去哪儿了？

方小英：我和金中一去看电影了。

安　娜：什么电影？有意思吗？

方小英：是个美国电影，很有意思。昨天下课以后，你找我了吗？

安　娜：找你了。我想约你去听音乐。

方小英：是吗？我也很想听音乐。你想什么时候去？

安　娜：今天晚上我们一起去，好不好？

方小英：好啊。

安　娜：现在我去打电话，订两张票……

方小英：不用，我们到那儿再买吧！

安　娜：没问题吗？

方小英：没问题。昨天晚上你做什么了？去图书馆了吧？

安　娜：没有，没去图书馆。我一个人去散步了。

方小英：你喜欢一个人散步？

安　娜：对，我很喜欢一个人散步。

方小英：今天晚上我们几点钟去听音乐？

安　娜：六点半吧！

方小英：在哪儿见面？

安　娜：在学校门口儿，怎么样？

方小英：好，六点半，在学校门口儿。不见不散。

生词语

1.	想	xiǎng	(o.v)		to want to, to think
		a. 我今天想吃中国饭。			
		b. 我现在很想去散步，不想看书。			
2.	约	yuē	(v)		to set (a time), to make an appointment
		a. 他约我下课以后去书店。			
		b. 我们约她一起去散步。			
3.	听	tīng	(v)		to listen
4.	音乐	yīnyuè	(n)	[种 zhǒng]	music
5.	以后	yǐhòu	(n)		afterwards, later
6.	了	le	(part)		(modal particle, indicating a completed action)
7.	有意思	yǒu yìsi	(vo)		to be interesting
		a. 这本书很有意思，你想看吗？			
		b. 今天的电影没有意思。			
8.	找	zhǎo	(v)		to look for
		a. 你找什么？— 我找我的书，我的书呢？			
		b. 星期六上午我同学来找我复习课文。			
9.	啊	ā	(part)		(modal particle, added to verbs, adjectives or sentences to emphasize assurance or agreement, or stress the speaker's point of view)

10.	打	dǎ	(v)		(in context) to send, transmit as a phone call; to hit
11.	电话	diànhuà	(n)	[个]	telephone
12.	订	dìng	(v)		to book, reserve (a ticket); to subscribe (to a newspaper, etc.)
13.	张	zhāng	(m)		a sheet of (for flat surfaced object, including paper, tables and tortillas)
14.	票	piào	(n)	[张]	ticket
15.	怎么样	zěnmeyàng	(pro)		How is it? How does it go? How about it?
16.	不用	búyòng	(o.v)		need not

a. 我们不用买汉语词典，图书馆有。

b. 你不用来，我马上去。

c. 我们不用打电话订票，到电影院买，没问题。

17.	到	dào	(v)		to arrive
18.	那儿	nàr	(pro)		there
19.	再	zài	(adv)		then (opens a second clause, the action of which is done only when the action of the first clause has taken place), again, once more
20.	没问题	méi wèntí	(vo)		it's fine, no problem
	没	méi	(v)		not any (a contraction of méiyǒu)
	问题	wèntí	(n)	[个]	problem
21.	没(有)	méi (you)	(adv)		(negative of completed action)
22.	散步	sànbù	(vo)		to stroll, take a walk

23.	喜欢	xǐhuan	(v)		to like, enjoy
24.	钟	zhōng	(n)		(in time expressions, follows words such as diǎn to indicate time "of the clock"); a clock
25.	见面	jiàn miàn	(vo)		to meet
	见	jiàn	(v)		to see
	面	miàn	(n)		the face
		a. 今天老师跟新同学见面。			
		b. 我们在图书馆门口儿见面，好不好？			
26.	学校	xuéxiào	(n)	[个]	school
27.	门口儿	ménkǒur	(n)		entrance
28.	不见不散	bú jiàn bú sàn	(fixed expression)		"Don't leave until I get there." "Wait there till I arrive."

补充生词

音乐会	yīnyuèhuì	(n)	[个]	concert

语法点

1. Yǐhòu 以后 "later, afterwards"

"以后"

Yǐhòu can be used independently or following a time or action to create an "after" clause.

"以后"可以单独使用，也可以用在表示时间的词语或动词词组等的后面，一起做时间状语。

a. Wǒ jīntian bú qù kàn diànyǐng, yǐhòu zài qù.

我今天不去看电影，以后再去。

I won't go to see a film today; I'll go sometime later.

b. Sān tiān yǐhòu wǒ qù nǐ jiā.

三天以后我去你家。

I'll go to your house three days from now (= later).

c. Xià kè yǐhòu, wǒmen yìqǐ qù chī fàn ba.

下课以后，我们一起去吃饭吧。

Let's go to eat together after class.

2. The particle le 了

(Le is the most protean of Chinese particles and will complicate your lives for a while. Be patient. It can be conquered. We'll chip away gradually at its various functions.)

The modal particle le 了 (1)

语气助词“了”(1)

The modal particle le 了 (also called "sentence end le") appears after verbal predicates indicating that something has already come about or taken place. In such conditions, le must be used. The sentence may also contain a time word indicating that the occurrence is finished, e.g., yesterday or last week.

语气助词“了”(也可以叫做句尾“了”)出现在动词谓语句的句尾，表示某件事已在过去实现或完成。句中常有表示过去的时间词语，如“昨天”“上星期”等做状语。

Time word + S + V + O + 了

S + Time word + V + O + 了

a. Zuótian nǐmen qù nǎr le?

昨天你们去哪儿了？

Where did you go yesterday?

b. Wǒ qù túshūguǎn le; tā qù péngyou jiā le.

我去图书馆了，他去朋友家了。

I went to the library, he went to a friend's house.

To negate such sentences, méi(yǒu) is placed before the verb, and sentence end le is deleted. Méiyǒu alone can be used in response if one is in a mood to be economical with words. In the affirmative-negative question form, add méiyǒu at the end.

这种句子的否定式是在动词前用"没(有)"，同时去掉句尾的"了"。正反疑问式是在句尾"了"后加上"没有"。

S + 没(有) + V + O

S + V + O + 了 + 没有？

c. Zuótian nǐ kàn diànyǐng le méiyǒu?

昨天你看电影了没有？

Did you see a film yesterday?

d. Méiyǒu, wǒ zuótian méi(you) kàn diànyǐng.

没有，我昨天没(有)看电影。

No, I didn't see a film yesterday.

* In such sentences, the object *cannot* be modified by a measure word or quantifier. What is emphasized is that the whole event has been completed or come about, not the number or quantity of that event. Therefore, this sentence is WRONG: Zuótian wǒ kàn yí ge diànyǐng le.
在这类句子里，宾语不能受数量词修饰，因为"了"强调的是整个事件已经完成或实现，而并不是要说明完成了多少量，所以宾语不能带数量词。下面的句子是错误的："昨天我看一个电影了。"

3. Omission of yī 一 with measure words

"一"在量词前的省略

When a noun object is modified by <u>yī</u> plus a measure word, the <u>yī</u> can be omitted.

当动词后的名词宾语受“一”加量词修饰时，“一”可以省略。

a. Wǒ qù shūdiàn mǎi běn shū.

我去书店买本书。

I'm going to the bookshop to buy a book.

b. Nǐ dǎ ge diànhuà, dìng zhāng diànyǐng piào.

你打个电话，订张电影票。

Make a phone call and reserve a ticket for the film.

4. Modal particle <u>ba</u> (2) (see also Lesson 4, p. 110)

语气助词“吧”(2)（见第四课，页110）

The modal particle <u>ba</u> can also be used to express a question. It is not a simple interrogative, but indicates surmise or guess. The speaker isn't 100% sure of the issue, so uses <u>ba</u>.

语气助词“吧”也可以表示疑问，但往往不是单纯提问，而是带有揣测的语气。当说话人对某一事实没有百分之百的把握时，就可以用“吧”来提问。

a. Nǐ shi Fāng Xiǎoyīng ba?

你是方小英吧？

You're Fang Xiaoying, aren't you?

b. Tā méi lái ba?

他没来吧？

He didn't come, did he?

c. Nàge diànyǐng hěn yǒu yìsi ba?

那个电影很有意思吧？

That film is interesting, I'll bet?

d. Ānnà qù sànbù le ba?

安娜去散步了吧？

Anna probably went for a walk, I assume?

5. Verb constructions as objects

动词结构做宾语

In general, objects are nominals or pronominals in Chinese. Other constructions can play that role, as here with verbals (and Lesson 8, with the S-P construction).

汉语中，一般是由名词或代词充任宾语的，但其他结构也可以充当，如下面所举的动词结构(和第八课的主谓结构)。

a. Wǒ xǐhuan wǎnshang sànbù.

我喜欢晚上散步。

I like to take walks in the evening.

b. Wǒ bù xǐhuan kàn diànyǐng, wǒ xǐhuan tīng yīnyuè.

我不喜欢看电影，我喜欢听音乐。

I don't like to watch films. I like to listen to music.

NOTES 注释

1. Wǒmen dào nàr zài mǎi ba 我们到那儿再买吧 "Let's buy it when we get there". Zài 再, "and then", functions to delay something until a given time later. Note these examples:

"我们到那儿再买吧"："再"表示把事情推延到某个时间之后再做。例如：

a. Jīntiān shàngwǔ wǒmen yìqǐ qù túshūguǎn, zěnmeyàng?

今天上午我们一起去图书馆，怎么样？

Let's go to the library together this morning.

Shàngwǔ wǒ yǒu kè, xiàwǔ zài qù ba.

上午我有课，下午再去吧。

I have a class in the morning, let's go in the afternoon.

b. Xiànzài búyòng dìng piào, wǒ xiǎng míngtiān qù kàn diànyǐng de shíhou zài mǎi.

现在不用订票，我想明天去看电影的时候再买。

We don't have to book tickets now. I'd rather buy them tomorrow when we go to see the film.

c. Wǒmen jīntiān wǎnshang yìqǐ yùxí xīn kè, hǎo ma?

我们今天晚上一起预习新课，好吗？

Shall we prepare the new lesson together this evening?

Míngtiān bù xué xīn kè, hòutiān xué. Wǒmen míngtiān wǎnshang zài yùxí ba.

明天不学新课，后天学。我们明天晚上再预习吧。

We don't study the new lesson tomorrow; it's the day after tomorrow. Let's prepare tomorrow night.

2. Wǒ hěn xǐhuan yí ge rén sànbù 我很喜欢一个人散步. In this sentence, yí ge rén is an adverbial adjunct that describes the manner of the stroll.

"我很喜欢一个人散步"："一个人"在这里做状语，说明散步的方式。

词组和句子

1. 两年以后　三个月以后　两天以后　2000年以后
三月以后　二号以后　十点钟以后　看电影以后
吃饭以后　来中国以后　学生下课以后　我们散步以后
他们有新书以后

2. 喜欢这位老师　喜欢中国学生　不喜欢那个人
喜欢听音乐　喜欢去书店　不喜欢看电影
喜欢跟朋友一起散步　不喜欢在图书馆做作业

3. 上午他去散步了吗？

4. 上午他没去散步。
5. 吃饭以后他去散步吗？
6. 吃饭以后他不去散步。
7. 上星期六你约朋友去吃饭了吧？
8. 没有，我没约。我去老师家了。
9. 昨天中午大卫来找我了，我们一起复习生词和课文了。
10. 下午四点半以后你没有课吧？
11. 下课以后，我到学校门口儿等你，好吗？
12. 不用。下课以后，我到二班找你吧！
13. 来中国以后，我有很多新朋友。
14. 两个星期以后，他回英国，我也回国。
15. 以后，我不想学音乐，我想学汉语。
16. 我们以后一起预习生词吧！
17. 星期日我喜欢一个人在家看书。
18. 我喜欢在这儿买书，不喜欢去那儿买。
19. 我有个问题，想去问老师。
20. 他想打个电话订张票，明天晚上去听音乐。

参考资料

拼音课文

Wǒ xiǎng yuē nǐ qù tīng yīnyuè

Ānnà: Fāng Xiǎoyīng. Zuótian xià kè yǐhòu, nǐ qù nǎr le?

Fāng Xiǎoyīng: Wǒ hé Jīn Zhōngyī qù kàn diànyǐng le.

Ānnà: Shénme diànyǐng? Yǒu yìsi ma?

Fāng Xiǎoyīng: Shì ge Měiguo diànyǐng, hěn yǒu yìsi. Zuótian xià kè yǐhòu, nǐ zhǎo wo le ma?

Ānnà: Zhǎo ni le. Wǒ xiǎng yuē ni qù tīng yīnyuè.

Fāng Xiǎoyīng: Shì ma? Wǒ yě hěn xiǎng tīng yīnyuè. Nǐ xiǎng shénme shíhou qù?

Ānnà: Jīntian wǎnshang wǒmen yìqǐ qù, hǎo bu hǎo?

Fāng Xiǎoyīng: Hǎo a.

Ānnà: Xiànzài wǒ qù dǎ diànhuà, dìng liǎng zhāng piào ...

Fāng Xiǎoyīng: Búyòng, Wǒmen dào nàr zài mǎi ba!

Ānnà: Méi wèntí ma?

Fāng Xiǎoyīng: Méi wèntí. Zuótian wǎnshang nǐ zuò shénme le? Qù túshūguǎn le ba?

Ānnà: Méiyou, méi qù túshūguǎn. Wǒ yí ge rén qù sànbù le.

Fāng Xiǎoyīng: Nǐ xǐhuan yí ge rén sànbù?

Ānnà: Duì, wǒ hěn xǐhuan yí ge rén sànbù.

Fāng Xiǎoyīng: Jīntian wǎnshang wǒmen jǐ diǎnzhōng qù tīng yīnyuè?

Ānnà: Liù diǎn bàn ba!

Fāng Xiǎoyīng: Zài nǎr jiàn miàn?

Ānnà: Zài xuéxiào ménkǒur, zěnmeyàng?

Fāng Xiǎoyīng: Hǎo, liù diǎn bàn, zài xuéxiào ménkǒur. Bú jiàn bú sàn.

英译课文

I'd like to ask you to go hear some music with me

Anna: Fang Xiaoying, where did you go after class yesterday?

Fang Xiaoying: I went with Kim Chung-il to see a film.

Anna: What film? Was it interesting?

Fang Xiaoying: It was an American film and very interesting. Were you trying to find me after class yesterday?

Anna: Yes. I wanted to ask you to go hear some music with me.

Fang Xiaoying: Oh? I'd very much like to go to hear some music, too. When do you want to go?

Anna: Let's go together tonight!

Fang Xiaoying: Fine.

Anna: I'll go and make a phone call now to reserve two tickets …

Fang Xiaoying: You don't have to. We'll buy them when we get there.

Anna: There won't be any problem?

Fang Xiaoying: No. What did you do last night? Did you go to the library?

Anna: No, I didn't. I went for a walk by myself.

Fang Xiaoying: You like going for walks alone?

Anna: Right, I'm rather fond of going for walks alone.

Fang Xiaoying: What time do we go this evening?

Anna: 6:30, I think!

Fang Xiaoying: Where shall we meet?

Anna: How about at the school entrance?

Fang Xiaoying: Fine. 6:30 at the school entrance. We won't leave without each other.

课堂活动

I. yǐhòu

"以后"

A. Students form pairs for Q and A. yǐhòu must be used in responses.

二人一组，互相问答。一人持表A，一人持表B，回答时必须用"以后"。

Example:

A: Ānnà shénme shíhou qù tīng yīnyuè?

安娜什么时候去听音乐？

B: Ānnà xià kè yǐhou qù tīng yīnyuè.

安娜下课以后去听音乐。

A

	去听音乐？	去散步？	预习？
安娜			
山本	三天	跟朋友见面	买本子
大卫			
方小英	散步	打电话	回宿舍
金中一			
张老师	看电影	买书	（不用预习）

B

	去听音乐？	去散步？	预习？
安娜	下课	做作业	订电影票
山本			
大卫	两个星期	买词典	去图书馆
方小英			
金中一	半个月	吃饭	回家
张老师			

B. Copy the information below onto slips, two slips for each group of eight students (1, 2, 3 & 4). Each student takes a slip, then ask questions, beginning with "Míngtiān xiàkè yǐhòu nǐ qù zuò shénme?" Answer in the slip order, then ask again until finding the student whose ordering of activities matches. Yǐhòu must be used in answering.

八人一组，每人持一卡片，卡片上所示为各人明天要做的事情及其顺序。根据卡片内容互相问答，直至找到持有相同卡片者为止。问句是“明天下课以后你去做什么？”卡片有四种，内容都一样，仅所列事项的次序不同。每种卡片有两张。回答时必须用“以后”。四种卡片的内容如下：

1)	A 订电影票	B 听音乐	C 跟朋友吃饭	D 散步
2)	A 订电影票	B 跟朋友吃饭	C 听音乐	D 散步
3)	A 订电影票	B 听音乐	C 散步	D 跟朋友吃饭
4)	A 订电影票	B 跟朋友吃饭	C 散步	D 听音乐

C. Students form pairs, one student taking chart A and the other chart B, then ask and answer questions. Students each ask “X jīntiān tīng yīnyuè yǐhòu xiǎng zuò shénme?” Answers should be on the basis of the numbers (1st, 2nd, etc.) on the chart, and the questioner should enter the answers in the blanks. Once finished, students check to see whose plans match.

二人一组，一人持表A，一人持表B，互相问“某某人今天听音乐以后想做什么？”回答时请按照阿拉伯数字的顺序把该人想做的事说出，让提问的人写在空格内。最后一起看看谁和谁的计划一样。

Example:

Q: Zhāng Shān jīntiān tīng yīnyuè yǐhòu xiǎng zuò shénme?
张山今天听音乐以后想做什么？

A: Zhāng Shān jīntiān tīng yīnyuè yǐhòu xiǎng huí xuéxiào zhǎo rén.
张山今天听音乐以后想回学校找人。

Q: ... huí xuéxiào zhǎo rén hǐhòu xiǎng zuò shénme?
……回学校找人以后想做什么？

A: ... huí xuéxiào zhǎo rén yǐhòu xiǎng qù shūdiàn mǎi cídiǎn.
(and so on)
……回学校找人以后想去书店买词典。
(以此类推)

A

	回学校找人	打电话订书	去书店买词典	买电影票
张山				
金一				
方明				
韩新				
安山	2	4	1	3
马同	4	1	3	2
张汉	1	2	4	3
文英	1	3	2	4

B

	回学校找人	打电话订书	去书店买词典	买电影票
张山	1	3	2	4
金一	4	1	3	2
方明	2	4	1	3
韩新	1	2	4	3
安山				
马同				
张汉				
文英				

II. Verbal Expressions as Objects

动词结构作宾语

Students form pairs, each with a chart. A asks the question "Xǐhuān zuò shénme" (with its time antecedent) then B answers with the information from chart B. A checks the "same?" column if the item is the same on the A chart. Students holding C and D charts also ask and answer their questions. Since the contents of charts are all different, A, B and C, D can then switch to go through the exercise again.

老师分组，二人一组。学生A持表A，学生B持表B。先由A提问，B按表中"喜欢做什么？"一项下面的答案回答，A将二人相同的活动，在"是否相同"一项下做记号（如相同的划"✓"）。然后由B提问，作法同前。C，D两位同学可同时用C，D两表问答。因内容各不相同，A，B同学和C，D同学可以交换表格各自再做一遍。

A

Time 时间	What do you like to do? 喜欢做什么？	Same? 是否相同
1. 下午下课以后	散步	
2. 星期五晚上	跟朋友吃饭	
3. 星期六下午	预习新课	
4. 晚上七点以后	去图书馆	
5. 星期六晚上	看电影	
6. 星期日上午	复习课文和生词	

B

Time 时间	What do you like to do? 喜欢做什么？	Same? 是否相同
1. 下午下课以后	复习课文和生词	
2. 星期五晚上	跟朋友吃饭	
3. 星期六下午	看电影	
4. 晚上七点以后	去图书馆	
5. 星期六晚上	散步	
6. 星期日上午	预习新课	

C

Time 时间	What do you like to do? 喜欢做什么？	Same? 是否相同
1. 下午下课以后	去吃中国饭	
2. 星期五晚上	听音乐	
3. 星期六下午	去朋友家	
4. 晚上七点以后	做作业	
5. 星期六晚上	跟朋友散步	
6. 星期日上午	预习生词	

D

Time 时间	What do you like to do? 喜欢做什么？	Same? 是否相同
1. 下午下课以后	做作业	
2. 星期五晚上	听音乐	
3. 星期六下午	去吃中国饭	
4. 晚上七点以后	预习生词	
5. 星期六晚上	跟朋友散步	
6. 星期日上午	去朋友家	

After the Q & A, students will discover that two of them enjoy two of the activities at the same time. Then A and B (or C and D) may practice the following dialogue:

问答以后，同学可发现有两项活动进行的时间与对方相同。那么A，B(或C，D)即可进行下面的对话，如：

A: Xīngqīwǔ wǎnshang nǐ xǐhuan …, wǒ yě xǐhuan …. Wǒmen yìqǐ qù … ba!

星期五晚上你喜欢……，我也喜欢……。我们一起去……吧！

B: Hǎo. Wǒmen yìqǐ qù … ba!

好。我们一起去……吧！

B: Wǎnshang qī diǎn yǐhòu, nǐ xǐhuan …, wǒ yě xǐhuan …. Wǒmen yìqǐ qù … ba!

晚上七点以后，你喜欢……，我也喜欢……。我们一起去……吧！

A: Hǎo, wǒmen yìqǐ qù … ba!

好。我们一起去……吧！

III. Modal particle le (indicating an action has already been realized or concluded)

语气助词"了"(表示过去实现或完成)

Students form pairs, each holding a chart. The assumption is that both parties had the same plan at some time in the past and are now checking on it to see what may have been done and what not done. Reasons must be given for what hasn't been concluded. ✓ indicates something was done or happened, ✗ that it was not.

老师分组，二人一组。一人持表A，一人持表B。假设双方都在某一段过去的时间里有一样的计划，现在正在进行回顾，看看哪些做了，哪些没做。没做的要说出原因。✓ 表示做了，✗ 表示没做。

Example:

B asks: Nǐ qiántian zhōngwǔ gēn lǎoshī jiàn miàn le ma?

你前天中午跟老师见面了吗？

A answers: Méiyǒu.

没有。

B asks: Wèi shénme méiyǒu gēn lǎoshī jiàn miàn?

为什么没有跟老师见面？

A answers: Lǎoshī de péngyou lái le.

老师的朋友来了。

A

Time 时间	Original plan 原订计划	Concluded 是否完成	Why not? 为什么没有……？
9月20日（前天）上午	预习新课了吗？	✓	
（例）→中午	跟老师见面了吗？	✗	老师的朋友来了。
下午	订电影票了吗？	✓	
晚上	听音乐了吗？	✓	
9月21日（昨天）上午	做作业了吗？	✗	前天做了。
中午	约同学吃饭了吗？	✗	同学没来。
下午	去图书馆看书了吗？	✗	同学来找我了。
晚上	复习生词和课文了吗？	✓	
9月22日（今天）上午	去朋友的学校了吗？	✗	朋友有课。
中午	打电话订词典了吗？	✓	
下午	跟你朋友去散步了吗？	✗	我朋友去美国了。
晚上	去看电影了吗？	✗	复习生词了。
（现在是9月22日晚上十一点钟）			

B

Time 时间	Original plan 原订计划	Concluded 是否完成	Why not? 为什么没有……？
9月20日（前天）上午	预习新课了吗？	✗	去朋友家了。
（例）→中午	跟老师见面了吗？	✓	我跟老师见面了。
下午	订电影票了吗？	✓	
晚上	听音乐了吗？	✗	没有票。
9月21日（昨天）上午	做作业了吗？	✗	前天没有作业。
中午	约同学吃饭了吗？	✓	
下午	去图书馆看书了吗？	✓	
晚上	复习生词和课文了吗？	✗	预习新课了。
9月22日（今天）上午	去朋友的学校了吗？	✗	复习课文了。
中午	打电话订词典了吗？	✗	明天我去书店买。
下午	跟你朋友去散步了吗？	✓	
晚上	去看电影了吗？	✗	那个电影不好。
（现在是9月22日晚上十一点钟）			

第七课

给老师打电话

汉字课文

(一)

接电话人：喂？

金 中 一：喂，请问张老师在吗？

接电话人：什么？你找谁？

金 中 一：我找张老师。

接电话人：你打错了。

金 中 一：您的电话号码是不是25116084？

接电话人：不是。

金 中 一：对不起。

接电话人：没关系。

(二)

张老师：喂？您找哪一位？

金中一：喂，是张老师家吗？请张老师接电话。

张老师：我就是。

金中一：张老师，您好。我是金中一。

张老师：你好，金中一。

金中一：张老师，我朋友明天从德国来，我想去接他。明天我能不能请假？

张老师：你几点去接他？

金中一：他十点零五分到，我八点四十五去。

张老师：上午和下午你都请假吗？

金中一：不，下午我不请假。上午从九点到十一点是您的课，我请假。

张老师：你大概什么时候回来？

金中一：我大概十一点回来。第三节课我能上。

张老师：好，你去接朋友吧。明天我们学习第八课，你好好儿预习一下儿。

金中一：谢谢您，张老师。再见！

张老师：再见。

生词语

1. 给 gěi (v, prep) to give; to, for (instrumental function word often untranslatable)

   a. 请今天晚上给我打个电话。

   b. 你去书店吗？请给我买一本《汉语小词典》。

2. 接 jiē (v) to receive

   a. 大卫，你的电话，你去接电话吧！

   b. 我明天去接朋友。

3. 喂 wèi (i) hello (telephone usage)

4. 请问 qǐngwèn (v) excuse me (in asking a question; lit., please may I ask)

   a. 请问，您是不是韩老师？

   b. 请问，在哪儿买票？

5. 错 cuò (adj) to be wrong

6. 号码 hàomǎ (n) [个] number

7.	对不起	duìbuqǐ		I'm sorry, I beg your pardon
8.	没关系	méi guānxi		that's alright, no problem
9.	位	wèi	(m)	(polite measure word for people)
10.	请	qǐng	(v)	to request
11.	就	jiù	(adv)	(often with the equational shi, and often handled through voice emphasis in English) precisely, that's it

a. 她就是我的中国朋友。

b. 这本书就是我的。

c. 你找小图书馆吗？这个就是小图书馆。

12.	从	cóng	(prep)	from
13.	能	néng	(o.v)	(before verb) to be able to
14.	请假	qǐng jià	(vo)	to request leave, ask to be absent
	请	qǐng	(v)	to request
	假	jià	(n)	leave, time off

a. 你星期几请假？

b. 他下星期请两天假，我不请假。

c. 明天你不来上课，你今天请假了没有？

15.	大概	dàgài	(adv, adj)	probably

a. 今天他大概没来。

b. 她大概后天回日本。

16.	第	dì	(pref)	(ordinal prefix)
17.	节	jié	(m)	a section of a whole, as "a class hour"
18.	学习	xuéxí	(v)	to study
19.	好好儿	hǎohāor	(adj)	well, wholeheartedly

a. 我想好好儿复习一下儿。

b. 你回宿舍好好儿找一下儿你的本子。

20. 一下儿	yíxiàr		one time, once (as a counter following many verbs, it lightens an action or takes the edge off what might be taken as an order otherwise)
21. 谢谢	xièxie	(v)	thanks
22. 再见	zàijiàn	(v)	goodbye

专有名词

德国	Déguó	Germany

补充生词

回电话	huí diànhuà	return a phone call

语法点

1. The adverb <u>jiù</u> 就 (1)

副词"就"(1)

This adverb, which generally speaking translates as "then" ("since such and such is the case, then …"), will be explained in more detail at Lesson Fifteen (see p. 359). Here it functions to affirm that the subject is none other than X or Y and one need look no further. Voice stress is on the subject.

这个副词，在一般情况下可以译做英语里的"then"。在第十五课我们将学习它的其他用法(见359页)。本课的"就"起强调作用，表示主语已经符合谓语所提的条件，不需要另外寻找。主语要重读。

a. Zhè jiù shi wǒ de shū.

这就是我的书。

<u>This</u> is my book.

b. Wǒ jiù jiào Dàwèi.

我就叫大卫。

<u>I'm</u> the one named David.

c. Tā jiù shi Ānnà.

她就是安娜。

<u>She</u> is Anna.

2. The preposition <u>cóng</u> 从

介词"从"

<u>Cóng</u> draws attention to the starting point, i.e., "from" a place or point in time. It forms part of an adverbial adjunct.

"从"表示起点，后面常带处所词或时间词，组成介宾结构"从……"，充任状语。

从 + Place word + V

a. Wǒ de péngyou cóng Měiguo lái.

我的朋友从美国来。

My friend is coming from the U.S.

b. Shānběn cóng sùshè qù.

山本从宿舍去。

Yamamoto is going from the dormitory.

<u>Cóng</u> ... <u>dào</u> ... 从……到…… "From ... to ..." This pattern defines the boundaries of the time or space discussed. It can be used as an adverbial adjunct, or as an attributive.

"从……到……"这个结构用来限定时间、处所或范围。在句中经常充任状语，有时也做定语。

c. Jīntian shàngwǔ wǒ cóng qī diǎn bàn dào bā diǎn yùxí xīn kè.

今天上午我从七点半到八点预习新课。

This forenoon, from 7:30 until 8:00, I'll prepare the new lesson.

d. Cóng 1990 nián dào 1992 nián, wǒ zài Zhōngguo xué Hànyǔ.

从1990年到1992年，我在中国学汉语。

I studied Chinese in China from 1990 through 1992.

e. Cóng yībān dào sìbān de tóngxué dōu lái le.

从一班到四班的同学都来了。

Classmates from the first through fourth sections all came.

3. The optative verbs néng 能 and xiǎng 想

能愿动词"能"和"想"

The optative verbs neng 能 and xiang 想, expressing a wish, desire or the wherewithal to do something. They are auxiliaries to the main verb, with xiǎng expressing a wish or desire (somewhere between "like to" and "want to"), and néng expressing that the wherewithal exists for, or conditions permit, an action.

"能"和"想"都是能愿动词，它们出现在句中主要动词前。"想"表示有做某事的希望或愿望（介乎英语的"like to"和"want to"之间）。"能"表示具备了某种资格或条件有可能或被允许去做某事。

a. Wǒ xiǎng qù túshūguǎn.

我想去图书馆。

I'd like to/want to go to the library.

b. Wǒ xiǎng kàn diànyǐng.

我想看电影。

I'd like to/want to see a film.

c. Míngtian bú shàng kè, wǒ néng qù jiē péngyou.

明天不上课，我能去接朋友。

I don't attend class tomorrow, so can go to pick up (our) friend.

Optative verbs are directly negated with bù, and alternative type questions are expressed with the side by side affirmative and negative forms of the optative verb.

否定式是在能愿动词之前加“不”。正反疑问式是由它的肯定式和否定式并列而构成。

d. Wǒ bù xiǎng mǎi nèi běn cídiǎn.

我不想买那本词典。

I don't want to buy that dictionary.

e. Ānnà bù néng kàn diànyǐng, tā qù péngyou jiā.

安娜不能看电影，她去朋友家。

Anna can't go to the movies. She's going to a friend's house.

f. Nǐ xiǎng bu xiǎng yùxí dì-bā kè?

你想不想预习第八课？

Do you want to prepare Lesson Eight?

g. Wǒ néng bu néng xiànzài qù zhǎo ni?

我能不能现在去找你？

Can I call on you right now?

4. Dì 第, the ordinalizing prefix

序数词词头“第”

We have seen dì at the head of each of our lessons ("First Lesson", "Lesson One", etc.). It precedes a number which can, dependent on context, then be followed by a measure word.

我们已经看到了在每一课前边的“第”（“第一课”等）。“第”可以用在整数的前边表示次序。后面可以再跟量词。

a. Dào Zhōngguo yǐhòu de dì-èr tiān, wǒ qù kàn wǒ de Zhōngguo péngyou le.

到中国以后的第二天，我去看我的中国朋友了。

On the second day after arriving in China, I went to see my Chinese friend.

b. Dì-èr jié kè jǐ diǎn zhōng xià?

第二节课几点钟下？

When do we finish the second (class) period?

* Some nouns, when expressing order, do not use dì, e.g., liùbān de xuésheng 六班的学生 "the students of Section Six", cóng yī lóu dào wǔ lóu 从一楼到五楼 "from the first to the fifth floors". There aren't many of them, and they must be learned individually when encountered.

有些名词在表示次序时可以不用"第"，如"六班的学生"、"从一楼到五楼"。这种情况不多见，只能在遇到时一个一个学习。

* Èr 二 and NOT liǎng 两 is used for "the second", irrespective of whether or not it is followed by a measure word, e.g., èrbān 二班 Section Two, èr lóu 二楼 "the second floor (= "level two")", dì-èr ge tóngxué 第二个同学 "the second classmate", dì-èr jié kè 第二节课 "the second class period".

当表示"第二"这个意思时，不论后面有没有量词出现，一律用"二"不用"两"。如"二班"、"二楼"、"第二个同学"、"第二节课"。

NOTES 注释

1. Dăcuò le 打错了 "Wrong number". This is common telephone usage. There will be more said on the particular structure in Lesson Twelve.

   "打错了"是一个常见的电话用语。"打错"这种结构将在第十二课详细介绍。

2. Wèi 位 is a respect measure for a person or people. Wèi cannot modify rén alone. Zhèi wèi rén 这位人, Nèi wèi rén 那位人 are incorrect. Rén itself must be modified before wèi is used, as in (c).

   量词"位"用于人，表示尊敬。但它不能修饰名词"人"，不能说"这位人""那位人"。但"人"前有其他修饰语时，仍可用量词"位"，如例c。

a. Zhèi wèi shi Shānběn.

这位是山本。

This (gentleman/lady) is Yamamoto.

b. Nèi wèi shi Zhōngguorén.

那位是中国人。

That (gentleman/lady) is Chinese.

c. Nà liǎng wèi Zhōngguorén shi Zhāng lǎoshī de péngyou.

那两位中国人是张老师的朋友。

Those two Chinese people are Mr. Zhang's friends.

* When context is adequately clear, the noun following either a number plus measure word or a demonstrative pronoun plus measure word can be elided.

在上下文清楚的情况下，名词前有数量词或指示代词加量词时，名词可以省略。

3. Huílai 回来 "to return, come back" (to where the speaker is). This form is a verb with "directional complement" and will be explained in more detail at Lesson Thirteen.

"回来"(回到说话人所在地)，这个结构是由一个动词和一个趋向补语组合而成，这种结构将在第十三课里解释。

4. Yíxiàr 一下儿. This is placed after an action verb to indicate the shortness of the action, or the sense of giving it a try, doing something informally or as one is so inclined, e.g., lái yíxiàr 来一下儿 "come for a second", kàn yíxiàr 看一下儿 "have a glance", yùxí yíxiàr 预习一下儿 "prepare for a while", wèn yíxiàr 问一下儿 "try asking".

"一下"，用在动词后表示动作短促或含有尝试的意思或表示随意、非正式，如"来一下儿""看一下儿""预习一下儿""问一下儿"。

词组和句子

1. 第八课　第十二班　第三节课　第五个生词
第一个人　第十本书　第三位老师　第七个同学
第六年　第九个月　第二天　第四个星期
2. 他就叫金中一。
3. 你找张老师吗？那位老师就姓张。
4. 这个电话号码就是安娜的，那个不是，那个是方小英的。
5. 大卫从宿舍来，方小英从她家来。
6. 我朋友后天从美国去日本。
7. 从七点到八点我预习新课。
8. 从第一课到第三课的生词不多，大概有八十个。
9. 我们现在从第四课复习。
10. 我想去图书馆看书。
11. 书店有没有新书？我想去看一下儿。
12. 我想好好儿复习一下课文和生词。
13. 我不想散步，我想在宿舍做作业。
14. 你想不想看那个电影？我们一起去，怎么样？
15. 下午下课以后，你能跟我一起去听音乐吗？
16. 对不起，我不能跟你一起去，我朋友下午来找我。
17. 星期五晚上你能不能给我打个电话？
18. 老师，我现在能不能问问题？
19. 下星期二，我能不能请一天假？
20. 上午你不能请假，下午能请(假)。

参考资料

拼音课文

Gěi lǎoshī dǎ diànhuà

(I)

Jiē diànhuà rén: Wèi?

Jīn Zhōngyī: Wèi, qǐngwèn Zhāng lǎoshī zài ma?

Jiē diànhuà rén: Shénme? Nǐ zhǎo shéi?

Jīn Zhōngyī: Wǒ zhǎo Zhāng lǎoshī.

Jiē diànhuà rén: Nǐ dǎcuò le.

Jīn Zhōngyī: Nín de diànhuà hàomǎ shì bu shì èr wǔ yī yī liù líng bā sì (25116084)?

Jiē diànhuà rén: Bú shì.

Jīn Zhōngyī: Duìbuqǐ.

Jiē diànhuà rén: Méi guānxi.

(II)

Zhāng lǎoshī: Wèi? Nín zhǎo nǎ yí wèi?

Jīn Zhōngyī: Wèi, shì Zhāng lǎoshī jiā ma? Qǐng Zhāng lǎoshī jiē diànhuà.

Zhāng lǎoshī: Wǒ jiùshì.

Jīn Zhōngyī: Zhāng lǎoshī, nín hǎo. Wǒ shi Jīn Zhōngyī.

Zhāng lǎoshī: Nǐ hǎo, Jīn Zhōngyī.

Jīn Zhōngyī: Zhāng lǎoshī, wǒ péngyou míngtian cóng Déguo lái, wǒ xiǎng qù jiē ta. Míngtian wǒ néng bu néng qǐng jià?

Zhāng lǎoshī: Nǐ jǐ diǎn qù jiē ta?

Jīn Zhōngyī: Tā shí diǎn líng wǔ fēn dào, wǒ bā diǎn sìshi wǔ qù.

Zhāng lǎoshī: Shàngwǔ hé xiàwǔ nǐ dōu qǐng jià ma?

Jīn Zhōngyī: Bù, xiàwǔ wǒ bù qǐng jià. Shàngwǔ cóng jiǔ diǎn dào shíyī diǎn shì nín de kè, wǒ qǐng jià.

Zhāng lǎoshī: Nǐ dàgài shénme shíhou néng huílai?

Jīn Zhōngyī: Wǒ dàgài shíyī diǎn huílai. Dì-sān jié kè wǒ néng shàng.

Zhāng lǎoshī: Hǎo, nǐ qù jiē péngyou ba. Míngtian wǒmen xuéxí dì-bā kè, nǐ hǎohāor yùxí yíxiàr.

Jīn Zhōngyī: Xièxie nín, Zhāng lǎoshī. Zàijiàn!

Zhāng lǎoshī: Zàijiàn!

英译课文

Telephoning the teacher

(I)

Telephone voice: Hello?

Kim Chung-il: Hello. Is Mrs. Zhang there please?

Telephone voice: What? Whom do you want?

Kim Chung-il: I'm trying to get Mrs. Zhang.

Telephone voice: You've got the wrong number.

Kim Chung-il: Is your number 25116084?

Telephone voice: No.

Kim Chung-il: I'm sorry.

Telephone voice: That's all right.

(II)

Mrs. Zhang: Hello? Whom are you looking for?

Kim Chung-il: Hello. Is this Mrs. Zhang? I'd like to talk to Mrs. Zhang.

Mrs. Zhang: I am Mrs. Zhang.

Kim Chung-il: Mrs. Zhang, how are you? This is Kim Chung-il.

Mrs. Zhang: How are you, Kim Chung-il.

Kim Chung-il: Mrs. Zhang, my friend is coming from Germany tomorrow and I'd like to go to meet him. May I be excused tomorrow?

Mrs. Zhang:	What time are you going to meet him?
Kim Chung-il:	He arrives at 10:05. I'm going at 8:45.
Mrs. Zhang:	Do you want to be excused both morning and afternoon?
Kim Chung-il:	No, I'm not asking to be excused in the afternoon. Your class is in the morning from 9:00 to 11:00 and I'm asking to be excused from that.
Mrs. Zhang:	About when will you return?
Kim Chung-il:	I'll return about 11:00. I can attend the third period.
Mrs. Zhang:	All right. Go meet your friend. We'll be studying lesson 8 tomorrow. Prepare well for it.
Kim Chung-il:	Thank you. Mrs. Zhang. Good bye!
Mrs. Zhang:	Good bye.

课堂活动

I. jiù
"就"

Students form pairs for Q & A. Cut up slips copied from A and B below and give one to each student. Student answers must include jiù.

二人一组，一人持表A，一人持表B。互相问答，回答时必须用"就"。

1. Example:

A: Něige rén shi Shānběn?

哪个人是山本？

B: Dì-sān ge rén jiùshi Shānběn.

第三个人就是山本。

A　山本？马同？安娜？张山？金一？

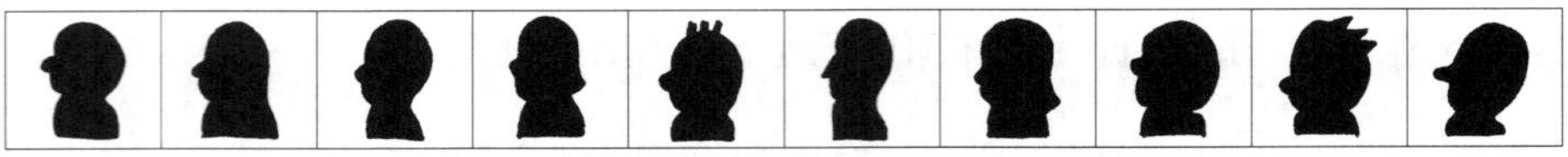

大卫 ____ ____ 小英 ____ 谢文 方明 ____ 韩新 ____

B　大卫？韩新？方明？小英？谢文？

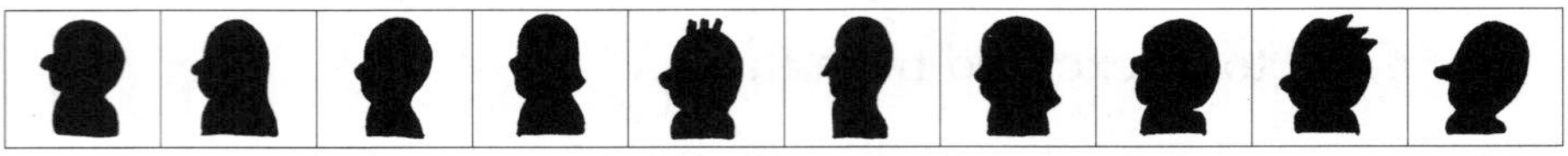

____ 安娜 山本 ____ 马同 ____ ____ 金一 ____ 张山

2. Example: (following the same directions)

A: Něige diànhuà hàomǎ shi Shānběn de?

哪个电话号码是山本的？

B: Dì-sān ge diànhuà hàomǎ jiùshi Shānběn de.

第三个电话号码就是山本的。

A: (a) Něige diànhuà hàomǎ shi Ānnà/Dàwèi de?

哪个电话号码是安娜/大卫的？

(b) Něi jié kè shi Zhāng lǎoshī/Xiè lǎoshī de?

哪节课是张老师/谢老师的？

(c) Něi běn cídiǎn shi zuì xīn de/zuì jiù de/Ānnà de?

哪本词典是最新的/最旧的/安娜的？

B: (a) Něige diànhuà hàomǎ shi Fāng Xiǎoyīng/Zhāng Shān/Jīn Zhōngyī de?

哪个电话号码是方小英/张山/金中一的？

(b) Něi jié kè shi Jīn lǎoshī/Mǎ lǎoshī de?

哪节课是金老师/马老师的？

(c) Něi běn cídiǎn shi zuì hǎo de/zuì bù hǎo de/lǎoshī de?

哪本词典是最好的/最不好的/老师的？

A

(1)

26336412 _______
26336423 _______
26336431 山本
27453125 金中一
28908618 方小英
23405190 张山

(2)

8:30– 9:20 _______
9:30–10:20 金老师
10:30–11:20 方老师
11:30–12:20 _______
12:30– 1:20 马老师
1:30– 2:20 _______

(3)

- xxxxx词典
- xxxxx词典 ← 老师的
- xxxxx词典
- xxxxx词典
- xxxxx词典 ← 最好的
- xxxxx词典 ← 最不好的
- xxxxx词典
- xxxxx词典 ← 图书馆的

B

(1)

26336412 安娜
26336423 大卫
26336431 山本
27453125 _______
28908618 _______
23405190 _______

(2)

8:30– 9:20 谢老师
9:30–10:20 _______
10:30–11:20 _______
11:30–12:20 张老师
12:30– 1:20 _______
1:30– 2:20 韩老师

(3)

- xxxxx词典 ← 你朋友的
- xxxxx词典
- xxxxx词典 ← 最旧的
- xxxxx词典 ← 安娜的
- xxxxx词典
- xxxxx词典
- xxxxx词典 ← 最新的
- xxxxx词典

II. cóng ... dào
“从……到”

A. Students form groups of eight, each student holding one card (as below). They ask each other “Nǐ cóng jǐ diǎn dào jǐ diǎn zài jiā?” until they hit another with the same card. (The first group below practices the sì/shí pronounciation distinction, while the second focuses on èr/liǎng usage).

八人一组，各持下列其中一张卡片，互相问："你从几点到几点在家？"直至找到持相同卡片者为止。(活动1集中练4和10，活动2集中练èr和liǎng)。

1)

4:14–4:40	4:40–10:14	4:14–4:40	4:40–10:14
10:10–4:40	10:40–4:14	10:14–4:40	10:40–4:14

2)

12:02–2:12	12:02–2:22	12:02–2:12	12:02–2:22
2:02–2:22	2:02–2:12	2:02–2:22	2:02–2:12

B. Students form groups of eight, each student holding one card (as below). They ask each other "Nǐ cóng dì-jǐ jié dào dì-jǐ jié yǒu kè?" until coming upon another with the same card.

八人一组，各持下列其中一张卡片，互相问："你从第几节到第几节有课？"直至找到持相同卡片者为止。

1–4	2–4	1–4	2–4	1–7	2–7	1–7	2–7

III. dōu

"都"

Students form groups of eight, each student with one card (as below). They ask each other "Nī xīngqí X hé xīngqí X dōu qǐng jià ma?" until coming upon another with the same card.

八人一组，各持下列其中一张卡片，互相问："你星期X和星期X都请假吗？"直到找到持相同卡片者为止。

星期一 星期二	星期一 星期四	星期二 星期四	星期二 星期三	星期一 星期二	星期一 星期四	星期二 星期四	星期二 星期三

IV. Q & A asking "X de diànhuà hàomǎ shi duōshǎo?"

以"某某人的电话号码是多少？"互相问答

A.

姓名	电话号码
张老师	26058493
金中一	25504021
安娜	27599214
方小英	
山本	
谢老师	

B.

姓名	电话号码
张老师	
金中一	
安娜	
方小英	23872190
山本	26018559
谢老师	28549597

V. Optative verbs xiǎng and néng

能愿动词"想"和"能"

Students form pairs, each student with one chart. Student A will ask the xiǎng and néng questions from slip 1. Student B will answer affirmatively (✓) or negatively (✗) using the information on the chart. A then asks "Why?". B answers according to the chart. B then asks A from slip 2 in the same manner. A then asks B again from slip 3, and then the other way round from slip 4.

老师分组，二人一组，各持一表。学生A先就第1项中用"想"和用"能"两种问题提问，学生B根据表上提示用肯定式或否定式句子回答（"✓"表肯定式"✗"表否定式），再从"为什么"栏里的(1) (2)两项答案中选择相应的一项。然后，学生B就第2项中的问题提问，作法同A。同样，第3项由A问B答，第4项由B问A答。

A

Question 问题	Aff/Neg 肯定或否定	Why? 为什么（选择其中一个答案）
1. 明天下午你想（能）去听音乐吗？		
2.	✗	(1) 那个电影不好。 (2) 我朋友星期六晚上来找我。
3. 今天中午你想（能）回家吗？		
4.	✗	(1) 我朋友约我跟他去。 (2) 我不喜欢吃中国饭。

B

Question 问题	Aff/Neg 肯定或否定	Why? 为什么（选择其中一个答案）
1.	✗	(1) 我不喜欢听音乐。 (2) 我明天下午有课。
2. 星期六晚上你能（想）去看那个电影吗？		
3.	✗	(1) 我十二点下课，下午没有课。 (2) 我想回家吃饭。
4. 星期日晚上能（想）跟我去吃中国饭吗？		

阅读练习

(一)

今天是九月二十号，星期六。

我想约几个朋友中午去吃饭，下午看电影。上午九点半，我给小张打电话，约小张，小张去图书馆看书了，不在家，十二点回来。我给小王打电话，小王从十点半到一点有课，不能请假。我给大卫打电话，大卫有一个朋友今天上午十一点四十五分从美国来，他想去接这个朋友，中午也不能去吃饭。我想 (to think)，我们中午不能去吃饭，没关系，我们下午去看电影，晚上去吃饭。

(二)

昨天下课以后，安娜给方小英打电话，想约她一起去听音乐。方小英不在家，她和金中一去看电影了。那是一个美国电影，很有意思。

昨天晚上安娜一个人去散步了，她没去图书馆。散步以后，她回宿舍做作业，复习旧课和预习新课。

安娜喜欢听音乐，方小英也很喜欢听音乐。今天晚上安娜和方小英想一起去听音乐。安娜约方小英下午六点半在学校门口儿见面。她们没有打电话订票，想到那儿再买 (票)。晚饭以后，安娜和方小英一起去听音乐了。

我来介绍一下儿

汉字课文

(在教室里，马丁是新同学，从德国来，是金中一的朋友。)

金中一：大卫，我来介绍一下儿，这是我的朋友马丁，这是我的同学大卫。

大　卫：你好！我叫大卫。

马　丁：你好！大卫。我叫马丁，从德国来。

大　卫：我是美国人。你在哪个班上课？

金中一：他是我们班的新同学。

大　卫：好啊！欢迎你！

马　丁：你们都学中文吗？

大　卫：是的，我们都学中文。

马　丁：我们班有多少同学？

大　卫：现在十一个。

金中一：你看，外边儿有三个同学，他们也都是六班的。

大　卫：左边儿的是方小英，右边儿的是山本。

马　丁：中间的女同学叫什么名字？

大　卫：叫安娜。

马　丁：她是哪国人？

大　卫：英国人，怎么啦？

马　丁：你给我介绍一下儿，可以吗？

大　卫：当然可以。

金中一：你不想认识别的人吗？

马　丁：当然想认识。别的人呢？

大　卫：大概都去厕所了。

(下课以后)

大　卫：马丁，你去食堂吃饭吗

马　丁：食堂在哪儿？

大　卫：在大礼堂后边儿。我们宿舍前边儿也有一个。

马　丁：安娜，我们一起去吧！

安　娜：我今天不在学校吃饭。我觉得学校食堂的饭不好吃。

马　丁：你每天都不在学校吃饭吗？

安　娜：不，有的时候在学校吃，有的时候在外边儿吃。

马　丁：大卫，我们今天也在外边儿吃吧！

生词语

1.	介绍	jièshào	(v)		to introduce
		a. 请你介绍一下儿，这位同学姓什么？			
		b. 我给你们介绍一下儿。			
		c. 老师给学生介绍了一本好书。			
2.	教室	jiàoshì	(n)	[个；间 jiān]	classroom
3.	里	lǐ	(n - pw)		inside
4.	欢迎	huānyíng	(v)		to welcome
5.	外边儿	wàibianr	(n - pw)		outside
6.	左边儿	zuǒbianr	(n - pw)		left side, to the left
7.	右边儿	yòubianr	(n - pw)		right side, to the right

8.	中间(儿)	zhōngjiān (zhōngjiànr)	(n - pw)	in the middle, at the center
9.	怎么啦	zěnme la		What's up? Is ther something wrong? Have you got a problem with that?

a. 他怎么啦？今天为什么没来？

b. 怎么啦？
—我的本子呢？我没拿本子！本子大概在宿舍。

10.	可以	kěyǐ	(o.v)	(before another verb) may, can; not bad, pretty good
11.	当然	dāngrán	(adj, adv)	certainly, of course

a. 你认识她吗？
—当然认识。一九九零年的时候她是我的中文老师。

b. 那本词典好吗？
—当然很好，那是一本最新的，也是最好的词典。

12.	认识	rènshi	(v)	to recognize
13.	别的	biéde	(pro)	other

a. 我不认识她，她大概是别的学校的。

b. 你认识这个班的老师，也认识别的班的老师吗？

14.	厕所	cèsuǒ	(n) [个]	Toilet. As in all languages, roundabout terms are available for the squeamish. Xǐshǒujiān "washroom" (see below) is one.
15.	食堂	shítáng	(n) [个]	canteen, dining hall
16.	大	dà	(adj)	to be big
17.	礼堂	lǐtáng	(n) [个]	auditorium
18.	后边儿	hòubianr	(n - pw)	at the back, to the rear
19.	前边儿	qiánbianr	(n - pw)	at the front

20.	觉得	juéde	(v)	to feel, be of the opinion
21.	好吃	hǎochī	(adj)	to be tasty
22.	每	měi	(pro)	each

专有名词

1.	马丁	Mǎdīng	Martin
2.	中文	Zhōngwén	Chinese (usually, but not always, refers to the written language)

补充生词

1.	英文	Yīngwén	(n)		English
2.	日文	Rìwén	(n)		Japanese
3.	德文	Déwén	(n)		German
4.	法文	Fǎwén	(n)		French
5.	餐厅	cāntīng	(n)	[个，家，间]	restaurant
6.	洗手间	xǐshǒujiān	(n)	[个]	washroom

语法点

1. Locality words

方位名词

Locality words, such as wàibianr 外边儿 "outside", zuǒbianr 左边儿 "left side" and zhōngjiān 中间 "middle" are nouns and can therefore function as subject or object, modify or be modified. When they serve as modifiers, de is used between them and the modified noun. If they themselves are modified, the intervening de can be eliminated.

"外边儿"、"左边儿"、"中间"等都是方位名词，它们可以充任主语或宾语，也可以修饰名词或受名词修饰。当它们修饰名词时，要用"的"，受名词修饰时"的"可以省略。

a. Qiánbianr shi túshūguǎn.

前边儿是图书馆。

At the front is the library. (as subject)

b. Cèsuǒ zài zuǒbianr.

厕所在左边儿。

The toilet is at the left. (as object)

c. Zhōngjiān de nǚ tóngxué shi Ānnà.

中间的女同学是安娜。

The female student in the middle is Anna. (as modifier)

d. Túshūguǎn (de) hòubianr yǒu yí ge shítáng.

图书馆(的)后边儿有一个食堂。

There is a cafeteria in back of the library. (as modified noun)

2. <u>You</u> 有 and <u>shi</u> 是

"有"和"是"

<u>Yǒu</u> 有 and <u>shì</u> 是 can both describe existence. However, the object of <u>yǒu</u> is generally indefinite, while the object of <u>shì</u> may either be definite or indefinite.

"有"和"是"都表示存在。二者的区别是"有"的宾语是无定的，而"是"的宾语既可以是有定的，又可以是无定的。

S (location) + 有 + O (indefinite person/thing)

a. Xuéxiào (de) hòubianr yǒu yí ge diànyǐngyuàn.

学校(的)后边儿有一个电影院。

There is a theater behind the school.

b. Wàibianr méiyǒu rén.

外边儿没有人。

Nobody is outside.

S (location) + 是 + O (definite or indefinite person/thing)

c. Túshūguǎn hé lǐtáng (de) zhōngjiān shi yí ge shūdiàn.

图书馆和礼堂(的)中间是一个书店。

There is a bookshop between the library and the auditorium.

d. Fāng Xiǎoyīng (de) qiánbianr shi Shānběn, bú shi Jīn Zhōngyī.

方小英(的)前边儿是山本，不是金中一。

It is Yamamoto who is in front of Fang Xiaoying, not Kim Chung-il.

The differences can be further illustrated with this trio:
从下面一组句子里可以更清楚地看出它们的区别：

e. Fāng Xiǎoyīng (de) qiánbianr yǒu yí ge Rìběn tóngxué.

方小英(的)前边儿有一个日本同学。

There is a Japanese student in front of Fang Xiaoying. (indefinite)

f. Fāng Xiǎoyīng (de) qiánbianr shi yí ge Rìběn tóngxué.

方小英(的)前边儿是一个日本同学。

There is a Japanese student in front of Fang Xiaoying. (indefinite)

g. Fāng Xiǎoyīng (de) qiánbianr shi Shānběn.

方小英(的)前边儿是山本。

It is Yamamoto who is in front of Fang Xiaoying. (definite)

Use shì when it is clearly known that the someone or something is where you are saying it is. In 2(f) above, for example, it is known to the speaker and listener that someone is in front of Fang Xiaoying. What is being clarified in 2(g) is that the someone is Yamamoto. 2(e) is making the point that there is someone in front of Fang Xiaoying, a fact that might not have been known.

用“是”时，说话人已知某处存在着某人或某物，如上述的例(f)和例(g)，说话人与听话人均已知道方小英前边有个人，例(f)是进一步说明这个人是一个日本同学。例(g)是进一步说明这个人是山本。用“有”时，只是陈述一个事实，如例(e)，在说这句话时，只是告诉听话人“方小英的前边有一个日本同学”这个事实。

3. The optative verb kěyǐ 可以

Kěyǐ “may, can” expresses permission to do. The preferred negative form is bù néng 不能 (although bù kěyǐ is accepted by some speakers) “may not, cannot”. A lone “no!” is best expressed with bùxíng 不行.

能愿动词“可以”经常用来表示“许可”，否定式是“不能”(有些人也说“不可以”)，单独回答问题时，要说“不行xíng”。

a. Wǒ xiànzài kěyǐ wèn wèntí ma?

我现在可以问问题吗？

May I ask a question now?

Xiànzài bù néng wèn. Xià kè yǐhòu kěyǐ wèn.

现在不能问。下课以后可以问。

Not now. You may ask after class.

b. Wǒ kěyǐ bu kěyǐ zài zhèr zuò zuòyè?

我可以不可以在这儿做作业？

May I do homework here?

Bù xíng. Qǐng nǐ dào nàr qù zùo ba.

不行。请你到那儿去做吧。

No. Please go over there to do it.

c. Jīntian xiàwǔ méiyǒu kè. Wǒmen kěyǐ yìqǐ qù kàn diànyǐng.

今天下午没有课。我们可以一起去看电影。

There is no class this afternoon. We can go together to see a movie.

4. Subject-predicate construction as object

主谓结构作宾语

We have seen (Lesson Six, see p. 94) verbal expressions as objects, and now observe S-P constructions in that role. The S-P construction could be an independent sentence itself.

我们学习了动词结构作宾语(见第六课94页)，本课学习主谓结构作宾语。在汉语里，主谓结构自身可以独立成为一个句子。

a. Wǒmen dōu juéde zhège diànyǐng hěn yǒu yìsi.

我们都觉得这个电影很有意思。

We all feel that this film is very interesting.

b. Nǐ juéde zhège shítáng de fàn hǎochī ma?

你觉得这个食堂的饭好吃吗？

Do you think that the food at this restaurant is good?

Note that English must use a "that" type subordinate clause for this purpose.

注意：在汉语里，主谓结构可以直接跟在动词后作宾语，在英语里，要用"that" 引出充任宾语的从句。

5. Wǒ měi tiān dōu qù dǎ 我每天都去打 "I go to play everyday".

Měi 每 is a demonstrative pronoun. It is followed by a number, measure word and noun, and is usually summed up with the adverb dōu. The number may be omitted if it is "one". We met dōu in this summing up role in Lesson Four. Dōu emphasizes the entirety of the referent of měi.

"每"是一个指示代词，指全体中的任何个体。它常常修饰数量词及名词，后面常用"都"总括"每"所指的对象，说明情况没有例外。"都"的用法见第四课。

a. Měi ge tóngxué dōu yǒu yì běn cídiǎn.

每个同学都有一本词典。

Each student has a dictionary.

b. Wǒ měi tiān wǎnshang dōu qù sànbù.

我每天晚上都去散步。

I go for a walk every night.

c. Wǒ měi tiān wǎnshang (cóng) jiǔ diǎn bàn dào shí diǎn yùxí dì-èr tiān de xīn kè.

我每天晚上(从)九点半到十点预习第二天的新课。

I prepare the next day's new lesson every evening from 9:30 to 10:00.

NOTES 注释

1. When shàngbiānr 上边儿 and lǐbiānr 里边儿 are modified, the -biānr is often omitted. E.g., sùshè lǐ yǒu guǐ 宿舍里有鬼 "There's a ghost in the dorm" (guǐ 鬼 = "ghost"); shūshang yǒu cāngying 书上有苍蝇 "There's a fly on the book" (cāngying 苍蝇 = "fly"). It must be included if the location is very specific: Shū (de) shàngbianr yǒu cāngying 书(的)上边儿有苍蝇 "There's a fly on the top side of the book".

   "上边儿""里边儿"作中心语时，"边儿"经常省略。例如："教室里有鬼"，"书上有苍蝇"。如果"上边儿"指特定的方位，"边儿"就不能省略。例如："书(的)上边儿(靠上部份)有苍蝇"。

2. Wǒ lái jièshào yíxiàr 我来介绍一下儿. In this context, the lái 来 loses its directional sense and, coming immediately before another verb, indicates that the actor will take it upon him/herself to do it. E.g. Wǒ lái zuò 我来做 "I'll do it" or wǒ lái mǎi piào 我来买票 "I'll buy the tickets".

   "我来介绍一下儿"。在这里，"来"不表示动作的方向，它出现在另一动词前，只表示作者将要去做这件事。例如"我来做"、"我来买票"。

词组和句子

1. 礼堂外边儿　书店左边儿　学校右边儿
   我前边儿　老师后边儿　山本和他中间
2. 食堂里　宿舍里　教室里
   家里　学校里　电影院里
3. 前边儿的大图书馆　后边儿的学生宿舍
   里边儿的人　右边儿的书店
4. 学校外边儿的书店　宿舍前边儿的食堂
   礼堂里的学生　我家右边儿的电影院
   安娜左边儿的男同学　一班和三班中间的教室
5. 觉得很好　觉得怎么样　觉得很有意思
   觉得没问题　觉得对不起　觉得不好吃
   觉得那个电影没意思　觉得那本书不很好
6. 书店在前边儿，食堂在后边儿，学生宿舍在中间。
7. 前边儿是书店，后边儿是食堂，中间是学生宿舍。
8. 前边儿有一个书店，后边儿有一个食堂，中间有一个学生宿舍。
9. 他在左边儿，我在右边儿，山本在中间。
10. 左边儿是他，右边儿是我，中间是山本。
11. 这儿是我们的宿舍，宿舍前边有一个小书店。
12. 礼堂左边儿有一个小图书馆，右边儿是大图书馆。
13. 前边的宿舍是女同学的，右边儿的宿舍是男同学的。中间是他们的食堂。
14. 我不认识那个同学，你可以给我们介绍一下儿吗？
15. 我可以在这儿打个电话吗？

16. 我可以去厕所吗？
17. 现在教室里没有人，我们可以去那儿复习。
18. 星期五你可以跟我们一起去听音乐吗？
19. 星期五不能去，那天我有课。
20. 每个同学都认识他。
21. 每课都有二十到二十五个生词。
22. 他每天下课以后都去图书馆。
23. 每个星期六马丁都约朋友去吃饭。
24. 我觉得那本书很好，他觉得不很好。
25. 她很喜欢晚上吃饭以后跟好朋友一起去散步。

参考资料

拼音课文

Wǒ lái jièshào yíxiàr

(I)

(Zài jiàoshì li, Mădīng shi xīn tóngxué, cóng Déguo lái, shi Jīn Zhōngyī de péngyou.)

Jīn Zhōngyī:	Dàwèi, wǒ lái jièshào yíxiàr, zhè shi wǒ de péngyou Mădīng. Zhè shi wǒ de tóngxué Dàwèi.
Dàwèi:	Nǐ hǎo! Wǒ jiào Dàwèi.
Mădīng:	Nǐ hǎo! Dàwèi. Wǒ jiào Mădīng, cóng Déguo lái.
Dàwèi:	Wǒ shi Měiguorén. Nǐ zài něige bān shàng kè?
Jīn Zhōngyī:	Tā shi wǒmen bān de xīn tóngxué.
Dàwèi:	Hǎo a! Huānyíng ni!
Mădīng:	Nǐmen dōu xué Zhōngwén ma?
Dàwèi:	Shì de, wǒmen dōu xué Zhōngwén.

Mădīng:	Wŏmen bān yŏu duōshao tóngxué?
Dàwèi:	Xiànzài shíyī ge.
Jīn Zhōngyī:	Nĭ kàn, wàibianr yŏu sān ge tóngxué, tāmen yĕ dōu shi liùbān de.
Dàwèi:	Zuŏbianr de shi Fāng Xiăoyīng, yòubianr de shi Shānbĕn.
Mădīng:	Zhōngjiān de nǚ tóngxué jiào shénme míngzi?
Dàwèi:	Jiào Ānnà.
Mădīng:	Tā shi nĕi guó rén?
Dàwèi:	Yīngguorén, zĕnme la?
Mădīng:	Nĭ gĕi wŏ jièshào yíxiàr, kĕyĭ ma?
Dàwèi:	Dāngrán kĕyĭ.
Jīn Zhōngyī:	Nĭ bù xiăng rènshi biéde rén ma?
Mădīng:	Dāngrán xiăng rènshi. Biéde rén ne?
Dàwèi:	Dàgài dōu qù cèsuŏ le.
(Xià kè yĭhòu)	
Dàwèi:	Mădīng, nĭ qù shítáng chī fàn ma?
Mădīng:	Shítáng zài năr?
Dàwèi:	Zài dà lĭtáng hòubianr. Wŏmen sùshè qiánbianr yĕ yŏu yí ge.
Mădīng:	Ānnà, wŏmen yìqĭ qù ba!
Ānnà:	Wŏ jīntian bú zài xuéxiào chī fàn. Wŏ juéde xuéxiào shítáng de fàn bù hăochī.
Mădīng:	Nĭ mĕi tiān dōu bú zài xuéxiào chī fàn ma?
Ānnà:	Bù, yŏude shíhou zài xuéxiào chī, yŏude shíhou zài wàibianr chī.
Mădīng:	Dàwèi, wŏmen jīntian yĕ zài wàibianr chī ba!

英译课文

I'll introduce you

(In the classroom. Martin is a new student, from Germany, and Kim Chung-il is his friend.)

Kim: David, I'll introduce you. This is my friend, Martin. This is my classmate, David.

David: How are you! I'm David.

Martin: How are you, David? I'm Martin, from Germany.

David: I'm an American. Which section are you in?

Kim: He's in our section.

David: Great! Welcome to you!

Martin: Are you all studying Chinese?

David: Yes, we all study Chinese.

Martin: How many students are there in our section?

David: Eleven now.

Kim: Look, there are three students outside. They're all Section 6 students, too.

David: The one on the left is Fang Xiaoying and the one on the right is Yamamoto.

Martin: What's the girl in the middle's name?

David: Anna.

Martin: Where is she from?

David: She's English, why?

Martin: Can you introduce us?

David: Of course.

Kim: Don't you want to know the others?

Martin: Of course I do. Where are they?

David: They're probably all gone to the toilets.

(After class)

David: Martin, are you going to the cafeteria to eat?

Martin: Where is the cafeteria?

David: In back of the large auditorium. There is another one in front of our dorm.

Martin: Anna, let's go together.

Anna: I'm not eating at school today. I don't think the school cafeteria food is very good.

Martin: You never eat at school? (= You don't eat at school every day?)

Anna: No, sometimes I eat at school and sometimes I eat outside.

Martin: David, why don't we eat outside today, too?

课堂活动

I. Placewords
方位词

A. Placewords as attributives. Students form pairs, one student with chart A and the other chart B. Information is missing from both charts. Ask each other and answer questions in accordance with the example until the missing information is found.
方位词作定语：二人一组，一人持图A，一人持图B，双方图上各缺少一些资料。按照下列例子互相问答，直至找到所有资料为止。

Example:

A: Zuǒbianr de (jiàoshì) shi něi bān de?
左边儿的(教室)是哪班的？

B: Zuǒbianr de (jiàoshì) shi yībān de.
左边儿的(教室)是一班的。

A: Yòubianr de shi nĕi bān de?

右边儿的是哪班的？

B: Yòubianr de shi èrbān de.

右边儿的是二班的。

A: Zhōngjiān de shi nĕi bān de?

中间的是哪班的？

B: Zhōngjiān de shi sānbān de.

中间的是三班的。

Those following ask about shéi, shéme, nĕi-, etc.

A

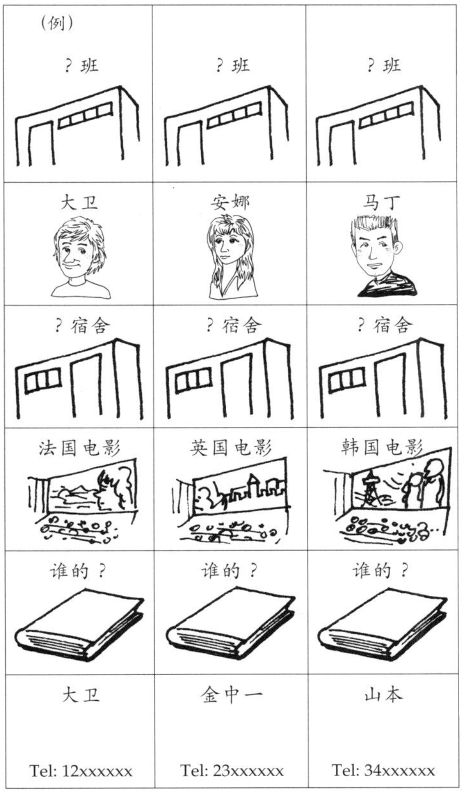

(例) ？班	？班	？班
大卫	安娜	马丁
？宿舍	？宿舍	？宿舍
法国电影	英国电影	韩国电影
谁的？	谁的？	谁的？
大卫 Tel: 12xxxxxx	金中一 Tel: 23xxxxxx	山本 Tel: 34xxxxxx

B

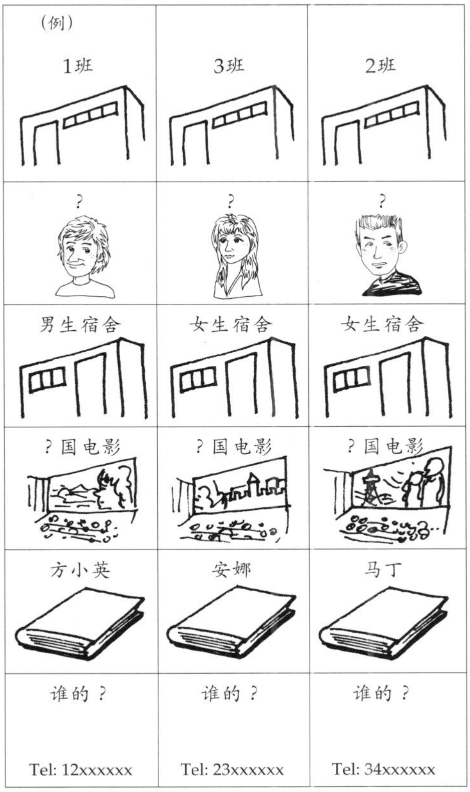

(例) 1班	3班	2班
？	？	？
男生宿舍	女生宿舍	女生宿舍
？国电影	？国电影	？国电影
方小英	安娜	马丁
谁的？ Tel: 12xxxxxx	谁的？ Tel: 23xxxxxx	谁的？ Tel: 34xxxxxx

B. Placewords as central word. Exercise as above.

方位词作中心语：二人一组，一人持图A，一人持图B，双方图上各缺少一些资料。按照下列例子互相问答，直至找到所有资料为止。

1. Example:

   A: Lǐtáng de qiánbianr shi shénme?

   礼堂的前边儿是什么？

   B: Lǐtáng de qiánbianr shi shítáng.

   礼堂的前边儿是食堂。

A

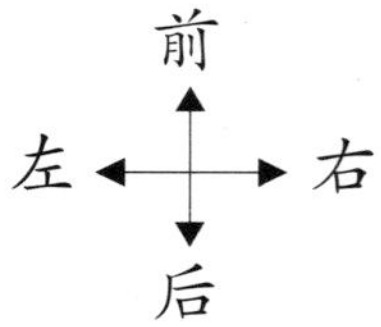

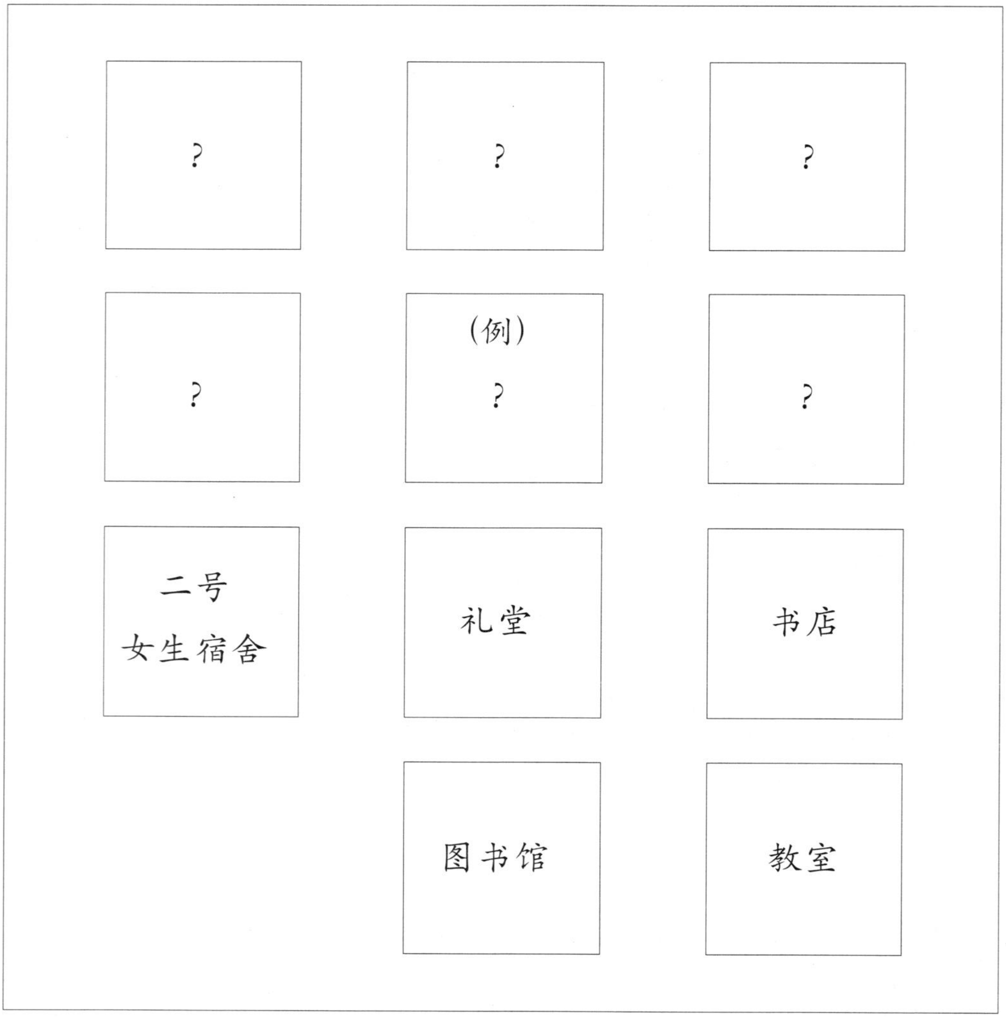

B

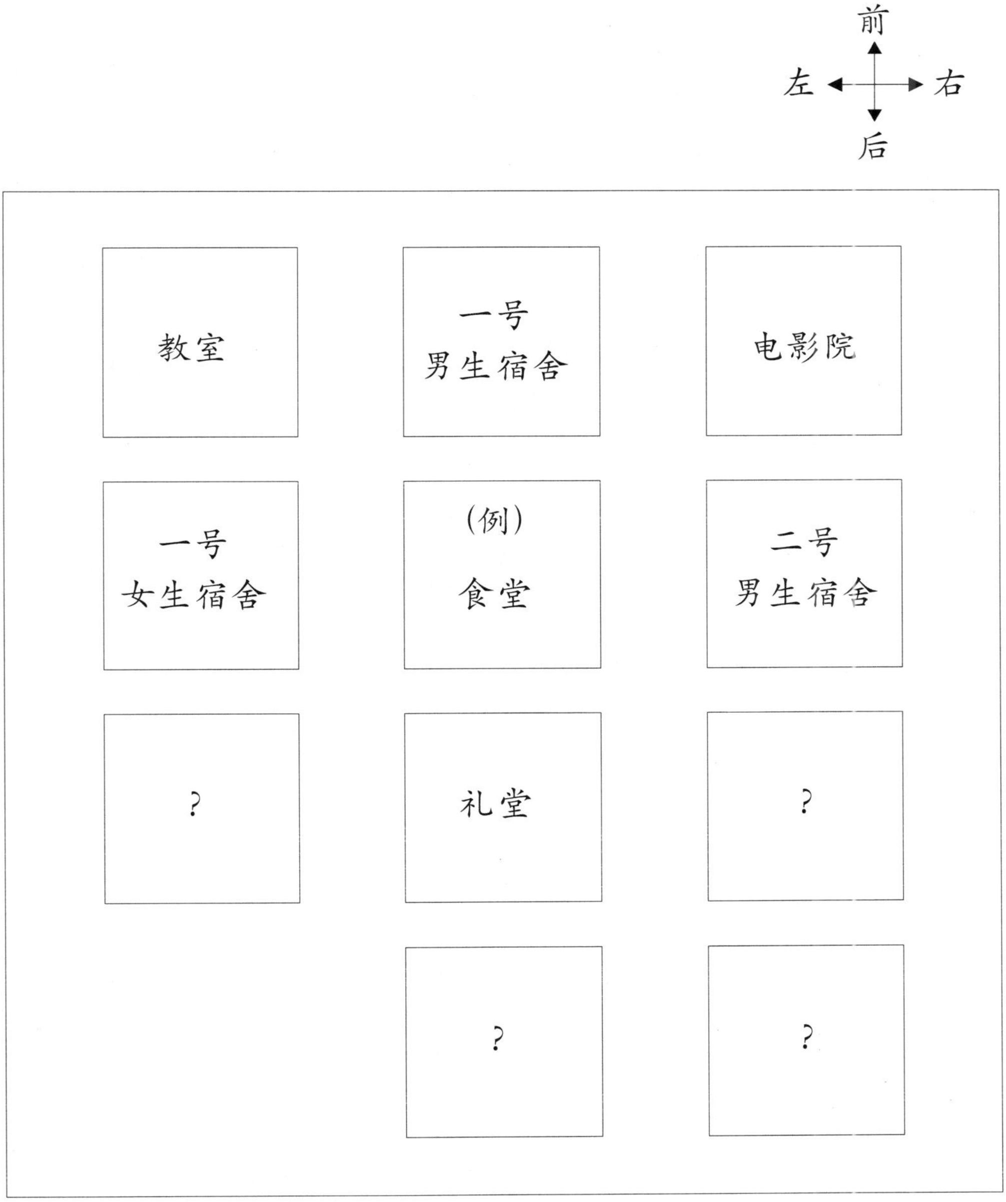

2. Example:

A: Dàwèi de qiánbianr yǒu jǐ ge rén?

大卫的前边儿有几个人？

B: Dàwèi de qiánbianr yǒu ….

大卫的前边儿有……

A: Tāmen shi něi guó rén?

他们是哪国人？

B: Zuǒbianr shi yí ge ... yòubianr shi yí ge ....

左边儿是一个……，右边儿是一个……。

A

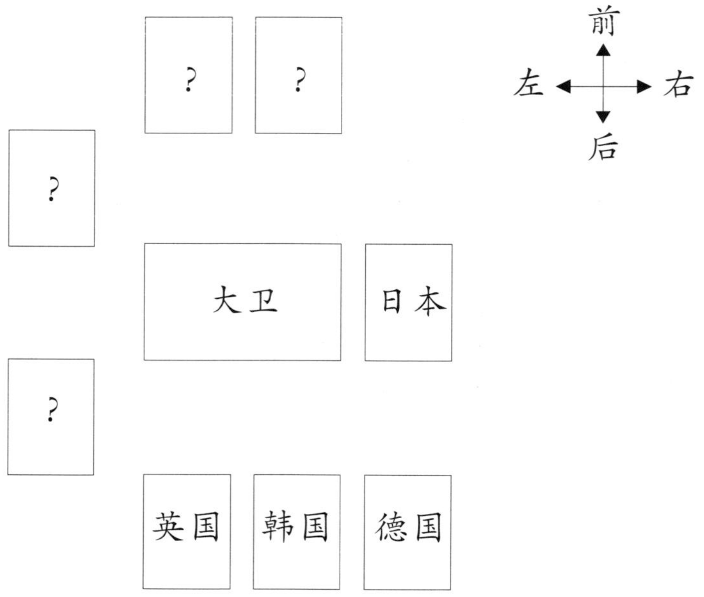

B

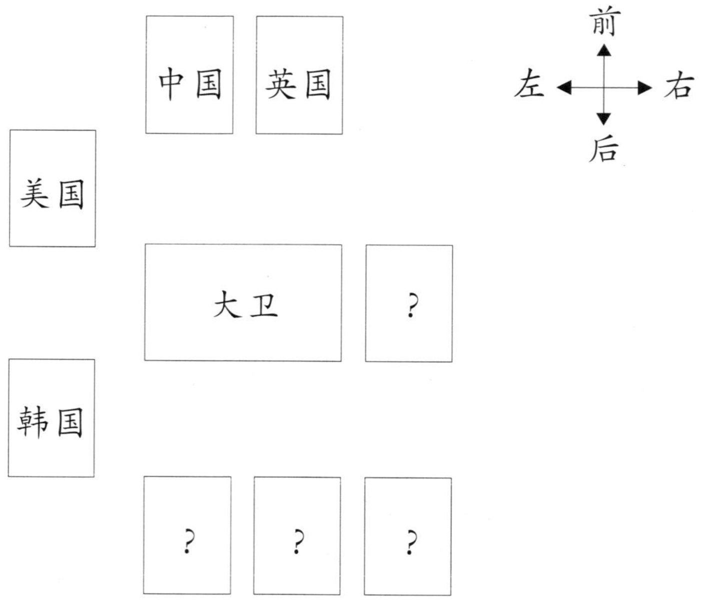

C. Placewords as subjects. Students form pairs, one student with chart A and the other B. Each chart lacks certain data. Questions are asked on the basis of the example here until that information is found.
方位词作宾语：二人一组，一人持卡片A，一人持卡片B，双方图上各缺少一些资料。按照下列例子互相问答，直至找到所有资料为止。

Example:

A: Shítáng zài nǎr?
食堂在哪儿？

B: Shítáng zài lǐtáng qiánbianr.
食堂在礼堂前边儿。

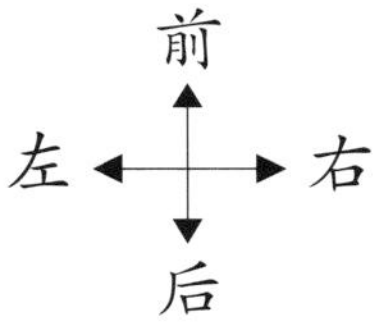

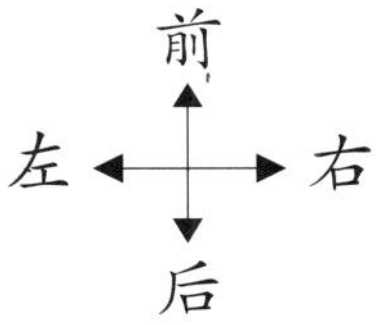

A

食堂、书店、教室、图书馆和女生宿舍在哪儿？			
	男生宿舍	(例)	
老师的食堂	小礼堂	礼堂	
电影院			

B

小礼堂、电影院、男生宿舍和老师的食堂在哪儿？			
		食堂(例)	女生宿舍
		礼堂	书店
		教室	图书馆

D. Placewords as subjects. Exercise as above.
方位词作主语：二人一组，一人持卡片A，一人持卡片B，双方图上各缺少一些资料。按照下列例子互相问答，B就第一、二项提问，A就第三、四项提问，直至找到所有资料为止。

Example:

A: Jiàoshì lǐbianr hé wàibianr dōu yǒu xuésheng ma?

教室里边儿和外边儿都有学生吗？

B: Lǐbianr yǒu xuésheng, wàibianr méiyou xuésheng.

里边儿有学生，外边儿没有学生。

A

(例)	[教室: 学生？ 里] 外 学生？
1.	教室✓ 左 [礼堂] 右 教室✓
2.	学校？ 后 [电影院] 前 学校？
3.	书店✓ 前 [学校: 书店✓ 里] 后 书店✗
4.	[宿舍: 电话？ 里] 外 电话？

B

(例)	教室 里：学生✓ 外：学生✗
1.	礼堂 左：教室？ 右：教室？
2.	电影院 后：学校✓ 前：学校✗
3.	学校 前：书店？ 里：书店？ 后：书店？
4.	宿舍 里：电话✓ 外：电话✓

II. měi ... dōu ...
每……都……

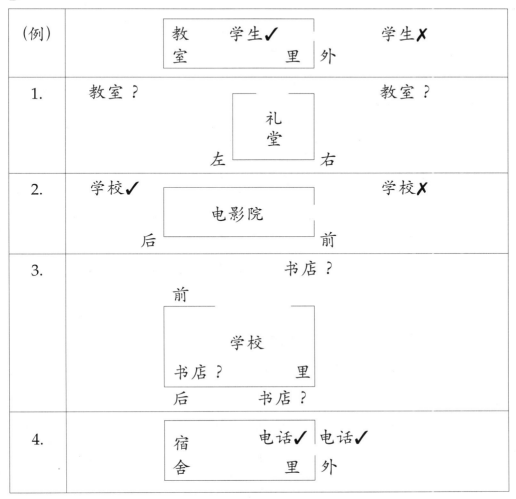

Students form pairs, each student with one of the groups of eight questions below. Following the example, students ask and answer, at the end checking to see which answers are the same.

二人一组，各持有八个相同的问题，但二人问题后的答案不同。根据自己的答案互相问答，最后看看有几项相同。

Example:

A: Nǐ měi tiān dōu zài xuéxiào shítáng chī fàn ma?

你每天都在学校食堂吃饭吗？

B: ✓ Wǒ měi tiān dōu zài xuéxiào shítáng chī fàn.

我每天都在学校食堂吃饭。

✗ Wǒ měi tiān dōu bú zài xuéxiào shítáng chī fàn.

我每天都不在学校食堂吃饭。

✓✗ Yǒushíhou zài xuéxiào shítáng chī, yǒushíhou bú zài xuéxiào shítáng chī.

有时候在学校食堂吃，有时候不在学校食堂吃。

A

1. 你每天都在学校食堂吃饭吗？ ✓
2. 你每天都有中文课吗？ ✓
3. 我们班每个人你都认识吗？ ✓✗
4. 你觉得今天每节课都很有意思吗？ ✓
5. 每个星期你都去书店买书吗？ ✓✗
6. 每天晚上你都给同学打电话吗？ ✗
7. 每位老师你都认识吗？ ✓
8. 每个星期六你都去外边吃饭吗？ ✗

B

1. 你每天都在学校食堂吃饭吗？ ✗
2. 你每天都有中文课吗？ ✓
3. 我们班每个人你都认识吗？ ✓✗
4. 你觉得今天每节课都很有意思吗？ ✗
5. 每个星期你都去书店买书吗？ ✓

6. 每天晚上你都给同学打电话吗？　✓
7. 每位老师你都认识吗？　✗
8. 每个星期六你都去外边吃饭吗？　✓

第九课

我们一起去打网球

汉字课文

大　卫：金中一，七点钟我们一起去打网球，好不好？

金中一：好啊。你也喜欢打网球吗？

大　卫：对，我每天都去打。

金中一：你今天打了没有？

大　卫：还没打呢。你知道网球场在哪儿吗？

金中一：不知道，网球场在哪儿？

大　卫：在体育馆的旁边儿。

金中一：体育馆在哪儿？

大　卫：我们学校有一个大体育馆，一个小体育馆，大的在北边儿，网球场都在大体育馆的旁边儿。

金中一：小体育馆在哪边儿呢？

大　卫：在那边儿。

金中一：那边儿是——西南？

大　卫：对。

金中一：我们的学校真大。打网球的人一定不少吧？定网球场容易吗？

大　卫：不太难。我下午定了一个，时间是从七点到八点。

金中一：我们学校有没有游泳池？

大　卫：有，小体育馆东边儿有个游泳池。你喜欢游泳吗？

金中一：喜欢。你呢？

大　卫：我也喜欢。你看，食堂到了，我们先去吃饭吧！

金中一：我吃了饭了。你还没吃吗？

大　卫：没有。我吃了饭去找你。

金中一：好，一会儿见。

生词语

1.	打	dǎ	(v)		to hit, strike; to play (with objects indication sports, etc.)
2.	网球	wǎngqiú	(n)	[个]	tennis
3.	了	le	(part)		(aspect particle, attached to V indicating a completed action)
4.	还	hái	(adv)		still yet

a. 我做了作业了，还没预习呢。

b. 你还没吃饭吧？跟我一起吃，好吗？

5.	知道	zhīdao	(v)		to know

a. 安娜不知道他家的电话号码。

b. 我知道方小英今天不来，她昨天和今天都请假了。

c. 你知道山本为什么不去吗？

d. 我不知道山本为什么不去。

e. 你知道不知道我们星期几有马老师的课？

6.	网球场	wǎngqiúchǎng	(n)	[个]	tennis court
7.	体育馆	tǐyùguǎn	(n)	[个]	gymnasium
8.	旁边儿	pángbiānr	(n)		side, beside
9.	北边儿	běibianr	(n)		northside
10.	边儿	biānr	(n)		side

a. 他在哪边儿？

		b. 他在这边儿看课文，我在那边儿复习生词。			
11.	西南	xīnán	(n)		southwest
12.	真	zhēn	(adv)		genuinely, truly, really
13.	一定	yídìng	(adv; adj)		definitily; to be definite, certain
		a. 下了课我一定给家里打电话。			
		b. 明天他不一定来。			
		c. 这个学校的学生一定很多吧？			
14.	定	dìng	(v)		to reserve, fix, sign up for
15.	容易	róngyi	(adj)		to be easy
16.	太	tài	(adv)		too
17.	难	nán	(adj)		to be difficult
18.	时间	shíjiān	(n)		time
19.	游泳池	yóuyǒngchí	(n)	[个]	swimming pool
20.	东边儿	dōngbianr	(n)		eastside
21.	游泳	yóuyǒng	(v)		to swim
22.	先	xiān	(adv)		first, beforehand
		a. 他先做容易的作业。			
		b. 我先去图书馆，一会儿回宿舍。			
23.	一会儿	yíhuìr; yìhuǐr	(n)		a while, a moment
		a. 你在这儿等我，我一会儿回来。			
		b. 我们一会儿去吃饭吧！			
24.	见	jiàn	(v)		to see, meet

补充生词

1.	足球	zúqiú	(n)	[个]	soccer
2.	篮球	lánqiú	(n)	[个]	basketball

3. 乒乓球 pīngpāngqiú (n) [个] ping pong
4. 高尔夫球 gāo'ěrfūqiú (n) [个] golf

* Note that all of these are used also as the events themselves: soccer match, basketball game, ping pong game, golf match

语法点

1. Aspect particle le 了

动态助词"了"

(Distinguish this from the MODAL PARTICLE le we met in Lesson Six. See p. 149.)

The aspect of a verb refers to the stage it is at in its progress or development. For example, it could be about to occur, in progress, completed or continuing. DISTINGUISH this from TENSE, which refers to the time an action occurs (present, past, future, etc.) from the perspective of when it is being described. Tense is not a feature of Chinese. Time words are used in Chinese for this purpose (now, yesterday, next year, etc.) We refer in grammar notes to the progressive aspect, the completed aspect, the continuous aspect, etc.

动词的态是指动作在整个发生的过程中所处的阶段。比如，一个动作有进行阶段、完成阶段、持续阶段等，我们就叫它进行态、完成态、持续态等。动词的态与动词的时不同，时是表示动作所发生的时间(现在、过去、将来等)与说话时间之间的关系，在汉语中，时的概念用时间词来表示(现在、昨天、明年等)。

Aspect particle le (sometimes called "verbal le") follows a verb to express that an action has been completed.

在动词后加上动态助词"了"(有时也叫动词后"了")，就可以表示动作的完成，这就是动作的完成态。

a. Tā qù le.

他去了。

He went.

b. Tóngxuémen dōu lái le.

同学们都来了。

Our classmates have all come.

c. Wǒ húilái le.

我回来了。

I have returned.

If the verb plus aspect particle has an object, one or another of the FOLLOWING CONDITIONS must be met so that the utterance will be complete and not a dangling thought.

如果带上动态助词“了”的动词后面又有宾语，就必须符合下列条件之一，才能使句子所表达的意思完整。

I. The object must be preceded by a number or other modifier.
宾语前有数量词或其他定语。

S + V + 了 + Attr + O

a. Jīntian shàngwǔ wǒ mǎile yì běn Hànyǔ cídiǎn.

今天上午我买了一本汉语词典。

I bought a Chinese dictionary this morning.

b. Zuótian wǒ mǎile hěn duō Zhōngwénshū.

昨天我买了很多中文书。

Yesterday I bought a lot of Chinese books.

II. When the sentence has a simple object, there is follow-up action to the completed action.
如果宾语简单，后面要有后续成分。

S + V + 了 + O + follow-up action

c. Míngtian wǎnshang wǒmen chīle fàn qù kàn diànyǐng.

明天晚上我们吃了饭去看电影。

After we've eaten tomorrow evening, we'll go to see a film.

d. Wǒ xiàle kè jiù qù túshūguǎn.

我下了课就去图书馆。

I'll go to the library after class.

III. When the sentence has a simple object, a modal le is used at the end of the sentence.
如果宾语简单，可在句尾再用上语气助词"了"。

S + V + 了 + O + 了

e. Wǒ chīle fàn le.

我吃了饭了。

I've eaten.

f. Dàwèi zuòle zuòyè le.

大卫做了作业了。

David did homework.

IV. When the sentence has a simple object, there is a long or somewhat involved adverbial adjunct preceding the verb.
如果宾语简单，动词前要有较长或复杂的状语。

g. Tā zuótian gēn Dàwèi yìqǐ zài shūdiàn lǐ mǎile shénme?

他昨天跟大卫一起在书店里买了什么？

What did he buy when he was together with David at the bookstore yesterday?

h. Xiàwǔ wǒ gēn wǒmen bān tóngxué yìqǐ yùxíle kèwén.

下午我跟我们班同学一起预习了课文。

I prepared the lesson together with classmates from our section in the afternoon.

* Remember that if le follows the verb, the sentence must meet one of the above conditions in order to stand alone.
牢记：动词带"了"的句子，必须符合上述条件之一，否则句子就不能独立。

The negative of sentences with aspect le is expressed with méi (you) before the verb and eliminating the le, thereby stating that the action has not happened or not been completed，
否定式则把副词"没(有)"放在动词前，去掉"了"，表示动作没有发生或没有完成。

S + 没(有) + V + O

a. Tāmen xiūxi le, wǒmen méi (you) xiūxi.

他们休息了，我们没(有)休息。

They took a break. We didn't take a break.

b. Zuótian wǒ mǎile yì běn cídiǎn, méi (you) mǎi biéde shū.

昨天我买了一本词典，没(有)买别的书。

I bought a dictionary yesterday, no other books.

To express that an action has not yet happened or been completed, but will shortly, use hái méiyǒu ... ne 还没有……呢 "still not ...", "yet to ...". This type of action ordinarily is one that should under normal circumstances have occurred.
如果动作尚未实现或完成，但可能很快即将实现或完成，就可以用"还没(有)……呢"。这种动作往往是本应实现或按常规该实现的。

S + 还 + 没(有) + V + O + 呢

c. Xiànzài hái méi shàng kè ne.

现在还没上课呢。

Class hasn't begun yet at this time.

d. Wǒ hái méi zuò zuòyè ne, nǐ xiān qù ba.

我还没做作业呢，你先去吧。

I haven't done the homework yet. You go on ahead.

The affirmative-negative question form of V + le sentences is as follows:

"动词＋了"的正反疑问式是

S + V + O + 了 + 没有?	or	S + V + 了 + O + 没有?

e. Nǐ chī fàn le méiyou?

你吃饭了没有？

Have you eaten?

f. Nǐmen mǎi shū le méiyou?

你们买书了没有？

Did you buy books?

g. Nǐ zuòle zuòyè méiyou?

你做了作业没有？

Have you done the homework?

The aspect particle le simply expresses the completion of an action, not the time that it happened. The completion can occur in the past, or it may also occur in future.

动态助词"了"只表示动作的完成，但不表示动作发生的时间，一个完成的动作可以发生在过去，也可以发生在将来。

a. Zuótian wǎnshang wǒ kànle yí ge diànyǐng.

昨天晚上我看了一个电影。

I saw a film last night.

b. Wǒ chīle fàn qù zhǎo ni, hǎo ma?

我吃了饭去找你，好吗？

I'll look for you after eating, alright?

c. Míngtian xiàwǔ xiàle kè, wǒmen qù yóuyǒng.

明天下午下了课，我们去游泳。

We're going swimming after class tomorrow.

* In sentences with verbal constructions in series (4.1) describing the purpose of an action, le generally comes after the last verb.
在表示目的的连动句中，“了”一般放在最后一个动词的后面。

a. Dàwèi lái wènle wǒ liǎng ge wèntí.

大卫来问了我两个问题。

David asked me two questions.

b. Wǒ zuótiān qù shūdiàn mǎile yì běn cídiǎn.

我昨天去书店买了一本词典。

I went to the bookstore and bought a dictionary yesterday.

2. Verb constructions and subject-predicate constructions as modifiers
动词结构和主谓结构作定语

They must be followed by a de 的. Note that English treats this form as a relative clause.
这两种结构作定语时，后面要用“的”。这种定语在英语中是用关系子句来表达的。

a. Shàngwǔ yóuyǒng de rén bù duō.

上午游泳的人不多。

There aren't many people (who are) swimming in the morning. (V)

b. Wǎnshang zài shítáng chī fàn de rén hěn shǎo.

晚上在食堂吃饭的人很少。

There are very few people (who are) eating in the cafeteria in the evening. (V)

c. Zài túshūguǎn kàn shū de nàge tóngxúe jiào shénme míngzi?

在图书馆看书的那个同学叫什么名字？

What's the name of that classmate (who is) studying in the library? (V)

d. Xǐhuan dǎ wǎngqiú de tóngxúe dōu qù wǎngqiúchǎng le.

喜欢打网球的同学都去网球场了。

Classmates who enjoy playing tennis have all gone to the tennis courts. (V)

e. Tā mǎi de cídiǎn hěn hǎo.

她买的词典很好。

The dictionary that she bought is good. (S-O)

f. Tā zuò de zuòyè dōu duì.

他做的作业都对。

The homework (that) he did is all correct. (S-O)

词组和句子

1. 昨天我去书店了，买了三本书。
2. 上星期日我在朋友家认识了一位中文老师。
3. 我们下了课去打网球吧，上午我定了一个网球场。
4. 下了课你先去网球场等我，我一定来。
5. 上星期五晚上我和马丁吃了饭去看电影了。
6. 明天我订了电影票去你家找你。
7. 昨天上午你们上了几节课？
8. 昨天我没上课，我请假了，上午他上了三节课。
9. 你去了大体育馆了没有？

10. 没有，我没去大体育馆，我去了小体育馆了。
11. 下午打网球的学生很多，游泳的人也不少。
12. 体育馆旁边儿的游泳池大不大？在那儿游泳的同学多不多？
13. 晚上从八点到九点是我做作业的时间，九点到十点是我预习的时间。
14. 在教室里看书的那个同学是谁？
15. 我想知道您什么时候在家。您在家的时候，我给您打电话，可以吧？
16. 他买的本子真好，别的人一定也想买。
17. 你做作业了没有？你觉得今天的作业怎么样？
18. 还没有呢，不过，我看了一下儿，我觉得今天的作业很难。
19. 作业太难不好，太容易也不好。
20. 你还没吃饭吧？在我家吃怎么样？
21. 谢谢，我吃了饭了。
22. 你还没做作业吧？我们一起做吧！

参考资料

拼音课文

Wǒmen yìqǐ qù dǎ wǎngqiú

Dàwèi:	Jīn Zhōngyī, qī diǎnzhōng wǒmen yìqǐ qù dǎ wǎngqiú, hǎo bu hǎo?
Jīn Zhōngyī:	Hǎo a. Nǐ yě xǐhuan dǎ wǎngqiú ma?
Dàwèi:	Duì, wǒ měi tiān dōu qù dǎ.
Jīn Zhōngyī:	Nǐ jīntian dǎle méiyou?
Dàwèi:	Hái méi dǎ ne. Nǐ zhīdao wǎngqiúchǎng zài nǎr ma?
Jīn Zhōngyī:	Bù zhīdào, wǎngqiúchǎng zài nǎr?

Dàwèi: Zài tǐyùguǎn de pángbiānr.

Jīn Zhōngyī: Tǐyùguǎn zài nǎr?

Dàwèi: Wǒmen xuéxiào yǒu yí ge dà tǐyùguǎn, yí ge xiǎo tǐyùguǎn, dà de zài běibianr, wǎngqiúchǎng dōu zài dà tǐyùguǎn de pángbiānr.

Jīn Zhōngyī: Xiǎo tǐyùguǎn zài něibiānr ne?

Dàwèi: Zài nèibianr.

Jīn Zhōngyī: Nèibianr shi — xīnán?

Dàwèi: Duì.

Jīn Zhōngyī: Wǒmen de xuéxiào zhēn dà. Dǎ wǎngqiú de rén yídìng bù shǎo ba? Dìng wǎngqiúchǎng róngyi ma?

Dàwèi: Bú tài nán. Wǒ xiàwǔ dìngle yí ge, shíjiān shi cóng qī diǎn dào bā diǎn.

Jīn Zhōngyī: Wǒmen xuéxiào yǒu meiyǒu yóuyǒngchí?

Dàwèi: Yǒu, xiǎo tǐyùguǎn dōngbianr yǒu ge yóuyǒngchí. Nǐ xǐhuan yóuyǒng ma?

Jīn Zhōngyī: Xǐhuan. Nǐ ne?

Dàwèi: Wǒ yě xǐhuan. Nǐ kàn, shítáng dào le, wǒmen xiān qù chī fàn ba!

Jīn Zhōngyī: Wǒ chīle fàn le. Nǐ hái méi chī ma?

Dàwèi: Méiyou. Wǒ chīle fàn qù zhǎo nǐ.

Jīn Zhōngyī: Hǎo, yìhuǐr jiàn.

英译课文

We go together to play tennis

David: Kim Chung-il, let's go together to play tennis at 7:00!

Kim: Fine. Do you like playing tennis, too?

David: Yes, I go to play every day.

Kim: Have you played today?

David: Not yet. Do you know where the tennis courts are?

Kim: No, where are they?

David: Beside the gym.

Kim: Where is the gym?

David: There is a large gym at our school and a small one. The large one is to the north and the tennis courts are beside the large gym.

Kim: And on which side is the small gym?

David: Over there.

Kim: That is — the south-west.

David: Right.

Kim: Our school is really big. Quite a few people play tennis, I imagine. Is it easy to reserve a court?

David: Not too hard. I reserved one for the afternoon, the time from 7:00 until 8:00.

Kim: Is there a swimming pool at our school?

David: Yes. There's a swimming pool on the eastern side of the small gym. Do you like to swim?

Kim: Yes, and you?

David: I like to swim, too. Look, we're at the cafeteria. Let's eat first!

Kim: I've eaten. Haven't you eaten yet?

David: No. I'll look for you after I've eaten.

Kim: All right. I'll see you in a while.

课堂活动

I. Aspect particle le

动态助词“了”

Students form pairs, one student with card A and the other B. They ask each other questions using the pattern S + TIMEWORD + V + le + NUMBER with MEASURE WORD + O.

二人一组，一人持卡片A，一人持卡片B，以“S＋时间词＋数量词＋0”的句型互相问答。

Example:

A: Dàiwèi zuótian mǎile jǐ běn shū?

大卫昨天买了几本书？

B: Dàiwèi zuótian mǎile sān běn shū.

大卫昨天买了三本书。

A

时间	做什么？	大卫	山本
昨天	买书（本）（例）		2
前天	上课（节）		4
今天	订票（张）		8
昨天	打电话（个）		2
上星期	请假（天）		2
上个月	认识新朋友（位）		3
昨天	约朋友打球（个）		4
昨天晚上	复习课文（课）		2
昨天	定网球场（个）		1

B

时间	做什么？	大卫	山本
昨天	买书（本） （例）	3	
前天	上课（节）	5	
今天	订票（张）	7	
昨天	打电话（个）	2	
上星期	请假（天）	1	
上个月	认识新朋友（位）	2	
昨天	约朋友打球（个）	5	
昨天晚上	复习课文（课）	2	
昨天	定网球场（个）	2	

II. Aspect particle <u>le</u> (with elements following it)

动态助词“了”（带后续成分）

As above.

做法同练习 I。

Example:

A: Ānnà xiàle kè qù zuò shénme?

安娜下了课去做什么？

B: Ānnà xiàle kè qù fùxí kèwén.

安娜下了课去复习课文。

A: Tā fùxíle kèwén qù zuò shénme?

她复习了课文去做什么？

B: Tā fùxíle kèwén qù shūdiàn.

她复习了课文去书店。

A

(例)	安娜	下课→复习课文→去书店
	小金	下课→　　　　→
	马丁	下课→吃饭　　→散步
	小方	下课→　　　　→
	山本	下课→预习生词→游泳
	大卫	下课→　　　　→
	小明	下课→做作业　→打网球

B

(例)	安娜	下课→复习课文→去书店
	小金	下课→吃饭　　→买词典
	马丁	下课→　　　　→
	小方	下课→买本子　→去图书馆
	山本	下课→　　　　→
	大卫	下课→预习课文→游泳
	小明	下课

III. Subject-Predicate Construction as Object

主谓结构作宾语

A. Students form pairs. A asks B if he/she knows where the main gymnasium/main swimming pool/Dormitory One/Dormitory Two/Dormitory Five/bookstore/Canteen Two/Tennis Courts Seven through Fourteen is/are. (Nǐ zhīdao bù zhīdao dà tǐyùguǎn (etc.) zài nǎr?)

二人一组，一人持卡片A，一人持卡片B。A问B“你知道不知道大体育馆／大游泳池／一号宿舍／二号宿舍／五号宿舍／书店／二号食堂／七到十四号网球场在哪儿？”

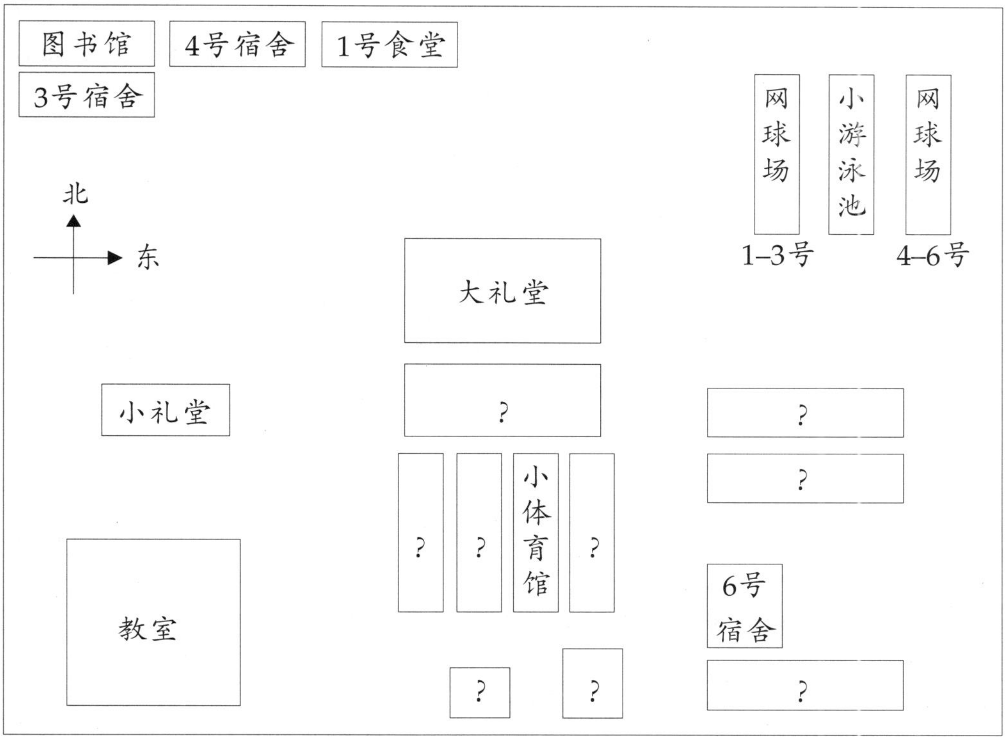

B. Students form pairs. B asks A if he/she knows where the small auditorium/Dormitory Three/Dormitory Four/Dormitory Six/Canteen One/the small swimming pool/Tennis Courts one through six is/are.

B问A“小礼堂／教室／三号宿舍／四号宿舍／六号宿舍／一号食堂／小游泳池／一到六号网球场在哪儿？”

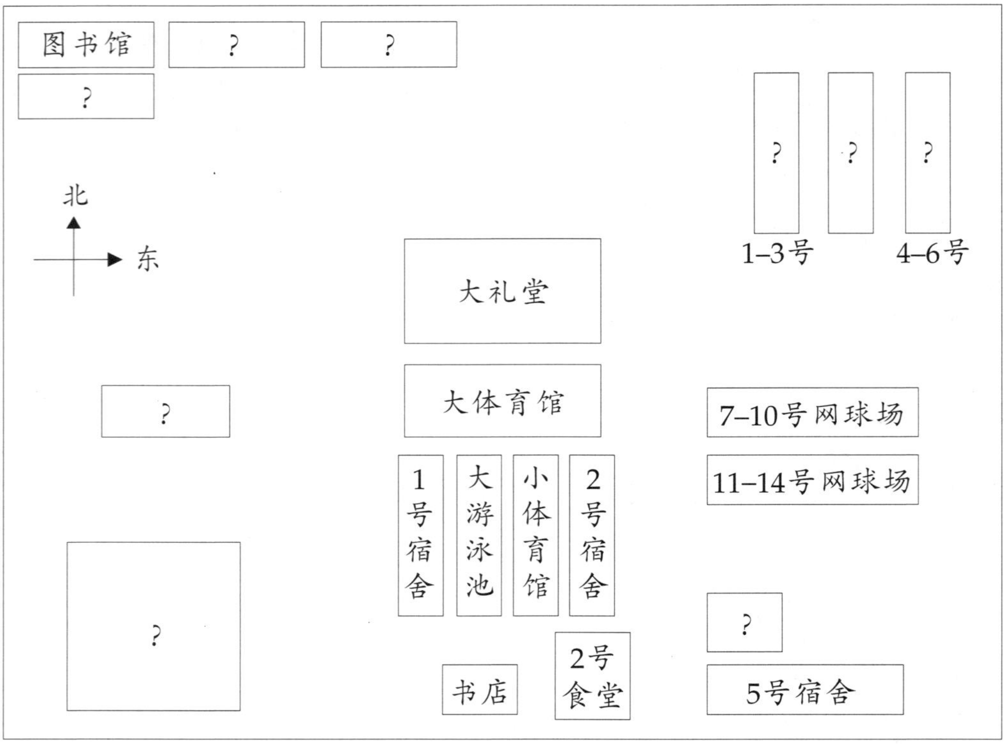

IV. Subject-Predicate Construction as attributive

主谓结构作定语

A. Students form pairs, then ask and answer questions. Convert question marks into the appropriate question particle.

二人一组，互相问答。

Example:

A: Ānnà zuótian kàn de diànyǐng yǒu yìsi ma?

安娜昨天看的电影有意思吗？

B: Ānnà zuótian kàn de diànyǐng hěn yǒu yìsi.

安娜昨天看的电影很有意思。

A

	昨天看电影	上星期订网球场	认识朋友	想问问题	买词典
安娜	有意思？	是新的？	多？	难？	汉英词典？
山本	有意思	是旧的	多	不难	日韩词典
大卫	没有意思	是新的	多	容易	汉英词典
马丁	有意思？	是旧的？	多？	难？	德韩词典？

B

	昨天看电影	上星期订网球场	认识朋友	想问问题	买词典
安娜	有意思	是新的	多	难	英汉词典
山本	有意思？	是新的？	多？	难？	日汉词典？
大卫	有意思？	是新的？	多？	难？	汉英词典？
马丁	没有意思	是旧的	少	不容易	德汉词典

B. Students ask and answer the question:

"What is the building at the eastern/southern/western/northern side of X?"

"Zài ... dōng/nán/xī/běibianr de shi shénme?"
以"在……东/南/西/北边的是什么？"互相问答。

The first time, student A holds card A1 and student B card B1. B asks and A answers. The second time, student A holds card A2 and student B holds card B2. A asks and B answers.

第一轮学生A看A1，学生B看B1，B问A答。第二轮学生A看A2，学生B看B2，A问B答。

A1

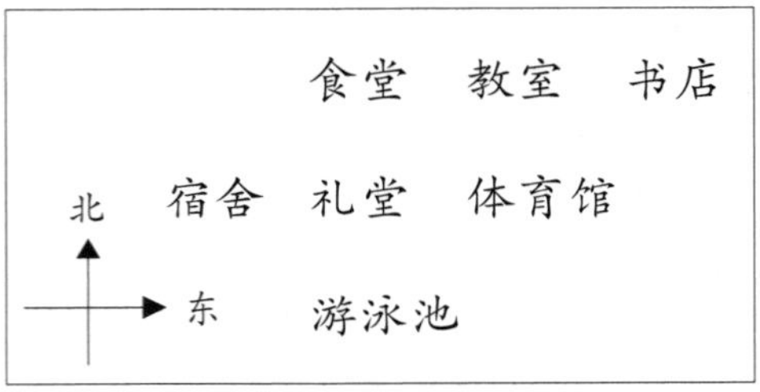

B1

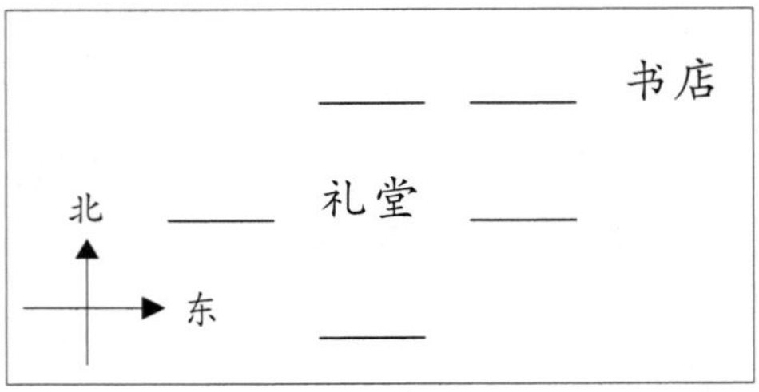

A2

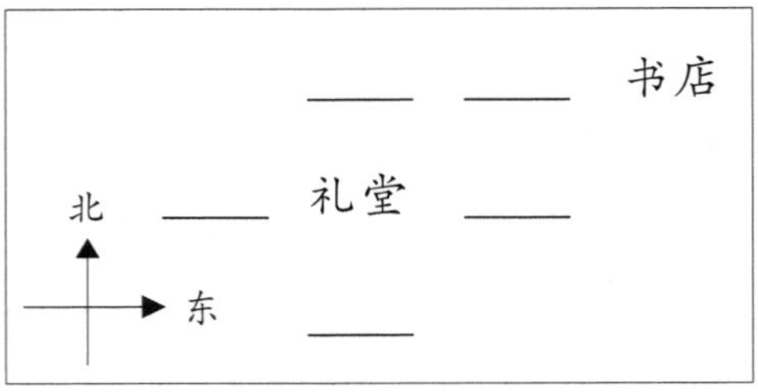

B2

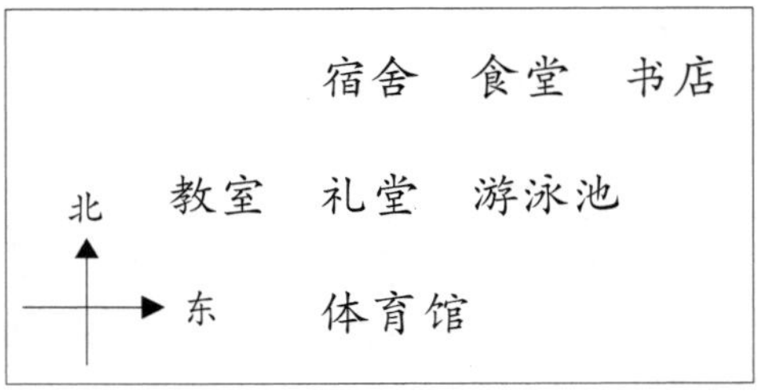

第十课

谁教我们写字？

汉字课文

（一）

马　丁：大卫，我们每课都要听写吗？

大　卫：对，每课都要听写。你昨天练习写汉字了吗？

马　丁：练习了，不过，我写得太慢。

大　卫：日本同学写字写得快。

安　娜：韩国同学写得也很快。

马　丁：是啊，他们写得又快又好看。

安　娜：我觉得汉字不难，如果每天都练习，就一定没问题。

马　丁：教我们写字的老师姓什么？

安　娜：姓王。

马　丁：王老师教得真好，她写的字也很好看。

方小英：是，同学们都喜欢她。

马　丁：昨天的作业你做了吗？

方小英：还没呢。我想下午去图书馆做。

马　丁：什么时候交？

方小英：明天交。

马　丁：给哪位老师？

方小英：谢老师。

马　丁：谢老师？

方小英：就是那位男老师，说话说得比较慢，上课的时候常常问我们："懂了吗？""有问题没有？"

(二)

大　卫：山本，快来告诉我"说话"的"说"怎么写。

山　本：你们为什么不休息啊？

大　卫：一会儿听写。

山　本：什么？听写？我怎么不知道？——完了！完了！

安　娜：别紧张，别紧张。日本同学写汉字一定没问题。

山　本：什么没问题！如果不练习，我也不会写。快告诉我，听写哪课的。

生词语

1.	教	jiāo	(v)		to teach
		a. 这位老师教什么课？他教哪个班？			
		b. 这位老师教二班汉字课。			
2.	写字	xiě zì	(vo)		to write
	写	xiě	(v)		to write
	字	zì	(n)	[个]	graph, character
3.	要	yào	(o. v)		should, be supposed to
		a. 你们要好好儿听，不要说话。			
		b. 今天我们要交作业吗？			
4.	听写	tīngxiě	(v, n)		to take dictation; dictation
5.	练习	liànxí	(v, n)	[个]	to practice; practice
		a. 你觉得今天的练习多不多？			
		b. 我们要练习听，练习说，也要练习写。			

6. 得	de	(part)		(structural particle, placed between verb or adjective and a complement of degree)
7. 慢	màn	(adj)		to be slow
8. 快	kuài	(adj)		to be quick, fast
9. 又……又……	yòu … yòu …			both … and …

a. 那个礼堂又大又好。

b. 他说得又快又好，我说得又慢又不好。

10. 好看	hǎokàn	(adj)		to be attractive (to look at)
11. 如果……就……	rúguǒ … jiù …			if … then …

a. 你如果每天练习，就能写得很好。

b. 你如果不懂，就来问我吧。

12. 交	jiāo	(v)		to hand in, give over to

a. 我还没交作业本子呢，下午交可以吗？

b. 你的作业交谢老师了吗？

13. 给	gěi	(v)		to give

a. 山本给我两本中文书。

b. 那本汉语词典你给谁了？

14. 说话	shuō huà	(vo)		to talk, speak
说	shuō	(v)		to talk
话	huà	(n)	[句 jù]	speech
15. 比较	bǐjiào	(adv; v)		comparatively, to compare

a. 今天的课比较难，生词也比较多。

b. 他说中文的时候，比较紧张，常常说的不对。

16. 常常 chángcháng (adv) frequently, always (hyperbolic)

17. 懂 dǒng (v) to understand

18. 告诉 gàosu (v) to tell

a. 请告诉我你的电话号码。

b. 这个问题你告诉老师了没有？

19. 怎么 zěnme (pro) how, in what way

a. 这个字怎么写？

b. "没问题"英文怎么说？

c. 昨天你怎么没来上课？

20. 休息 xiūxi (v) to rest

21. 完 wán (v) to finish, complete (does not take a direct object); <u>wán le</u>! 完了！as used in the text is an idiomatic expression, meaning "I'm finished" or "I'm in trouble".

22. 别 bié (o. v) don't

a. 你别告诉她我在这儿。

b. 明天的课很有意思，你别请假。

23. 紧张 jǐnzhāng (adj) to be tense, nervous

a. 现在我学习中文，每天都很紧张，星期日要好好儿休息一下。

b. 听写的时候，你紧张吗？别紧张，我想不难。

24. 会 huì (o. v) to know how to

a. 方小英会游泳，也会打网球。

b. 我会说英文，不会说日文。

c. 他会不会写汉字？

专有名词

1.	汉字	Hànzì		[个]	Chinese characters
2.	王	Wáng			(a surname)
3.	谢	Xiè			(a surname)

补充生词

1.	念	niàn	(v)		to read aloud
2.	句子	jùzi	(n)	[个]	sentence

语法点

1. Verbal Predicate Sentences with two objects

双宾语动词谓语句

Some verbs are frequently followed by two objects, the first indirect and most often a person, the second direct and generally referring to a thing or an event.

有些动词可以带两个宾语。第一个宾语是间接宾语，通常指人。第二个宾语是直接宾语，通常指事物。

S + V + Indirect O + Direct O

a. Xiè lǎoshī jiāo wǒmen Hànyǔ.

谢老师教我们汉语。

Mr. Xie teaches us Chinese.

b. Dàwèi gàosu wo míngtian tīngxiě.

大卫告诉我明天听写。

David told me that we have dictation tomorrow.

c. Mădīng wèn wo wǒmen bān xīngqīliù shàng bu shàng kè.

马丁问我我们班星期六上不上课。

Martin asked me if our section had class or not on Saturday.

2. Complement of degree

程度补语

A complement follows a verb or adjective, supplying description to the given action or quality. The degree complement describes the degree or extent that the action or quality reaches, and is commonly an adjective. The suffix de 得 must be used between the verb and its complement. The action described by verbs with complements of degree is often already completed, or frequently occurs and reaches some kind of degree or result. Thus, the speaker is able to evaluate the subject as he does.

动词或形容词后边的补充说明成分叫作补语。补充说明动作或性质所达到的程度的补语叫程度补语。程度补语一般由形容词担任。动词和补语之间要用结构助词"得"。带程度补语的动词，它所表示的动作常常是已经完成或经常发生并达到某种程度、结果的，所以说话人才能据此作出对主语的这种评价。

S + V + 得 + {很} + Adj

a. Tāmen xué de hěn kuài.

他们学得很快。

They learn very fast.

b. Wáng lǎoshī jiāo de zhēn hǎo.

王老师教得真好。

Mrs. Wang teaches really well.

Watch these features of the complement of degree:

请注意程度补语以下几个特点：

I. An adverb of degree (minimally hěn 很) must precede the complement adjective. Otherwise, the expression will be comparative in nature.

当形容词充任程度补语时，形容词前要有程度副词，如"很"。如果没有程度副词，一般含有对比或比较的意思。

a. Tā xiě de hěn kuài.

他写得很快。

He writes very fast.

b. Tā xiě de kuài, wǒ xiě de mà.

他写得快，我写得慢。

He writes fast and I write slowly.

II. One negates the complement and not the verb in this construction.

否定式是把"不"放在补语前，而不是放在动词前。

S + V + 得 + 不 + Adj

a. Tāmen xiě de bú kuài.

他们写得不快。

They don't write fast.

b. Wǒ xué de bú tài hǎo.

我写得不太好。

I don't learn very well.

III. Similarly, the affirmative-negative question is asked with the complement.

正反疑问是并列程度补语的肯定形式和否定形式。

S + V + 得 + Adj 不 Adj ?

a. Tāmen xué de kuài bu kuài?

他们学得快不快？

Do they learn fast?

b. Zuótian nǐ xiūxi de hǎo bu hǎo?

昨天你休息得好不好？

Did you rest well yesterday?

IV. If, in this construction, the verb has an object, the following forms are used.

如果动词后带有宾语，有以下两种形式。

A. The verb is repeated.
重复动词后再加"得"和补语。

S + V + O + V + 得 + CD

a. Tāmen zuò zuòyè zuò de hěn kuài.

他们做作业做得很快。

They do homework quickly.

b. Wǒmen xiě Hànzì xiě de bǐjiào màn.

我们写汉字写得比较慢。

We write Chinese characters rather slowly.

B. The receiver of the action is placed BEFORE the verb or at the head of the sentence. This creates another sentence type which we call on S-P predicate sentence. See the grammar point that follow.
把动词的受事放到动词前或句首构成另一种句式，我们称之为主语谓语句(见下文语法点)。

O + S + V + 得 + CD

S + O + V + 得 + CD

a. Zuòyè tāmen zuò de hěn kuài.

作业他们做得很快。

They do homework fast.

b. Wǒmen Hànzì xiě de bǐjiào màn.

我们汉字写得比较慢。

We write Chinese characters rather slowly.

* "Do homework fast" is an evaluation of "they" in regard to homework in example (a), just as "write rather slowly" is an appraisal of "we" regarding "Chinese characters" in example (b).

例 (a) 的"做得很快"是在"作业"方面对"他们"的评价，例 (b) 的"写得比较慢"是指在"汉字"方面对"我们"的评价。

3. S-P predicate sentence

主谓谓语句

The usual order of a Chinese sentence, as we know, is

SUBJECT – VERB – OBJECT

However, the object may be brought to the head of the sentence in a contrastive situation, or when one wishes to draw the listener's attention to it.

汉语中的动词谓语句，最常见的语序是主语—动词—宾语。如果为了要使听话人特别注意宾语或表示对比时，就可以把宾语放在主语或动词前。

S = Object of the verb + (S + P)

a. Zuótian de zuòyè nǐ zuò le ma?

昨天的作业你做了吗？

Have you done yesterday's homework?

b. Wǒ zuótian de zuòyè zuò le, (wǒ) jīntian de zuòyè hái méi (you) zuò ne.

我昨天的作业做了，(我) 今天的作业还没 (有) 做呢。

I've done yesterday's homework, but haven't done today's yet.

The S-P predicate sentence is one in which an S-P construction serves as the predicate. There are three types of this sentence, of which we will introduce two here:
主谓谓语句是指主谓结构做谓语的句子，有三种情况，这里介绍两种：

I. The subject of the entire sentence is the object of the minor predicate (meaning the predicate of the S-P construction).
全句主语是小谓语（即主谓结构中的谓语）的受事。

II. The object of the minor predicate is the minor subject.
主语结构中的小主语是小谓语的受事。

S + (S = object of the verb) + P

a. Tā Hànzì xiě de hěn hǎo.
他汉字写得很好。
He writes Chinese characters well.

b. Wǒ zuòyè hái méi zuò ne.
我作业还没做呢。
I haven't done the homework yet.

* We may also think of this construction as one that states the object at the head of a sentence, or before the verb.
也可以认为这种句式是把动词的宾语移到句首或动词前。

NOTES 注释

1. <u>... de shíhou</u> ……的时候 "when, at the time of". This time expression is most often preceded by a verbal phrase, together forming an adverbial adjunct.
"……的时候"经常受动词或动词结构修饰，在句中作状语。

a. Xiūxi de shíhou, wǒ zài gàosu ni.

休息的时候，我再告诉你。

I'll tell you at break time.

b. Zuótian tā lái de shíhou, wǒ méi zài jiā.

昨天她来的时候，我没在家。

When she came yesterday, I wasn't at home.

c. Tā xǐhuan chī fàn de shíhou tīng yīnyuè.

他喜欢吃饭的时候听音乐。

He likes to listen to music when he's eating.

2. Wán le 完了. The direct meaning of this utterance is "It's finished now". Idiomatically, as in our lesson text, it expresses a reaction to a situation out of hand or a potential headache.

"完了"的本来意思是表示事情完结、结束，在本课则是表示遇到的事情、情况不好、不利于自己。

3. Shénme méi wèntí 什么没问题！"What do you mean 'don't have any problem'?". Putting shénme 什么 before a repeated or quoted portion as Yamamoto does here indicates disagreement with that quoted portion.

"什么没问题"，在对话中，当一方不同意另一方的某个观点时，可以重复此观点或应用观点中的一部分，并在前面用上"什么"。"什么没问题"的意思是山本不同意安娜的观点："日本同学写汉字一定没问题"。

词组和句子

1. 马老师教他们中文，他教得很好。
2. 谢老师教中国学生英文，她教得很快，学生学得也很快。
3. 我朋友给我一本新词典。
4. 下课以后，我问了老师两个问题。
5. 大卫问我们明天去不去游泳。

6. 今天下午王老师在网球场教我们打网球。
7. 你快告诉我这个练习怎么做。
8. 星期日你们休息得怎么样？
9. 他们休息得都很好，我休息得不好。
10. 听写的时候你写得快不快？
11. 我写得不快，有的字我不会写。
12. 上课的时候，老师常常问问题吗？他问得多不多？
13. 有的时候问得多，有的时候问得比较少。
14. 方小英游泳游得好，我游得不好。
15. 那个同学写字写得又快又好看，我写得又慢又不好看。
16. 我练习得少，中文说得不太好。
17. 我中文说得很不好，说话的时候，我常常很紧张。
18. 今天的练习，你们都交了吗？
19. 今天的练习，别的人都交了，我还没交呢。有的练习我不会做。
20. 这个问题，我还没问老师呢。我觉得这个问题不难，我们要好好儿想一下儿。
21. 他不会写的字，你告诉他了没有？
22. 先别告诉我，我可以想一下儿。那个汉字我一定会写。

参考资料

拼音课文

Shuí jiāo wǒmen xiě zì?

(I)

Mǎdīng: Dàwèi, wǒmen měi kè dōu yào tīngxiě ma?

Dàwèi: Duì, měi kè dōu yào tīngxiě. Nǐ zuótiān liànxí xiě Hànzì le ma?

Mǎdīng: Liànxíle, búguò, wǒ xiě de tài màn.

Dàwèi: Rìběn tóngxué xiě zì xiě de kuài.

Ānnà: Hánguo tóngxué xiě de yě hěn kuài.

Mǎdīng: Shì a, tāmen xiě de yòu kuài yòu hǎokàn.

Ānnà: Wǒ juéde Hànzì bù nán, rúguo měi tiān dōu liànxí, jiù yídìng méi wèntí.

Mǎdīng: Jiāo wǒmen xiě zì de lǎoshī xìng shénme?

Ānnà: Xìng Wáng.

Mǎdīng: Wáng lǎoshī jiāo de zhēn hǎo, tā xiě de zì yě hěn hǎokàn.

Fāng Xiǎoyīng: Shì, tóngxuémen dōu xǐhuan ta.

Mǎdīng: Zuótian de zuòyè nǐ zuò le ma?

Fāng Xiǎoyīng: Hái méi ne. Wǒ xiǎng xiàwǔ qù túshūguǎn zuò.

Mǎdīng: Shénme shíhou jiāo?

Fāng Xiǎoyīng: Míngtian jiāo.

Mǎdīng: Gěi něi wèi lǎoshī?

Fāng Xiǎoyīng: Xiè lǎoshī.

Mǎdīng: Xiè lǎoshī?

Fāng Xiǎoyīng: Jiùshi nèi wèi nán lǎoshī, shuō huà shuō de bǐjiào màn, shàng kè de shíhou chángcháng wèn wǒmen: "Dǒng le ma?" "Yǒu wèntí méiyǒu?"

(II)

Dàwèi: Shānběn, kuài lái gàosu wo "shuō huà" de "shuō" zěnme xiě.

Shānběn: Nǐmen wèishénme bù xiūxi a?

Dàwèi: Yìhuǐr tīngxiě.

Shānběn: Shénme? Tīngxiě? Wǒ zěnme bù zhīdào? — Wán le! Wán le!

Ānnà:	Bié jǐnzhāng, bié jǐnzhāng. Rìběn tóngxué xiě Hànzì yídìng méi wèntí.
Shānběn:	Shénme méi wèntí! Rúguǒ bú liànxí, wǒ yě bú huì xiě. Kuài gàosu wo, tīngxiě něi kè de.

英译课文

Who's teaching us writing?

(I)

Martin:	David, do we have dictation in every lesson?
David:	Yes, dictation in every class. Did you practice writing Chinese characters yesterday?
Martin:	Yes, but I write too slowly.
David:	The Japanese students write fast.
Anna:	The Korean students write fast, too.
Martin:	Yea, they write fast and attractively.
Anna:	I don't think that Chinese characters are difficult. There's definitely no problem if you practice every day.
Martin:	What's the last name of the teacher who teaches us writing?
Anna:	Wang.
Martin:	Ms. Wang's a good teacher, and she writes beautifully.
Fang Xiaoying:	Yes, all the students like her.
Martin:	Did you do yesterday's homework?
Fang Xiaoying:	Not yet. I'm going to the library to do it in the afternoon.
Martin:	When do we hand it in?
Fang Xiaoying:	Tomorrow.
Martin:	To which teacher?
Fang Xiaoying:	Mr. Xie.
Martin:	Mr. Xie?

Fang Xiaoying: That male teacher who speaks somewhat slowly, the one who always asks us in class: "Do you understand?" and "Are there any questions?"

(II)

David: Yamamoto, tell me quickly how to write the "shuo" in "shuo hua."

Yamamoto: Why aren't you taking a break?

David: We're having dictation in a minute.

Yamamoto: What? Dictation? Why don't I know about it? I'm in deep trouble!

Anna: Take it easy. Japanese students certainly don't have any trouble with Chinese characters.

Yamamoto: What do you mean we don't have any trouble? If I don't practice I don't know how to write them either. Hurry up and tell me which lesson's characters we're taking dictation on.

课堂活动

I. Verbal Predicate Sentence with Two Objects

双宾语动词谓语句

Students in pairs, ask questions from their cards, A and B, in the form of the example. Boxes with characters are for questions, those with diagonal lines are not to be asked or answered. A asks when a name appears in the row, B answers, etc.

二人一组，一人持卡片A，一人持卡片B，互相问答。凡有"／"的格，不需提问。

Example:

A: Dàwèi jiāo shéi Yīngwén?

大卫教谁英文？

B: Dàwèi jiāo Ān Shān Yīngwén.

大卫教安山英文。

A

	英文	日文	韩文	德文	法文	写汉字	打网球	游泳
大卫	(例) 安山	／	／	／	／	／	／	马同
方小英	／	／	／	／	韩新	／	方明	
山本	／		／	／	／			／
安娜	张汉	／	／	／	／	／	／	
马丁	／	／	／	金一	／	／		王常
金中一	／	／	方明	／	／	大卫	／	

B

	英文	日文	韩文	德文	法文	写汉字	打网球	游泳
大卫	(例) 安山	／	／	／	／	／	／	
方小英	／	／	／	／		／		韩新
山本	／	张山	／	／	／	马丁	方明	／
安娜		／	／	／	／	／	／	王常
马丁	／	／	／		／	／	金一	
金中一	／	／		／	／		／	金一

II. Verb-object Construction as Attributive

动宾结构做定语

Use the cards above again. Cover the column on the extreme left that contains names, then make six questions from the material, asking and answering back and forth.

利用上表，轮流遮住左边第一行（即大卫等六人的名字），然后各造六个问句，互相问答。

Example:

A: Jiāo Ān Shān Yīngwén de rén shi shéi?

教安山英文的人是谁？

B: Jiāo Ān Shān Yīngwén de shi Dàwèi.

教安山英文的人是大卫。

III. Verbal Predicate Sentence with Two Objects

双宾语动词谓语句

Students in pairs, ask and answer questions, one from the content of chart A and the other from chart B.

二人一组，一人持卡片A，一人持卡片B，互相问答。可根据表中不同的要求采用下列三种问句之一。

Example:

1. Dàwèi jiāo shéi Yīngwén?

   大卫教谁英文？

2. Shéi jiāo Ān Shān Yīngwén?

   谁教安山英文？

3. Dàwèi jiāo Ān Shān shénme?

   大卫教安山什么？

A

谁		谁	什么
马丁	教	金一	德文
山本	教	方明	？
安娜	教	王常	游泳
？	教	韩新	法文
金中一	教	大卫	写汉字

大卫	告诉	马丁	?
马丁	告诉	大卫	明天要听写
山本	告诉	?	今天的作业不难
安娜	告诉	山本	马丁写字写得不好看
?	告诉	老师	大卫常常很紧张
安娜	告诉	老师	她的作业还没做完
大卫	问	?	什么时候听写
马丁	问	老师	星期几交作业
山本	问	安娜	?
安娜	问	方小英	那个字怎么写
?	问	方小英	谁想学韩文
方小英	问	马丁	有没有最新的词典
山本	问	大卫	?
方小英	问	金中一	金一是不是韩国人

B

谁		谁	什么
马丁	教	金一	?
山本	教	方明	打网球
安娜	教	?	游泳
方小英	教	韩新	法文
?	教	大卫	写汉字
大卫	告诉	马丁	山本汉字写得很好
?	告诉	大卫	明天要听写
山本	告诉	安山	今天的作业不难

安娜	告诉	山本	？
金一	告诉	老师	大卫常常很紧张
安娜	告诉	？	她的作业还没做完
大卫	问	老师	什么时候听写
？	问	老师	星期几交作业
山本	问	安娜	大卫为什么很紧张
安娜	问	方小英	？
金中一	问	方小英	谁想学韩文
方小英	问	马丁	？
山本	问	大卫	安娜有没有男朋友
方小英	问	？	金一是不是韩国人

IV. Complement of Degree
程度补语

Group students into pairs, one student holding card A and the other B. Students take Q & A turns with the information on their cards in the following sequence.

二人一组，一人持卡片A，一人持卡片B，轮流以下列句型互相问答。

A. Shéi + V + O + V + de + Adj? Go through the whole set with this question (B answering Jīn Zhōngyī, then asking who writes fast, then A answers Dàwèi, etc.)

第一次，请用：谁 + V + O + V + 得 + Adj？

B. Nǐ + O + V + de + Adj + ma? (or)

_______________ Adj + bu + Adj? Again, go through the whole set (B answering Jīn Zhōngyī ..., then asking Nǐ shuō huà shuō de kuài bù kuài? etc.)

第二次，请用：你 + V + O + V + 得 + Adj + ma？

或者 Adj + bu + Adj？

C. Wǒmen bān shéi + V + O + V + de + zuì + Adj? (go through the whole, B answering Jīn Zhōngyī, etc.)

第三次，请用：我们班谁 + V + O + V + 得 + 最 + Adj？

A

______	写汉字	好看
大卫	说话	快
______	打网球	好
安娜	游泳	慢
______	学中文	快
张山	教英文	好
______	做饭	好吃
金一	吃饭	快

B

金中一	写汉字	好看
______	说话	快
马丁	打网球	好
______	游泳	慢
方小英	学中文	快
______	教英文	好
山本	做饭	好吃
______	吃饭	快

阅读练习

我们的学校很大，学生也很多。我们有一个很大的图书馆，在学校的中间，同学们都喜欢去图书馆看书，做作业。我们学校有两个体育馆：一个在北边儿，一个在东边儿。北边儿的比较大，东边儿的比较小。大体育馆前边儿是网球场，我们没有课的时候，常常去网球场打网球。学校里有三个宿舍：两个男生宿舍，一个女生宿舍。每个宿舍下边儿都有一个食堂，小体育馆后边儿也有 一个食堂，老师们都在那个食堂吃饭。

我们班不大，有八个人。同学们中文都学得很好。有的人说话说得快，有的人写字写得好。韩国同学和日本同学汉字写得又快又好看，我写得最不好，又慢又不好看。我每天都和我的同学一起练习说中国话，一起练习写汉字。

我们的课比较多，每天都有很多作业，做了作业，要交老师。老师今天告诉我们，以后每课都要听写。他说，听写不难，如果能常常练习，就一定没有问题，不用紧张。

第二单元复习

1. The completion of an action

   动作的完成

   I. The modal particle <u>le</u> expressing completion.

      语气助词“了”表示完成

      a. Did you go back home (to your country) last year?

         你去年回国了吗？

         I went back home last year.

         我去年回国了。

         I didn't go back home last year.

         我去年没回国。

      b. Did you see a film last week?

         上星期你们看电影了吗？

         We saw a film last week.

         上星期我们看电影了。

         We didn't see a film last week.

         上星期我们没看电影。

   II. The aspect particle <u>le</u> expressing completion.

      动态助词“了”表示完成

      a. How many films did you see last week?

         上星期你们看了几个电影？

         He didn't see a film, but I saw two.

         他没看电影，我看了两个。

b. Are you going to the canteen to eat after class?

你下了课去食堂吃饭吗？

No, I'm going swimming after class.

不，我下了课去游泳。

c. Did you go swimming after class yesterday?

昨天你下了课去游泳了吗？

No, I didn't go swimming after class yesterday. I went to the library after class yesterday.

没有，昨天我下了课没去游泳。我下了课去图书馆了。

d. Have you done the exercises?

你做了练习了吗？

I've done the exercises.

我做了练习了。

e. Whom did Kim Chung-il introduce to his classmate in the classroom?

金中一在教室里给他的同学们介绍了谁？

Kim Chung-il introduced Martin to his classmate in the classroom yesterday.

金中一在教室里给他的同学介绍了马丁。

2. Optative (= auxiliary) verbs

能愿动词

I. xiǎng

想

a. I'd like to set a date to go to eat with you.

我想约你去吃饭。

b. I'd like to ask you a question.

我想问你一个问题。

c. Do you want to swim?

你想不想游泳？

I don't want to swim. I want to play tennis.

我不想游泳，我想打网球。

d. I very much want to study Chinese.

我很想学汉语。

II. néng

能

a. Who is he? Can you introduce him to me?

他是谁？你能不能给我介绍一下儿？

Sure, I'll introduce you.

可以，我来介绍一下儿。

b. I can't come tomorrow, he can come.

明天我不能来，他能来。

c. Can I go to make a phone call now?

我能不能现在去打电话？

No, go after class.

不行 (xíng = all right; bù xíng = no)，下课以后再去打吧。

III. kěyǐ

可以

a. That bookstore has this dictionary. You can go to buy it tomorrow.

那个书店有这本词典，明天你可以去买。

b. You can eat at school at noon, or you can also eat outside.

中午你可以在学校吃饭，也可以到外边儿吃。

c. May I ask questions?

我可以问问题吗？

Of course you may.

当然可以。

d. May I go to look for him this afternoon?

今天下午我可以去找他吗？

No, this afternoon he's going to a friend's house.

不行 (xíng = all right; bù xíng = no)，他今天下午去朋友家。

IV. huì

会

a. I know how to speak Chinese.

我会说中文。

b. He doesn't know how to write that character.

他不会写那个字。

c. Do you know how to swim?

你们会不会游泳？

She doesn't, I do. But I don't swim well.

她不会，我会。不过，我游得不好。

V. yào

要

a. Everyday I must review the old lesson and prepare the new one.

我每天都要复习旧课，预习新课。

b. Should we write our names on the notebooks?

我们要在本子上写名字吗？

Of course.

当然要。

c. Must we hand in homework notebooks today?

今天我们要不要交作业本子？

You needn't today. Hand them in tomorrow.

今天不用交，明天交。

3. Localizers

方位词

I. As subject and object

作主语和宾语

a. The auditorium is in the front, and the gymnasium is at the back. The dormitory is at the north, the canteen is to the south and the library is in between.

前边儿是礼堂，后边儿是体育馆。宿舍在北边儿，食堂在南边儿，图书馆在中间儿。

b. Are there no cafeteria on the western and eastern sides?

西边儿和东边儿没有食堂吗？

Not on the west side, but there is one on the eastern side. But that cafeteria is rather small. Not many people eat there.

西边儿没有，东边儿有一个。不过，那个食堂很小，在那儿吃饭的人不多。

c. He went out for a walk. The others are all inside.

他去外边儿散步了，别的人都在里边儿。

II. As attributive and central word

作定语和中心语

a. There is a bookshop in the school. To the left of the bookshop is an auditorium, and to the right of the bookshop is the student dormitory.

学校里有一个小书店，书店的左边儿是个礼堂，书店的右边儿是学生宿舍。

b. There are two cafeteria there. The one in the front is the instructors' and the one in the back is the students'.

那边儿有两个食堂，前边儿的食堂是老师的，后边儿的是学生的。

c. There is a Chinese book beside that dictionary, and there is a small notebook inside the book. Take a look and see what's inside the little notebook.

那本词典的旁边儿有一本中文书，书里有一个小本子。

你看一下，小本子里有什么？

4. "是""有""在"

Place + shì + the thing/object/person (indefinite/definite)

处所 + 是 + 存在的事物（无定/有定）

Place + yǒu + the thing/object/person (usually indefinite)

处所 + 有 + 存在的事物（一般为无定）

The thing/object/person (usually definite) + zài + place

存在的事物（一般为有定）+ 在 + 处所

a. There is a theater at the west side of my house.

我家西边儿是一个电影院。

b. There are two Chinese students in the classroom.

教室里是两个中国同学。

c. The Star Theater is at the west of my house.

我家西边儿是天星电影院。

d. David and Yamamoto are in the classroom.

教室里是大卫和山本。

e. There is a theater to the east of my house.

我家东边儿有一个电影院。

f. There are two Chinese students in the classroom.

教室里有两个中国同学。

g. The Star Theater is to the west of my house.

我家西边儿有天星电影院。(✗)

h. David and Yamamoto are in the classroom.

教室里有大卫和山本。(✗)

i. The star Theater is at the west of my house.

天星电影院在我家西边儿。

j. David and Yamamoto are in the classroom.

大卫和山本在教室里。

k. To the west of my house is a theater.

一个电影院在我家西边儿。(✗)

l. Two Chinese classmates are in the classroom.

两个中国同学在教室里。(✗)

Sentences followed by (✗) are not normally correct by themselves, but only in specific contexts.

(✗)：表示一般不能说，只有在一定的语言环境下才可以说。

5. Verbal construction and S-P construction

动词结构和主谓结构

I. Verbal construction as attributive

动词结构作定语

a. The new classmate from Germany is called Martin.

从德国来的新同学叫马丁。

b. Are there many students studying Chinese?

学中文的学生多不多？

c. Don't talk during class.

上课的时候不要说话。

d. Is that classmate taking a walk outside David?

在外边散步的那个同学是大卫吗？

e. Lots of people want to see that film.

想看那个电影的人不少。

f. There is nobody in our section who studies badly.

我们班没有学得不好的人。

g. A lot of people were looking for you this afternoon, and a lot of people telephoned you.

今天下午找你的人很多，给你打电话的人也很多。

II. S-P construction as attributive

主谓结构作定语

a. Is that book you read interesting?

你看的那本书有意思吗？

b. The dictionary you bought isn't bad.

你买的词典不错。

c. What question did David ask?

大卫问的问题是什么？

d. The exercises Martin did today are all correct.

马丁今天做的练习都对。

e. I like his writing.

我喜欢他写的字。

III. Verbal construction as object

动词结构作宾语

a. Fang Xiaoying likes listening to music.

方小英喜欢听音乐。

b. Anna told me that there was no class on Saturday.

安娜告诉我星期六没有课。

c. He asked me if I would go for a walk.

他问我去不去散步。

d. I don't know if the class has begun.

我不知道上课了没有。

IV. S-P construction as object

主谓结构作宾语

a. He knows where the gymnasium is.

他知道体育馆在哪儿。

b. I didn't know that he would request absence today.

我不知道他今天请假。

c. Yamamoto asked me who was going swimming tomorrow.

山本问我明天谁去游泳。

d. Kim Chung-il told Fang Xiaoying that he would wait for her at the school entrance.

金中一告诉方小英他在学校门口儿等她。

e. She said she understood.

她说，她懂了。

Optative Verbs
能愿动词表

Usage & meaning 用法和词义 / 能愿动词 Optative Verbs	肯定式 Affirm-ative	否定式 Nega-tive	正反疑问式 Affirm-ative negative	单独回答肯定式 Used in Affirm-ative response	单独回答否定式 Used in Negative response	词义 Meaning	出现课数 Lesson
想 want	想	不想	想不想	想	不想	打算、希望 plan to, hope to	6
能 can	能	不能	能不能	可以	不行	环境上许可、准许 conditions permit or allow	7
可以 can, may	可以	不能 不可以	可以不可以	可以	不行	许可 is/are allowed to	8
会 can, know how to	会	不会	会不会	会	不会	懂得怎样做或有能力做(多指需要学习的事情) know how to or have the ability to	10
要 must, have to	要	不用	要不要	要	不用	须要、应该 must, should	10
得 must, need to	得	不用	X	X	不用	必须，情理上或事实上需要 required by reason or circumstance	11
应该 should	应该	不应该	应该不应该	应该	不应该	情理上必须如此 action dictated by reason	14
该 will surely	该	X	X	X	X	估计情况应该如此 conditions should bring about this result	20

阅读

大　卫：明天是星期天，你想做什么？

马　丁：我想好好儿休息一下儿。

大　卫：怎么休息？

马　丁：上午吃了早饭，先去游泳。

大　卫：去体育馆西边儿的那个游泳池吗？

马　丁：对！

大　卫：你为什么不下午去游？

马　丁：上午去，人少；下午去，人太多。那个游泳池比较小。

大　卫：你买游泳票了吗？

马　丁：买了，买了三张。你去不去？给你一张。

大　卫：谢谢，我不想去。明天下午你做什么？

马　丁：明天午饭以后，我先在宿舍里听一会儿音乐，三点钟的时候去打网球。

大　卫：跟谁打？

马　丁：跟山本打。你有时间，欢迎也来。我知道你网球打得很好？

大　卫：你定网球场了吗？

马　丁：还没定呢，一会儿我打电话定一个。

大　卫：晚上你做什么？

马　丁：晚上我去学校外边儿吃晚饭。星期六和星期日，我喜欢在外边儿吃饭。

大　卫：你一个人去吗？

马　丁：不，我喜欢跟别的人一起吃。每个星期都有人约我去吃晚饭。

大　卫：是吗？这个星期谁约你了？

马　丁：你啊！

大　卫：我？我什么时候约你了？

马　丁：你现在可以约啊！

第十一课

我还想买一双鞋

汉字课文

(一)

马　丁：安娜，附近有没有商店？我想买一点儿东西。

安　娜：你想买什么？

马　丁：我想买一件衣服和一个箱子。

安　娜：学校东边儿有一个商场，那个商场比较大。

马　丁：离学校远不远？

安　娜：不远，很近。

马　丁：要走多长时间？

安　娜：出了学校，走十分钟，就到了。

马　丁：怎么样？那儿的东西多不多？

安　娜：还可以。

马　丁：你和我一起去，好吗？

安　娜：好，一个小时以后你来找我。

(二)

马　丁：卖衣服的地方在哪儿？

安　娜：在楼上。

马　丁：几楼啊？

安　娜：大概是三楼。

马　丁：我们上楼吧。

（他们上楼去买衣服）

马　丁：安娜，你看这件衣服怎么样？

安　娜：不太好。我觉得上边儿那件好。

马　丁：我也喜欢那件，可是太贵了。下边儿这件比较便宜。

安　娜：下边儿这件便宜，可是不好看。你穿上边儿那件好。

马　丁：是吗？你说好，我就买。

（马丁买了一件衣服）

马　丁：在哪儿买箱子？

安　娜：买箱子得到楼下，在一楼。我们下楼吧。

（他们下楼买了箱子）

马　丁：我还想买一双鞋。

安　娜：什么？买鞋得到四楼，我们还得上楼！

生词语

1.	双	shuāng	(m)		a pair
2.	鞋	xié	(n)	[双，只 zhī]	shoes
3.	附近	fùjìn	(n)		vicinity
		a. 请问附近有没有大商场？			
		b. 他家附近有一个电影院。			
4.	商店	shāngdiàn	(n)	[个，家]	shop, store
5.	（一）点儿	(yì)diǎnr	(m)		some, a little
		a. 我会说一点儿中文，不过，说得不好。			
		b. 我昨天复习了两课课文和一点儿生词。			
6.	东西	dōngxi	(n)	[件]	thing

7.	件	jiàn	(m)	an item of, article of (clothing, business matter, etc.)
8.	衣服	yīfu	(n) [件]	clothing
9.	箱子	xiāngzi	(n) [个，只]	suitcase, valise, box
10.	商场	shāngchǎng	(n) [个]	shopping center, arcade
11.	离	lí	(prep)	(distance) from

a. 商店离我家很近。

b. 学校离那个书店远不远？

12.	远	yuǎn	(adj)	to be far, distant
13.	近	jìn	(adj)	to be near, close
14.	走	zǒu	(v)	to walk

a. 去教室的时候，他走得很慢，去食堂的时候，他走得很快。

b. 八点半上课，我们走吧！

15.	多	duō	(adv)	how (questioning degree)
16.	长	cháng	(adj)	to be long
17.	出	chū	(v)	to go out of (a place), to exit
18.	分钟	fēnzhōng	(m)	a minute of time
19.	小时	xiǎoshí	(n, m) [个]	hour
20.	卖	mài	(v)	to sell

a. 请问，卖票的地方在哪儿？

b. 商店里卖的东西我不想买，我想买的东西，商店里不卖。

c. 这个书店也卖本子，有的书店不卖。

21.	地方	dìfang	(n) [个]	place
22.	楼上	lóushàng	(n)	upstairs

23. 楼	lóu	(n)	[个，座zuò]	storied building; floor (1, 2 etc.) of a building
24. 上楼	shàng lóu	(vo)		to go upstairs, to upper floors
上	shàng	(v)		to go up, ascend
楼	lóu	(n)		storied building
25. 上边儿	shàngbianr	(n)		topside
26. 可是	kěshì	(c)		but

a. 今天的练习比较难，可是很有意思。

b. 他说得比较快，可是我都懂了。

27. 贵	guì	(adj)		to be expensive
28. 下边儿	xiàbianr	(n)		bottomside, under side
29. 便宜	piányi	(adj)		to be inexpensive
30. 穿	chuān	(v)		to wear (clothing)
31. 得	děi	(o.v)		must, have to

a. 上个星期我们学得比较多，这个星期我得好好儿复习一下儿。

b. 我的书大概在宿舍，我得回宿舍去拿。

32. 楼下	lóuxià	(n)		downstairs
33. 下楼	xià lóu	(vo)		to go downstairs
下	xià	(v)		to go down
楼	lóu	(n)	[层céng]	storied building

补充生词

1. 衬衫	chènshān	(n)	shirt
2. 裙子	qúnzi	(n)	skirt
3. 裤子	kùzi	(n)	pants

4.	牛仔裤	niúzǎikù	(n)	jeans
5.	大衣	dàyī	(n)	overcoat
6.	皮鞋	píxié	(n)	shoes (leather)
7.	球鞋	qiúxié	(n)	tennis or athletic shoes

语法点

1. The preposition lí 离 "(distance) from"

介词"离"

This construction is used to express degree of distance in space or time.

"离"用在下面的句型里表示空间上(或时间上)的"距离"。

S + 离 + Place/Time Word + Adj

a. Túshūguǎn lí shítáng hěn jìn.

图书馆离食堂很近。

The library is close to the cafeteria.

b. Xuéxiào lí shāngdiàn bù yuǎn.

学校离商店不远。

The school isn't far from the shop.

c. Xiànzài lí shàng kè (de shíjiān) hái yǒu shí fēnzhōng.

现在离上课(的时间)还有十分钟。

There is still ten minutes until class (time).

2. Complement of time

时量补语

A numeral together with a noun expressing a unit of time (e.g., shí fēnzhōng 十分钟 "ten minutes", bàn ge xiǎoshí 半个小时 "half an hour", yí ge bàn yuè 一个半月 "a month and a half", yìhuǐr 一会儿 "a while") can also constitute a complement, following the verb. The construction describes how long the action continues or will be continued.

数词加表示时间单位的名词(如“十分钟、半个小时、一个半月、一会儿”)可以出现在动词后作补语，补充说明行为动作已经持续或将要持续多长时间。

a. Tā měi tiān fùxí yí ge bàn xiǎoshí.

他每天复习一个半小时。

He studies for an hour and a half every day.

b. Xiànzài xiūxi yí kèzhōng!

现在休息一刻钟！

Take a quarter hour break now!

If the verb has a pronoun as an object, that pronoun comes BEFORE the complement.

如果动词带人称代词宾语，人称代词放在时量补语前。

S + V + O (Pro) + CT

c. Nǐ děng wǒ yìhuǐr, wǒ mǎshang lái.

你等我一会儿，我马上来。

Wait for me a minute. I'll come right away.

d. Tā bú huì yóuyǒng, wǒ měi tiān jiāo tā yí ge xiǎoshí.

他不会游泳，我每天教他一个小时。

He can't swim. I teach him for an hour every day.

If it has a noun object, the object comes AFTER the complement.

如果动词带名词宾语，名词宾语要放在时量补语后。

S + V + CT (+ 的) + O

e. Míngnián wǒ yào xué yì nián Zhōngwén.

明年我要学一年中文。

Next year I'm going to study a year of Chinese.

f. Wǒ měi tiān dōu dǎ bàn ge xiǎoshí (de) wǎngqiú.

我每天都打半个小时(的)网球。

I play a half hour of tennis every day.

* A de 的 can be used after the time expression.

可以在时间词语后用上结构助词“的”。

If the verb has a noun object, that verb can be repeated and the time complement placed after the repeated verb.

动词带名词宾语时，也可以重复动词，把时量补语放在重复的动词后。

S + V + O + V + CT

g. Nǐ měi tiān zuò zuòyè yídìng yào zuò sìshí fēnzhōng ma?

你每天做作业一定要做四十分钟吗？

Must you do forty minutes of homework each day?

h. Tā xué yǒuyǒng děi xué yí ge xīngqī.

他学游泳得学一个星期。

He has to learn swimming for a week.

* If there are adverbial adjuncts or optative verbs, they must come before the repeated verb.

如果有状语或能愿动词，都要放在重复的动词前。

In a completed action situation with the aspect particle le 了, the le follows the verb. And if the verb is repeated, le follows the repeated verb.

如果句子里有表示完成的动态助词“了”，“了”要紧跟在动词后；如果有重复的动词，“了”在重复的动词后。

i. Wǒmen xiūxile shí fēnzhōng.

我们休息了十分钟。

We rested for ten minutes.

j. Tā qǐngle sān tiān jià.

她请了三天假。

She took three days leave.

k. Tā kàn shū kànle yí ge xiǎoshí.

她看书看了一个小时。

She read for an hour.

If the modal particle le 了 finishes the sentence, this indicates that the action most likely still goes on: as of now, such and such has been done.

如果句尾同时用上语气助词"了"，则表示到说话时（或某时）为止动作已持续了多长时间，有可能还要持续下去。

S + V + 了 + CT (+ O) + 了

l. Wǒmen xiūxile shí fēnzhōng le, hái yào xiūxi ma?

我们休息了十分钟了，还要休息吗？

We've rested for ten minutes (up to now). Do you want to go on?

m. Tā qǐngle sān tiān jià le, hái děi qǐng liǎng tiān.

她请了三天假了，还得请两天。

She has already (or, up to now) taken three days off and has to take two more.

n. Tā qǐng jià qǐngle sān tiān le, míngtiān hái bù néng lái.

她请假请了三天了，明天还不能来。

She has already taken three days off and still can't come in tomorrow.

3. Clock time and duration of time

时点和时段

To express time of the clock, we use ... diǎn (zhōng) ……点（钟）"hour", ... fēn ……分 "minute", ... kè ……刻 "quarter of an hour", etc.

在表示时间上的某一点时（时点），我们用"……点（钟）"、"……分"、"……刻"，还有"今天""明年""三月""这个星期"。

liǎng diǎn (zhōng)	两点（钟）	2:00
shí'èr diǎn (zhōng)	十二点（钟）	12:00
liǎng diǎn shí fēn	两点十分	2:10
sān diǎn líng wǔ (fēn)	三点零五（分）	3:05
wǔ diǎn èrshí (fēn)	五点二十（分）	5:20
shí'èr diǎn yī kè	十二点一刻	12:15

To express an interval or duration of time, use ... xiǎoshí ……小时 "hour", ... fēnzhōng ……分钟 and ... kèzhōng ……刻钟 (and other units that will be introduced in later lessons).

在表示一段时间时（时段），我们用"……小时"、"……分钟"、"……刻钟"，还有"一天""两年""三个月""一个星期"等。

liǎng ge xiǎoshí	两个小时	two hours
shí'èr ge xiǎoshí	十二个小时	twelve hours
yí kèzhōng	一刻钟	a quarter of an hour
shí fēnzhōng	十分钟	ten minutes
èrshí fēnzhōng	二十分钟	twenty minutes

4. The operative verb děi 得 "must", "have to"

能愿动词"得"

The optative verb děi 得 "must", "have to" (written with the same character as the complement of degree suffix de 得 introduced in Lesson 10, pp. 236–239). Its usage is straightforward, except that it is not negated with bu 不. Instead, búyòng 不用 is used.

"得"（在写法上，与程度补语的结构词"得 de"汉字相同，但发音和意义不同）的用法比较明确，需要注意的是，"得"的否定是"不用"，而不是"不得"。

a. Mǎi xiāngzi děi shàng lóu ma?

买箱子得上楼吗？

Do you have to go upstairs for luggage?

Búyòng, mài xiāngzi de dìfang zài lóuxià.

不用，卖箱子的地方在楼下。

No, the place where they sell luggage is downstairs.

b. Wǒmen jīntiān wǎnshang děi yùxí dì-shí'èr kè ma?

我们今天晚上得预习第十二课吗？

Must we prepare Lesson 12 tonight?

Búyòng yùxí, hòutiān xué dì-shí'èr kè, míngtiān zài yùxí ba.

不用预习，后天学第十二课，明天再预习吧。

No, we'll study Lesson 12 day after tomorrow. It'll be all right to prepare it tomorrow.

NOTE 注释

Kěshi tài guì le 可是太贵了 "But it's too expensive". The modal particle le here affirms, adds a "definitely" sense to a statement. It is often used where emphatics such as tài 太 "too", zuì 最 "most", etc. precede the verb or adjective.

"可是太贵了"。这里的语气助词"了"表示肯定的语气。常用在"太……了""最……了"等格式里。

a. Nàge dìfang tài yuǎn le.

那个地方太远了。

That place is too far away.

b. Wǒ zuì xǐhuan dǎ wǎngqiú le.

我最喜欢打网球了。

I'm most fond of playing tennis.

c. Zhège wèntí tài nán le, wǒ bú huì huídá.

这个问题太难了，我不会回答。

This question is too hard, I can't answer it.

d. Wǒ zuì bù xǐhuan yóuyǒng le.

我最不喜欢游泳了。

I dislike swimming most. (or) I hate to swim!

词组和句子

1. 五分钟　十五分钟　一刻钟
二十分钟　三刻钟　四十五分钟
半(个)小时　一(个)小时　一个半小时
两(个)小时零一刻钟　三(个)小时零四十五分钟
2. 那个大商场离我们学校很近。
3. 那家电影院离这儿远不远？要走多长时间？
4. 那家电影院离这儿不太远。走一会儿就到了。
5. 那个地方比较远，我们大概走了半个小时。
6. 今天上午我预习了二十分钟。
7. 我今天上了五节课，现在想休息一会儿。
8. 我们每天上午上四节课，每两节课中间休息十分钟。
9. 方小英下午在图书馆看了两个小时书。
10. 星期六晚上方小英和安娜听了两个半小时音乐。
11. 我学了两年中文，两年半日文，可是，我的中文比较好，日文不太好。
12. 大卫写了四十分钟的汉字，做了一个小时的作业，复习了半个小时的生词。

13. 今天下午我上了一个小时的汉字课，一个小时的日文。
14. 金中一游泳游了一个半小时。
15. 张老师教中文教了三年了。
16. 她学游泳学了一个星期了，现在还不会游。
17. 马丁复习课文复习了一个下午。
18. 他打电话打了二十五分钟，打的时间太长了。
19. 我的新衣服在楼上，我得上楼去穿。
20. 她给我的那双鞋太小，不能穿，我得去买一双新的。
21. 那个商店的东西比较贵，我得到一个(东西)便宜的商店去买。
22. 我的朋友从英国来了，我得请两天假。

参考资料

拼音课文

Wǒ hái xiǎng mǎi yì shuāng xié

(I)

Mǎdīng: Ānnà, fùjìn yǒu méiyǒu shāngdiàn? Wǒ xiǎng mǎi yìdiǎnr dōngxi.

Ānnà: Nǐ xiǎng mǎi shénme?

Mǎdīng: Wǒ xiǎng mǎi yí jiàn yīfu he yí ge xiāngzi.

Ānnà: Xuéxiào dōngbianr yǒu yí ge shāngchǎng, nàge shāngchǎng bǐjiào dà.

Mǎdīng: Lí xuéxiào yuǎn bu yuǎn?

Ānnà: Bù yuǎn, hěn jìn.

Mǎdīng: Yào zǒu duō cháng shíjiān?

Ānnà: Chūle xuéxiào, zǒu shí fēnzhōng, jiù dào le.

Mǎdīng: Zěnmeyàng? Nàr de dōngxi duō bu duō?

Ānnà: Hái kěyi.

Mădīng:　Nǐ hé wǒ yìqǐ qù, hǎo ma?

Ānnà:　Hǎo, yí ge xiǎoshí yǐhòu nǐ lái zhǎo wo.

(II)

Mădīng:　Mài yīfu de dìfang zài nǎr?

Ānnà:　Zài lóushàng.

Mădīng:　Jǐ lóu a?

Ānnà:　Dàgài shi sān lóu.

Mădīng:　Wǒmen shàng lóu ba.

(Tāmen shàng lóu qù mǎi yīfu)

Mădīng:　Ānnà, nǐ kàn zhèi jiàn yīfu zěnmeyàng?

Ānnà:　Bú tài hǎo. Wǒ juéde shàngbianr nèi jiàn hǎo.

Mădīng:　Wǒ yě xǐhuan nèi jiàn, kěshì tài guì le. Xiàbianr zhèi jiàn bǐjiào piányi.

Ānnà:　Xiàbianr zhèi jiàn piányi, kěshì bù hǎokàn. Nǐ chuān shàngbianr nèi jiàn hǎo.

Mădīng:　Shì ma? Nǐ shuō hǎo, wǒ jiù mǎi.

(Mădīng mǎile yí jiàn yīfu)

Mădīng:　Zài nǎr mǎi xiāngzi?

Ānnà:　Mǎi xiāngzi děi dào lóuxià, zài yī lóu. Wǒmen xià lóu ba.

(Tāmen xià lóu mǎile xiāngzi)

Mădīng:　Wǒ hái xiǎng mǎi yì shuāng xié.

Ānnà:　Shénme? Mǎi xié děi dào sì lóu, wǒmen hái děi shàng lóu.

英译课文

I still have to buy a pair of shoes

(I)

Martin:　Anna, is there a store nearby? I want to buy a few things.

Anna:　What do you want to buy?

Martin: I want to buy clothing and a suitcase.

Anna: There's a shopping center east of the school. It's fairly big.

Martin: Is it far from school?

Anna: No, it's close.

Martin: How long a walk is it?

Anna: Once you're out of the school, you're there in a ten minute walk.

Martin: How is it? Is it well stocked?

Anna: Not bad.

Martin: Why don't you come with me?

Anna: All right, come get me in an hour.

(II)

Martin: Where do they sell clothes?

Anna: Upstairs.

Martin: Which floor?

Anna: Probably the third floor.

Martin: Let's go upstairs.

(They go upstairs to buy clothes)

Martin: Anna, what do you think of this one?

Anna: That's not very good. That one up above it is all right, in my opinion.

Martin: I like that one, too, but it's too expensive. This one down below is cheaper.

Anna: It's cheaper, but not so good looking. The one up above would be good on you.

Martin: Oh? If you say it's good I'll buy it.

(Martin buys one item of clothing)

Martin: Where do you buy a suitcase?

Anna: You have to go downstairs to buy suitcases, on the first floor. Let's go down.

(They go downstairs and buy a suitcase)

Martin: I still have to buy a pair of shoes.

Anna: What? You have to go to the fourth floor to buy shoes. We have to go up again!

课堂活动

I. Preposition lí

介词"离"

Paired students will ask each other question using the ... lí ... yuǎn/jìn ma? pattern, then write the answers in the blank spaces on their charts. Student A is given the first chart (with A, B and scale) and B the second. Answers must follow the distances indicated on the scale, moving from the reference point to hěn yuǎn hěn yuǎn.

Example:

A: Yóuyǒngchí lí tǐyùguǎn yuǎn ma?

游泳池离体育馆远吗？

B: Yóuyǒngchí lí tǐyùguǎn hěn jìn.

游泳池离体育馆很近。

Hěn jìn because the distance between the two is only one space. If there are two spaces between, it is bǐjiào jìn, three spaces bù yuǎn yě bú jìn, etc.

The object is to discover the correct positions of the nine buildings on each other's charts. Some juggling of initial placements will be required but the exercise can be completed with the two buildings provided.

二人一组，以“……离……远/近吗？”互相问答并把答案填在自己的表上。练习的目的是运用包含“离”的句式，找出对方手上九个建筑物的排列顺序。回答时须参照下面的比例尺。例如，A问B“游泳池离体育馆远吗？”B应该回答：“游泳池离体育馆很近”（因两者相距一格，故答“很近”。若相距两格则答“比较近”，相距三格答“不远也不近”，余此类推。另，双方表上有相同的九个建筑物，仅相对位置不同。）

A：

宿舍	游泳池	网球场	商店	食堂	礼堂	体育馆	商场	图书馆

B：

				体育馆		商店		

SCALE:

很远很远	很远	比较远	不远也不近	比较近	很近	Reference point

B：

宿舍	商场	图书馆	游泳池	体育馆	礼堂	商店	食堂	网球场

A：

				食堂			商场	

SCALE:

很远很远	很远	比较远	不远也不近	比较近	很近	Reference point

II. Complement of Time

时量补语

A. Students divide into pairs. Assume that each student knows what the other did yesterday, and the order in which it was done, but not how long it took. Ask how long using the pattern Nǐ zuótian V + O + V + le + duō cháng shíjiān? Then see at what time both people were doing the same thing. Start at 8:00 a.m. Only address the "how long" issue in the questions and answers. At the end, when this information is all known, students can then ask each other cóng jǐ diǎn dào jǐ diǎn (e.g. "From what time until what time in the morning were you buying shoes.").

二人一组，假设知道对方昨天做了什么，也知道各项事情的顺序，可是不知道用了多长时间。请以"你昨天 + V + O + V + 了 + 多长时间？"的句型互相问答，并对照一下哪段时间二人正在做同一件事(双方皆从上午8:00开始)。问答过程中只许提及"多长时间"，最后对答案时才可以提及"从几点到几点"。

A.	B.
08:00 am	08:00 am
↕ 买鞋	↕ 买衣服
09:30 am	
↕ 买衣服	↕ 买鞋
10:30 am	
↕ 跟朋友吃饭	↕ 买箱子
12:30 pm	
↕ 打电话	↕ 跟朋友吃饭
12:45 pm	
↕ 买箱子	↕ 听音乐
01:30pm	
↕ 看电影	↕ 看电影
04:00pm	

B.	A.
08:00 am	08:00 am
↕ 买衣服	↕ 买鞋
10:00 am	
↕ 买鞋	↕ 买衣服
11:00 am	
↕ 买箱子	↕ 跟朋友吃饭
11:30 am	
↕ 跟朋友吃饭	↕ 打电话
01:00 pm	
↕ 听音乐	↕ 买箱子
02:00 pm	
↕ 看电影	↕ 看电影
03:30 pm	

B. Students divide into pairs. Ask and answer questions using the pattern S + V + le + duō cháng shíjiān de + O. Fill in the answers, then ask questions of each other to verify.

二人一组，以"S + V + 了 + 多长时间的 + O"句型互相问答。

A

	学中文	学英文
金中一	半年	六年
马丁		
山本	十个月	十年
安娜		
方小英		
大卫	四年	不用学

B

	学中文	学英文
金中一		
马丁	两年半	十年
山本		
安娜	两年零四个月	不用学
方小英	十个星期	十四年
大卫		

C. Students divide into pairs, one asking the other the compass locations relative to the dormitory of the places on their cards, and how long it takes to walk to them from the dormitories.

问问你的同学以下各地方在学生宿舍的哪边儿，从学生宿舍到以下各地方要走多长时间。

First student: Qǐngwèn shítáng/lǐtáng/yóuyǒngchí/túshūguǎn zài xuéshēng sùshè de nǎibiānr? Yào zǒu duō cháng shíjiān?

请问食堂/礼堂/游泳池/图书馆在学生宿舍的哪边儿？要走多长时间？

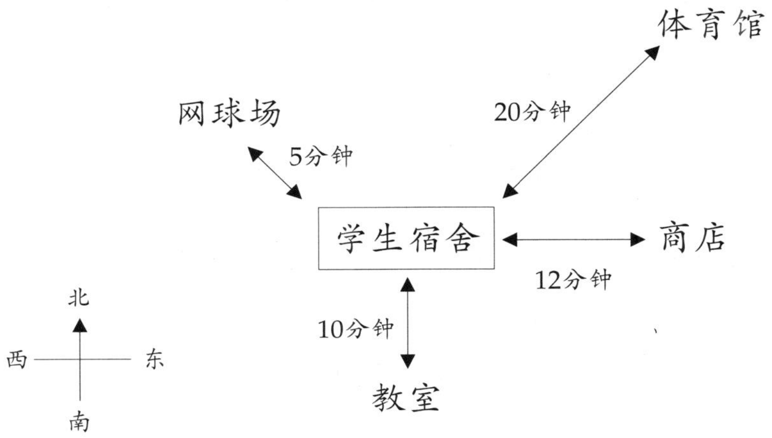

Second student: Qǐngwèn wǎngqiúchǎng/tǐyùguǎn/shāngdiàn/jiàoshì zài xuéshēng sùshè de něibiānr? Yào zǒu duō cháng shíjiān?

请问网球场/体育馆/商店/教室在学生宿舍的哪边儿？要走多长时间？

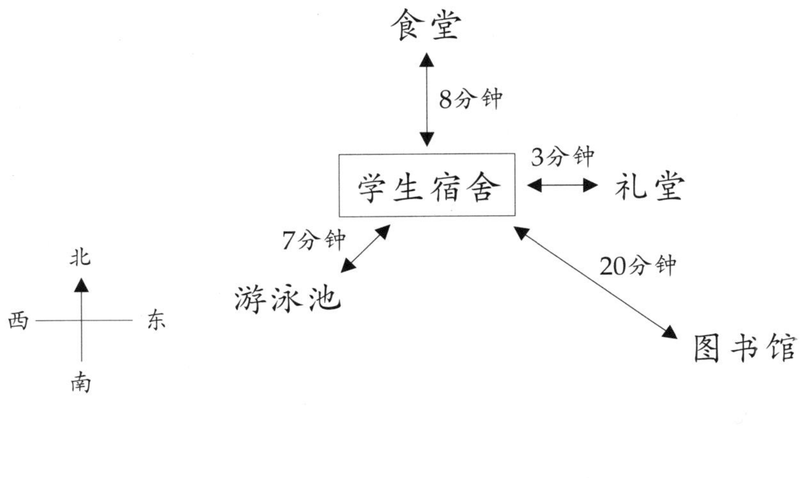

III. Preposition lí

介词"离"

Students divide into pairs, one with card A and the other card B. Alternately, they ask questions and answer according to the illustration. The questions asks "... lí ... yuǎn bù yuǎn?" or "... lí ... hěn jìn ma?"; the answerer uses "cóng ... dào ... hěn yuǎn" or "cóng ... dào ... bú tài yuǎn".

二人一组，一人持A表，一人持B表，二人轮流提问，并按照表下简图回答。提问的人用"……离……远不远？"或者"……离……很近吗？"等提问；回答的人用"从……到……很远。"或者"从……到……不太远。"等回答。

¼ hour = hěn jìn　　½ to ¾ of an hour = bú tài yuǎn

1 hour to 1½ hours = bǐjiào yuǎn　　2 hours = hěn yuǎn

一刻钟（很近）　　半小时到三刻钟（不太远）

一小时到一个半小时（比较远）　　两小时（很远）

A

	宿舍	朋友家	商场	图书馆	书店	学校
学校						
书店						
图书馆						
商场						
朋友家						
宿舍						

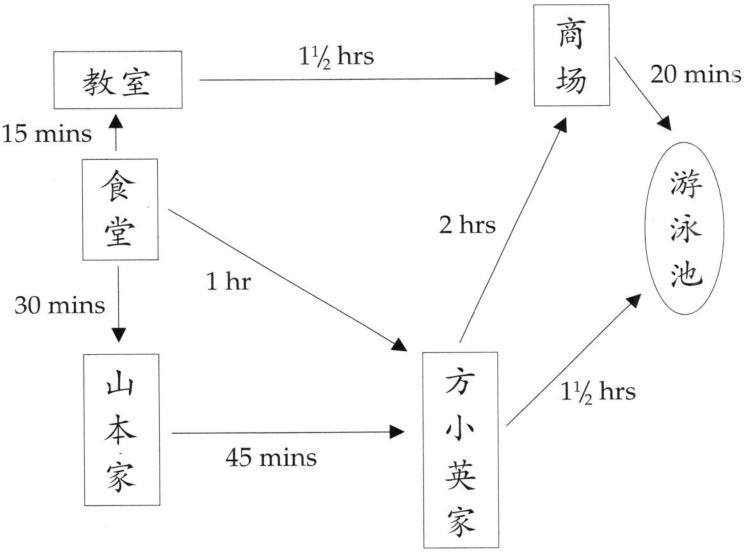

B

	教室	食堂	方小英家	游泳池	商场	山本家
山本家						
商场						
游泳池						
方小英家						
食堂						
教室						

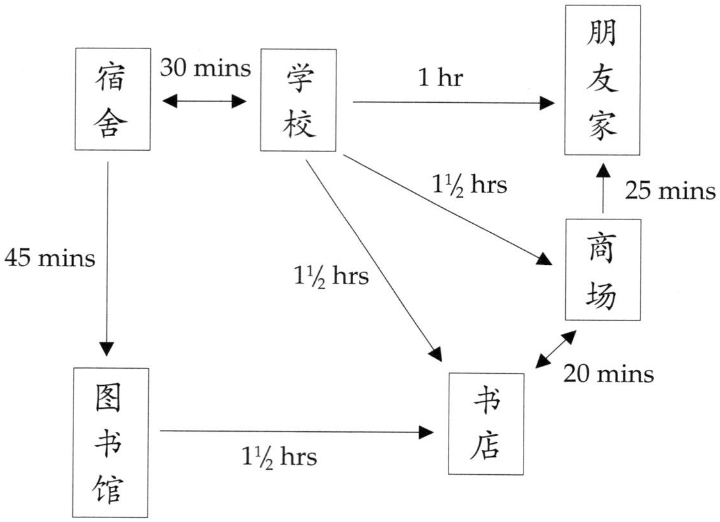

第十二课

这本词典多少钱？

汉字课文

（一）

金中一：今天上午你有时间吗？我们一起去书店，好吗？

方小英：你要买什么？

金中一：我要买一本《汉语小词典》。

方小英：上（个）星期你买了一本，为什么还要买？

金中一：我那本词典前天丢了。

方小英：丢了？你真行！

（二）

金中一：请问，有《汉语小词典》吗？

售货员：对不起，已经卖完了。

金中一：上星期我们来买过，那时候还有呢。

售货员：是。这种词典卖得很快。过几天，您再来看看。

金中一：有英汉词典吗？

售货员：有，有《新英汉词典》。

金中一：能给我们看一看吗？

售货员：可以。

方小英：（看了看）嗯，不错。

金中一：是吗？那我买一本吧。多少钱？

售货员：三十块零五毛八。（金中一拿出一张五十元的人民币）

售货员：您有零钱吗？

金中一：对不起，我没听清楚，你说什么？

方小英：他问你有没有零钱。

金中一：我只有一张五十块的。

售货员：有八分吗？

金中一：请等一等。哦，有，给你。

售货员：谢谢。找您十九块五，请您数一数。(问方小英) 您要买什么书？

方小英：我不买，我来看一看。请问，附近有卖本子和纸的地方吗？

售货员：有。出了这个书店，往右走……

金中一：哦，我去过那个商店。

方小英：我没去过。

金中一：我陪你去。

生词语

1. 钱 qián (n) [块，毛，分，元] money
2. 还 hái (adv) again (future repetition of an action)
3. 前天 qiántiān (n) day before yesterday
4. 丢 diū (v) to lose

   a. 他的电影票丢了。

   b. 我丢了九十块零五毛。
5. 行 xíng (adj) (here:) to be capable. (Often, as here, used ironically.)

   a. 她只学了半年汉语，现在说得很好，写得也很好。她真行。

b. 你昨天丢了一本词典，今天丢了两个本子，真行！

6.	售货员	shòuhuòyuán	(n) [个，位]	salesperson, clerk
7.	已经	yǐjīng	(adv)	already

a. 我已经写好汉字练习了。

b. 新售货员已经来(了)四个月了。

8.	过	guò	(part)	(aspect particle, attached to verbs and adjectives, expresses experience = "have done X")
9.	是	shì	(adj)	yes, right
10.	种	zhǒng	(m)	kind, sort
11.	过	guò	(v)	to pass by, to go by

a. 过几天，我们去新体育馆看看。

b. 我说时间过得真快，可是他说时间过得真慢。

12.	几	jǐ	(pro)	several
13.	嗯	ng	(i)	hm, mm (indicating affirmation or agreement)
14.	不错	búcuò	(adj)	pretty good, not bad; correct
15.	那	nà	(c)	then, in that case
	那么	nàme		

a. 他们都去，那(么)我们也去吧。

b. 这种衣服又便宜又好看。

—— 那(么)我买两件吧。

16.	块	kuài	(m)	dollar; a piece of
17.	毛	máo	(m)	tenth of a dollar, ten cents
18.	元	yuán	(m)	dollar (kuài above is not the normal written form, yuán is. Both are spoken.)

19. 人民币	rénmínbì	(n)	RMB, the designation of China's currency
20. 零钱	língqián	(n)	small change
21. 清楚	qīngchu	(adj)	to be clear

a. 他说得很慢，很清楚。

b. 书上的这个字不清楚，老师，您给我们写一下儿吧。

c. 他昨天没说清楚，你今天问一问他。

22. 只	zhǐ	(adv)	only (usually followed by a quantified noun that is not the subject)

a. 他只有十二块零五分。

b. 我只会说英文，不会说中文。

c. 他只做了作业，没有预习。

23. 分	fēn	(m)	cent
24. 哦	ǒ	(i)	oh (expressing discovery or a new realization)

a. 那边就是天星电影院。

——哦，我去过那儿。

b. 我是张老师的学生大卫。

——哦，你就是大卫。

25. 找	zhǎo	(v)	to give change; to look for

a. 请找我零钱，好吗？

b. 这是找您的五十一块二。

26. 数	shǔ	(v)	to count
27. 纸	zhǐ	(n)	paper
28. 往	wǎng, wàng	(prep)	toward, to (in the direction of)

a. 你找他吗？他往东（边儿）走了。

b. 别往那边儿走，那边儿没有商店。

c. 你往右看，那就是书店。

29. 右	yòu	(n-pw)	right
30. 陪	péi	(v)	to accompany, go along with, keep company

a. 你陪我去散步吧。

b. 明天她一个人在家，你去陪陪她吧。

专有名词

《新英汉词典》 Xīn Yīng Hàn Cídiǎn A New English-Chinese Dictionary

补充生词

1.	百	bǎi	(nu)	hundred
2.	千	qiān	(nu)	thousand
3.	万	wàn	(nu)	ten thousand
4.	角	jiǎo	(m)	written form of fen, "ten cents"
5.	交钱	jiāo qián	(vo)	to pay (money)
6.	信用卡	xìnyòngkǎ	(n)	credit card

语法点

1. Zài 再 and hái 还

"再"和"还"

These adverbs indicate that an action will be repeated. Watch that in general zài is used in declarative sentences for this function, while the interrogative form uses hái. An optative verb can follow hái.

这两个副词都表示动作将要重复。"再"一般用于陈述句。在疑问句中，则用"还"，后面还可以跟着能愿动词。

a. Shòuhuòyuán shuō, "Nèi zhǒng yīfu yǐjīng mài wán le, xiàxīngqī nín zài lái kànkan ba.

售货员说："那种衣服已经卖完了，下星期您再来看看吧。"

The salesperson said, "That kind of clothing is already sold out. Come back again next week to have a look (and see if new stock has come in)."

b. Nǐ chī de tài shǎo, zài chī yìdiǎnr ba.

你吃得太少，再吃一点儿吧。

You ate too little, have some more.

c. Zhèi zhǒng cídiǎn búcuò, wǒ zài mǎi yì běnr gěi wǒ péngyou.

这种词典不错，我再买一本儿给我朋友。

This dictionary isn't bad. I'll buy another to give to my friend.

d. Zhèi zhǒng dōngxi zěnmeyàng? Nǐ hái (yào) chī ma?

这种东西怎么样？你还(要)吃吗？

How is this thing? Do you want to eat more?

e. Nàge dìfang yuǎn bù yuǎn? Tā yǐhòu hái (xiǎng) qù ma?

那个地方远不远？他以后还(想)去吗？

Is that place far? Does he want to go again?

2. Aspect particle guò 过

动态助词"过"

Guò 过, aspect particle indicating that the subject has had the particular experience or has done such and such (one or more times) previously. Because of this, the subject knows the issue, can evaluate it and present views.

"过"表示施事者曾经有过某种经历（一次或多次），因此了解某事，或能对某事作出评论，提出看法。

S + V + 过 + O

a. Tā qùguo Měiguó.

他去过美国。

He has been to the United States.

b. Wǒ qùguo dà túshūguǎn, wǒ zhīdao dà túshūguǎn zài nǎr.

我去过大图书馆，我知道大图书馆在哪儿。

I've been to the main library, and/so know where the main library is. (= because I've been there, I know …)

c. Wǒ xuéguo Zhōngwén, Zhōngwén bú tài nán.

我学过中文，中文不太难。

I've studied Chinese, and it's not so difficult.
(= therefore, I know it's not …)

Méi (you) 没有 appears before the verb in the negative form, and the verbal guò is retained. The affirmative-negative question form is V + guò … méiyou.

否定式是在动词前用上副词"没（有）"，还保留"过"。正反疑问句是把"没有"放在句尾。

S + 没（有）+ V + 过

d. Wǒ méi kànguo nèige diànyǐng, wǒ xiǎng qù kàn.

我没看过那个电影，我想去看。

I haven't seen that film, so would like to see it.

S + V + 过 + O + 没有？

e. Q: Nǐ qùguo Zhāng Lǎoshī jiā méiyou?

你去过张老师家没有？

Have you been to Mrs. Zhang's house?

A: Méi qùguo.

没去过。

No, I haven't.

3. Complement of result

结果补语

This complement, a verb or an adjective, is affixed to the verb to describe the result that an action has created. Note that the completed action <u>le</u> 了 is most often attached.

结果补语是出现在动词后面补充说明动作的结果的。充任补语的是动词或形容词。补语后面常有表示完成的"了"。

S + V + CR (+了) + O

a. Jīntiān tīngxiě de shíhou, wǒ xiěcuò le liǎng ge zì.

今天听写的时候，我写错了两个字。

At dictation today, I wrote two characters wrong.

b. Nǐ de huà wǒ dōu tīngdǒng le.

你的话我都听懂了。

I understand what you say.

In Chinese, both action and result (V + CR) are necessary parts of the expression. The result alone is usually adequate in English, leaving the specific verbal action unstated. Thus, one can say "she finished today's homework" without specifying that she "finished writing" or "doing" it. In contrast, *她完了今天的作业 *<u>Tā wán le jīntiān de zuòyè</u> is WRONG. It must be expressed as <u>Tā zuòwán le jīntiān de zuòyè</u> 她做完了今天的作业.

在汉语里，当要说明一个动作有了结果时，需要用"动词＋结果补语"来表达。而英语往往只用表示结果的那个动词来表达。因此，汉语要说"她做完了今天的作业"，不能说"她完了今天的作业"。英语只需要说："she finished today's homework"，而不必说"finished writing" or "finished doing"。

An action with a result is usually brought to completion. Thus, the construction is negated with méi (yǒu). Only in the case of a hypothetical statement would bù be the negator.

有了结果的动作常常是已经完成了的。因此，否定式一般用"没(有)"。除非在假设句中，才能用"不"否定。

S + 没 (有) + V + CR

c. Wǒmen méiyǒu yuēhǎo jiànmiàn de shíjiān.

我们没有约好见面的时间。

We didn't/haven't arranged a meeting time.

d. Tā méi zuòwán jīntiān de zuòyè.

他没做完今天的作业。

He didn't finish today's homework.

The affirmative-negative question form is either:

正反疑问句有如下两种形式：

V + CR (+ O) + 了 + 没有？

or

V + CR + 了 (+ O) + 没有？

e. Nǐ yùxíhǎo le méiyǒu?

你预习好了没有？

Have you finished (to a good point) preparing?

f. Tā zuòguò le zhàn méiyǒu?

他坐过了站没有？

Did he go past (= ride past) the station?

g. Nǐ tīngqīngchu tā de huà le méiyǒu?

你听清楚他的话了没有？

Did you hear clearly what he said?

4. Reduplication of monosyllabic verbs

单音节动词重叠

Some, NOT ALL, single syllable verbs can be repeated. Repetition indicates that the action is brief or tentative. It carries a lighter, less formal flavor. NOTE that the second syllable is neutralized. Further, yī 一 "one, a" may be inserted between the two syllables.

一部分（而不是全部）单音节动词可以重叠，表示动作的短暂、尝试、轻松、或非正式。要注意的是，第二个音节应读轻声，重叠的音节之间可以插入"一"。

a. Wǒ xiǎng wènwen biéde ren.

我想问问别的人。

I want to ask someone else.

b. Qǐng nǐ děng yi děng.

请你等一等。

Please wait a minute. (or) One moment, please.

In a completed action situation, the le 了 indicating completion comes between the verbs: V le V, V le yī V.

如果动作已经完成，就要在重叠的动词之间插入"了"："动了动"或"动了一动"。

c. Xià kè yǐhòu, tā dǎle dǎ wǎngqiú, jiù qù túshūguǎn le.

下课以后，他打了打网球，就去图书馆了。

After class he played a bit of tennis, then went to the library.

d. Tā kànle yí kàn, juéde bú tài hǎo, méiyou mǎi.

他看了一看，觉得不太好，没有买。

He took a look, felt it wasn't very good, so didn't buy it.

5. Units of money

钱的计算单位

Chinese currency units are yuán 元 , jiăo 角 and fēn 分. In speech, the parallel set kuài 块, máo 毛 and fēn 分 is most commonly used.

中国的币制单位是“元、角、分”，口语中经常使用的是“块、毛、分”。

$2	èr yuán 二元	liăng kuài (qián) 两块(钱)
$.50	wŭ jiăo 五角	wŭ máo (qián) 五毛(钱)
$.09	jiŭ fēn 九分	jiŭ fēn (qián) 九分(钱)
$1.20	yì yuán èr jiăo 一元二角	yí kuài èr 一块二
$17.28	shíqī yuán èr jiăo bā fēn 十七元二角八分	shíqī kuài èr máo bā 十七块二毛八
$20.05	èrshí yuán líng wŭ fēn 二十元零五分	èrshí kuài líng wŭ fēn 二十块零五分
$30.60	sānshí yuán (líng) liù jiăo 三十元(零)六角	sānshí kuài líng liù máo 三十块零六毛

NOTE that with simpler, one unit figures, such as the first three above, the noun qián 钱 "money" may close the spoken form. Qián is unnecessary if there are two or more units. In everyday conversation, the final measure word can be omitted if the result is clear, as with $17.28 above.

注意：如果钱数中只包含一个单位，后边可以用一个“钱”字(如上述前三例)，如果有两个以上的单位，后边不需要用“钱”。而且，在口语里，只要不会产生误解，最后的量词也可以省略。

NOTES 注释

1. Nǐ zhēn xíng! 你真行！"You're really something!" Xíng 行 means "able" or "capable" and here is used sarcastically; literally "You're really capable".

   "你真行！"字面意思是"你真能干！""行"表示有能力，能干。这里是一句反话，含讽刺意味。

2. Note the use of jǐ 几 in the lesson text as an indefinite. It has the following uses: jǐ + measure word = "a few"; zhejǐ 这几 + measure word = "these"; shíjǐ 十几 + measure word = "ten odd, ten some", and so forth. Recall that jǐ is generally used in reference to numbers within the one to ten range.

   注意："几"在课文里表示不定量，它的用法："几 + 量词" = "一些"，"这几 + 量词" = "这些"，"十几 + 量词" = "十多"等等。"几"一般表示从一到十的数目。

3. Búcuò 不错 can mean either (1) "right, not incorrect" or (2) the commonly uttered descriptive "pretty good".

   "不错"有两个意思：(1) 对，正确；(2) 通常用来表示不坏，好。

词组和句子

1. 两块钱 (2.00元)　两毛钱 (0.20元)　两 (二) 分钱 (0.02元)
   一块两 (二) 毛五 (1.25元)　二十二块三毛七 (22.37元)
   十二块零两 (二) 分 (12.02元)　十块零五毛 (10.50元)
   九十块零八分 (90.08元)　九十块零两毛 (90.20元)

2. (1) 做完　学完　听写完　介绍完
   复习完　练习完　没预习完　没听完
   没卖完

   (2) 预习好　复习好　休息好　穿好

没写好　没做好　约好朋友　教好学生

订好票　没学好中文

(3) 写错　听错　看错　没说错

没做错　买错了词典　打错了电话　没找错钱

没拿错本子

(4) 做对　找对　没说对　没数对钱

(5) 听清楚　问清楚　没说清楚

写清楚你的名字　没看清楚他写的字

(6) 听懂　没看懂

(7) 教会　没教会

(8) 回到　看到　买到　找到

走到学校门口儿　没听到他说的话

3. 你已经订了两张电影票了，为什么还要订？
4. 生词和课文下午我都复习了，不过，晚上我还要复习一下儿。
5. 大卫上午已经打了一个小时网球了，下午他还打吗？
6. 这种东西真好，我还想吃。
7. 我没上过马老师的课，你上过没有？马老师的课怎么样？
8. 那个女售货员说，她穿过这种鞋，这种鞋又便宜又好。
9. 你去过那个商场没有？远不远？
10. 我们已经学完了第十二课，明天学第十三课。
11. 生词太多，昨天晚上我没复习完。
12. 今天听写了二十个字，我都写对了。
13. 书上边是不是你的名字？你看错了没有？
14. 你走错了，商店在东边儿，这是西边儿。
15. 他写了一个什么字？我没看清楚。

16. 你去问问张老师，要问清楚明天下午几点上课。

17. 你穿好衣服，我们去散散步，好不好？

18. 方小英订好电影票了没有？

19. 老师说，她一定要教会每一个同学。

20. 同学们说，如果我们好好儿学，就一定能学好。

21. 看懂课文以后，再做练习。

22. 你接完电话来找我一下儿。

23. 那种箱子已经卖完了，你买别的箱子吧。

24. 我不会游泳，你教教我吧！

25. 他只看了看那本书，没有买。

参考资料

拼音课文

Zhèi běn cídiǎn duōshao qián?

(I)

Jīn Zhōngyī: Jīntian shàngwǔ nǐ yǒu shíjiān ma? Wǒmen yìqǐ qù shūdiàn, hǎo ma?

Fāng Xiǎoyīng: Nǐ yào mǎi shénme?

Jīn Zhōngyī: Wǒ yào mǎi yì běn *Hànyǔ Xiǎo Cídiǎn*.

Fāng Xiǎoyīng: Shàng (ge) xīngqī nǐ mǎile yì běn, wèishénme hái yào mǎi?

Jīn Zhōngyī: Wǒ nèi běn cídiǎn qiántian diū le.

Fāng Xiǎoyīng: Diū le? Nǐ zhēn xíng!

(II)

Jīn Zhōngyī: Qǐngwèn, yǒu *Hànyǔ Xiǎo Cídiǎn* ma?

Shòuhuòyuán: Duìbuqǐ, yǐjīng màiwán le.

Jīn Zhōngyī: Shàng xīngqī wǒmen lái mǎiguo, nèi shíhou hái yǒu ne.

Shòuhuòyuán: Shì. Zhèi zhǒng cídiǎn mài de hěn kuài. Guò jǐ tiān, nín zài lái kànkan.

Jīn Zhōngyī: Yǒu Yīng Hàn cídiǎn ma?

Shòuhuòyuán: Yǒu, yǒu *Xīn Yīng Hàn Cídiǎn.*

Jīn Zhōngyī: Néng gěi wǒmen kàn yi kàn ma?

Shòuhuòyuán: Kěyǐ.

Fāng Xiǎoyīng: (Kànle kàn) Ng, búcuò.

Jīn Zhōngyī: Shì ma? Nà wǒ mǎi yì běn ba. Duōshao qián?

Shòuhuòyuán: Sānshi kuài líng wǔ máo bā. (Jīn Zhōngyī náchū yì zhāng wǔshi kuài de Rénmínbì)

Shòuhuòyuán: Nín yǒu língqián ma?

Jīn Zhōngyī: Duìbuqǐ, wǒ méi tīng qīngchu, nǐ shuō shénme?

Fāng Xiǎoyīng: Tā wèn ni yǒu méiyǒu língqián?

Jīn Zhōngyī: Wǒ zhǐ yǒu yì zhāng wǔshi kuài de.

Shòuhuòyuán: Yǒu bā fēn ma?

Jīn Zhōngyī: Qǐng děng yi děng. O, yǒu, gěi ni.

Shòuhuòyuán: Xièxie. Zhǎo nín shíjiǔ kuài wǔ, qǐng nǐ shǔ yi shǔ. (Wèn Fāng Xiǎoyīng) Nín yào mǎi shénme shū?

Fāng Xiǎoyīng: Wǒ bù mǎi, wǒ lái kàn yi kàn. Qǐngwèn, fùjìn yǒu mài běnzi hé zhǐ de dìfang ma?

Shòuhuòyuán: Yǒu. Chūle zhège shūdiàn, wàng yòu zǒu …

Jīn Zhōngyī: O, wǒ qùguo nàge shāngdiàn.

Fāng Xiǎoyīng: Wǒ méi qùguo.

Jīn Zhōngyī: Wǒ péi ni qù.

英译课文

How much is this dictionary?

(I)

Kim Chung-il: Do you have time this morning? Let's go to the bookstore together.

Fang Xiaoying: What do you want to buy?

Kim Chung-il: I want to buy a copy of the *Concise Chinese Dictionary*.

Fang Xiaoying: You bought one last week, why are you buying another one?

Kim Chung-il: I lost that one the day before yesterday.

Fang Xiaoying: Lost it? You're really something!

(II)

Kim Chung-il: Excuse me, do you have the *Concise Chinese Dictionary*?

Salesperson: Sorry, we're sold out.

Kim Chung-il: We came last week and it was still here then.

Salesperson: Yes, but this sort of dictionary sells quickly. Check again in a few days.

Kim Chung-il: Do you have an English-Chinese dictionary?

Salesperson: Yes, we have the *New English-Chinese Dictionary*.

Kim Chung-il: Can you let us have a look?

Salesperson: Sure.

Fang Xiaoying: (Looks at it) Hm, not bad.

Kim Chung-il: Oh? I'll buy one then. How much?

Salesperson: $30.58. (Kim Chung-il takes out one 50 RMB bill.)

Salesperson: Do you have change?

Kim Chung-il: Excuse me, I didn't understand. What did you say?

Fang Xiaoying: He asked you if you had change.

Kim Chung-il: I only have that one RMB 50.

Salesperson: Do you have eight cents?

Kim Chung-il: Just a minute, please. Mm, yes, here you are.

Salesperson: Thanks, here's $19.50 change. Please count it. (Asks Fang Xiaoying) Is there a book that you'd like to buy?

Fang Xiaoying: No, I just came to look. Could you tell me if there is someplace nearby that sells notebooks and paper?

Salesperson: Yes, go right when you get out of this store ...

Kim Chung-il: Oh, I've been to that store.

Fang Xiaoying: I haven't.

Kim Chung-il: I'll go along with you.

课堂活动

I. Calculating money

钱的计算

Pairs of students ask and answer questions of each other, following the example below. A in the pair is given chart A and B chart B. When B answers, A jots down those answers, and so on.

二人一组，互相问答。A持表A问B，B按表B回答，A记下答案。B持表B问A，A按表A回答，B记下答案。

Example:

A: Xié duōshao qián yì shuāng?

鞋多少钱一双？

B: Jiǔshísì kuài wǔ yì shuāng. Nǐ mǎi jǐ shuāng?

94.50（九十四块五）一双，你买几双？

A: Wǒ mǎi yì shuāng, zhè shì jiǔshíwǔ kuài.

我买一双，这是95.00（九十五块）。

B: Zhǎo nǐ wǔ máo qián. Xièxie!

找你0.50（五毛钱）。谢谢！

A	多少钱＋“一”＋量词	“几”＋量词	这是…钱	找你
(例) 鞋		1	95.00	
电影票	8.00			18.00
本子		3	2.00	
纸	0.15			2.50
小词典		1	20.00	
中文书	11.88			3.12
小箱子		1	80.00	
英汉词典	22.90			0.20
游泳衣		2	58.00	

B	多少钱＋“一”＋量词	“几”＋量词	这是…钱	找你
(例) 鞋	94.50			0.50
电影票		4	50.00	
本子	0.63			0.11
纸		50	10	
小词典	18.20			1.80
中文书		1	15.00	
小箱子	79.80			0.20
英汉词典		2	46.00	
游泳衣	28.6			0.80

II. Aspect particle guò

动态助词“过”

Students group into fours. Each student is given a chart and a slip showing three responses. Students with chart A ask the other students questions (a) and (b) from chart A. Those three students answer, selecting the appropriate response from their slip. A fills in those answers on his/her chart, then students B, C and D ask questions in similar fashion in rotation. Finally, each student will relate in connected form the information given by the answers as filled in on the charts.

四人一组，每人有一张表格卡片及三组答案。持卡片A的同学先按照表格中的(a)，(b)两个问题向同组同学提问，被提问的人要从三组答案中选出最合适的回答。持卡片A的同学需将答案填在表上。然后由持卡片B，C，D的人轮流提问，做法同前。最后，每人根据表上所填向老师及全班同学转述。

Example: Chart X

Question 问题 / Name 姓名	a. Nǐ zài nàge túshūguǎn kànguo shū ma? 你在那个图书馆看过书吗？	b. Nàge túshūguǎn zěnmeyàng? 那个图书馆怎么样？
Dàwèi 大卫	kànguo 看过	yòu dà yòu hǎo 又大又好
Ānnà 安娜	méi zài nàge túshūguǎn kànguo 没在那个图书馆看过	(bù zhīdào) (不知道)
Shānběn 山本	kànguo 看过	shū hěn duō, yě hěn xīn 书很多，也很新

Recount: Ānnà méi zài nèige túshūguǎn kànguo shū. Tā bù zhīdào nèige túshūguǎn zěnmeyàng. Dàwèi hé Shānběn dōu zài nàr kànguo shū. Tāmen shuō nèige túshūguǎn yòu dà yòu hǎo. Shū hěn duō, yě hěn xīn.

转述：安娜没在那个图书馆看过书，她不知道那个图书馆怎么样。大卫和山本都在那儿看过书，他们说那个图书馆又大又好。书很多，也很新。

卡片A

问题 / 姓名	a. 你在那个饭馆儿吃过饭没有？	b. 那个饭馆儿怎么样？
B		
C		
D		

A 对别人提问的答案：

回答B：a. 没在… + 买过	b.（不知道）
回答D：a. 上过	b. 很新
回答C：a. 游过	b. 很好，离学生宿舍很近

卡片B

问题 / 姓名	a. 你在那个商店买过东西没有？	b. 那个商店怎么样？
A		
C		
D		

B 对别人提问的答案：

回答A：a. 吃过	b. 很好，离我们学校也不远
回答D：a. 没在…+上过	b.（不知道）
回答C：a. 游过	b. 很大，游泳的人也不多

卡片C

问题 / 姓名	a. 你在那个游泳池游过泳没有？	b. 那个游泳池怎么样？
A		
B		
D		

C 对别人提问的答案：

回答B：a. 买过	b. 东西很多
回答C：a. 上过	b. 又大又好
回答D：a. 没在…+吃过	b.（不知道）

卡片D

问题 / 姓名	a. 你在那个教室上过课没有？	b. 那个教室怎么样？
A		
B		
C		

D 对别人提问的答案：

回答A：a. 吃过	b. 那个饭馆儿的饭很好吃
回答C：a. 没在…+游过	b.（不知道）
回答B：a. 买过	b. 很大，东西也很便宜

III. Reduplicated verbs

动词重叠

Use reduplicated verbs in answering the questions. Please refer to the illustration below.

请用动词重叠的形式来回答问题。可以参考下面的图画。

Example:

A: Xīngqītiān nǐ xǐhuan zuò shénme?

星期天你喜欢做什么？

B: Wǒ xǐhuan qù shūdiàn mǎi yi mǎi shū. (use "VV" or "V yī V")

我喜欢去书店买一买书。(用"VV"或"V一V")

A: Zuótian shī xīngqírì, nǐ zuò shénme le?

昨天是星期日，你做什么了？

B: Zuótian wǒ qù shūdiàn mǎile mǎi shū. (use "V le V")

昨天我去书店买了买书。(用"V了V")

IV. Complement of Result

结果补语

Pairs of students question and answer each other in dialogue. Students can freely create what they wish for the underlined portion.

二人一组，互相问答，进行对话。(划线部分可由学生自由发挥。)

Example 1:

A: Tā xiě de zì, nǐ kàn qīngchu le méiyou?

他写的字，你看清楚了没有？

B: Tā xiě de zì, wǒ méi kàn qīngchu, nǐ kàn qīngchu le ma?

他写的字，我没看清楚。你看清楚了吗？

A: Wǒ kàn qīngchu le.

我看清楚了。

B: Nǐ kěyǐ gàosù wǒ tā xiě de shì shénme ma?

你可以告诉我他写的是什么吗？

A: Dāngrán kěyǐ, tā xiě de shì "jīntiān" de "tiān".

当然可以。他写的是"今天"的"天"。

(1) B: Tā shuō de huà, nǐ tīngdǒng le méiyou?

他说的话，你听懂了没有？

A: ______________________________?

B: ______________________。

A: ______________________________?

B: ______________________________。

(2) A: Lǎoshī xiě de nèi jǐ ge shēngcí, nǐ kàn qīngchu le méiyou?

老师写的那几个生词，你看清楚了没有？

B: ______________________________?

A: ____ 。

B: ____ ?

A: ____ 。

(3) B: Lǎoshī wèn de wèntí, nǐ huídá duì le méiyou?

老师问的问题，你回答对了没有？

A: ____ ?

B: ____ 。

A: ____ ?

B: ____ 。

Example 2:

A: Jīntiān de zuòyè, nǐ zuòwán le méiyou?

今天的作业，你做完了没有？

B: Jīntiān de zuòyè wǒ méi zuòwán, nǐ zuòwán le méiyou?

今天的作业，我没做完。你做完了吗？

A: Wǒ zuòwán le. Nǐ wèi shénme méi zuòwán?

我做完了。你为什么没做完？

B: Wǒ xiàwǔ qù dǎ wǎngqiú le.

我下午去打网球了。

(1) A: Jīntiān de shēngcí, nǐ fùxí wán le méiyou?

今天的生词，你复习完了没有？

B: ____ ?

A: ____ ?

B: ____ 。

(2) B: Dì-shísānkè de kèwén, nǐ yùxí hǎo le méiyou?

第十三课的课文，你预习好了没有？

A: ____？

B: ____？

A: ____。

(3) A: Nèi kè de Hànzì nǐ xiěhuì le méiyou?

那课的汉字你写会了没有？

B: ____？

A: ____？

B: ____。

阅读练习

新新商场离学校不远，就在学校附近，出了学校，往东走，走一刻钟就到了。这个商场不很大，可是东西比较多。

一楼是卖书的地方。我有的时候去看看有什么新书、好书，如果有我喜欢的，就买一本。二楼是卖衣服的地方。那儿的衣服都很好看，有男人的，也有女人的，可是不便宜。三楼卖鞋。有的鞋很贵，有的鞋比较便宜。四楼卖箱子。买箱子的人不太多，不过，他们的箱子都不错。

这个商场我来过很多次，可是，小王和小张还没来过。下午我陪他们来看看。今天是星期日，人很多。小王买了一件衣服，不太贵，五十五块二。小王有两张五十块的人民币，售货员问他有没有零钱。小王数了数自己的零钱，说："有，给你五十五块二，不用找钱了。"小张买了一双鞋，这双鞋又便宜又好看。我呢？我买了一本汉英词典，我的那本丢了。

买完东西，五点半，我说："我们在外边儿吃饭吧！"小王说他已经和朋友约好了，得去朋友家。小张说他得回宿舍等一个电话。我想：自己一个人在外边儿吃饭，没有意思。就跟小张一起回学校了。

祝你生日快乐

汉字课文

马　丁：金中一，安娜找你，她在山本那儿，让你去一下儿。

金中一：到山本那儿去？好吧。

(金中一到了山本的房间)

金中一：欸，你们怎么都在这儿？张老师，您也在这儿！

安　娜：一、二、三！

大　家：祝你生日快乐！

金中一：哦，你们叫我来，就是要给我过生日啊！谢谢，谢谢。

马　丁：大家随便坐吧。张老师，您坐这儿。你们喝点儿什么？

方小英：我们自己来吧。

老　师：金中一，这是我送给你的生日礼物。

金中一：《汉语小词典》！太好了！谢谢老师。我的那本丢了。老师，您怎么知道我的词典丢了？

老　师：(看方小英，笑) 这是个秘密，不能告诉你。

安　娜：昨天晚上我给你做了一张生日卡，送给你。祝你生日快乐！

金中一：真好看！你用了很多时间吧？

安　娜：差不多一个晚上。

方小英：我也送你一件礼物。

金中一：啊，一支笔！真漂亮！谢谢你。

马　　丁：大卫和山本到商店去买生日蛋糕了，他们一会儿就回来。

（大卫和山本回来了）

方小英：他们来了。

马　　丁：生日蛋糕来了！

山　　本：什么生日蛋糕来了！谁是生日蛋糕？（大家都笑了）

马　　丁：金中一，快切蛋糕吧。我饿了。

方小英：还没唱生日歌儿呢！

大　　卫："祝你生日快乐……"

大　　家："祝你生日快乐……"

生词语

1.	祝	zhù	(v)	to wish, offer wishes
2.	生日	shēngri	(n) [个]	birthday
3.	快乐	kuàilè	(adj)	to be happy
4.	让	ràng	(v)	to let, to have do (in the sense of "to cause to do")

a. 马丁让（叫）大家去他的房间坐坐。

b. 老师让（叫）我们下午交作业。

5.	房间	fángjiān	(n) [个]	room
6.	欸	é; éi	(i)	(surprise exclamation)

a. 欸，我的本子呢？你看到没有？

b. 欸，山本怎么没来？他去哪儿了？

7.	叫	jiào	(v)	to have do (cause to do)
8.	过	guò	(v)	go through the process of, to celebrate

9.	大家	dàjiā	(pro)	everyone
10.	随便	suíbiàn	(adj)	to be casual, informal; as one likes

a. 我们在他家很随便。

b. 他不是一个很随便的人。

c. 你想喝点儿什么？—— 随便。

d. 请大家随便坐，请随便吃一点儿。

e. 上课的时候，别随便说话。

11.	坐	zuò	(v)	to sit

a. 你有时间到我家坐一坐。

b. 你坐这儿，我坐那儿，他坐我旁边儿。

12.	喝	hē	(v)	to drink
13.	自己	zìjǐ	(pro)	oneself

a. 这是我自己的书，不是图书馆的。

b. 自己的东西，自己拿。

14.	来	lái	(v)	(replaces another verb, creating a familiar or casual tone)

a. 我饿了，先来块蛋糕，等一会儿再吃饭。

b. 这种笔真便宜，我来一支，你也来一支吧！

15.	送	sòng	(v)	to present, give (a gift)
16.	礼物	lǐwù	(n) [件，个]	gift, present
17.	笑	xiào	(v)	to laugh, smile
18.	秘密	mìmì	(adj, n) [个]	secret
19.	生日卡	shēngrìkǎ	(n) [张，个]	birthday card
20.	用	yòng	(v)	to use, to spend

a. 你每天做作业，用多少时间？

b. 你用过这种笔吗？

c. 你会用这本词典吗？

21.	差不多	chàbuduō	(adj)	almost, nearly

a. 这两种词典差不多，都不太好。

b. 我今天用了差不多八十块钱。

c. 老师说的话，我差不多都懂。

22.	支	zhī	(m)	measure for slender objects, e.g., chopsticks, pens
23.	笔	bǐ	(n) [支]	writing instrument
24.	漂亮	piàoliang	(adj)	to be attractive, pretty
25.	蛋糕	dàngāo	(n) [个，块]	cake
26.	切	qiē	(v)	to cut

a. 谁来切蛋糕？—— 我来切吧。

b. 他切得又快又好。

27.	饿	è	(v)	to be hungry

a. 我太饿了，有吃的东西吗？

b. 我不饿，你们饿不饿？

28.	唱歌儿	chàng gēr	(vo)	to sing
	唱	chàng	(v)	to sing
	歌儿	gēr	(n) [个，支]	song

补充生词

1.	岁	suì	(m)	years of age
2.	铅笔	qiānbǐ	(n)	pencil
3.	圆珠笔	yuánzhūbǐ	(n)	ball pen

语法点

1. Pivotal sentences

兼语句

Pivotal sentences have predicates which include two verbs. The object of the first verb is the subject of the second. Formulaically put, they look like this:

兼语句的谓语中包含两个主要动词，而且第一个动词的宾语同时又是第二个动词的主语，用句型表示就是：

$$S_1 + V_1 + O_1 (S_2) + V_2 + O_2$$

The first verb is most often of the "cause to" or "have X do" type.

第一个动词常常是表示使令意义的“请”、“让”、“叫”……等。

a. Lǎoshī ràng wǒ huídá jǐ ge wèntí.

老师让我回答几个问题。

The teacher has/had me answer a few questions.

b. Shòuhuòyuán qǐng Fāng Xiǎoyīng shǔ yi shǔ qián.

售货员请方小英数一数钱。

The sales clerk asks/asked Fang Xiaoying to count the change.

c. Lǎoshī jiào nǐ qù yíxiàr.

老师叫你去一下儿。

The teacher wants you to go by.

d. Dàwèi qǐng nǐ jīntiān xiàwǔ gěi tā dǎ ge diànhuà.

大卫请你今天下午给他打个电话。

David asked you to phone him this afternoon.

2. Gěi 给 as a preposition, "to, for"

介词"给"

Preposition + object constructions with gěi 给 are often adverbial adjuncts. They are similar to "for ..." or "to ..." clauses in English.
由介词"给"组成的介宾结构在句中经常作状语。相当于英语的"to"、"for"。

I. "To":

a. Jīn Zhōngyī gěi Zhāng Lǎoshī dǎle yí ge diànhuà.
金中一给张老师打了一个电话。
Kim Chung-il telephoned (to) Mrs. Zhang.

b. Tā gěi wǒ nálái yí kuài dàngāo.
他给我拿来一块蛋糕。
He brings (to) me a piece of cake.

c. Zhāng Lǎoshī yào gěi wǒmen shuō yí ge gùshi.
张老师要给我们说一个故事。
Mrs. Zhang is going to tell (to) us a story.

II. "For":

d. Nǐ gěi nǐ zìjǐ qǐng jià le ma?
你给你自己请假了吗？
Did you ask for leave for yourself?

e. Nǐ gěi tā wèn yi wèn, tā shénme shíhou kěyi lái xuéxí.
你给他问一问，他什么时候可以来学习。
Ask for him (= on his behalf) as to when he can come to study.

f. Xīngqīrì wǒ gěi nǐmen zuò Zhōngguófàn, hǎo bu hǎo?
星期日我给你们做中国饭，好不好？
I'll make Chinese food for you on Sunday, all right?

3. <u>Gěi</u> 给 as complement of result

结果补语"给"

The basic meaning is "give". Through various actions (handing over, presenting, etc.), the result is that someone is given something. In such a context, the verb and complement may take indirect and direct objects.

动词"给"的基本词义是"give"，用在别的动词后面作结果补语时，表示交与、付出等意义。"动词 + 给"总含有使某人得到某些东西的意思，后面可以带双宾语。

S + V + 给 + Indirect O + Direct O

a. Tā jiāogěi lǎoshī bā ge běnzi.

他交给老师八个本子。

He handed over eight notebooks to the teacher.

b. Fāng Xiǎoyīng sònggěi tā yí jiàn hěn hǎokàn de yīfu.

方小英送给她一件很好看的衣服。

Fang Xiaoying gave her an attractive article of clothing.

4. Simple directional complements

简单趋向补语

The attachment of a <u>lái</u> 来 "come" or <u>qù</u> 去 "go" to verbs is a distinctive feature of Chinese. These directionals serve to indicate whether an action "comes" toward the speaker or "goes" away from the speaker. We call them simple directional complements in contrast to more complex directionals (e.g., "down onto" or "upwards" [in a direction toward the speaker]) which will be introduced later.

动词"来"和"去"常常用在别的动词后表示动作的趋向，称为简单趋向补语。如果动作向着说话人进行，用"来"，如果离开说话人，用"去"。以后我们还将进一步学习复合趋向补语的用法。

a. Tā shànglái le.

他上来了。

He came up. (toward the speaker)

b. Tā chūqù le.

他出去了。

He went out. (away from the speaker)

c. Tā chūlái le.

她出来了。

She went out. (toward the speaker)

NOTE usage when the verb + complement construction has an object.
注意：如果动词有宾语，有两种情况。

I. When the object is a place, it comes before the <u>lái</u> or <u>qù</u>.
处所宾语要放在“来”或“去”之前。

S + V + O + CDI

a. Tā huí jiā qù le.

他回家去了。

He returned home. (away from the speaker)

b. Tā huí jiā lái le.

他回家来了。

He returned home. (toward the speaker)

c. Ānnà dào jiàoshì qù le.

安娜到教室去了。

Anna went to the classroom. (where the speaker is not)

d. Ānnà dào jiàoshì lái le.

安娜到教室来了。

Anna came to the classroom. (where the speaker is)

II. When the object is a thing, it may either come before the lái or qù or after them.
一般指事物的宾语，既可放在“来”或“去”之前，也可放在“来”或“去”之后。

S + V + CDI + O

a. Tā jīntiān nálái le yì běn xīn cídiǎn.
他今天拿来了一本新词典。
He brought a new dictionary today.

b. Qǐng dàjiā míngtiān ná *Hànyǔ Xiǎo Cídiǎn* lái.
请大家明天拿《汉语小词典》来。
Will everyone please bring *The Concise Chinese Dictionary* tomorrow.

c. Tāmen sòngqù yí ge hěn dà de shēngri dàngāo.
他们送去一个很大的生日蛋糕。
They are sending a big birthday cake.

d. Tā hòutiān guò shēngri. Wǒ xiǎng míngtiān gěi tā sòng yí jiàn lǐwù qù.
她后天过生日。我想明天给她送一件礼物去。
Her birthday is day after tomorrow. I think I'll bring a gift to her tomorrow.

If an action is completed, the object is most often placed after the directional. If the action will be realized in the future, the object is often placed before the directional.
如果动作已经完成，事物宾语多放在“来”或“去”之后，动作尚未完成，常常放在“来”或“去”之前。

NOTES 注释

1. Tā zài Shānběn nàr 她在山本那儿 “She is there where Yamamoto is”. Zhèr and nàr can be added to nouns essentially making place words out of

them, with zhèr referring to items close to the speaker and nàr items farther away. E.g., Tā dào Mădīng nàr qù le 她到马丁那儿去了 "He went over there where Martin is". Nĭde cídiăn zài wŏ zhèr 你的词典在我这儿 "Your dictionary is here where I am".

在一般名词之后用上"这儿"或"那儿"就可以成为一个处所词。近指用"这儿"，远指用"那儿"。如"她到马丁那儿去了"，"你的词典在我这儿"。

2. Zěnme 怎么 "why", an interrogative about the same as wèishénme 为什么, just a shade more colloquial.

"怎么"跟"为什么"意思相同，只是更口语化。

3. Wŏmen zìjĭ lái ba 我们自己来吧 "We'll serve ourselves". Lái substitutes for a more specific verb, much like "do" might in English. In this case, it refers to the picking up of the wine bottle or the pouring of the wine.

"我们自己来吧"，汉语里的"来"能代替一些意义更具体的动词，很像英语里的"do"。在本课是指(自己去)拿酒或倒酒。

4. Tài hăo le 太好了, a fixed expression meaning "terrific" or "great".

"太好了！"是一个固定用法，意思是"太棒了"、"妙极了"。

5. A 啊. A modal particle placed at a pause point or the end of an utterance to indicate a range of feelings, in this case (jiùshi yào gěo wŏ guò shēngrì a 就是要给我过生日啊) the sense of "Oh so that's it".

语气助词"啊"可以用在句尾或句中停顿处，表示各种不同的语气或感情。本课是表示一种感叹的语气，有"原来如此"的意思。

词组和句子

1. 老师让我们下课以后问问题。
2. 张老师叫我们明天拿词典来。
3. 你拿的是什么东西？让我看一看。
4. 今天他过生日，他请我们到他家去吃饭。

5. 他不让我们送他礼物。
6. 售货员请我们到那边儿看一看。
7. 安娜叫我坐她旁边儿。
8. 他让我告诉他什么时候有时间。
9. 他只给了小王几本中文书，没给英文书。
10. 你只给了小王几本中文书，没给小张。
11. 如果你去书店，给我买一本《汉语小词典》，好吗？
12. 今天晚上我得给老师打个电话，请一天假。
13. 你给我拿一点儿吃的东西来，我饿了。
14. 她交给我五十块钱，叫我给她买几张好看的生日卡。
15. 小王卖给我很多旧书。
16. 我认识一位很好的中文老师，我很想介绍给你。
17. 他们买来了一个很大的生日蛋糕，送给金中一，给他过生日。
18. 请你拿一张纸来，我想让大家写一下自己的名字。
19. 小英不在家，她到商场去了，大概一个小时以后回来。
20. 马丁到山本那儿去了，不在我这儿。
21. 我看到他从图书馆出来了，现在大概回家去了。
22. 你从学校出去以后，往南，差不多走五分钟，就到那个商店了。

参考资料

拼音课文

Zhù nǐ shēngrì kuàilè

Mǎdīng: Jīn Zhōngyī, Ānnà zhǎo ni. Tā zài Shānběn nàr, ràng nǐ qù yíxiàr.

Jīn Zhōngyī:	Dào Shānběn nàr qù? Hǎo ba.

(Jīn Zhōngyī dàole Shānběn de fángjiān)

Jīn Zhōngyī:	Ế, nǐmen zěnme dōu zài zhèr? Zhāng lǎoshī, nín yě zài zhèr!
Ānnà:	Yī, èr, sān!
dàjiā:	Zhù nǐ shēngrì kuàilè!
Jīn Zhōngyī:	Ò, nǐmen jiào wǒ lái, jiùshi yào gěi wo guò shēngri a! Xièxie, Xièxie.
Mǎdīng:	Dàjiā suíbiàn zuò ba. Zhāng lǎoshī, nín zuò zhèr. Nǐmen hē diǎnr shénme?
Fāng Xiǎoyīng:	Wǒmen zìjǐ lái ba.
Zhāng lǎoshī:	Jīn Zhōngyī, zhè shi wǒ sònggei nǐ de shēngri lǐwù.
Jīn Zhōngyī:	*Hànyǔ Xiǎo Cídiǎn*! Tài hǎo le! Xièxie lǎoshī. Wǒ de nèi běn diū le. Lǎoshī, nín zěnme zhīdao wǒ de cídiǎn diū le?
Zhāng lǎoshī:	(Kàn Fāng Xiǎoyīng, xiào) Zhè shi ge mìmi, bù néng gàosu ni.
Ānnà:	Zuótian wǎnshang wǒ gěi nǐ zuòle yì zhāng shēngrikǎ, sònggei nǐ. Zhù nǐ shēngri kuàilè.
Jīn Zhōngyī:	Zhēn hǎokàn! Nǐ yòngle hěn duō shíjiān ba?
Ānnà:	Chàbuduō yí ge wǎnshang.
Fāng Xiǎoyīng:	Wǒ yě sòng nǐ yí jiàn lǐwù.
Jīn Zhōngyī:	À, yì zhī bǐ! Zhēn piàoliang! Xièxie nǐ.
Mǎdīng:	Dàwèi hé Shānběn dào shāngdiàn qù mǎi shēngri dàngāo le, tāmen yìhuǐr jiù huílai.

(Dàwèi hé Shānběn huílai le)

Fāng Xiǎoyīng:	Tāmen lái le.
Mǎdīng:	Shēngri dàngāo lái le!
Shānběn:	Shénme shēngri dàngāo lái le! Shéi shi shēngri dàngāo? (dàjiā dōu xiào le)
Mǎdīng:	Jīn Zhōngyī, kuài qiē dàngāo ba. Wǒ è le.

Fāng Xiǎoyīng: Hái méi chàng shēngri gēr ne!

Dàwèi: "Zhù nǐ shēngri kuàilè ..."

dàjiā: "Zhù nǐ shēngri kuàilè ..."

英译课文

Happy Birthday to you

Martin: Kim Chung-il, Anna's looking for you. She's in Yamamoto's room and wants you to go over for a minute.

Kim Chung-il: Go to Yamamoto's room? All right.

(Kim goes to Yamamoto's room)

Kim Chung-il: Hey, what are you doing here? Mrs. Zhang, you're here, too!

Anna: One, two, three!

Group: Happy Birthday!

Kim Chung-il: Ah, you got me here for my birthday! Thanks, thank you!

Martin: Sit down everyone! Please sit here, Mrs. Zhang. What would you all like to drink?

Fang Xiaoying: We'll serve ourselves.

Teacher: Kim Chung-il, this is my birthday present for you.

Kim Chung-il: A *Concise Chinese Dictionary*! This is great! Thank you! I lost mine. Mrs. Zhang, how did you know that my dictionary was lost?

Teacher: (Looking at Fang Xiaoying, laughing) It's a secret. I can't tell you.

Anna: Here, I made a birthday card for you last night. Happy birthday!

Kim Chung-il: Neat, it must have taken you a long time!

Anna: Almost all night!

Fang Xiaoying: Here's a gift from me.

Kim Chung-il: Wow! A pen! It's beautiful! Thank you!

Anna: David and Yamamoto will be right back. They went to the store to buy a birthday cake.

(David and Yamamoto return)

Fang Xiaoying: They're back!

Martin: The birthday cake has arrived!

Yamamoto: What do you mean "the birthday cake has arrived"? Who's "the birthday cake"? (= "We" have arrived, not "the birthday cake".) (All laugh)

Martin: Hurry up and cut the cake, Kim Chung-il! I'm hungry.

Fang Xiaoying: We haven't sung "Happy Birthday" yet!

David: Happy Birthday to you ...

Group: Happy Birthday to you ...

课堂活动

I. The preposition gěi

介词"给"

Students split into groups of three or four, each student with an individual card. A "✓" following an entry on the card signifies that it is something that can be done. "✗" indicates that it cannot be done. Tomorrow is the birthday of a student in your section. You want to celebrate the birthday for that student. Ask the others in your group what you can do for the birthday person. Each in the group asks one question.

三人或四人一组，一人一张卡片，卡片上有"✓"表示是你能做的事，有"✗"是表示你不能做的。明天是你们班一位同学的生日，你们想给他过生日。现在请你问问同组同学谁能给他做什么。一人问一个问题。

Example:

A: Nǐ néng gěi tā zuò shēngrìkǎ ma?

你能给他做生日卡吗？

B: Wǒ bù néng gěi tā zuò shēngrìkǎ.

我不能给他做生日卡。

C: Wǒ néng gěi tā zuò shēngrìkǎ.

我能给他做生日卡。

D: Wǒ yě néng gěi tā zuò shēngrìkǎ.

我也能给他做生日卡。

When the questioning and answering by turns is finished, the instructor may ask a student from each group to report, e.g.:
轮流问答完毕以后，老师可请每组的一位同学报告一下。例如：

C tóngxué hé D tóngxué néng gěi tā zuò shēngrìkǎ.

C同学和D同学能给他做生日卡。

A.	给他买礼物	✓
	给他订生日蛋糕	✓
	给他做生日卡	✗
	给他唱生日歌儿	✗
	给他打电话	✓

B.	给他买礼物	✗
	给他订生日蛋糕	✓
	给他做生日卡	✗
	给他唱生日歌儿	✓
	给他打电话	✓

C.	给他买礼物	✗
	给他订生日蛋糕	✓
	给他做生日卡	✓
	给他唱生日歌儿	✓
	给他打电话	✗

D.	给他买礼物	✓
	给他订生日蛋糕	✗
	给他做生日卡	✓
	给他唱生日歌儿	✓
	给他打电话	✗

II. The complement of result <u>gěi</u>

结果补语"给"

Practice <u>zhèi</u> + measure word + object + <u>mǎi</u> + <u>gěi</u> + person. In pairs, students ask each other questions along the lines of the illustrations and prompts below.

练习"这 + 量词 + 物件名 + 买 + 给 + person"。两人一组，按照下图及提示提问和回答。

A.

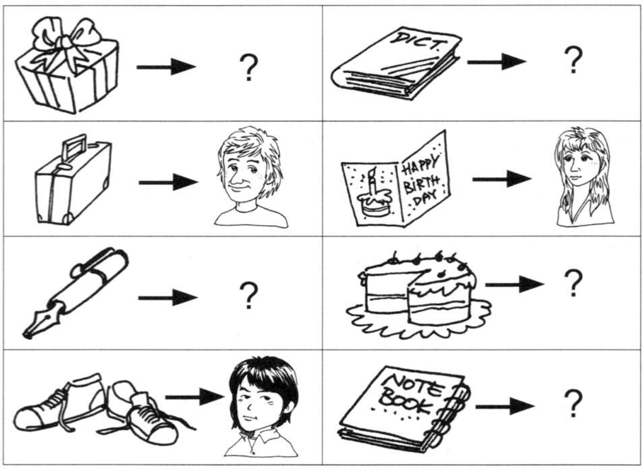

B.

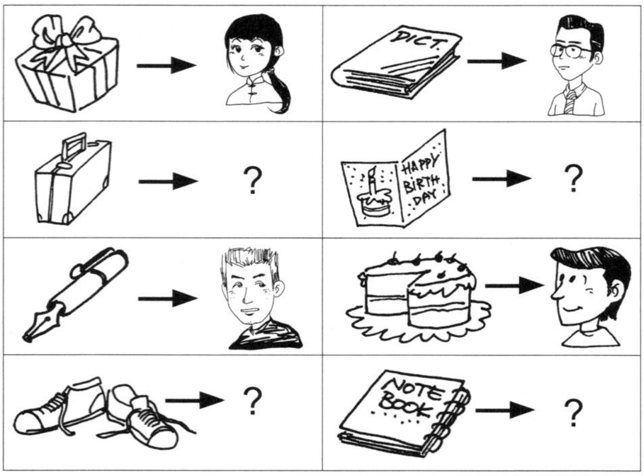

III. Simple directional complements

简单趋向补语

A. Pairs of students each play the roles of A and B to complete the dialogues below. Follow this example.

请和你的一位同学一起，模仿下例，分别扮演A和B的角色，完成下列对话。

Example:

A: Tā shànglái le.

他上来了。

B: Tā shàngqù le.

他上去了。

1：A：______________________.

B：______________________.

2：A：______________________.

B：______________________.

3：A：______________________.

B：______________________.

4：A：______________________,

______________________.

B：______________________,

______________________.

5：A：________________________________，

________________________________。

B：________________________________，

________________________________。

B. Pairs of students ask each other questions along the lines of the illustrations and prompts below to complete the dialogue.
二人一组，根据下图和提示，互相问答，完成对话。

Example:

A: Tā dào nàr qù?
他到哪儿去？

B: Tā dào jiàoshì qù.
他到教室去。

A: Tā dào jiàoshì qù zuò shéme?
他到教室去做什么？

B: Tā dào jiàoshì qù jiāo běnzi.
他到教室去交本子。

a)

c)

b)

d)

第十四课

你点菜吧

汉字课文

山　本：安娜，今天晚上我们一起去吃饭，怎么样？

安　娜：好啊！

山　本：你喜欢吃中餐还是喜欢吃西餐？

安　娜：今天我想吃中餐。

山　本：好，我们去吃中餐。

(在饭馆儿里)

服务员：你们二位吃点儿什么？这是菜单。

山　本：谢谢。安娜你喜欢吃什么？今天我请你，你点菜吧！

安　娜：真的？那我就点最贵的。

山　本：没问题。

安　娜：你别担心，我跟你开玩笑。我不常吃中国菜，不知道应该点什么，你来点吧。

山　本：好吧。一个糖醋鱼，一个家常豆腐。你喜欢吃辣的吗？

安　娜：有的时候也吃一点儿。

山　本：那么，我们要个辣子鸡丁儿吧。小姐，几个菜了？

服务员：三个了。(念了一遍菜名) 你们还要什么？

山　本：再要一个青菜。

服务员：一共四个菜。(又念了一遍菜名) 要不要来个汤？

安　娜：不要汤了。要一点儿饮料吧。

服务员：喝什么饮料？是啤酒还是可乐？

安　娜：我要可乐。你呢？

山　本：我要一瓶啤酒。

安　娜：山本，你常来这个饭馆吃饭吗？

山　本：是，我来过很多次了。这儿的菜做得不错。

安　娜：你再说一遍那四个菜的名字，我记一记。

山　本：不用记，我回学校给你写一遍。

(服务员送来饮料和菜)

山　本：啤酒是我的，可乐是你的。我们尝尝辣子鸡丁儿吧。

安　娜：好。嗯，很好吃。哎呀，真辣！

生词语

1.	点	diǎn	(v)		to order (food)
		a. 我不常来中国饭馆，不会点菜，你来点吧。			
		b. 他点了三个菜一个汤。			
2.	菜	cài	(n)	[个]	items of good, dishes; green vegetables
3.	中餐	zhōngcān	(n)	[顿 dùn]	Chinese food
4.	还是	háishi	(c)		or (used in alternative questions)
5.	西餐	xīcān	(n)	[顿]	western food
6.	饭馆儿	fànguǎnr	(n)	[个，家]	restaurant
7.	服务员	fúwùyuán	(n)	[个，位]	attendant (general term for those who wait on customers at restaurants and elsewhere in the service industry)
8.	菜单	càidān	(n)	[张，份fèn]	menu

9. 请 qǐng (v) to invite; to request (polite)

10. 真的 zhēnde (adj) really

a. 她明天过生日。

—— 真的？我们应该送她一件礼物。

b. 我朋友一九八四年在这儿学中文的时候，也是谢老师的学生。

—— 真的？太有意思了。

11. 担心 dān xīn (vo) to be concerned, worry

a. 她不会游泳，今天一个人去游泳了，我们很担心。

b. 你别担心衣服太贵，我今天拿了很多钱。

12. 开玩笑 kāi wánxiào (vo) to jest, joke

开 kāi (v) to make (limited contexts)

玩笑 wánxiào (n) joke

a. 他不喜欢别人跟他开玩笑。

b. 我们今天跟他开了个小玩笑。

13. 常 cháng (adj) often

14. 应该 yīnggāi (o.v) should, ought to

a. 你有不懂的地方，应该去问老师。

b. 你不应该告诉他怎么做，应该让他自己做。

15. 辣 là (adj) to be (spicy) hot

16. 要 yào (v) to ask for

a. 我们要了两个菜一个汤，还要了两瓶啤酒。

b. 他的钱不多，常常要跟家里要钱。

c. 我去商店，你们要什么？

—— 我要一个本子。他要什么，我不知道。

17.	小姐	xiǎojie	(n)	[位，个]	Miss (used for addressing service personnel and younger women in general)
18.	念	niàn	(v)		to read, read aloud

a. 他念课文念得很清楚。

b. 这个字念什么？

c. 这个字怎么念？

—— 我知道怎么写，可是不知道怎么念。

19.	遍	biàn	(m)		number of times
20.	菜名	cài míng			name of a dish, item of prepared food
21.	青菜	qīngcài	(n)		vegetables, greens, dish without meat
22.	一共	yígòng	(adv)		altogether, in all
23.	又	yòu	(adv)		once again (repetition which has taken place)
24.	汤	tāng	(n)	[个]	soup
25.	饮料	yǐnliào	(n)	[瓶，杯 bēi]	beverages, drinks
26.	啤酒	píjiǔ	(n)	[瓶，杯]	beer
27.	可乐	kělè	(n)	[瓶，杯]	cola
28.	瓶	píng	(m)		bottle
29.	次	cì	(m)		number of times
30.	记	jì	(v)		to write down

a. 请再说一遍你的电话号码，我要记一下儿。

b. 老师说的话，他都在本子上记了。

31.	送	sòng	(v)		to bring (to someone)
32.	尝	cháng	(v)		to taste, to try
33.	哎呀	āiyā	(i)		Yow! Wow! Ah!

专有名词

1.	糖醋鱼	tángcùyú	Sweet and sour fish
2.	家常豆腐	jiāchángdòufu	Homestyle bean curd
3.	辣子鸡丁	làzijīdīng	Diced chicken with chili peppers

补充生词

1.	茶	chá	(n)	tea
2.	咖啡	kāfēi	(n)	coffee
3.	牛奶	niúnǎi	(n)	milk
4.	汽水儿	qìshuǐr	(n)	soda pop, soft drinks
5.	果汁	guǒzhī	(n)	fruit juice
6.	鸡	jī	(n)	chicken
7.	鱼	yú	(n)	fish
8.	牛肉	niúròu	(n)	beef
9.	羊肉	yángròu	(n)	mutton
10.	猪肉	zhūròu	(n)	pork

语法点

1. <u>(shì) ... háishi</u> (是)……还是, "A or B"

"(是)……还是……"

This construction is used to ask about a choice. <u>Shì</u> 是 generally precedes the first item proposed in the choice, and <u>háishi</u> 还是 the second. The first <u>shì</u> is optional.

"(是)……还是……"用在选择句里。要选择的前一项目放在"是"后，后一项目放在"还是"后。前面的"是"也可以省略。

a. Q: Nǐ shì yào píjiǔ háishi yào kělè?

你是要啤酒还是要可乐？

Do you want beer or cola?

A: (Yào) kělè.

(要) 可乐。

(I want) cola.

b. Q: Shì nǐ diǎn cài háishi tā diǎn cài?

是你点菜还是他点菜？

Will you order or will he?

A: Qǐng tā diǎn ba.

请他点吧。

Ask him to order.

c. Q: Nǐ chī zhōngcān háishi xīcān?

你吃中餐还是西餐？

Will you eat Chinese or western food?

A: (Chī) xīcān.

(吃) 西餐。

(I'll eat) western food.

2. Yìdiǎnr 一点儿 "a little"

"一点儿"

This is a number-measure word construction that is often in a modifier position.

"一点儿"是一个数量词，表示少量，经常作定语。

a. Wǒ xiǎng chī yìdiǎnr dòufu.

我想吃一点儿豆腐。

I'd like to eat some beancurd.

The yī may be elided when yìdiǎnr is the object or an attributive of the object. Compare Lesson 6, Structure note 3 (p. 151).

如果“一点儿”作动词后的宾语或宾语的定语时，“一”可以省略。参看第六课语法点3（151页）。

b. Zài lái diǎnr cài.

再来点儿菜。

Bring some more vegetables.

If the context is adequately clear, the central word modified by yìdiǎnr can be left unstated.

如果上下文很清楚时，“一点儿”所修饰的中心语也可以省略。

c. Tángcùyú hén hǎochī, nǐ chī (yì) diǎnr ba.

糖醋鱼很好吃，你吃（一）点儿吧。

The sweet and sour fish is tasty. Eat a bit of it.

3. The model particle le 了 (2)

语气助词“了”(2)

The modal particle le 了 (2) expressing change of state. In addition to its function at sentence end affirming that something has already occurred (Lesson 6), it also very frequently indicates a change or emergence of a new situation.

在第六课我们学习了语气助词“了”的一个用法：出现在句尾，表示行为动作已经发生。此外，语气助词“了”也可以表示变化或出现新的情况。

a. Wǒ è le.

我饿了。

I'm hungry.

b. Zhè jiàn yīfu jiù le.

这件衣服旧了。

This item of clothing is (has gotten) old.

c. Wǒ huì xiě Hànzì le.

我会写汉字了。

I know how to write Chinese characters now.

d. Tā xiànzài kàn zhōngwénshū kàn de kuài le.

她现在看中文书看得快了。

She reads Chinese books with speed now.

e. Jīntiān yǐjīng shì xīngqīwǔ le.

今天已经是星期五了。

Today is Friday already.

f. Wǒ méiyou qián le, bù néng qù fànguǎnr le.

我没有钱了，不能去饭馆儿了。

I don't have any money and can't go to the restaurant.

NOTE that it is often in sentences with adjectival predicates (a, b), equational (shì 是) sentences (e) and sentences with complements of degree (d) and negated VO predicate sentences (f) that le may function in this manner.

注意：这种句子的主要类型有：形容词谓语句（例a、b），“是”字句（例e），带程度补语的句子（例d），否定形式的动词谓语句（例f）。

4. Verb measure words as complements

动量补语

Nouns take measure words in Chinese, and so do verbs. Cì 次 is an example of a verbal measure word. A numeral combined with a verbal measure word can serve as a verbal complement. The verbal measure as complement serves to describe a quantitative feature of the action, e.g., how many times it happened.

名词有量词，动词也有量词。“次”就是一个常见的动量词。“数词 + 动量词”能作动量补语，补充说明动作的量，如：动作的次数。

a. Tā láiguo sì cì le.

他来过四次了。

He has been (to this place) four times now.

b. Wǒ méi tīng qīngchu nín shuō de huà, qǐng nín zài shuō yí biàn.

我没听清楚您说的话，请您再说一遍。

I didn't catch what you said, please say it again.

c. Qǐng nǐ měi ge zì xiě liǎng biàn.

请你每个字写两遍。

Please write each character twice.

If the verb takes a nominal object, the object follows the complement. If it takes a pronoun object, the object precedes the complement.

如果动词后带有名词宾语，宾语放在补语后，如果是代词宾词，就要放在补语前。

S + V (+了) + CM + O

d. Zhèige yuè wǒ kànle sì cì diànyǐng.

这个月我看了四次电影。

I've seen four movies this month.

S + V (+了) + O (Pro) + CM

e. Wǒ qǐng jià de shíhou, tā lái kànle wǒ liǎng cì.

我请假的时候，他来看了我两次。

He came to see me twice while I was off on leave.

5. The adverbs <u>yòu</u> 又, <u>zài</u> 再 and <u>hái</u> 还

"又""再"和"还"

<u>Yòu</u> expresses a repeated occurrence of an action or condition. Compare it with <u>zài</u> and <u>hái</u>.

<u>yòu</u>: the occurence has <u>already</u> been repeated.

<u>zài</u>: the occurrence <u>will</u> be repeated.

<u>hái</u>: the occurrence <u>will</u> be repeated, but <u>hái</u> is used in interrogative contexts (see Lesson 12).

“又”表示行为或情况重复出现，它和“再”“还”的不同是：“又”表示已经重复，“再”表示将要重复，“还”也是表示将要重复，但它用来提问(见第十二课)。

a. Tā zuótiān lái le, jīntiān yòu lái le.

他昨天来了，今天又来了。

He came yesterday, and again today.

b. Tā zuótiān méi lái shàng kè, jīntiān yòu méi lái shàng kè.

她昨天没来上课，今天又没来上课。

She didn't come to class yesterday, and again today didn't come to class.

c. Shàng xīngqī tā tīngle yí cì yīnyuè, zhèige xīngqī yòu tīngle yí cì yīnyuè.

上星期他听了一次音乐，这个星期又听了一次音乐。

He listened to music once last week, and listened once again this week.

d. Nèige diànyǐng zhēn hǎo, wǒ shàng xīngqī kànle yí cì, zuótiān yòu kànle yí cì, xià xīngqī wǒ xiǎng zài kàn yí cì.

那个电影真好，我上星期看了一次，昨天又看了一次，下星期我想再看一次。

That film is really good, I saw it once last week, again yesterday, and next week I want to see it once more.

e. Zhèi zhǒng shū wǒ mǎile hěn duō běn le, yǐhòu bú zài mǎi le.

这种书我买了很多本了，以后不再买了。

I bought many of these books and won't buy any more after this (= won't buy them again afterwards).

f. Nǐ niàn de bú duì, qǐng nǐ zài niàn yí biàn.

你念得不对，请你再念一遍。

You read it incorrectly, please read it once again.

g. Tā jīntiān lái le, míngtiān tā hái lái ma?

他今天来了，明天他还来吗？

He came today. Will he come again tomorrow?

h. Zhèige gēr tā yǐjīng tīngle sān biàn le, tā hái yào tīng ma?

这个歌儿她已经听了三遍了，她还要听吗？

She already listened to this song three times. Is she going to listen to it still more?

NOTES 注释

Nǐmen èr wèi chī yìdiǎnr shénme? 你们二位吃(一)点儿什么？ "What would the two of you like?" Èr wèi is an unusual variant of liǎng wèi 两位, with no semantic difference. As in our example, it is only used as a discrete nominal. It is often used as a more polite variant in beckoning to or introducing two people.

"你们二位吃点什么？"中的"二位"是"两位"的一种不常用的形式。二者语义相同，但"二位"常在较客气地招呼对方(两个人)或作介绍时用。后面多不出现名词，如"这二位"、"他们二位"等。

词组和句子

1. 今天下午你游泳还是打网球？
2. 你喝可乐还是喝啤酒？
3. 下课以后，你去图书馆还是回宿舍？
4. 他是中国人还是日本人？
5. 你是懂还是不懂？如果不懂，就问一问老师。

6. (是)你去，还是他去？还是你们都去？
7. 西餐好吃，还是中餐好吃？还是两种都好吃？
8. 你喜欢吃辣的还是不辣的？
9. 我的鞋已经很旧了，应该买一双新的了。
10. 今天已经是星期四了，后天就可以休息了。
11. 我有词典了，不用买了。
12. 去年我还是学生，今年我已经是老师了。
13. 今天晚上我不去听音乐了。
14. 他现在念课文念得很清楚了。
15. 他中文已经说得很好了。
16. 上星期天我打了两次网球，上午打了一次，下午又打了一次。
17. 我问了他两次，他都没听清楚。
18. 他没在家，请你明天再来吧。
19. 第一遍你念得不清楚，请你再念一遍。
20. 他昨天来了，今天又来了。
21. 他昨天没来，今天又没来。
22. 那本书我已经看了两遍了，上星期又看了一遍。
23. 那本书我已经看了两遍了，我想下星期再看一遍。
24. 那个汉字我昨天已经写了三遍，今天上午又写了两遍。我想下午再写五遍，大概就会写了。

参考资料

拼音课文

Nǐ diǎn cài ba

Shānběn: Ānnà, jīntian wǎnshang wǒmen yìqǐ qù chī fàn, zěnmeyàng?

Ānnà: Hǎo a!

Shānběn: Nǐ xǐhuan chī zhōngcān háishi xǐhuan chī xīcān?

Ānnà: Jīntian wǒ xiǎng chī zhōngcān.

Shānběn: Hǎo, wǒmen qù chī zhōngcān.

(Zài fànguǎnr li)

Fúwùyuán: Nǐmen èr wèi chī diǎnr shénme? Zhè shi càidān.

Shānběn: Xièxie. Ānnà nǐ xǐhuan chī shénme? Jīntian wǒ qǐng ni. Nǐ diǎn cài ba!

Ānnà: Zhēnde? Nà wǒ jiù diǎn zuì guì de.

Shānběn: Méi wèntí.

Ānnà: Nǐ bié dān xīn, wǒ gēn nǐ kāi wánxiào. Wǒ bù cháng chī Zhōngguo cài, bù zhīdào gāi diǎn shénme, nǐ lái diǎn ba.

Shānběn: Hǎo ba. Yí ge tángcùyú, yí ge jiāchángdòufu. Nǐ xǐhuan chī là de ma?

Ānnà: Yǒude shíhou yě chī yìdiǎnr.

Shānběn: Nàme, wǒmen yào ge làzijīdīngr ba. Xiǎojie, jǐ ge cài le?

Fúwùyuán: Sān ge le. (Niànle yí biàn cài míng) Nǐmen hái yào shénme?

Shānběn: Zài yào yí ge qīngcài.

Fúwùyuán: Yígòng sì ge cài. (Yòu niànle yí biàn cài míng) Yào bu yào lái ge tāng?

Ānnà: Bú yào tāng le. Yào yìdiǎnr yǐnliào ba.

Fúwùyuán: Hē shénme yǐnliào? Shì píjiǔ háishi kělè?

Ānnà: Wǒ yào yì bēi kělè. Nǐ ne?

Shānběn: Wǒ yào yì píng píjiǔ.

Ānnà: Shānběn, nǐ cháng lái zhèige fànguǎnr chī fàn ma?

Shānběn: Shì, wǒ láiguo hěn duō cì le. Zhèr de cài zuò de búcuò.

Ānnà: Nǐ zài shuō yí biàn nà sì ge cài de míngzi, wǒ jì yí jì.

Shānběn: Búyòng jì, wǒ huí xuéxiào gěi nǐ xiě yí biàn.

(Fúwùyuán sònglái yǐnliào hé cài)

Shānběn: Píjiǔ shi wǒ de, kělè shi nǐ de. Wǒmen chángchang làzijīdīngr ba.

Ānnà: Hǎo. Ng, hěn hǎochī. Āiyā, zhēn là!

英译课文

Why don't you choose the food!

Yamamoto: Anna, let's eat together tonight!

Anna: All right!

Yamamoto: Would you like to eat Chinese or western?

Anna: I'd like to eat Chinese today.

Yamamoto: All right, let's eat Chinese.

(In the restaurant)

Waitress: What would the two of you like? Here's the menu.

Yamamoto: Thanks. What would you like, Anna? It's on me today. You make the selection!

Anna: Really? Then I'll choose the most expensive things.

Yamamoto: No problem.

Anna: Don't worry, I'm joking. I don't eat Chinese that much and don't know what to order. You order.

Yamamoto: All right. A sweet and sour fish and a homestyle beancurd. Do you eat spicy hot things?

Anna: Sometimes I do.

Yamamoto: Then let's have the spicy hot diced chicken. How much have we ordered, Miss?

Waitress: Three. (She reads the names of the dishes) Do you want anything else?

Anna: Let's add a vegetable dish.

Waitress: Four in all. (She reads the order again) Would you like a soup?

Anna: No, but we'd like something to drink, I think.

Waitress: What would you like? Beer or cola?

Anna: I'd like cola. And you?

Yamamoto: I'd like a bottle of beer.

Anna: Yamamoto, do you come to this restaurant often to eat?

Yamamoto: Yes, I've been here often. The food here is (cooked) not bad.

Anna: Say the names of those four dishes again. I'll note them down.

Yamamoto: You don't have to note them down. When we get back to school I'll write them for you.

(The waitress brings the drinks and food)

Yamamoto: The beer is mine and the cola yours. Let's try the hot chicken.

Anna: All right. Mm, it's good. Yow, it's hot!

课堂活动

I. (shi) … háishi …

(是)……还是……

Students divide into pairs, one with illustration A and the other with B. "?" in the illustration indicates that the holder should ask a question. "✗" asks for a negative response, "✓" for a positive response. Students should use the (shi) … háishi … pattern in questions, and (bu)xiǎng/ (bu)yào/(bu)xǐhuan in answers. When hearing the response, the questioner should then decide what they will to do, or eat, or where they will go together.

二人一组，一人持A图，一人持B图。图中有"？"表示提问；有"✗"表示否定回答，有"✓"表示肯定回答。请学生按照图示用"(是)……还是……"提问，用"(不)想／(不)要／(不)喜欢……"回答，得到答案后，提问的人决定他们一起去做什么或吃什么或去哪儿。

A

(是)…… 还是……？	他 { 想…… 要…… 喜欢……	那么…… 就……吧。

B

(是)…… 还是……？	他 { 想…… 要…… 喜欢……	那么…… 就……吧。

II. The modal particle le expressing change of state

表示变化的语气助词"了"

Students group into pairs and make sentences using le according to the prompts on their slips.

二人一组，根据下图和所给的提示造句。

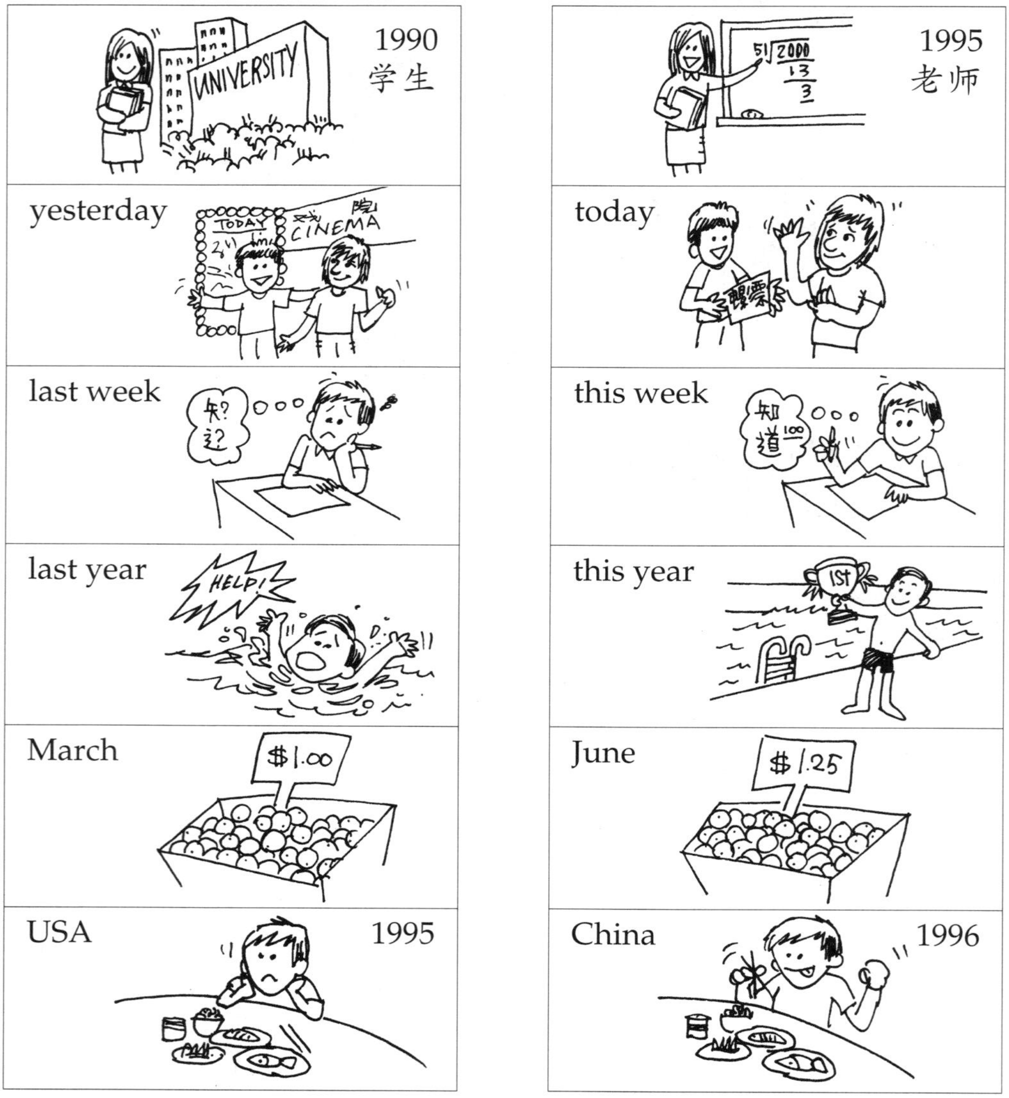

III. Number plus verbal measure word as complement

动量补语

Students group into twos or threes, ask each other the following questions and jot down the answers. The instructor can check answers by asking other questions.

二人或三人一组，用以下问题互相问答，并将答案记下。做完后，老师可以用提问的方式来检查答案。

Example:

Zhège yuè shéi kàn diànyǐng kàn de zuì duō?

这个月谁看电影看得最多？

Shéi zuì xǐhuan kàn zhège diànyǐng?

谁最喜欢看这个电影？

1. 这个月你看了几次电影？
2. 这个电影你看了几遍？
3. 上个星期你去了几次书店？
4. 那本书你看了几遍？
5. 每个生词你写几遍？
6. 下个星期你要交几次作业？
7. 这课的课文你念过几遍？
8. 你在那家商店买过几次衣服？

IV. Adverbs zài and yòu

“再”和“又”

Students group into pairs and, with information in the illustrations, complete the blank line statements or questions using zài + V or yòu + V.

二人一组，根据下图及提示，用“再 + V”或“又 + V”完成对话。

(1)

A：你怎么回来了？

B：我没带书。

A：________________？

B：我没带钱。

(2)

A：这个电影怎么样？

B：这个电影真好。________________________。

(3)

A：________________________。

B：我吃得很多了，不吃了。

(4)

A：我知道你的词典丢了，那么，这本词典是谁的？

B：是我的，我昨天__________________________。

(5)

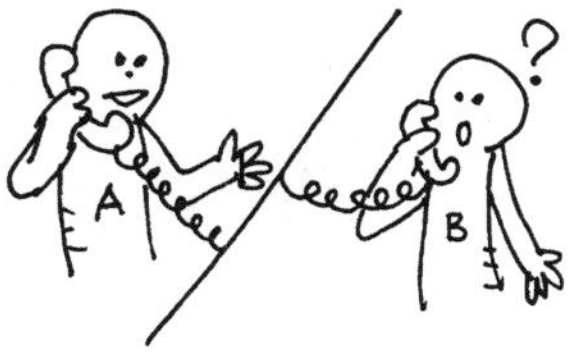

A：请告诉我张老师的电话……

B：对不起，我没听清楚，__________________________。

(6)

A：张老师在吗？

B：对不起，他不在，请三点钟__________。

A：张老师在吗？

B：对不起，他还没回来。请四点以后_______________。

C：你给张老师打电话了吗？

A：打了，我十二点打了一次，三点______，可是他都不在，接电话的人让我四点以后__________。

第十五课

你家里都有什么人？

汉字课文

（马丁去找安娜）

马　丁：安娜，在吗？

安　娜：谁啊？请进！是你啊！请坐。

马　丁：你做什么呢？

安　娜：我在给家里写信呢。

马　丁：写了半天了吧？

安　娜：没有，吃了饭，我先看了一会儿书，才开始写信。

马　丁：你家里都有什么人？

安　娜：我家一共有六口人，你看看那张桌子上的照片。

马　丁：这是你爸爸吗？

安　娜：对，他是个医生。

马　丁：左边儿坐着的是你妈妈吧？

安　娜：不，左边儿的是我奶奶，右边儿的是我妈妈。

马　丁：真的？你妈妈和你奶奶都那么年轻，我以为你奶奶是你妈妈，你妈妈是你姐姐呢。

安　娜：是吗？我妈妈和我奶奶听见一定很高兴。

马　丁：你爷爷呢？

安　娜：他一九九零年就去世了。

马　丁：你妈妈做什么工作？

安　娜：她是个中学老师。

马　丁：后边儿站着的都是谁？

安　娜：这边儿是我哥哥，我哥哥已经大学毕业了。

马　丁：他在哪儿工作？

安　娜：在一个贸易公司工作。那边儿是我妹妹，她正在念中学。

马　丁：你妹妹长得真漂亮，跟你一样。这是你弟弟吧？

安　娜：不是，我没有弟弟。他是朋友。

马　丁：朋友！？

生词语

1. 进 jìn (v) to enter
   a. 请进！请进来！
   b. 同学们都进教室来了。
   c. 我看见他进了一家商店，不到一刻钟，他又从商店出来了。
   d. 我走进书店，看到了很多新书。
   e. 他大学毕业以后，进了一家贸易公司工作。
2. 在 zài (adv) (before verb or verb phrase, indicates that the action is in progress)
3. 信 xìn (n) [封 fēng] letter
4. 半天 bàntiān (n) a long time (in the users perception, often exaggerated)
5. 才 cái (adv) then, just at that time
6. 开始 kāishǐ (v) to begin
   a. 我从一九九五年开始学中文，已经学了两年了。

b. 每天晚上我七点半开始复习，九点半以后开始预习。

c. 我八月三十一号到这儿，九月一号开始上课。

7.	口	kǒu	(m)		measure for (number of) people, as in a family
8.	桌子	zhuōzi	(n)	[张，个]	table, desk
9.	照片	zhàopiàn	(n)	[张]	photograph
10.	爸爸	bàba	(n)	[个]	dad, papa
11.	医生	yīshēng	(n)	[个，位]	doctor
12.	着	zhe	(part)		(continuous aspect verbal suffix)
13.	妈妈	māma	(n)	[个]	mom, ma
14.	奶奶	nǎinai	(n)	[个]	paternal grandmother
15.	那么	nème, nàme	(adv)		so, that degree

a. 他学得那么好，真是一个好学生。

b. 我不知道你那么喜欢吃中餐，以后我请你吃中餐吧！

c. 那件衣服那么小，只能给弟弟穿了。

16.	年轻	niánqīng	(adj)		to be youthful
17.	以为	yǐwéi	(v)		to assume, take (incorrectly) that

a. 你来了，真好！我以为你不来了。

b. 今天听写我以为都写对了，老师告诉我，我写错了两个字。

c. 你的中文说得那么好，我以为你是中国人呢。

18.	姐姐	jiějie	(n)	[个]	older sister
19.	听见	tīngjian	(v)		to hear

a. 我听见他们在楼下唱歌儿呢。

b. 你听见没听见他说的话？

20. 高兴	gāoxìng	(adj)		to be happy, to be delighted
21. 爷爷	yéye	(n)	[个]	paternal grandfather
22. 去世	qùshì	(v)		to pass away (death euphemism)
23. 工作	gōngzuò	(v, n)	[个]	to work, work

a. 您做什么工作？在哪儿工作？

b. 他的工作很不错，我也想找一个跟他一样的工作。

24. 中学	zhōngxué	(n)	[个]	middle school, high school
25. 站	zhàn	(v)		to stand
26. 哥哥	gēge	(n)	[个]	older brother
27. 大学	dàxué	(n)	[个]	university
28. 毕业	bìyè	(vo)		to graduate (from school)
29. 贸易	màoyì	(n)		trade
30. 公司	gōngsī	(n)	[个，家]	company
31. 妹妹	mèimei	(n)	[个]	younger sister
32. 正在	zhèngzài	(adv)		in the process of (same as zài above, except that zhèngzài is used for immediate ongoing actions)
33. 长	zhǎng	(v)		to grow

a. 弟弟和妹妹都长大了。

b. 他长得跟他爸爸一样。

34. 一样	yíyàng	(adj)		to be the same
35. 弟弟	dìdi	(n)	[个]	younger brother

补充生词

1. 父亲	fùqin	(n)	father
2. 母亲	mǔqin	(n)	mother

3. 儿子	érzi	(n)	son
4. 女儿	nǚ'ér	(n)	daughter
5. 大哥	dàgē	(n)	eldest brother
6. 二姐	èrjiě	(n)	second older sister
7. 高	gāo	(adj)	to be tall
8. 老	lǎo	(adj)	to be old
9. 死	sǐ	(v)	to die

语 法 点

1. <u>Zài</u> 在, <u>zhèngzài</u> 正在, <u>zhèng</u> 正, … <u>ne</u> 呢

"在"、"正在"、"正"和"……呢"

These adverbs are used to indicate that an action is, will be or was in progress. <u>Zài</u> alone, or <u>zhèng</u> alone may be used, the resultant sentence may end with <u>ne</u> or, with less precision, the sentence end <u>ne</u> alone can express the idea. If <u>zài</u> is used by itself, the sense need not necessarily be that the action is going on just at that given moment, but the duration can be longer. E.g., it might be used in a statement that "the earth is (in the process of) revolving around the sun".

副词"在"、"正在"、"正"表示动作正处于进行阶段。进行的动作可能发生在现在，可能发生在将来，也可能发生在过去。"……呢"前三个词各自可以单独使用，也可以跟语气词数"呢"一起用。有的时候，只在句尾加上"呢"也表示动作正在进行。"在"和"正在"、"正"的区别是，用"在"的句子不强调动作正在进行，它可以用于持续时间较长的情况，如"地球在围绕着太阳转"。

S + 正/正在/在 + V + O (+ 呢)

Sentence + 呢

a. Tā zhèngzài chī fàn.

她正在吃饭。

She is eating (right now in the process of).

b. Tā zuò shénme ne?

他做什么呢？

What is he doing?

c. Tā zài gěi jiāli xiě xìn.

他在给家里写信。

He's writing a letter home.

d. Zuótiān zǎoshang wǒ jìn jiàoshì de shíhou, tā zài xiě Hànzì ne.

昨天早上我进教室的时候，他在写汉字呢。

Yesterday morning when I went into the classroom he was (in the midst of) writing Chinese characters.

e. Míngtiān xiàwǔ sāndiǎn zhōng de shíhou wǒ yídìng zhèngzài kàn diànyǐng ne.

明天下午三点钟的时候我一定正在看电影呢。

At three tomorrow afternoon I'll definitely be watching a movie.

2. The aspect particle zhe 着

动态助词"着"

V + zhe 着 indicates that the action goes on, is sustained (as in example a below). The actual action may have been completed (as in examples b, c below) but the result of it goes on.

动词后面紧跟上"着"，表示动作未结束，仍在持续（例a），或者动作已经结束了，而结果在持续中（例b、c）。

a. Wǒ zài wàibiānr děngzhe nǐ, hǎo ma?

我在外边儿等着你，好吗？

I'll wait/be waiting for you outside, all right?

b. Wǒ mèimei chuānzhe yí jiàn hěn piàoliang de xīn yīfu.

我妹妹穿着一件很漂亮的新衣服。

My younger sister is wearing an attractive new outfit.

c. Tā názhe yì zhī bǐ, zhèngzài wèn dàjiā “zhè shì shéi de?”

他拿着一支笔，正在问大家“这是谁的”？

He is holding a pen and asking everybody “Whose is this?”

In sentences where zhèng 正 … ne 呢 and other such variants described above are used to indicate that an action is in progress, zhe 着 can be attached to the verb. Zhe doesn't express “in progress”. However, because of the fact that actions in progress are often continuing, the two forms (zhèng and zhe) can appear in the same sentence.

“着”可以和上边介绍的表示动作正在进行的“正在”、“呢”等一起用。“着”仍紧跟在动词后。“着”并不表示进行，但因正在进行的动作往往也是持续着的动作，所以这两种形式可以同时出现在一个句子中。

d. Lǎoshī zhèng gēn tóngxuémen shuōzhe huà ne, nǐ děng yìhuǐr zài jìnqù.

老师正跟同学们说着话呢，你等一会儿再进去。

The teacher is talking to the students now. Wait a while before you go in.

3. The adverbs jiù 就 (2) (see Lesson 7, p. 170) and cái 才 (1)

副词“就”(2)(见第七课，170页)和“才”(1)

The adverb jiù as an adjunct expresses the speaker's sense that an action takes place early, quick, or progresses smoothly, e.g. “right on time”. Cái conversely expresses the speaker's view that the action is late, slow or progresses with some wrinkles, e.g. “not until”.

副词“就”作状语表示说话者认为动作发生得早、快或事情进行得顺利。“才”正相反，表示说话者认为动作发生得晚、慢或事情进行得不顺利。如：“not until”(直到……才……)。

a. Tā qī diǎn bàn jiù lái le, wǒ bā diǎn cái lái.

她七点半就来了，我八点才来。

She was here at 7:30 and I didn't come until eight.

b. Nǐmen jiǔ diǎn bàn cái shàng kè ne, nǐ lái de tài zǎo le.

你们九点半才上课呢，你来得太早了。

You don't go to class until 9:30. You've come too early.

c. Wǒ liǎng diǎn jiù zài zhèr děng tā, tā liǎng diǎn bàn cái lái.

我两点就在这儿等他，他两点半才来。

I was here at 2:00 waiting for him and he didn't arrive until 2:30.

When an action has already been realized or completed, use jiù … le or cái; when an action will be realized or completed, use jiù or cái … (ne).

如果动作已经实现或完成，要用"就……了"或"才"。如果动作将要实现或完成，多用"就"或"才……呢"。

d. Wǒ jiā liù diǎn chī fàn. Māma wǔ diǎn bàn jiù huílái le. Bàba lái diànhuà shuō tā qī diǎn cái huílai ne.

我家六点吃饭。妈妈五点半就回来了，爸爸来电话说他七点才回来呢。

Our family eats at 6:00. Ma was home at 5:30, but pa phoned to say that he won't get back until 7:00.

e. Xiànzài shi liù diǎn. Māma liù diǎn yīkè jiù huílai. Bàba qī diǎn cái huílai ne.

现在是六点。妈妈六点一刻就回来，爸爸七点才回来呢。

It's 6:00. Ma will be back at 6:15 but pa won't get back until 7:00.

f. "Hòutiān" shàngge xīngqī jiù xué le, "qiántiān" zuótiān cái xué.

"后天"上个星期就学了，"前天"昨天才学。

We learned "the day after tomorrow" last week, but just learned "the day before yesterday" yesterday.

* In sentences using cái, even if the action has been realized do not add le.
在用"才"的句子里，即使动作已经实现或完成，也不能用"了"。

4. The comparative form "A gēn B (bu) yíyàng" A 跟 B（不）一样
表示比较的"（不）一样"

Note how it works.
这种句式如下：

a. Ānnà de mèimei gēn Ānnà yíyàng, yě hěn piàoliang.
安娜的妹妹跟安娜一样，也很漂亮。
Anna's younger sister is like Anna, also very pretty.

b. Wǒ gēn nǐ bù yíyàng, wǒ bùxǐhuan chī zhōngcān.
我跟你不一样，我不喜欢吃中餐。
I'm not like you, I don't like Chinese food.

An adjective or verbs of cognition and feeling can follow yíyàng.
在"跟……一样"后面也可以跟着形容词或感知动词。

c. Tā xiě de gēn wǒ yíyàng kuài.
他写得跟我一样快。
He writes as fast as I do.

d. Zhège dàngāo gēn nèige dàngāo bù yíyàng dà.
这个蛋糕跟那个蛋糕不一样大。
This cake isn't as big as that cake.

e. Zhōngcān gēn xīcān yíyàng hǎochī.
中餐跟西餐一样好吃。
Chinese food and western food are equally delicious.

f. Tā gēn wǒ yíyàng xǐhuan tīng yīnyuè.
他跟我一样喜欢听音乐。
He, as I, likes listening to music.

NOTES 注释

Nǐ jiā dōu yǒu shénme rén?

你家都有什么人？

Who all are there in your family?

Dōu 都, as we have noted, sums up a number of things that usually come before it, as in Nǐmen dōu qù ma? 你们都去吗？(Are you all going?) In interrogative sentences, it can sum up what comes after it. There must be an interrogative pronoun in what follows, such as nǎr 哪儿, shénme 什么, nǎxiē 哪些 etc. HOWEVER, in responses the dōu is NOT used. As the awkward translation here indicates, it is difficult to express the same concept neatly in English.

我们已经学了"都"的一般用法：总括它前面的事物，如"你们都去吗？"但是在疑问句中，它可以总括动词后面的宾语，宾语中往往有疑问代词，如"哪儿""什么""哪些"等。不过，答句不再用"都"。英语里没有与之相应的表达方式。

词组和句子

1. 你们做什么呢？
2. 我在写信呢，她在看照片呢。
3. 你不能进去，他们正在上课。
4. 他进教室的时候，我正跟安娜说话呢。
5. 昨天我去他家的时候，他正在吃饭。
6. 你明天晚上八点钟去找她，她一定正在做作业。
7. 妹妹穿着我送给她的那件衣服，非常漂亮。
8. 这是我爸爸和我妈妈年轻时候的照片，我爷爷和奶奶在前边儿坐着，他们在后边儿站着。
9. 他拿着很多书，从图书馆出来。
10. 昨天晚上你给我打电话的时候，我正写着信呢。

11. 我们正点着菜，看到马丁也到饭馆儿来了。
12. 星期天中午我们十二点就吃完饭了，他一点才吃完。
13. 我约她六点在电影院门口儿见面，我五点三刻就来了，她六点十分才来。
14. 今天的练习很容易，我只做了半个小时，就做完了。
15. 今天的练习太难，我做了一个半小时，才做完。
16. 我等了他半天，他才来。
17. 请你坐一会儿，我马上就来。
18. 你在我房间里等她一会儿，她四点半就下课。
19. 你如果没有时间，就别等她了，她四点半才下课呢。
20. 我现在要预习明天的课，八点以后才能陪你去散步呢。
21. 我用的本子跟他用的一样。
22. 他看的这本书跟老师介绍的那本不一样。
23. 他买的衣服跟你买的衣服一样长。
24. 小王穿的鞋跟小谢穿的鞋不一样大，小王穿的大，小谢穿的小。
25. 小张家里的人跟我家里的人一样多，他家有四口，我家也有四口。

参考资料

拼音课文

Nǐ jiāli dōu yǒu shénme rén?

(Mǎdīng qù zhǎo Ānnà)

Mǎdīng: Ānnà, zài ma?

Ānnà: Shéi a? Qǐng jìn! Shì nǐ a! Qǐng zuò.

Mădīng: Nǐ zuò shénme ne?

Ānnà: Wǒ zài gěi jiāli xiě xìn ne.

Mădīng: Xiěle bàntiān le ba?

Ānnà: Méiyou, chīle fàn, wǒ xiān kànle yìhuǐr shū, cái kāishǐ xiě xìn.

Mădīng: Nǐ jiāli dōu yǒu shénme rén?

Ānnà: Wǒ jiā yígòng yǒu liù kǒu rén, Nǐ kànkan nèi zhāng zhuōzi shang de zhàopiàn.

Mădīng: Zhè shi nǐ bàba ma?

Ānnà: Duì, tā shi ge yīshēng.

Mădīng: Zuǒbianr zuòzhe de shi nǐ māma ba?

Ānnà: Bù, zuǒbianr de shi wǒ nǎinai, yòubianr de shi wǒ māma.

Mădīng: Zhēnde? Nǐ māma hé nǐ nǎinai dōu nàme niánqīng, wǒ yǐwéi nǐ nǎinai shi nǐ māma, nǐ māma shi nǐ jiějie ne.

Ānnà: Shì ma? Wǒ māma hé wǒ nǎinai tīngjian yídìng hěn gāoxìng.

Mădīng: Nǐ yéye ne?

Ānnà: Tā yī jiǔ jiǔ líng nián jiù qùshì le.

Mădīng: Nǐ māma zuò shénme gōngzuò?

Ānnà: Tà shi ge zhōngxué lǎoshī.

Mădīng: Hòubianr zhànzhe de dōu shi shéi?

Ānnà: Zhèibianr shi wǒ gēge, wǒ gēge yǐjīng dàxué bìyè le.

Mădīng: Tā zài nǎr gōngzuò?

Ānnà: Zài yí ge màoyì gōngsī gōngzuò. Nèibianr shi wǒ mèimei, tā zhèngzài niàn zhōngxué.

Mădīng: Nǐ mèimei zhǎng de zhēn piàoliang, gēn ni yíyàng. Zhè shi nǐ dìdi ba?

Ānnà: Bú shi, wǒ méi yǒu dìdi. Tā shi péngyou.

Mădīng: Péngyou!?

英译课文

Tell me about the people in your family

(Martin looks for Anna)

Martin: Anna, are you there?

Anna: Who is it? Come in, please. Oh, it's you. Have a seat.

Martin: What are you doing?

Anna: I'm writing a letter to my family.

Martin: You've been writing for a while, I'll bet.

Anna: No, I read a bit after eating, then started writing.

Martin: Tell me about the people in your family.

Anna: There are six of us. Look at the photo on that table.

Martin: Is this your father?

Anna: Yes. He's a doctor.

Martin: Is the person seated on the left your mother?

Anna: No, the one on the left is my (paternal) grandmother. The one on the right is my mother.

Martin: Really? Your mother and your grandmother are both so young. I thought your grandmother was your mother and your mother was your older sister.

Anna: Oh? My grandmother and mother would be delighted to hear that.

Martin: How about your grandfather?

Anna: He passed away in 1990.

Martin: What does your mother do?

Anna: She's a high school teacher.

Martin: Who are those standing in the back?

Anna: My older brother is on this side. My brother has already graduated from university.

Martin: Where does he work?

Anna: In a trading company. My younger sister is on that side. She is in middle school.

Martin: Your sister is pretty, like you. Is this your younger brother?

Anna: No, I don't have a younger brother. He's a friend.

Martin: A friend?

课堂活动

I. zhèng, zhèngzài, ne

"正"/"正在"/"呢"

A. Students form pairs and ask and answer each other's questions as prompted by the illustrations.

二人一组，根据下图，互相问答。

Example:

A: Zhāng lǎoshī zhèngzài zuò shénme?

张老师正在做什么？

B: Zhāng lǎoshī zhèngzài bā bān shàng kè.

张老师正在八班上课。

B. As above.

二人一组，根据下图，互相问答。

Example:

A: Zhāng lǎoshī shàng kè de shíhou, Jīn Zhōngyī zhèngzài zuò shénme?

张老师上课的时候，金中一正在做什么？

B: Zhāng lǎoshī shàng kè de shíhou, Jīn Zhōngyī zhèngzài zhǎo cídiǎn.

张老师上课的时候，金中一正在找词典。

II. Jìu and cái

“就”和“才”

Students form pairs and make sentences as prompted by the illustrations, using jìu or cái.

二人一组，根据下图，用“就”或“才”造句。

(1) 11:30 am — 午饭

小安 

2:30 pm — 午饭

小娜 

(2)

他：上课→去商店买饮料→回家

我：上课→回家

(3) 1 hr.

学校 → 商场

10 min.

学校 → 饭馆儿

(4) 应该9:30 am 开始工作

小谢8:40am 小方10:15 am

(5) 姐姐的中学，9月1号，开始上课。

哥哥的大学，9月15号，开始上课。

(6) 爸爸，9:10去公司。

妈妈，8:45去学校。

(7) 这个歌儿很容易，她只学了两次，现在会唱了。

那个歌儿很难，她学了四次，现在会唱了。

(8) 这些汉字，他写了三遍，现在会写了。

这些汉字，我写了五遍，现在会写了。

III. gēn … yíyàng

跟……一样

Answer your partner's questions as prompted by the illustrations.

二人一组，互相问答。

Example:

B: Xiǎoyīng mǎi le shénme?

小英买了什么？

B: Jīn Zhōngyī ne?

金中一呢？

B: Xiǎoyīng mǎi de gēn Jīn Zhōngyī mǎi de yíyàng ma?

小英买的跟金中一买的一样吗？

A then similarly answers B's questions.

A. 根据下图回答B的问题。　按照以下指示提问。

(1) a “安娜在做什么？”
“小英呢？”
b 请用“安娜看的／小英看的／一样”提问。

(2) a “马丁买了什么？”
“山本呢？”
b 请用“马丁买的／山本买的／一样”提问。

(3) a “小明在做什么？”
“小王呢？”
b 请用“小明看的／小王看的／一样”提问。

B. 根据下图回答A的问题。　按照以下指示提问。

(1) a “小英买了什么？”
“金中一呢？”
b 请用“小英买的／金中一买的／一样”提问。

(2) a “大卫在做什么？”
“安娜呢？”
b 请用“大卫打得／安娜打得／一样”提问。

(3) a “王先生有工作吗？”
“金先生呢？”
b 请用“王先生的工作／金先生的／一样”提问。

阅读练习

昨天上午我们班听写第十四课的生词。山本说这次听写最好的人得请同学们吃饭，大家都说好，我也没说不好。我想每次听写都是山本和金中一最好，这次最好的一定不会是我。

今天下午第二节下课以后，我们去找张老师，问她昨天听写得怎么样。同学们问："最好的是谁？"张老师说最好的是我。我想，完了！完了！这次我得请大家吃饭了。同学们听见张老师的话，就问我："你请我们吃中餐，还是吃西餐？"

上完最后一节课，我们一起去一个中餐饭馆儿。饭馆儿的服务员给我们每个人一个菜单，让我们点菜。同学们一共点了七个菜一个汤。有辣的，有不辣的；有鱼，有鸡；有青菜，也有豆腐。点完了菜，大卫说，还得要点儿饮料，同学们又要了啤酒和可乐。

吃完最后一个菜，我说，我得先去一下儿厕所。从厕所出来，我就出了饭馆的后门，一个人回宿舍了。今天我听写得最好，同学们应该请我吃饭。你们说对不对？

第三单元复习

1. The prepositions cóng and lí

介词"从"和"离"

Cóng 从 expresses the starting point (in space or time) of an action.
"从"表示动作的起点(空间的，时间的)。

a. She is coming from home and I'm coming from the dormitory.

她从家里来，我从宿舍来。

b. You swim from that side of the pool and I'll swim from this side of the pool. We'll see who gets to the middle first.

你从游泳池那边儿游，我从游泳池这边儿游，看谁先到中间。

c. I'm asking for time off from Monday, asking four days leave. I'll come to class on Friday.

我从星期一请假，请四天假，星期五来上课。

d. We attend class every morning from 9:30 up to 12:20; we attend three sessions. In the afternoon we attend class from 1:30, also three sessions.

我们每天上午从九点半上课，到十二点二十，上三节课；下午从一点半开始上课，也上三节课。

Lí 离 expresses distance (in space or time).
"离"表示距离(空间的，时间的)。

a. The mall is close to the bookstore.

商场离书店很近。

The bookstore is close to the mall.

书店离商场很近。

b. My home isn't far from school.

我家离学校不远。

School isn't far from my home.

学校离我家不远。

c. It is now 9:10, so there are still twenty minutes until class.

现在是九点十分，离上课还有二十分钟。

d. I'm going home (back to my country) on April 15. Today is the first of April, already very close to the time I go home. There is a half month left.

我四月十五号回国，今天四月一号，离我回国已经很近，还有半个月了。

2. Complements

补语

I. Complement of degree

程度补语

a. On Sunday everyone in our family had a good rest.

星期天，我家里的人都休息得很好。

b. I didn't do yesterday's homework well.

昨天的作业我做得不好。

c. My older brother swims well, and his tennis isn't bad either.

我哥哥游泳游得很好，打网球也打得不错。

d. Does his younger brother write Chinese attractively?

他弟弟汉字写得好看不好看？

e. How is his mother's Chinese cooking?

他妈妈做中国菜做得怎么样？

II. Resultative complement

结果补语

a. How about my notebook? Who picked up the wrong homework notebook?

我的本子呢？谁拿错了作业本子？

b. Did you hear what he said?

他说的话你听见了吗？

I did, but I didn't hear him clearly. He talked too fast.

听见了，不过，我没听清楚，他说得太快。

c. If you don't review the lesson text thoroughly you can't do the exercise.

不复习好课文，就不能做练习。

d. Have you learned how to swim?

你学会游泳了没有？

e. Did you understand the questions the teacher asked?

老师问的问题，你听懂没听懂？

III. Simple directional complement

简单趋向补语

a. Dad is going to the company now and will come back after 5:30 in the afternoon.

爸爸现在到公司去，下午五点半以后回来。

b. Mom went upstairs and older sister came downstairs.

妈妈上楼去了，姐姐下楼来了。

c. He bought a big birthday cake.

他买来了一个很大的生日蛋糕。

d. Today Kim Chung-il didn't bring the *New Chinese Dictionary*. He lost his.

今天，金中一没带《汉语小词典》来，他那本丢了。

e. Tomorrow he's going to come to buy a satchel.

明天他要买一个箱子来。

IV. Complement of time

时量补语

a. Every morning we attend class from 9:30 until 12:20. Each session is fifty minutes, and between every two sessions we take a ten-minute break.

我们每天上午从九点半到十二点二十上课，每节课上五十分钟，每两节课中间休息十分钟。

b. I'm studying Chinese now. Every day is pressured. In the evenings I often have to review an hour and a half of vocabulary and lesson text, write Chinese characters for a quarter of an hour and do a half hour of exercises. Then I still have to prepare the new lesson.

我现在学习中文，每天都很紧张，晚上常常要复习一个半小时生词和课文，写一刻钟汉字，做半个小时练习，还要预习新课。

c. I started studying from last January, so have already studied Chinese for a year and a half.

我从去年一月开始学，已经学了一年半汉语了。

d. How many hours has younger sister been making the birthday card?

妹妹做生日卡做了几个小时了？

e. How long did you wait for her at the entrance of the auditorium? Did you wait for her for ten minutes?

你在礼堂门口儿等了她多长时间？等了她十分钟吗？

I didn't wait for ten minutes, only five.

我没等十分钟，只等了五分钟。

V. V measure word complement

动量补语

a. He came once this morning and again once in the afternoon, but was unable to find you either time.

他今天上午来了一次，下午又来了一次，都没找到你。

b. David read the lesson text twice and wrote the Chinese characters three times.

大卫念了两遍课文，写了三遍汉字。

c. I asked her that question once but she didn't know either.

那个问题我问过她一次，她也不知道。

3. Past experience

过去的经验

a. I've been to his house and know where it is.

我去过他家，知道他家在哪儿。

b. None of us joked with him.

我们都没跟他开过玩笑。

c. I've never eaten this dish. Is it tasty? Hot?

我没吃过这个菜，好吃吗？辣不辣？

d. The food at this restaurant isn't bad. Have you been to try it?

这家饭馆儿的菜做得还可以，你去吃过没有？

4. An ongoing action
   动作的进行

   a. The doctor is talking with Dad now. Don't go in just yet.
      医生正在跟爸爸说话，你先别进去。

   b. Fang Xiaoying is looking at photos and Anna is singing. What is Martin doing?
      方小英在看照片，安娜在唱歌儿，马丁在做什么呢？

   c. When he came to our house we were listening to music.
      他来我家的时候，我们正在听音乐呢。

   d. When we were listening to music he wrote a letter.
      我们听音乐的时候，他在写信。

5. Continuation of an action
   动作的持续

   a. He is sitting behind the table and we are standing beside him.
      他在桌子儿边儿坐着，我们在他旁边儿站着。

   b. Younger sister is wearing a pair of attractive new shoes.
      妹妹穿着一双很漂亮的新鞋。

   c. Mom is cooking. Go after you eat.
      妈妈做着饭呢，你吃完饭再走吧。

6. 再、又、还

   a. He bought a dictionary last week and bought another one this week.
      他上个星期买了一本词典，这个星期又买了一本。

b. She didn't come yesterday, or again today. If she doesn't come again tomorrow we'll have to go to look in on her.

她昨天没来，今天又没来，如果明天再不来，我们就得去看看她了。

c. Did you only buy two film tickets? Why don't you buy another one? Younger brother wants to go to see it, too.

你只买了两张电影票吗？再买一张吧，弟弟也想去看。

d. He saw that film last week. Why does he want to see it again?

那个电影他上星期看过了，为什么还要看？

He said that the film was very interesting and that he wanted to see it another time.

他说那个电影很有意思，他想再看一次。

7. 才、就

a. He'll go now. I'll go after I've eaten.

他现在就去，我吃完饭才去呢。

b. My older brother started work immediately after graduating from college, but I didn't work until two years after graduating from college.

我哥哥大学毕业以后马上就工作了，可是我大学毕业两年以后才工作。

c. Just a short time passed when the waiter brought drinks and dishes.

只过了一会儿，服务员就送来了饮料和菜。

d. The waiter only brought drinks and dishes after some time had passed.

过了半天，服务员才送来饮料和菜。

阅读

爸爸送儿子小亮到学校里去念书。

第一天，老师教了三个字——我、你、他。老师说："我，我是你的老师。你，你是我的学生。"又指着小亮旁边儿的同学说："他，他是你的同学。"

下课以后，小亮回家了。晚上爸爸从公司里回来，看到了小亮，就问他："今天你在学校里学了什么？"

"老师教了我们三个字——我、你、他。"

"这三个字你都懂吗？"爸爸问。

"懂，我都懂。我，我是你的老师，你，你是我的学生。"这时候小亮的弟弟进来了，他就指着弟弟说："他，他是你的同学。"

爸爸说："胡说！我是你的爸爸，你是我的儿子，他是你的弟弟。"

第二天，小亮又去学校了。上课的时候，老师要复习昨天学的字，就问："小亮，昨天我教的三个字你都懂了吗？"

"懂了。不过，老师，您昨天教错了，应该是：我是你的爸爸，你是我的儿子。"又指着旁边儿的同学说："他是你的弟弟。"

老师听了，一句话也说不出来。

生词语

1.	儿子	érzi	(n)	son
2.	指	zhǐ	(v)	to point at
3.	胡说	húshuō	(v)	to talk nonsense
4.	一句话也说不出来 yí jù huà yě shuō bu chūlái			couldn't say a word, speechless

去南湖公园怎么走？

汉字课文

马　丁：明天我们去南湖公园划船，怎么样？

金中一：划船？好啊！

安　娜：南湖公园离这儿远吗？

马　丁：从这儿骑自行车去，大概要四十分钟；坐公共汽车去，半个小时就能到。

方小英：我住在假日饭店旁边儿，离南湖公园很近，我可以走着去。

金中一：南湖公园我没去过，不知道怎么走。

马　丁：我认识路，你跟我一起骑车去吧！

金中一：好。安娜，你怎么去？

马　丁：你也跟我们骑车去吧！

安　娜：骑车太累，我想坐公共汽车去。不过，我不认识路。

方小英：别着急，我告诉你，非常方便。你在学校门口儿坐十六路车，坐到总站，然后换地铁。

安　娜：地铁坐几站？在哪个站下车？

方小英：坐四站，在南湖公园站下车。

安　娜：从地铁站出来以后呢？

方小英：出来以后，往左拐，一直走，五分钟就到了。

马　丁：明天我们在公园门口儿见面吧！早上九点怎么样？晚不晚？

安　娜：不晚，我觉得太早。

马　丁：那么，九点半吧。

方小英：九点半比较合适。

安　娜：山本和大卫去不去？

马　丁：我去问问他们。

生词语

1.	公园	gōngyuán	(n)	[个]	park
2.	划船	huá chuán	(vo)		to row a boat
	划	huá	(v)		to row
	船	chuán	(n)	[只，条 tiáo]	boat
3.	骑	qí	(v)		to ride astride (bicycle, horse)

a. 我每天都看见他骑自行车到公司去，他骑得非常快。

b. 我每天早上骑自行车去学校，路上要骑半个小时。

4.	自行车	zìxíngchē	(n)	[辆 liàng]	bicycle
5.	公共	gōnggòng	(adj)		public

a. 我家附近有个公共图书馆，我常常去那儿看书。

b. 公共游泳池在哪儿？骑车去方便，还是坐车去方便？

6.	汽车	qìchē	(n)	[辆]	car, automobile
7.	住	zhù	(v)		to live in, to reside

a. 去年我在那个饭店住了三个月。

b. 山本住楼上还是楼下？他住几号房间？

c. 你住在学生宿舍，还是住在家里？

8.	饭店	fàndiàn	(n)	[家，个]	hotel

9. 车　chē　(n)　[辆]　vehicle (wheeled)

10. 路　lù　(n)　road

11. 累　lèi　(adj)　to be tired

12. 着急　zháo jí　(vo)　to be anxious, nervous

a. 别着急，我马上告诉你，你先坐一会儿。

b. 昨天妹妹很晚才回来，爸爸妈妈着了半天急。

13. 非常　fēicháng　(adv)　unusually

14. 方便　fāngbiàn　(adj)　to be convenient

a. 住在别人家，有时候不方便。

b. 从这儿坐公共汽车去很方便，上了车，一直坐到总站，不用换车。

15. 路　lù　(m)　route (of buses, etc.)

16. 总站　zǒngzhàn　(n)　[个]　terminus, last stop

17. 然后　ránhòu　(adv)　afterwards, after that

a. 上课的时候，老师先问问题，然后听写。

b. 星期天，我们先去公园划船，然后去饭馆儿吃饭，吃完饭，去看电影，你们看，怎么样？

c. 去假日饭店，你先坐两站六路汽车，然后坐三站地铁，就到了。

18. 换　huàn　(v)　to change, change to

19. 地铁　dìtiě　(n)　underground transport

20. 站　zhàn　(n, m)　[个]　station, stop

21. 下车　xià chē　(vo)　get off a vehicle

下　xià　(v)　to get down from

车　chē　(n)　[辆]　wheeled vehicle

22. 左　zuǒ　(n-pw)　left

23. 拐　guǎi　(v)　to turn (a corner, etc.), make a turn

a. 请问，去天星电影院往哪边儿拐？往东边儿还是往西边？

b. 你们要拐到那条 (tiáo) 路上，就行了。

24. 一直	yìzhí	(adv)		directly, straight on
25. 早上	zǎoshang	(n)	[个]	morning
26. 晚	wǎn	(adj)		to be late
27. 早	zǎo	(adj)		to be early
28. 合适	héshì	(adj)		to be fitting, appropriate

a. 这件衣服太长，我穿不合适。

b. 这本书比较容易，你们现在学很合适。

c. 明天我九点半来行不行？

——你九点来吧！来得太晚不合适。

专有名词

1.	南湖公园	Nánhú Gōngyuán	Southlake Park
2.	假日饭店	Jiàrì Fàndiàn	Holiday Inn

补充生词

1.	出租(汽)车	chūzū (qì)chē	(n)	taxi
2.	计程车	jìchéng chē	(n)	taxi (Taiwan expression)
3.	的士	díshì	(n)	taxi (Hong Kong expression, transliteration of English "taxi")
4.	旅馆	lǚguǎn	(n)	inn
5.	酒店	jiǔdiàn	(n)	hotel, restaurant (Southern Chinese influenced expression)

语法点

1. Verbal expressions in series (2)

连动句(2)

In Lesson 4 (pp. 107–108) we saw the second verb/verb construction as expressing the objective of the going, coming, returning, etc. first verb. Here, the first verb/verb construction expresses the manner in which, or implement with which the second is carried out. The first verb construction is in the nature of an adverbial adjunct.

我们在第四课(107–108页)学习了连动句(1)：后一个动词(或动词结构)表示前一动作的目的，前一动词一般是表示"来""去""回"等意义的。本课学习的连动句(2)，前一个动词(或动词结构)表示后一个动作进行的方式或使用的工具，前一动词结构带有状语的性质。

a. Tāmen qí zìxíngchē qù gōngyuán, wǒmen zuò qìchē qù.

他们骑自行车去公园，我们坐汽车去。

They are going to the park by bicycle; we are going by car.

b. Nǐ yòng něi zhī bǐ xiě xìn? Wǒ yòng zhèi zhī bǐ xiě.

你用哪支笔写信？我用这支笔写。

Which pen do you use to write letters? I use this pen.

c. Gěi Zhōngguo lǎoshī de xìn, nǐ yòng Zhōngwén xiě háishi yòng Yīngwén xiě?

给中国老师的信，你用中文写还是用英文写？

Are you writing in Chinese or English in the letter to the Chinese teacher?

2. The resultative complement zài 在

结果补语"在"

S + V + 在 + O (place)

When zài follows the verb, it indicates that, as a result of the verbal action, someone or something exists in the stated place.
“在”可以跟在动词后作结果补语，表示通过动作而使人或事物存在于某处。

a. Tā jìnlái yǐhòu jiù zuò zài wǒ pángbiānr le.

他进来以后就坐在我旁边儿了。

He sat beside me when he came in.

b. Nǐmen zhù zai nǎr? Wǒ zhù zai xuéshēng sùshè, tā zhù zai xuéxiào wàibianr.

你们住在哪儿？我住在学生宿舍，他住在学校外边儿。

Where do you live? I live in the student dormitory and he lives outside the school.

* In this postpositional form, nothing can come between the verb and zài. Xiě míngzi zài zhǐshang 写名字在纸上 IS WRONG!
动词和“在”之间不能插入别的成分，不能说：“写名字在纸上”。

When zài (and its object) is in front of the verb as modifier, the situation described is that something happens at a certain place.
“在”和它的宾语组合后放在动词前作状语时，说明某动作在某处发生。

c. Zài shū shang xiě míngzi.

在书上写名字。

Write the name on the book. (= carrying out the “writing” action “on the book”)

3. Dào 到 as a resultative complement (1)

结果补语“到”(1)

Dào following the verb indicates that the action has taken someone or something to a given point. The object is inevitably a place or place expression.
“到”跟在动词后作补语，说明某人或某物通过动作而到达某处，“到”后的宾语是处所词。

S + V + 到 + O (place)

a. Wǒ měi tiān qí zìxíngchē qù xuéxiào, cóng jiāli qídào xuéxiào, zhǐ yào shíwǔ fēnzhōng.

我每天骑自行车去学校，从家里骑到学校，只要十五分钟。

I ride a bike to school everyday. Riding from home to school only takes fifteen minutes.

b. Wǒ kěyǐ cóng yóuyǒngchí zhèibiānr yóudào nèibiānr.

我可以从游泳池这边儿游到那边儿。

I can swim from here in the pool to over there.

c. Lǎoshī zǒudào wǒ pángbiānr, kàn wǒ xiě de zěnmeyàng.

老师走到我旁边儿，看我写得怎么样。

The teacher walks/walked over beside me and observes/observed how well I was writing.

If sentences with resultative complements <u>zài</u> 在 and <u>dào</u> 到 plus a place word have an object, that object is brought to the head of the sentence, forming an S-P predicate sentence.

在用"在"和"到"作结果补语的句子里，如果动词有受事宾语，要转换成主谓谓语句来表达。

d. Nà liǎng běn shū wǒ yǐjīng sòngdào nǐ jiāli le.

那两本书我已经送到你家里了。

I've already sent those books to your house.

e. Míngzi, nǐmen bú yào xiě zài zuǒbiānr, yào xiě zài yòubiānr.

名字，你们不要写在左边儿，要写在右边儿。

Don't write your names on the left, but on the right.

* The following would be INCORRECT:

下面的句子是错误的：

✗ Wǒ yǐjing sòng nèi liǎng běn shū dào nǐ jiāli le.

我已经送那两本书到你家里了。

✗ Nǐmen búyào xiě míngzi zài zuǒbiānr, yào xiě míngzi zài yòubiānr.

你们不要写名字在左边儿，要写名字在右边儿。

NOTE 注释

<u>Cóng zhèr qí zìxíngchē qù, dàgài yào sìshí fēnzhōng</u> 从这儿骑自行车去，大概要四十分钟 (You'll probably need forty minutes if you go by bike.) <u>Yào</u> 要 here is a verb meaning "to require", "to take".

"从这儿骑自行车去，大概要四十分钟"。这里的"要"是动词，意思是"需要"。

词组和句子

1. 明天上午我们走着去南湖公园，你去不去？
2. 走着去太累，我们想坐车去。
3. 你们坐什么车去？
4. 我坐公共汽车去，她坐地铁去。
5. 他怎么去？骑自行车去吗？
6. 上课的时候，老师用中文问问题，不用英文问。
7. 安娜用两个小时做了一张生日卡。
8. 马丁用七十块钱买了一个箱子，你说便宜不便宜？
9. 我很喜欢用这种纸写信，不过，这种纸比较贵。
10. 用这种笔写字，可以写得又快又好看。
11. 我的练习本子丢了，今天得用一个新本子做练习。
12. 她站着唱歌儿，我们都坐着听。
13. 谢老师拿着书进教室来了。

14. 张老师笑着说："这是个秘密。"
15. 在那张照片里，她姐姐坐在桌子旁边儿，她站在姐姐后边儿。
16. 山本住在楼上402号房间。
17. 我家离学校比较远，你从学校走到我家，一定很累了。
18. 公司离他家不近，每天下午七点以后，他才能回到家。
19. 你从这儿上车，坐到第四站下车，就是假日饭店。
20. 爸爸在饭馆儿订的菜，服务员已经送到家了。
21. 蛋糕，他已经拿到宿舍里请大家吃了。
22. 方小英的电话号码，我写在那张纸上了。
23. 老师问的问题，我都记在本子里了。

参考资料

拼音课文

Qù Nánhú Gōngyuán zěnme zǒu?

Mǎdīng: Míngtian wǒmen qù Nánhú Gōngyuán huá chuán, zěnmeyàng?

Jīn Zhōngyī: Huá chuán? Hǎo a!

Ānnà: Nánhú Gōngyuán lí zhèr yuǎn ma?

Mǎdīng: Cóng zhèr qí zìxíngchē qù, dàgài yào sìshi fēnzhōng; zuò gōnggòng qìchē qù, bàn ge xiǎoshí jiù néng dào.

Fāng Xiǎoyīng: Wǒ zhù zài Jiàrì Fàndiàn pángbiānr, lí Nánhú Gōngyuán hěn jìn, wǒ kěyǐ zǒuzhe qù.

Jīn Zhōngyī: Nánhú Gōngyuán wǒ méi qùguo, bù zhīdào zěnme zǒu.

Mǎdīng: Wǒ rènshi lù, nǐ gēn wǒ yìqǐ qí chē qù ba!

Jīn Zhōngyī: Hǎo. Ānnà, nǐ zěnme qù?

Mǎdīng: Nǐ yě gēn wǒmen qí chē qù ba!

Ānnà: Qí chē tài lèi, wǒ xiǎng zuò gōnggòng qìchē qù. Búguò, wǒ bú rènshi lù.

Fāng Xiǎoyīng: Bié zháojí, wǒ gàosu ni, fēicháng fāngbian. Nǐ zài xuéxiào ménkǒur zuò shíliù lù chē, zuòdào zǒngzhàn, ránhòu huàn dìtiě.

Ānnà: Dìtiě zuò jǐ zhàn? Zài něige zhàn xià chē?

Fāng Xiǎoyīng: Zuò sì zhàn, zài Nánhú Gōngyuán Zhàn xià chē.

Ānnà: Cóng dìtiězhàn chūlai yǐhòu ne?

Fāng Xiǎoyīng: Chūlai yǐhòu, wǎng zuǒ guǎi, yìzhí zǒu, wǔ fēnzhōng jiù dào le.

Mǎdīng: Míngtian wǒmen zài gōngyuán ménkǒur jiàn miàn ba! Zǎoshang jiǔ diǎn zěnmeyàng? Wǎn bu wǎn?

Ānnà: Bù wǎn, wǒ juéde tài zǎo.

Mǎdīng: Nàme, jiǔ diǎn bàn ba.

Fāng Xiǎoyīng: Jiǔ diǎn bàn bǐjiào héshì.

Ānnà: Shānběn hé Dàwèi qù bu qù?

Mǎdīng: Wǒ qù wènwen tāmen.

英译课文

How do you get to Southlake Park?

Martin: How about going rowing at Southlake Park tomorrow?

Kim Chung-il: Rowing? Great!

Anna: Is Southlake Park far from here?

Martin: By bike from here it probably takes forty minutes; by bus, you can get there in half an hour.

Fang Xiaoying: I live by the Holiday Inn which is very close to Southlake Park. I can walk there.

Kim Chung-il: I've never been to Southlake Park and don't know how to go.

Martin: I know the way. Why don't you bicycle there together with me?

Kim Chung-il: All right. Anna, how will you go?

Martin: Why don't you bicycle together with us?

Anna: Going by bike is too tiring. I want to go by bus, but I don't know the way.

Fang Xiaoying: Not to worry. I'll tell you. It's extremely easy. Take the 16 bus at the school entrance, go to the terminus and then switch to the subway.

Anna: How many stops do I go on the subway? At which stop do I get off?

Fang Xiaoying: Go four stops and get off at the Southlake Station.

Anna: And when I come out of the subway station?

Fang Xiaoying: Turn left when you come out, go straight ahead for five minutes and you're there.

Martin: Let's meet tomorrow at the entrance to the park! How about 9 am? Is that too late?

Anna: No, I think it's too early.

Martin: Then 9:30.

Fang Xiaoying: 9:30 is better.

Anna: Are Yamamoto and David going?

Martin: I'll go ask them.

课堂活动

I. The resultative complement zài

结果补语"在"

Students form pairs, asking each other "Where does X live?". They write answers they receive in the boxes containing question marks, then again query and answer each other as in the questions that follow.

二人一组，以"ＸＸ人住在哪儿？"互相问答，并将得到的答案填在有"？"的格里，最后读出附于下方的问题让对方回答。

A

ＸＸ人	住在哪儿？
小方	我们学校后边儿
小马	？
小金	学生宿舍三楼
小谢	？
小丁	朋友家
小文	？
小容	饭店里
小韩	？
小安	张老师家楼上
小园	？

请问：

几位同学住在学生宿舍？

谁住在王老师家楼下？

谁和老师住在一个楼里？

谁住在小方家旁边儿？

B

ＸＸ人	住在哪儿？
小方	？
小马	张老师家楼上
小金	？
小谢	饭店里
小丁	？
小文	王老师家楼下
小容	？
小韩	学生宿舍八楼
小安	？
小园	小方家旁边儿

请问：

几位同学住在饭店里？

几位同学住在张老师家楼上？

谁住在朋友家？

谁住在我们学校后边儿？

II. V + Resultative complement zài + location

V + 结果补语"在" + 处所

zhèng/zhèngzài

"正"/"正在"

Students form pairs. One student has "A" material, the other "B". They first identify five of the ten people in the picture on the basis of the descriptions provided, then ask questions using these patterns to identify the other five people:

二人一组，一人持资料A，一人持资料B。老师让A、B二人各自根据提示，写出图里其中五个人是谁，然后让A、B二人用下列格式提问以找出另外五个人是谁：

A: V + zài + location de (rén) shì shéi?

V + "在" + 处所的（人）是谁？

B: Zhèngzài + V + O de (rén) shì shéi?

"正在" + V + O 的（人）是谁？*

After this is done by both A & B, the remaining five people in the picture can be named.

找出图里另外的五个人是谁。

在小马家的房间里一共有十个人。

A

1. 坐在大桌子旁边儿的是小马。
2. 正在打电话的是小马的姐姐。
3. 正在喝啤酒的是小马的爸爸。
4. 站在门口儿的是小马的女朋友。
5. 站在奶奶后边儿的是小马的弟弟。

在小马家的房间里一共有十个人。

B

1. 坐在箱子上的是小马的哥哥。
2. 正在看照片的是小马的妈妈。
3. 站在桌子前边儿的是小马的小妹妹。
4. 站在小马妈妈旁边儿的是小马的同学。
5. 正切蛋糕的是小马的奶奶。

III. Verbal constructions in series (2)

连动句 (2)

Resultative complement dào

结果补语"到"

The figure in the illustration represents a railway station, a train or electric car stop, and numbers the bus stops of numbered bus routes (e.g. "the 21 bus", "the 18 bus").

这张图里代表地铁站，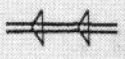代表电车站，(21)，(18)，(46)等代表21，18，46路等公共汽车站。

(1) The instructor asks a student "Cóng … dào … kěyǐ zuò shénme chē qù?"

The student responds after finding the information in the illustration.

老师问学生，"从……到……可以坐什么车去？"请学生看着图回答(可以用"先……然后……"格式)。

(2) The instructor asks a student "Cóng … dào … zuò dìtiě qù, zuòdào dì jǐ zhàn xià chē?"

"Going by subway from … to …, one goes to which stop and then gets off?" (= where does one get off?)

老师问学生，"从……到……，坐地铁去，坐到第几站下车？"请学生看着图回答。

(3) Students form pairs, asking each other a combination of the above questions, the instructor fixing a destination.

(1)和(2)两个练习也可以分组进行。由老师指定目的地，学生二人一组，轮流问答。

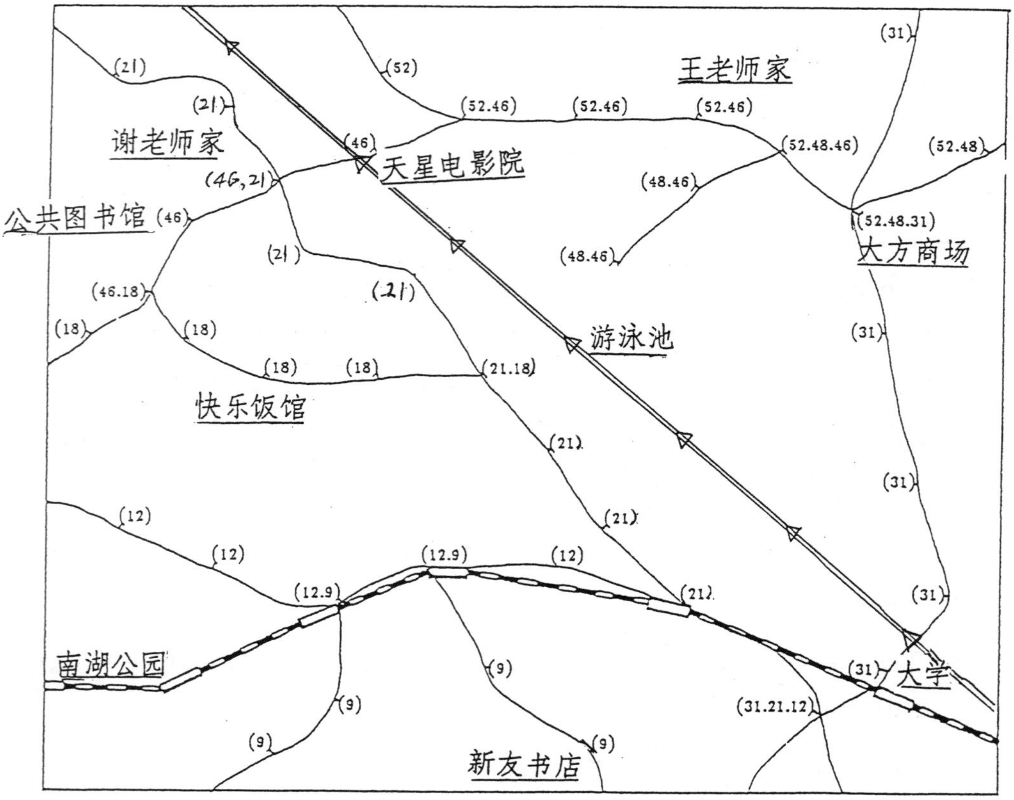
王老师家
谢老师家
天星电影院
公共图书馆
大方商场
游泳池
快乐饭馆
南湖公园
大学
新友书店
(21)
(52)
(31)
(52.46)
(46)
(46,21)
(52.48.46)
(52.48)
(48.46)
(52.48.31)
(46.18)
(18)
(21.18)
(12)
(12.9)
(9)
(31.21.12)

第十七课

我是坐公共汽车来的

汉字课文

(一)

(在南湖公园门口)

安　娜：你们来得真早！小英，你是什么时候到的？

方小英：大概十分钟以前吧。

金中一：她是第一个到的。

安　娜：你是跟马丁一起来的吗？

金中一：是啊，我们是一起骑车来的。

安　娜：你们都是从学校出发的吗？

金中一：对，我今天早上七点半起床，八点钟吃的早饭，八点三刻到的学校。然后跟马丁骑车出发，骑到这儿差不多九点半。

马　丁：安娜，你是怎么来的？

安　娜：我是坐公共汽车来的。小英，你是走着来的吗？

方小英：我不是走着来的，我是坐电车来的。今天早上我先去一个朋友家还书——上星期借的一本小说和两本杂志，还完书才来的。

安　娜：大卫和山本怎么还没来？

马　丁：大卫说，他最近非常忙，今天也要去办点儿事。山本要来，不过，今天早上他要到机场去送朋友，送完朋友，直接从机场来。

(二)

(半小时以后)

山　本：对不起，我来晚了。

安　娜：没关系。

方小英：我们等了你半个钟头了。你怎么啦?

山　本：别提啦！我在车上睡着了，坐过了站……

金中一：我以为你记错时间了呢。

马　丁：我以为你迷路了呢。

山　本：都没有，你们带了些什么好吃的？我又渴又饿。

方小英：我带了一些苹果、饼干什么的。苹果都洗干净了。

马　丁：没关系，不洗也能吃。

生词语

1. 以前 yǐqián (n) before
2. 出发 chūfā (v) to set out, set off
   a. 明天早上几点出发？九点还是九点半(出发)？
   b. 他们从学校出发，走了一刻钟，就到南湖公园了。
3. 起床 qǐ chuáng (vo) get out of bed, get up
   起 qǐ (v) to rise
   床 chuáng (n) [张，个] bed
4. 早饭 zǎofàn (n) [顿] breakfast
5. 电车 diànchē (n) [辆] electric streetcar, tram, trolley
6. 还 huán (v) to return (goods, books, etc.)
7. 借 jiè (v) to borrow; to lend
   a. 我从图书馆借来了两本新杂志。

b. 他借给我一本很好的小说。

c. 昨天我跟他借了五十块钱，今天我已经还 (给) 他了。

d. 我借了他五十块钱，今天我已经还 (给) 他了。

e. 我借 (给) 了他五十块钱，今天他已经还 (给) 我了。

8. 小说 xiǎoshuō (n) [本，部 bù] novel, fiction

9. 杂志 zázhì (n) [本] magazine

10. 最近 zuìjìn (n) recently

11. 忙 máng (adj) to be busy

12. 办 bàn (v) to manage, do

a. 那件事儿我还没有办完呢。

b. 他办事儿办得又快又好。

13. 事儿 shìr (n) [件，个] business, matter, a thing to do

14. 机场 jīchǎng (n) [个] airport

15. 直接 zhíjiē (adj) to be direct

16. 钟头 zhōngtóu (n) [个] hour

17. 别提啦 bié tí la It's a long story! Indescribable! What a mix-up! (lit., "Don't even bring it up.)

a. 他还给你钱了吗？

—— 别提啦，他是个有借没还的人。

b. 你今天怎么来晚了？

—— 别提啦，我的自行车丢了。我是走着来的。

18. 睡 shuì (v) to sleep

19. 着 zháo (v) (a verbal complement of result, indicating the successful attaining of an action)

a. 他每天睡下以后，半天才能睡着。

b. 他去买票了，可是没买着。

c. 我没借着那本书，想看那本书的人太多了。

20. 过 guò (v) to go past, to pass

a. 坐过了站，没关系。你下了车，再往回坐。

b. 我今天应该七点起床，可是我睡过了时间，七点半才起（床）。

21. 迷路 mí lù (vo) to get lost, go astray

22. 带 dài (v) to bring

a. 你带《汉语小词典》了吗？借给我用用。

b. 我今天没带本子，你如果带着新本子，借我一本，好吗？

c. 上星期姐姐带弟弟和妹妹去了一次公园。

23. （一）些 (yì) xiē (m) several, some (compare <u>jǐ-</u>, which is specifically "a few", less than ten. <u>Xiē</u> can be more, but less than the majority, "a portion.")

24. 渴 kě (v) to be thirsty

25. 苹果 píngguǒ (n) [个] apple

26. 饼干 bǐnggān (n) [块] cookie, biscuit

27. 什么的 shénmede (n) and so forth, etc.

a. 妈妈去商店买来很多东西，有蛋糕、饼干、苹果、可乐、啤酒什么的。

b. 打网球、游泳、骑自行车什么的，我都喜欢。

28. 洗 xǐ (v) to wash

29. 干净 gānjing (adj) to be clean

补充生词

1.	路口	lùkǒu	(n)	intersection (of a road), crossing road, street, avenue opposite
2.	马路	mǎlù	(n)	road, street, avenue
3.	对面	duìmiàn	(n)	opposite
4.	橘子	júzi	(n)	tangerine (popularly used for orange citrus in general)
5.	香蕉	xiāngjiāo	(n)	banana

语 法 点

1. Shì ... de 是……的

“是……的”句

When the completed nature of an act is known to be fact by both speaker and listener, the shì ... de construction can be used to emphasize some feature of that completed action, such as time, place or manner. The shì 是 may be eliminated in affirmative sentences.

当动作已经完成的事实成为听话人与说话人的共知信息以后，可以用“是……的”结构来着重说明与动作有关的某一方面，如：时间、处所、方式等。在肯定句中，“是”可以省略。

S + 是……的

a. Q: Tā yǐjīng lái le ma?

他已经来了吗？

Has he already come?

A: Tā yǐjīng lái le.

他已经来了。

He has already come.

Q: Tā shi shénme shíhou lái de?

他是什么时候来的？

When did he come?

A: Tā shi zuótiān lái de.

他是昨天来的。

He came yesterday.

b. Q: Nǐ shi cóng něi guó lái de?

你是从哪国来的？

What country are you from? (lit., You from what country came?)

A: Wǒ shi cóng Měiguó lái de.

我是从美国来的。

I'm from the United States.

If the verb in the sentence has an OBJECT, de can come before or after that object. Colloquial speech most often has it before the object.

如果"是……的"中间的动词带宾语，"的"在宾语的前后均可。口语中，"的"经常在宾语前。

S + 是……的 + O

c. Q: Tā chī fàn le ma?

他吃饭了吗？

Has he eaten?

A: Chī le.

吃了。

Yes.

Q: Tā shi zài nǎr chī de fàn?

他是在哪儿吃的饭？

Where did he eat?

A: Tā shi zài xuésheng shítáng chī de fàn.

他是在学生食堂吃的饭。

He ate in the student cafeteria.

d. Q: Tā mǎile nàme duō shū, tā shì shénme shíhou qù de shūdiàn?

他买了那么多书，他是什么时候去的书店？

He bought so many books. When did he go to the bookstore?

A: Tā shi zuótian xiàwǔ qù de shūdiàn.

他是昨天下午去的书店。

He went to the bookstore yesterday afternoon.

e. Wǒ shi qùnián lái Zhōngguo de.

我是去年来中国的。

I came to China last year.

The negative form is <u>bú shi</u> ... <u>de</u> 不是……的, and the affirmative-negative question form is <u>shì bu shì</u> ... <u>de</u> 是不是……的. Other question forms are routine.

否定式用“不是……的”，正反疑问形式用“是不是……的”。其他疑问形式与一般句型相同。

S + 不 + 是……的 (+ O)

S + 是不是……的 (+ O) ？

f. Q: Tā shì bu shì zuótiān lái de?

她是不是昨天来的？

Did she come yesterday?

A: Tā bú shi zuótiān lái de, shi shàng xīngqīliù lái de.

她不是昨天来的，是上星期六来的。

She didn't come yesterday; she came last Saturday.

2. Yǐqián

以前

<u>Yǐqián</u> 以前 functions the same as <u>yǐhòu</u> 以后 "later, afterwards". See Lesson 6, pp. 148–149.

"以前"和"以后"的用法相同，见第六课148–149页。

a. Yǐqián wǒ bùdǒng Zhōngwén.

以前我不懂中文。

I didn't understand Chinese before.

b. Shàngkè yǐqián yídìng xiān yùxí hǎo.

上课以前一定先预习好。

You must first prepare before going to class.

c. Wǒ qǐngjià yǐqián, tā yě qǐng guò yí cì jià.

我请假以前，他也请过一次假。

He asked for leave once before I did.

d. Sān nián yǐqián wǒ zài Měiguó kāishǐ xuéxí Zhōngwén.

三年以前我在美国开始学习中文。

Three years ago I began studying Chinese in the U.S.

3. Sentences that are passive in sense

意义上的被动句

The subject in most Chinese sentences is the agent or doer of the action, but in some instances it can be the receiver of the action. Thus, the sentence is passive. These subjects are definite, and most often inamimate.

汉语句子里的主语多数是施事或动作者，但在有些情况下，主语也可以是动作的受事，这种类型的主语一般是有定的，并且大多数是无生命的。

a. Nà běn shū jiāo gěi Fāng Xiǎoyīng le.

那本书交给方小英了。

That book was given to Fang Xiaoying.

b. Jiǎozi zuòhǎo le méiyou?

饺子做好了没有？

Are the dumplings done?

c. Nàge zì xiěcuò le.

那个字写错了。

That character is written incorrectly.

NOTES 注释

1. Bié tí la 别提啦. This expression indicates that the speaker finds whatever it is too painful, exasperating, embarrassing, etc. to talk about.

   "别提啦" 这是一个固定说法，是说话人告诉别人自己遇到了伤脑筋的事，或被某事困扰，陷入窘境。

2. Xiē 些 "several" is a measure word for an indefinite number. It is often prefaced with the number yī 一 "one": yìxiē 一些 for this indefinite sense.

   "些" 是一个不定量词，前边常常加上数词 "一"，说成 "一些"。

词组和句子

1. 两个小时以前　两天以前　两个月以前　两年以前

   两点以前　二号以前　二月以前　一九九二年以前

   出发以前　吃饭以前　来中国以前　哥哥工作以前

   姐姐大学毕业以前　我开始学习中文以前

2. 昨天晚上，我是十一点睡的。

3. 今天早上，你是几点起的(床)？
4. 你是什么时候来的？八点还是八点半？
5. 他是坐电车来的，还是坐地铁来的？
6. 她是从哪一站上的车？在哪一站下的车？
7. 你是不是在假日饭店(那一站)下的车？你下错车了，应该在前一站下。
8. 你是不是在家里吃的早饭？
9. 我不是在家里吃的早饭，是在食堂吃的。
10. 他是跟山本一起去的，还是跟大卫一起去的？
11. 王医生是什么时候打电话来的？
12. 你是下午五点到机场去的，他是五点十分打来的电话。
13. 王医生是给他来的电话，不是给你来的电话。
14. 我以前没学过中文，是最近才开始学的。
15. 我不是在中国学的中文，是在我们国家学的。
16. 下午上课以前，我很想睡一刻钟，休息一下儿。
17. 出发以前，请你看一看同学们都到了没有？
18. 你知道他们是在什么地方迷的路吗？
19. 我不知道他们是在什么地方迷的路。
20. 这些衣服是昨天洗的，都洗干净了。
21. 爸爸买的那种苹果真好吃，昨天都吃完了，是在哪儿买的？我再去买一些来。
22. 饮料都喝完了，可是我还渴，再去买一点吧！
23. 我上星期看的那本杂志借给安娜了，她还没还我呢。
24. 那本小说已经卖完了。

参考资料

拼音课文

Wǒ shì zuò gōnggòng qìchē lái de

(I)

(Zài Nánhú Gōngyuán ménkǒur)

Ānnà: Nǐmen lái de zhēn zǎo! Xiǎoyīng, nǐ shi shénme shíhou dào de?

Fāng Xiǎoyīng: Dàgài shí fēnzhōng yǐqián ba.

Jīn Zhōngyī: Tā shi dì-yī ge dào de.

Ānnà: Nǐ shi gēn Mǎdīng yìqǐ lái de ma?

Jīn Zhōngyī: Shì a, wǒmen shi yìqǐ qí chē lái de.

Ānnà: Nǐmen dōu shi cóng xuéxiào chūfā de ma?

Jīn Zhōngyī: Duì, wǒ jīntian zǎoshang qī diǎn bàn qǐ chuáng, bā diǎnzhōng chī de zǎofàn, bā diǎn sān kè dào de xuéxiào, ránhòu gēn Mǎdīng qí chē chūfā, qídào zhèr chàbuduō jiǔ diǎn bàn.

Mǎdīng: Ānnà, nǐ shi zěnme lái de?

Ānnà: Wǒ shi zuò gōnggòng qìchē lái de. Xiǎoyīng, nǐ shi zǒuzhe lái de ma?

Fāng Xiǎoyīng: Wǒ bú shi zǒuzhe lái de, wǒ shi zuò diànchē lái de. Jīntian zǎoshang wǒ xiān qù yí ge péngyou jiā huán shū — shàng xīngqī jiè de yì běn xiǎoshuō hé liǎng běn zázhì, huánwán shū cái lái de.

Ānnà: Dàwèi hé Shānběn zěnme hái méi lái?

Mǎdīng: Dàwèi shuō, tā zuìjìn fēicháng máng, jīntian yě yào qù bàn diǎnr shìr. Shānběn yào lái, búguò, jīntian zǎoshang tā yào dào jīchǎng qù sòng péngyou, sòngwán péngyou, zhíjiē cóng jīchǎng lái.

(II)

(bàn xiǎoshí yǐhòu)

Shānběn:	Duìbuqǐ, wǒ láiwǎn le.
Ānnà:	Méi guānxi.
Fāng Xiǎoyīng:	Wǒmen děngle ni bàn ge zhōngtóu le. Nǐ zěnme la?
Shānběn:	Bié tí la! Wǒ zài chēshang shuìzháo le, zuòguò le zhàn ...
Jīn Zhōngyī:	Wǒ yǐwéi nǐ jìcuò shíjiān le ne.
Mǎdīng:	Wǒ yǐwéi nǐ mí lù le ne.
Shānběn:	Dōu méiyou, nǐmen dàile xiē shénme hǎochī de? Wǒ yòu kě yòu è.
Fāng Xiǎoyīng:	Wǒ dàile yìxiē píngguǒ, bǐnggān shénmede. Píngguǒ dōu xǐ gānjing le.
Mǎdīng:	Méi guānxi, bù xǐ yě néng chī.

英译课文

I came by bus

(I)

(At the entrance to Southlake Park)

Anna:	You got here really early! Xiaoying, when did you get here?
Fang Xiaoying:	About ten minutes ago, I think.
Kim Chung-il:	She was the first to arrive.
Anna:	Did you come with Martin?
Kim Chung-il:	Yes, we rode together by bike.
Anna:	Did you all start out from school?
Kim Chung-il:	Yes, I got up at 7:30 this morning, had breakfast at 8:00 and got to school at 8:45. Then I started off by bike with Martin, getting here at about 9:30.

Martin: Anna, how did you get here?

Anna: I came by bus. Xiaoying, did you walk?

Fang Xiaoying: No, I didn't walk, I came by trolley. I first went to a friend's house this morning to return some books — a novel and two magazines that I'd borrowed last week — then came right after I returned them.

Anna: Why aren't David and Yamamoto here yet?

Martin: David said that he'd been terribly busy lately and that this morning he had something he had to do. Yamamoto is coming, but this morning he has to see a friend off at the airport and will come directly after doing that.

(II)

(A half hour later)

Yamamoto: I'm sorry I'm late.

Anna: That's all right.

Fang Xiaoying: We've waited a half an hour for you. What happened?

Yamamoto: Don't ask! I fell asleep on the train and went past the station ...

Kim Chung-il: I thought you got the time mixed up.

Martin: And I thought you got lost.

Yamamoto: Neither of those. What did you bring that's good to eat? I'm thirsty and hungry.

Fang Xiaoying: I brought some apples, cookies and that sort. The apples have been washed clean.

Martin: That's all right. You can eat them without washing them.

课堂活动

I. shì … de sentences

“是……的”句

A. Students separate into groups of two or three. They then describe their given situation to the class according to the prompts supplied, using shì ... de sentences. They should at the same time ask other students to take notes of the situation details that they are describing. At the end, two or three students who are responsible for describing the situations will ask the class several relevant questions. For example, Group A may ask the class how many hours Xiao Ying attended class, or how long it takes to get to school from home. Group B can ask the class to tell whose home is nearest or farthest from the park and why they assume so.

老师分组，二人或三人一组。每组有几个提示，请每组同学按照提示用“是……的”来向全班做简短的叙述，并要求全班记下细节，最后负责叙述的两三位同学问全班几个相关的问题。例如，A组可问全班小英上课上了几个小时，从家里到学校要多长时间等；B组可请全班估计安娜、大卫等人谁的家离公园最近或最远，并说出理由。

Group A Describe what Xiǎo Yīng did this morning and when it was done.

A组 请说说小英今天上午做了什么，是几点做的。

7:00am起床	7:30am吃早饭	8:15am上车
8:45am到学校	9:30am上课	12:20pm下课

Group B Tell how the various people came today.

B组 请告诉我们，他们今天都是怎么来公园的。

安娜/电车	大卫/地铁	山本/船
金中一/公共汽车	马丁/自行车	方小英/走着

Group C Tell in which bookstore they bought their magazines.

C组 请告诉我们，他们的杂志都是在哪个书店买的。

方小英/楼下	马丁/饭店旁边	金中一/学校附近
大卫/机场	山本/商场里	张老师/地铁站里

Group D "I Won't Come Home Today" is an old film that they have all seen. When did they see it?

D组 "今天不回家"是一个很旧的电影，他们都看过这个电影，请你告诉我们，他们是什么时候看的。

大卫/五年以前	山本/去年	金中一/上个星期
安娜/昨天	马丁/星期六	方小英/三个月以前

B. Students form pairs, one student with Card A and the other Card B. Based on hints in the pictures, answer the questions using <u>shì</u> ... <u>de</u> constructions. For example, A may ask B "Whom did you buy that drink for?" When the answer is known, connect the correct item at the left to the person on the right with a line. Then, "Where did you buy it?" may be asked, or "When did you buy it?"
二人一组，一人持A图，一人持B图，根据图上提示，用"是……的"句型来提问和回答。例如A问B"那杯饮料是给谁买的？"知道答案以后，请用线把左边的东西和右边的人连起来。然后再问，"是在哪儿买的？"或"是什么时候买的？"

A

买 	
借 	
买 	
买 	
买 	
借 	

 大卫	在哪儿？
 娜娜	什么时候？
 大中	什么时候？
 谢小姐	在哪儿？
 安安	在哪儿？
 小英	什么时候？

按照下图用“是……的”句型来回答B同学的问题：

 老王	 小张	 山本小姐	 方老师	 老丁	 小马
书店	饭馆儿	上午	上星期	商店	前天

B

买		 小张	在哪儿？
买		 老丁	在哪儿？
借		 山本小姐	什么时候？
借		 小马	什么时候？
买		 老王	在哪儿？
买		 方老师	什么时候？

按照下图用"是……的"句型来回答A同学的问题：

 谢小姐	 小英	 大中	 安安	 大卫	 娜娜
饭馆儿	今天上午	昨天	书店	商场	上个月

C. Students form pairs, then on the basis of the illustration information, use shì ... de sentences to ask questions and answer each other. Each of the four illustrations on students' cards have material for at least three questions.

二人一组，根据图上提示，用"是……的"句型提问和回答。每幅图最少提三个问题。

II. Preposed object, giving a passive sense

意义上的被动

Ask and answer questions back and forth on the basis of the illustrations. A "✓" indicates an affirmative answer, a "✗" negative. Note that you may use the resultative complements wán, hǎo, dào, zháo, etc. after the verb.

请同学看着图轮流提问并回答。"✓"表示答案是肯定的，"✗"表示答案是否定的。注意：动词后可用结果补语"完"、"好"、"到"、"着"等。

Example:

A: Qián dài lái le méiyǒu?

钱带来了没有？

B: Duìbuqǐ,méi dài lái.

对不起，没带来。

第十八课

在老师家过新年

汉字课文

(一)

(新年，同学们在张老师家的客厅里聊天儿。安娜、方小英在厨房里帮张老师做菜。大卫和山本进厨房来了。)

山　本：你们做什么菜呢？

大　卫：快做完了吧？

方小英：我正在做糖醋鱼。大卫，你帮我把糖拿来。

大　卫：汤就在你旁边儿，你还要什么汤？

安　娜：她要的是糖，不是汤。

大　卫：哦，"糖""汤"——不一样，是糖醋鱼，不是汤醋鱼。对不起，我没把发音学好。

安　娜：你平常发音很清楚啊！今天怎么啦？

山　本：他只想着吃饭了，把声调忘了。

张老师：大卫，山本，你们把水果沙拉和这两个菜端走吧。

大卫和山本：是！老师！

(二)

张老师：菜都做好了，大家吃吧，别客气！

马　丁：这么多菜！太好了。谢谢老师！

山　本：快把酒倒在杯子里。马丁，把这杯酒给张老师。

金中一：这个菜非常好吃。

马　丁：我也尝尝。大卫，递给我一双筷子。嗯，味道真不错。

张老师：忘了把饺子端来了。

马　丁：我去端。

金中一：我来，我来。

方小英：把饺子放到桌子中间，我们和老师一起照张相。金中一，照相机呢？

金中一：在这儿。我先给你们照。

(照完相，张老师尝了一个饺子。)

张老师：饺子不够咸，有一点儿淡。放点儿酱油吧。

安　娜：这儿有酱油、盐，还有醋。

大　卫：快把醋递给我，我爱吃醋。

(大家都笑了)

生词语

1. 新年 xīnnián (n) the new year; New Year's
2. 客厅 kètīng (n) [个，间] living room, parlor
3. 聊天儿 liáo tiānr (vo) to chat, have light conversation
   a. 我们聊了一会儿(天儿)，她就来了。
   b. 马丁很喜欢跟朋友聊天儿。
4. 厨房 chúfáng (n) [个，间] kitchen
5. 帮 bāng (v) to help
   a. 我今天要给大家做几个中国菜，你来帮帮我。
   b. 你去商店吗？帮我买一瓶酱油来，怎么样？
6. 把 bǎ (prep) (the pretransitive or disposal preposition)
7. 糖 táng (n) sweets, candy, sugar

8.	发音	fāyīn	(n)	pronunciation
9.	平常	píngcháng	(adj, n)	ordinary, ordinarily

a. 他平常早上七点就起床了，今天九点才起来。

b. 他平常下了课一定去打网球，今天为什么不去了？

c. 这是一件很平常的事。

10.	声调	shēngdiào	(n) [个]	tones (of Chinese)
11.	忘	wàng	(v)	to forget (since by its nature it is action that has occurred, wàng is always followed by le, a resultative complement, or negated with méi)

a. 你让我办的事，我忘了。真对不起！

b. 我的本子忘在宿舍里了。

c. 别忘了把名字写上。

d. 我忘了带照相机了，借你的用用，行吗？

12.	水果	shuǐguǒ	(n)	fruit
13.	沙拉	shālā	(n)	salad (often spoken as shālà)
14.	端	duān	(v)	to carry level with both hands, outstretched, as a tray, basin

a. 她端着两个菜，不知道放在哪儿好。

b. 请你把饼干和苹果端到桌子上。

c. 你把这两杯啤酒端走吧，没有人喝。

15.	走	zǒu	(v)	to go away, to leave; to walk

a. 安娜告诉我他要回国了，他什么时候走？

b. 下课以后他就走了，大概回家了吧？

c. 金中一，你别走，老师找你有事。

d. 请你把这些东西拿走，我要在这儿放箱子。

16.	客气	kèqi	(v, adj)		to act with politeness or modest restraint; to be polite
17.	酒	jiǔ	(n)		wine; generic noun for wines and spirits
18.	倒	dào	(v)		to pour
19.	杯子	bēizi	(n)	[个]	glass, cup
20.	递	dì	(v)		to pass to

a. 请递给我一个苹果。

b. 这个本子是他的，请递一下儿。

21.	筷子	kuàizi	(n)	[双，只]	chopsticks
22.	味道	wèidao	(n)		flavor, taste
23.	饺子	jiǎozi	(n)	[个]	Chinese dumplings
24.	放	fàng	(v)		to place, put

a. 把书放在那张桌子上吧！

b. 桌子上放着一本《汉语小词典》，是不是金中一的？

c. 快把东西放下吧！累不累？

25.	照相	zhào xiàng	(vo)		to take pictures, photograph
26.	照相机	zhàoxiàngjī	(n)	[个]	camera
27.	够	gòu	(adj)		to be enough, adequate

a. 每个月，你的钱够用吗？

——有的时候够用，有的时候不够用。

b. 这件衣服不够长，我穿不合适，给弟弟穿吧。

c. 一个人吃一个苹果够不够？

——我吃一个就够了。他不够，他得吃两个。

28.	咸	xián	(adj)		to be salty
29.	有(一)点儿	yǒu(yì)diǎnr	(adv)		slight, somewhat, a bit

30. 淡	dàn	(adj)	to be not salty; be insipid; be pale or light (of color)
31. 酱油	jiàngyóu	(n)	soy sauce
32. 盐	yán	(n)	salt
33. 醋	cù	(n)	vinegar
34. 爱	ài	(v)	to be fond of, like to; to love

a. 山本爱喝酒，也爱吃辣的。

b. 他爱打网球，不爱游泳。

c. 他上课的时候爱说话。

补充生词

1. 刀子	dāozi	(n)	[把]	knife
2. 叉子	chāzi	(n)	[个，把]	fork
3. 餐厅	cāntīng	(n)	[个]	restaurant
4. 洗手间	xǐshǒujiān	(n)	[个]	washroom
5. 甜	tián	(adj)		to be sweet
6. 酸	suān	(adj)		to be sour
7. 苦	kǔ	(adj)		to be bitter
8. 香	xiāng	(adj)		to be fragrant
9. 春节	Chūn Jié	(n)		Spring Festival — Lunar New Year's Day
10. 圣诞节	Shèngdàn Jié	(n)		Christmas

语法点

1. The <u>bă</u> 把 sentence (1)

"把"字句 (1)

In verbal predicate sentences that describe how the verb has "disposed" of a particular object or how the particular object has been affected by the verb, the bǎ construction is the preferred form. Bǎ is sometimes called the "transfer preposition" or "pretransitive".
"把"是标志处置意义的介词，或者说是有转移力的介词。当我们要说明动作如何处置一个特定的宾语或者如何使这个宾语受动作的影响时，就要用"把"字句。

S + 把 + O + Verbal phrase

NOTE these features:
注意"把"字句的下列特点：

- The verb is generally transitive and one that can control or affect the object of bǎ.
  动词一般是及物动词，从意义上看，可以处理或影响"把"的宾语。
- The verb has a complement (or is reduplicated, followed by le 了, etc.).
  动词往往带有补语（或是重叠形式，或者带"了"等）。
- The object is a particular one, not just "a dictionary", for example, but "the dictionary".
  宾语是确指的。比如，要说："这本词典"，而不要说"一本词典"。
- The negative (bù, méiyǒu) and optative verbs (néng 能, kéyǐ 可以, xiǎng 想, etc.) come before bǎ 把.
  否定副词（"不"，"没有"）和能愿动词（"能"、"可以"、"想"等）要放在"把"之前。

S + 不／没 + 能 + 把 + O + Verbal phrase

a. Míngtiān nǐmen dōu bǎ cídiǎn dàilái.

明天你们都把词典带来。

All of you bring your (= particularized) dictionaries tomorrow.

b. Dàwèi bǎ nèijiàn shì wàng le.

大卫把那件事忘了。

David forgot that matter.

c. Tā xiǎng bǎ xuéguo de Hànzì zài xiě yi xiě.

他想把学过的汉字再写一写。

He wants to write the Chinese characters he learned again.

d. Wǒ méi bǎ zuótiān de zuòyè zuòwán.

我没把昨天的作业做完。

I haven't finished yesterday's homework.

These example sentences can be spoken without bǎ, e.g. Míngtian nǐmen dōu dài cídiǎn lái 明天你们都带词典来. The difference is that, without bǎ, the sentence is a straightforward statement. Using bǎ spotlights the object following bǎ and emphasizes how it is/will be/was handled.

上述各例，也可以用不带"把"的句子表达，如"明天你们都带词典来"。所不同的是，不用"把"，只是对一件事情的一般叙述。用上"把"，就含有突出强调"把"的宾语，并表示(说话人)注意的重点在"把"后的宾语上，而且强调将要或已经如何处理它。

2. The bǎ 把 construction (2)

"把"字句(2)

We are now looking at sentences where bǎ must be used. When the main verb in the predicate not only has an object but also the resultative complement zài 在 or dào 到 followed by an object of location, the bǎ construction is generally required.

这是一种必须用"把"的句子。谓语主要动词有受事宾语，同时还带有结果补语"在"或"到"，"在""到"后面又有处所宾语时，一般就要用"把"字句来表达。

S + 把 + pO + V + 在／到 + O (place)

a. Nǐ bǎ míngzi xiězai zhèr ba.

你把名字写在这儿吧。

Write your name here, why don't you.

b. Nǐmen néng bǎ wǒ mǎi de dōngxi sòngdào wǒ jiāli ma?

你们能把我买的东西送到我家里吗？

Can you send the things I bought to my house?

* These sentences cannot be phrased as follows:
上述例句，不能说成：

✗ Nǐ xiě míngzì zài zhèr ba.

你写名字在这儿吧。

✗ Nǐmen néng sòng wǒ mǎide dōngxi dào wǒ jiāli ma?

你们能送我买的东西到我家里吗？

If the direct object is definite in sentences where the main verb has the resultative complement <u>gěi</u> 给 and at the same time direct and indirect objects, <u>bǎ</u> is preferred.

如果动词或动词 + "给" 带有双宾语，而且直接宾语是确指的（有定的），这时最好用"把"字句：

S + 把 + pO (direct) + V + 给 + O (indirect)

c. Qǐng bǎ zhèige liànxí běnzi jiāogěi Wáng lǎoshī.

请把这个练习本子交给王老师。

Please hand this practice notebook in to Mrs. Wang.

d. Qǐng bǎ zhè bēi píjiǔ nágěi Shānběn.

请把这杯啤酒拿给山本。

Please take this glass of beer to Yamamoto.

3. <u>Yǒu (yi) diǎnr</u> 有（一）点儿, "a little, somewhat"

"有（一）点儿"

The adjectival construction that follows this adverb usually has a negative or dissatisfying connotation.

"有（一）点儿"是副词，经常修饰形容词，被修饰的形容词或形容词结构通常表示不如意的情况或性质。

a. Lǎoshī wèn de wèntí yǒudiǎnr nán.

老师问的问题有点儿难。

The questions the teacher asked are a bit tough.

b. Nà jiàn yīfu bǐjiào hǎokàn, kěshi yǒudiǎnr guì.

那件衣服比较好看，可是有点儿贵。

That item of clothing is pretty good looking, but a bit expensive.

c. Jīntiān tīngxiě de shíhou wǒ yǒuyidiǎnr jǐnzhāng, dàgài xiěcuò le liǎng ge zì.

今天听写的时候我有一点儿紧张，大概写错了两个字。

During dictation today I was somewhat nervous and probably wrote a couple of characters wrong.

d. Tā jīntiān yǒudiǎnr bù gāoxing, nǐ zhīdao wèishénme ma?

她今天有点儿不高兴，你知道为什么吗？

She's a bit unhappy today. Do you know why?

NOTES 注释

1. Nǐ hái yào shénme tāng 你还要什么汤 "What do you mean 'get me some soup'?" When what someone has said is repeated with a shénme added, as here, it indicates disapproval or disagreement. Shénme is added after the repeated verb (or adjective).

"你还要什么汤？"：当说话人不赞成或不同意对方的做法或意见时，可以重复对方的话，并在被重复的动词(或形容词)后，加上"什么"。

A: Tā shuō tā xiǎng gēn wǒmen dǎ yìhuǐr wǎngqiú.

他说他想跟我们打一会儿网球。

He says he wants to play some tennis with us.

B: Tā dǎ shénme wǎngqiú, tā hái méi xuéhuì ne.

他打什么网球，他还没学会呢。

Him play tennis? He hasn't learned how yet!

2. Chī cù 吃醋 "to be jealous". This expression is used for jealousy between the sexes.

"吃醋"，指在男女关系上产生嫉妒情绪。

词组和句子

1. 他把我的姓写错了，不过，把名字写对了。
2. 妈妈把青菜沙拉做好了。
3. 爸爸最近很忙，今天中午他没把饭吃完，就到公司去了。
4. 明天我们去公园，你别忘了把照相机带去。
5. 她没把书带来，我把书借给她吧！
6. 别担心，妹妹能把水果洗得很干净。
7. 你把菜做得太淡了，再放一点儿盐吧。
8. 请你把生词再念一遍。
9. 我想把学过的生词好好儿复习一下儿。
10. 你如果有纸和笔，就把他的话记一记。
11. 我把他的电话号码忘了。
12. 明天你们去公园，把这些水果带着吧。
13. 别客气，随便坐，把东西放在我床上吧。
14. 请后天下午六点以前把蛋糕送到我家里。
15. 弟弟，快把这两杯酒端给爷爷和奶奶。
16. 这是一本非常好的小说，应该把这本书介绍给他们。
17. 明天他过生日，我想把这件礼物送给他。

18. 你能把电话号码告诉我吗？
19. 请你把酱油和醋递给我，我又爱吃酱油，又爱吃醋。
20. 这个菜有点儿咸，你能吃吗？
21. 这种酒有点儿辣，你能喝吗？
22. 姐姐今天有点儿不高兴，你知道为什么吗？
23. 他的发音有点儿不清楚，我没听懂他的话。

参考资料

拼音课文

Zài lǎoshī jiā guò Xīnnián

(I)

(Xīnnián, tóngxuémen zài Zhāng lǎoshī jiā de kètīng li liáo tiānr. Ānnà, Fāng Xiǎoyīng zài chúfáng li bāng Zhāng lǎoshī zuò cài. Dàwèi hé Shānběn jìn chúfáng lái le.)

Shānběn: Nǐmen zuò shénme cài ne?

Dàwèi: Kuài zuòwán le ba?

Fāng Xiǎoyīng: Wǒ zhèngzài zuò tángcùyú. Dàwèi, nǐ bāng wǒ bǎ táng ná lai.

Dàwèi: Tāng jiù zài nǐ pángbiānr, nǐ hái yào shénme tāng?

Ānnà: Tā yào de shi táng, bú shi tāng.

Dàwèi: O, "táng" "tāng" — bù yíyàng, shì tángcùyú, bú shì tāngcùyú. Duìbuqǐ, wǒ méi bǎ fāyīn xuéhǎo.

Ānnà: Nǐ píngcháng fāyīn hěn qīngchu a! Jīntian zěnme la?

Shānběn: Tā zhǐ xiǎngzhe chī fàn le, bǎ shēngdiào wàng le.

Zhāng lǎoshī: Dàwèi, Shānběn, nǐmen bǎ shuǐguǒ shālā hé zhè liǎng ge cài duānzǒu ba.

Dàwèi hé Shānběn: Shì! Lǎoshī!

(II)

Zhāng lǎoshī: Cài dōu zuòhǎo le, dàjiā chī ba, bié kèqi!

Mǎdīng: Zhème duō cài! Tài hǎo le. Xièxie lǎoshī!

Shānběn: Kuài bǎ jiǔ dàozai bēizi li. Mǎdīng, bǎ zhè bēi jiǔ gěi Zhāng lǎoshī.

Jīn Zhōngyī: Zhège cài fēicháng hǎochī.

Mǎdīng: Wǒ yě chángchang. Dàwèi, dìgěi wo yì shuāng kuàizi. Ng, wèidào zhēn búcuò.

Zhāng lǎoshī: Wàngle bǎ jiǎozi duānlái le.

Mǎdīng: Wǒ qù duān.

Jīn Zhōngyī: Wǒ lái, wǒ lái.

Fāng Xiǎoyīng: Bǎ jiǎozi fàngdào zhuōzi zhōngjiān, wǒmen hé lǎoshī yìqǐ zhào zhāng xiàng. Jīn Zhōngyī, zhàoxiàngjī ne?

Jīn Zhōngyī: Zài zhèr. Wǒ xiān gěi nǐmen zhào.

(Zhàowán xiàng, Zhāng lǎoshī chángle yí ge jiǎozi.)

Zhāng lǎoshī: Jiǎozi bú gòu xián, yǒuyìdiǎnr dàn. Fàng diǎnr jiàngyóu ba.

Ānnà: Zhèr yǒu jiàngyóu, yán, hái yǒu cù.

Dàwèi: Kuài bǎ cù dìgěi wo, wǒ ài chī cù.

(Dàjiā dōu xiaò le)

英译课文

Celebrating New Year's Day at the teacher's house

(I)

(New Year's Day, the students are chatting in Mrs. Zhang's living room. Anna and Fang Xiaoying are in the kitchen helping Mrs. Zhang cook. David and Yamamoto come into the kitchen.)

Yamamoto: What are you cooking?

David: Is it almost finished?

Fang Xiaoying: I'm making a sweet and sour fish. David, bring me the sugar.

David: The soup is right there by you. Why do you want me to bring you the soup?

Anna: She wants sugar, not soup.

David: Oh, "soup" and "sugar" are different. It's "sweet" and sour fish, not "soup" and sour fish. Sorry, I haven't got the pronunciation down.

Anna: Your pronunciation is usually pretty clear. What's wrong with you today?

Yamamoto: He's preoccupied with eating and has forgotten about pronunciation.

Mrs. Zhang: David, Yamamoto, take the fruit salad and these two dishes out.

David and Yamamoto: Yes, sir, Mrs. Zhang!

(II)

Mrs. Zhang: Everything is prepared. Eat up everyone, make yourselves at home!

Martin: So much! This is great! Thanks, Mrs. Zhang.

Yamamoto: Pour the wine. Martin, give this glass of wine to Mrs. Zhang.

Kim Chung-il: This dish is delicious.

Martin: Let me taste it. David, pass me a pair of chopsticks. Mm, it tastes great.

Mrs. Zhang: I forgot to bring out the dumplings.

Martin: I'll go bring them.

Kim Chung-il: I'll do it, I'll do it.

Fang Xiaoying: Put the dumplings in the middle. We'll take a picture together with Mrs. Zhang. Kim Chung-il, the camera?

Kim Chung-il: Here. I'll take one of you first.

(After the picture is taken, Mrs. Zhang tastes a dumpling.)

Mrs. Zhang: The dumplings are a bit bland, not salty enough. Add a bit (= dip them in a bit) of soy sauce.

Anna: The soy sauce, salt and vinegar are here.

David: Pass me the vinegar. I like vinegar.

(Everybody laughs)

课堂活动

I. Bǎ constructions

"把"字句

(1) In pairs, students A and B use information on Cards A and B to ask and answer questions using bǎ constructions.

老师分组，二人一组，一人持A图，一人持B图。请学生看着图，用"把"字句来提问及回答。

A

Example:

A: Shéi bǎ zì xiěcuò le?

谁把字写错了？

B: Mǎdīng bǎ zì xiěcuò le.

马丁把字写错了。

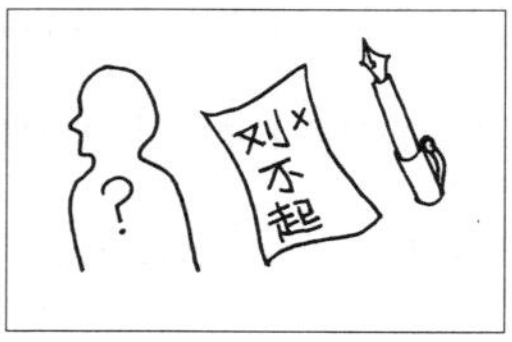

B

Example:

A: Shéi bǎ zì xiěcuò le?

谁把字写错了？

B: Mǎdīng bǎ zì xiěcuò le.

马丁把字写错了。

(2) The instructor writes <u>bǎ</u> construction sentences on cards for each member of the class. For example:

老师按照班上学生人数，写出若干"把"字句的卡片，如：

A. Qǐng bǎ nǐ de míngzi xiě zài běnzi shàng.

请把你的名字写在本子上。

B. Qǐng bǎ wǒ de cídiǎn gěi yí wèi nǚ tóngxué.

请把我的词典给一位女同学。

Ask students to do what the cards instruct them to. Once they have, ask other students in the class to describe what has been done.

然后发给学生，一人一句。请学生看了句子以后，按照指示完成动作，再让班上其他同学用“把”字句来说明他所做的动作。

(3) Students form pairs and, using information on their cards, aks each other questions in turn. The questioner must convert his question into a bǎ construction and the answering student must also use a bǎ construction together with the prompt information in response.

老师分组，二人一组，轮流问答。提问的人需将问题改成“把”字句来提问，回答的人需用“把”字句和所给的提示来回答。

A 例A：马丁为什么没把汤喝完？

B：大卫把那个汤端走了。

(例)

马丁	为什么没喝完汤？
山本	为什么没交来他的作业本子？
安娜	为什么没告诉大卫这件事？
金中一	为什么没带新书来？
大卫	为什么没喝完那杯啤酒？
方小英	洗／那件衣服
他朋友	还／那本小说／图书馆
小马	忘／今天要听写的事
美美	丢／自己的照相机

B　例A：马丁为什么没把汤喝完？

　　B：大卫把那个汤端走了。

(例)	大卫	端／那个汤
	山本	没做完／作业
	安娜	忘／这件事
	金中一	丢／那本新书
	马丁	喝／那半杯啤酒
	方小英	为什么没拿那件衣服来？
	小张	为什么没看完那本小说？
	小马	为什么没练习一下儿学过的汉字？
	美美	为什么没带照相机来？

II. <u>Yǒuyìdiǎnr</u>

“有一点儿”

Students make sentence with the <u>yǒuyìdiǎnr</u> adverbial on the basis of the illustration content.

请学生看着图，用“有一点儿”来造句。

阅读练习

(一)

南湖公园很大，在我们学校的南边儿，从学校门口儿坐公共汽车去，二十分钟就可以到了。公园里有一个大湖，叫南湖，湖里当然可以划船。公园里还有网球场、游泳池。每个星期日去南湖公园的人都不少。

昨天我跟几个同学约好了，一起去南湖公园划船。大家说今天早上九点四十在公园门口儿见面，然后一起进去。

今天我来得最早，我是九点二十五到的。小马家离公园不太远，可是他没来过这个公园，不认识路。今天他是跟小关一起来的，他们是骑自行车来的。小王和小丁都住校，他们是坐公共汽车来的。从学校外边儿上车，到公园门口儿下车。非常方便。

今天我们每个人都带了饮料和吃的东西。我们还带了照相机。大家可以在一起吃饭，照照相，划划船。说说笑笑，一定很高兴。

(二)

我二十三岁 (suì, year of age) 的时候，我妈妈说，我已经二十三了，应该找女朋友了。她请她的朋友帮我介绍了几个。为什么要介绍几个呢？我妈妈说可以比较一下儿，找个最好的。

照片我都看过了，有一个我觉得还不错，可是不知道人怎么样。听我妈妈说是一位小学老师。我想先跟她见见面。我妈妈的朋友给我们约好，在公园门口儿见面，星期六下午六点。五点半我就去了，我想：不能去晚了，让她等我。哎呀，这半个小时真长，我觉得时间过得太慢了。最后，来了一位小姐问我是不是姓“王”。她说她朋友今天有事儿，不能来了。我跟她说：“没关系。你来了，我们就进去散散步吧。”这个人就是我现在的太太。

第十九课

今天天气怎么样？

汉字课文

（一天下午，大卫打完网球回到宿舍，山本正在看电视）

大　卫：今天天气真不错。

山　本：是啊。这几天总是阴天，我以为会下雨呢。

大　卫：你看天气预报了吗？

山　本：刚看完。

大　卫：今天多少度？

山　本：10到15度。

大　卫：听说中国北方已经下雪了，我们这儿还这么暖和。

山　本：我最喜欢下雪了。

大　卫：你家是不是在日本的北方？

山　本：是，在北方。那儿冬天很冷，常常下大雪。

大　卫：常刮风吗？

山　本：有时候刮风。

大　卫：夏天没有这儿这么热吧？

山　本：比这儿凉快多了，气温跟这儿的秋天差不多。

大　卫：我家在美国中部，那儿夏天也比这儿凉快，天气比较干燥。春天天气更好。

山　本：这儿太潮湿了。

大　卫：山本，这是谁的雨伞？

山　本：雨伞？我看看，这是金中一的，我看见他打过。

大　卫：他刚来过吗？

山　本：没有，他昨天晚上来过，大概走的时候忘了带了。

大　卫：我今天下午也看见他了。他说他家的空调坏了，要去找人修理。

山　本：天气这么潮湿，没有空调真不舒服。

大　卫：如果我们的宿舍也有空调，那多好啊！

山　本：还用你说！

生词语

1.	天气	tiānqì	(n)		weather
2.	电视	diànshì	(n)	[个]	television
3.	总是	zǒngshì	(adv)		always

a. 你怎么回家以后总是写信？
—— 我接到了很多朋友的信，我要给他们回信啊！

b. 你的房间总是那么干净。

c. 他总是晚上十点半睡，早上六点半起(床)。

d. 上课的时候，他总是坐在中间的椅子上。

4.	阴天	yīntiān	(n)	[个]	overcast day, cloudy day
5.	下雨	xià yǔ	(vo)		to rain
	下	xià	(v)		to come down, fall
	雨	yǔ	(n)		rain
6.	预报	yùbào	(n,v)		forecast
7.	刚	gāng	(adv)		just

a. 刚吃完饭，不要去游泳。

b. 你来得真早，你是什么时候到的？

—— 我刚到，到了五分钟吧！

c. 刚下完雨，天气很凉快。

d. 我刚开始做作业，他就来了；他在这儿聊了半小时天儿，才走。

8.	度	dù	(m)		degree
9.	听说	tīngshuō	(v)		to have heard

a. 听说那儿的冬天非常冷，夏天非常热。

b. 我听说那位老师教中文教得非常好。

c. 这件事你听说过没有？

—— 没有，我没听说过。

10.	北方	běifāng	(n)		the north, northern part
11.	下雪	xià xuě	(vo)		to snow
	下	xià	(v)		to come down, fall
	雪	xuě	(n)		snow
12.	这么	zème; zhème	(pro)		to this degree, so

a. 天气怎么这么冷？

b. 他以前不知道饺子这么好吃。

13.	暖和	nuănhuo	(adj)		to be comfortably warm
14.	冬天	dōngtiān	(n)	[个]	winter
15.	冷	lěng	(adj)		to be cold (of weather)
16.	刮风	guā fēng	(vo)		to be windy
	刮	guā	(v)		to blow
	风	fēng	(n)		wind
17.	夏天	xiàtiān	(n)	[个]	summer
18.	热	rè	(adj)		to be hot (of weather) (sometimes, as with lěng, used metaphorically)

19.	比	bǐ	(prep, v)		comparative preposition; to compare, match against
20.	凉快	liángkuai	(adj)		to be cool (of the weather)
21.	气温	qìwēn	(n)		atmospheric temperature
22.	秋天	qiūtiān	(n)	[个]	autumn, fall
23.	中部	zhōngbù	(n)		central part
24.	干燥	gānzào	(adj)		to be dry (of the air and related phenomena)
25.	春天	chūntiān	(n)	[个]	spring
26.	更	gèng	(adv)		more, -er
27.	潮湿	cháoshī	(adj)		to be damp (of the air and related phenomena)
28.	雨伞	yǔsǎn	(n)	[把]	umbrella
29.	看见	kànjian			to see
30.	打	dǎ	(v)		to open, hold up (as an umbrella or flag)
31.	空调	kōngtiáo	(n)	[个]	air conditioner
32.	坏	huài	(adj)		to be bad, to be broken (malfunction), to go bad (as food)

a. 我的照相机坏了，要拿去修理一下儿。

b. 你怎么又来晚了？

—— 我的汽车在路上坏了。

c. 我的雨伞坏了，不能用了。

d. 晚上，这条路上有坏人吗？

e. 你说，这是件坏事，还是件好事？

33.	修理	xiūlǐ	(v)		to repair
34.	舒服	shūfu	(adj)		to be comfortable

a. 这种天气不潮湿，也不干燥，让人觉得很舒服。

b. 你昨天睡得怎么样？这种床舒服不舒服？

—— 不错，我睡得很舒服。

c. 老师，我有点儿不舒服，下一节课我想请假。

—— 好吧，你回宿舍休息一下。好了再来上课。

35. 多（么） duō (me) (adv) how (as in "how beautiful") — to that degree

补充生词

1.	晴天	qíngtiān	(n)	[个]	clear day
2.	晴	qíng	(adj)		to be clear (of the weather)
3.	季节	jìjié	(n)	[个]	season
4.	太阳	tàiyang	(n)	[个]	sun
5.	雨衣	yǔyī	(n)	[件]	raincoat, rainwear

语 法 点

1. Sentences without subjects

无主语句

The usual sentence in Chinese has both subject and predicate. However, in cases describing natural phenomena (viz. English "It is …") or where the subject is self-evident, a sentence can be subjectless.

汉语里一般句子都有主语和谓语两部分，但也有的句子没有主语，如叙述自然现象的（英语用"It is …"句式）或者是主语不言自明的。

a. Xià yǔ le.

下雨了。

It's raining.

b. Guā fēng le.

刮风了。

It's gotten windy.

c. Shàng kè le.

上课了。

(We will) start class now.

d. Xiànzài xià kè.

现在下课。

(We will) stop class.

e. Chī fàn le.

吃饭了。

(I/We'll) eat now.

2. The comparative preposition bǐ 比

表示比较的介词"比"

The bǐ sentence construction is:
用"比"的句型是:

A 比 B + Adj

a. Rìběn de běifāng bǐ nánfāng lěng.

日本的北方比南方冷。

The northern part of Japan is colder than the southern part.

b. Wǒ xuéguo hěn duō Hànzì. Tā xué de bǐ wǒ gèng duō.

我学过很多汉字。他学的比我更多。

I've learned many Chinese characters, but he has learned even more than me.

Some word expressing the degree of comparison can be placed after the adjective, such as yìdiǎnr 一点儿 "a bit", yìxiē 一些 "somewhat", or duōle 多了; de duō 得多 "much more".

某些表示比较程度的词语可以用在形容词之后，如"一点儿""一些""多了""得多"。

A 比 B + Adj + 一点儿/多了

c. Rìběn de běifāng bǐ nánfāng lěngduō le.

日本的北方比南方冷多了。

The northern part of Japan is much colder than the southern part.

d. Tā xuéguo de Hànzì bǐ wǒ xuéguo de duō yìdiǎnr.

他学过的汉字比我学过的多一点儿。

He has studied a few more Chinese characters than I have.

Or a more specific number may qualify the compared quality.

或者在形容词之后用上某些数量词语，具体说明比较的差别。

e. Tā xuéguo de Hànzì bǐ wǒ xuéguo de duō jǐshí ge.

他学过的汉字比我学过的多几十个。

He has studied a few dozen more Chinese characters than I have.

f. Zhèi běn cídiǎn bǐ nèi běn shū guì èrshí kuài qián.

这本词典比那本书贵二十块钱。

This dictionary is twenty yuan more expensive than that book.

In bǐ 比 sentences, do not use hěn 很 before the adjective.

在"比"字句中形容词前不能用"很"。

3. Méiyǒu ... (nème/zhème)

没有……（那么/这么）

A méiyǒu B (nème/zhème) ADJECTIVE, "A is not as Adjective as B". Its sense is that A does not reach the degree of B, and nème/zhème "that, this" often appear before the adjective to underscore the point.

"A没有B(那么／这么) + 形容词"句式表达的意思是：A没有达到B的程度。经常出现在形容词前的"那么／这么"强调指示的作用。

A 没有 B + (那么/这么) + Adj

a. Zuótiān de zuòyè méiyǒu jīntiān de nán.

昨天的作业没有今天的难。

Yesterday's homework wasn't as difficult as today's.

b. Rìběn de nánfāng méiyǒu běifāng nàme lěng.

日本的南方没有北方那么冷。

The southern part of Japan isn't as cold as the northern part.

c. Wǒ xuéguo de Hànzì méiyǒu tā xuéguo de nàme duō.

我学过的汉字没有他学过的那么多。

I haven't studied as many Chinese characters as he has.

d. Zhèige jiàoshì méiyǒu nèige jiaòshì nàme dà.

这个教室没有那个教室那么大。

This classroom isn't as big as that one.

e. Wǒ shuō Hànyǔ méiyǒu nǐ shuō de zhème hǎo.

我说汉语没有你说得这么好。

I don't speak Chinese as well as you do.

NOTES 注释

1. Nà duō hǎo a! 那多好啊！ "That's great!" or "Wouldn't that be great!" Here, the nà refers to the previous statement, in our text the presence of air conditioning in the dormitory rooms.

   "那多好啊！""那"用以指上文。本课是指"宿舍里有空调"。

2. Hái yòng nǐ shuō! 还用你说！"Isn't that the truth!" or "That goes without saying!" Hái 还 in such contexts is rhetorical, expressing irony or sarcasm. Here it is literally "is it still something you have to say?" See also the example at Lesson 21, note 2 below.

"还用你说！""还"在这里表示反问语气。这是一句反话，带有挖苦，讽刺的意味。从字面上讲是："还需要你说这句话吗？"

词组和句子

1. 阴天了，要下雨了。
2. 昨天下了一次大雪，我们去公园看看吧，一定非常好看。
3. 上课了，同学们快到教室里来吧。
4. 下课了。如果你们有问题，还可以问。
5. 我们学的课文比他们学的容易。
6. 他们学的课文比我们难多了。
7. 一班学了二十课，二班学了十八课，一班学得比二班快。
8. 二班比一班学得慢一点儿。
9. 六班有十一个学生，五班有十个，六班比五班多一个学生。
10. 五班的同学比六班少一个。
11. 北方的秋天比我们这儿凉快，可是冬天比这儿冷。
12. 这儿的夏天总是下大雨，不过不太热，比你们那儿舒服多了。
13. 昨天是14到17度，今天预报是15到18度。今天比昨天暖和一点儿，比前天暖和得多。
14. 他买的衣服比马丁买的便宜二十块钱，可是没有马丁买的好看。
15. 这种箱子比较贵，我想买便宜一点儿的。
16. 北方的天气没有南方这么潮湿。

17. 南方没有北方那么干燥。
18. 春天我们这儿常常刮风，没有你们那儿的天气好。
19. 在我们班里，方小英写字写得很快，金中一比她写得更快。
20. 大卫念课文念得最好，我们都没有他念得好。

参考资料

拼音课文

Jīntian tiānqì zěnmeyàng?

(Yì tiān xiàwǔ, Dàwèi dǎwán wǎngqiú huídao sùshè, Shānběn zhèngzài kàn diànshì)

Dàwèi: Jīntian tiānqì zhēn búcuò.

Shānběn: Shì a. Zhè jǐ tiān zǒngshi yīntiān, wǒ yǐwéi huì xià yǔ ne.

Dàwèi: Nǐ kàn tiānqì yùbào le ma?

Shānběn: Gāng kànwán.

Dàwèi: Jīntian duōshao dù?

Shānběn: Shí dù dào shíwǔ dù.

Dàwèi: Tīngshuō Zhōngguó běifāng yǐjing xià xuě le, wǒmen zhèr hái zème nuǎnhuo.

Shānběn: Wǒ zuì xǐhuan xià xuě le.

Dàwèi: Nǐ jiā shì bu shì zài Rìběn de běifāng?

Shānběn: Shì, zài běifāng. Nàr dōngtiān hěn lěng, chángcháng xià dà xuě.

Dàwèi: Cháng guā fēng ma?

Shānběn: Yǒu shíhou guā fēng.

Dàwèi: Xiàtiān méiyou zhèr zhème rè ba?

Shānběn: Bǐ zhèr liángkuai duōle, qìwēn gēn zhèr de qiūtiān chàbuduō.

Dàwèi:	Wǒ jiā zài Měiguó zhōngbù, nàr xiàtiān yě bǐ zhèr liángkuai, tiānqì bǐjiào gānzào, chūntiān tiānqì gèng hǎo.
Shānběn:	Zhèr tài cháoshī le.
Dàwèi:	Shānběn, zhè shi shéide yǔsǎn?
Shānběn:	Yǔsǎn? Wǒ kànkan, zhè shi Jīn Zhōngyī de, wǒ kànjian tā dǎguo.
Dàwèi:	Tā gāng láiguo ma?
Shānběn:	Méiyou, tā zuótian wǎnshang láiguo, dàgài zǒu de shíhou wàngle dài le.
Dàwèi:	Wǒ jīntian xiàwǔ yě kànjian ta le, tā shuō tā jiā de kōngtiáo huài le, yào qù zhǎo rén xiūlǐ.
Shānběn:	Tiānqì zhème cháoshī, méiyǒu kōngtiáo zhēn bù shūfu.
Dàwèi:	Rúguǒ wǒmen de sùshè yě yǒu kōngtiáo, nà duō hǎo a!
Shānběn:	Hái yòng nǐ shuō!

英译课文

What's the weather like today?

(One afternoon, David has returned to the dorm after a game of tennis and Yamamoto is watching TV.)

David:	It's a fine day today.
Yamamoto:	Yes. It's been cloudy these past few days. I thought we might even have rain.
David:	Did you watch the weather report?
Yamamoto:	I just watched it.
David:	How many degrees is it going to be today?
Yamamoto:	From 10 to 15 degrees.
David:	I hear that there's already snow in some places in northern China, and it's still so hot here.

Yamamoto: I love snow.

David: Is your home in northern Japan?

Yamamoto: Yes, in northern Japan. The winters are cold there and it often snows.

David: Is it often windy?

Yamamoto: Sometimes it's windy.

David: It's probably not as hot as here in summer.

Yamamoto: Much cooler than here. The temperature is about like the autumn here.

David: My home is in the central part of the United States. It's cooler there too in summer, and the weather is drier. The spring weather is better.

Yamamoto: It's too humid here.

David: Yamamoto, who's umbrella is this?

Yamamoto: Umbrella? Let me see it. It's Kim Chung-il's. I've seen him carrying it (lit. with it open).

David: Was he just here?

Yamamoto: No, he was here last night. He probably forgot it when he left.

David: I saw him on the way back from the tennis courts. He said that there was something wrong with the air conditioning at his place and he was on his way to get someone to fix it.

Yamamoto: It's really uncomfortable without air conditioning in weather as humid as this.

David: Wouldn't it be great if our dorm had air conditioning!

Yamamoto: Don't I know it!

课堂活动

I. Comparative constructions

Bǐ

"比"字句

… méiyǒu … (nàme/zhème) …

……没有……(那么/这么)……

Students form groups of two or three. Each group is given a few cards as prompts. Students then ask and answer in turn on the basis of card content.

老师分组，二人或三人一组。每组有几张图做为提示，请同学根据提示轮流问答。

Example:

A: Xiǎo Mǎ de zhàoxiàngjī bǐ Xiǎo Dīng de zhàoxiàngjī guì ma?

小马的照相机比小丁的照相机贵吗？

B: Duì, Xiǎo Mǎ de zhàoxiàngjī bǐ Xiǎo Dīng de (zhàoxiàngjī) guì.

对，小马的照相机比小丁的(照相机)贵。

A: Xiǎo Mǎ de zhàoxiàngjī méiyǒu Xiǎo Dīng de zhàoxiàngjī guì ma?

小马的照相机没有小丁的照相机贵吗？

B: Bù, Xiǎo Dīng de zhàoxiàngjī méiyǒu Xiǎo Mǎ de (zhàoxiàngjī) guì.

不，小丁的照相机没有小马的(照相机)贵。

(1) 天气 好

(2) 厕所 厨房 大

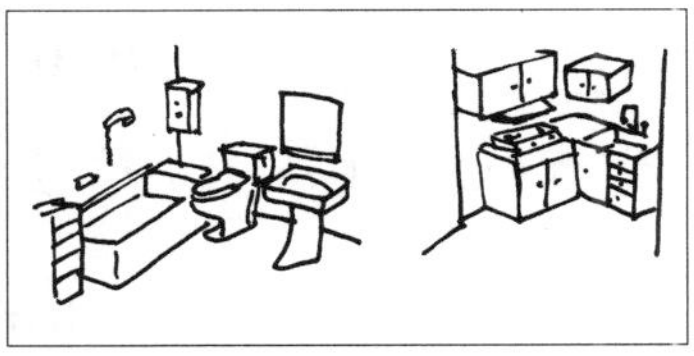

(3) 坐汽车　骑自行车　快

(4) 坐飞机　坐船　舒服

(5) 修理电视(机)
修理空调　容易

(6) 说中文　写汉字　难

(7) 伞　好看

(8) 春天　冷

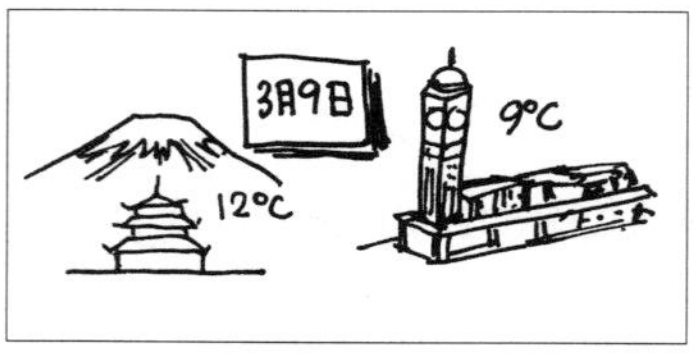

(9) 鱼　鸡　好吃

(10) 电影　有意思

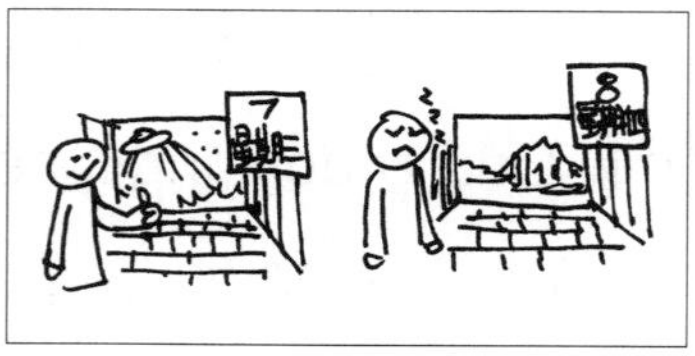

II. Comparative conjunctions

Bǐ

"比"字句

... méiyǒu ... (nàme/zhème)

……没有……(那么/这么)……

... gēn ... yíyàng

……跟……一样

Students form pairs, one holding Card A and the other B, then ask questions and answer in turn. Example questions are:

二人一组，一人持表A，一人持表B，轮流问答。问句如：

A: Xiànzài Guǎngzhōu shì chūntiān háishi xiàtiān?

现在广州是春天还是夏天？

B: Guǎngzhōu chūntiān de tiānqì zěnmeyàng?

Qìwēn shì duōshao?

广州春天的天气怎么样？气温是多少？

Then the instructor has students compare the weather in each place, e.g:

然后，老师可让同学比较一下各地的天气。如：

A: Něige dìfang de chūntiān bǐjiào nuǎnhuo?

哪个地方的春天比较暖和？

B: Něige dìfang hé něige dìfang de xiàtiān yíyàng rè?

哪个地方和哪个地方的夏天一样热？

Finally, the instructor has students discuss how accurate the information provided in this exercise is.

最后，老师可让学生讨论并指出本练习中各项资料的错处。

A

地名	天气	季节	地名	天气？	季节？
Xiānggǎng 香港		夏天	Guǎngzhōu 广州		
Běijīng 北京		冬天	Dōngjīng 东京		
Táiběi 台北		秋天	Hànchéng 汉城		
Màngǔ 曼谷		夏天	Lúndūn 伦敦		

B

地名	天气	季节	地名	天气?	季节 ?
Guǎngzhōu 广州		春天	Xiānggǎng 香港		
Dōngjīng 东京		秋天	Běijīng 北京		
Hànchéng 汉城		冬天	Táiběi 台北		
Lúndūn 伦敦		春天	Màngǔ 曼谷		

III. Negatives of comparative constructions

… bùbǐ … dà

……不比……大

… bǐ … dà yìdiǎnr

……比……大一点儿

… bǐ … dà de duō

……比……大得多

Students form pairs, one holding Card A and the other B. Asking along the suggested manner, discover who in the Wang or Zhang families is oldest, youngest or of the same age.

二人一组，一人持表A，一人持表B。用下列问题提问，找出王家/张家的人里谁最大，谁最小，谁跟谁一样大。

A: X bǐ Y dà ma?

X比Y大吗？

B: X bǐ Y xiǎo ma?

X比Y小吗？

C: X bǐ Y dà yìdiǎnr ma?

X比Y大一点儿吗？

D: X bǐ Y dà de duō ma?

X比Y大得多吗？

A

王家	名字	最大？ 最小？ 一样？	张家	名字	suì 岁 (age)
	文意	25		本礼	9
	文英			本中	9
	文美			本和	14
	文生			本先	15
	文真			本喜	12

B

王家	名字	suì 岁 (age)	张家	名字	最大？ 最小？ 一样？
	文意	25		本礼	9
	文英	22		本中	
	文美	27		本和	
	文生	30		本先	
	文真	25		本喜	

第二十课

学期快结束了

汉字课文

（一）

山　本：这个学期快结束了。后天考完最后两门，就要放假了。

大　卫：后天，可怕的后天！

山　本：怎么啦？后天为什么那么可怕？

大　卫：我怕后天的考试。

方小英：你中文学得很好啊，怕什么！

大　卫：我说得还马马虎虎，一写就不行了，我记不住那么多字。

山　本：别那么紧张，好好儿复习，你一定能考得很好。

方小英：开两天夜车就行了。

大　卫：开夜车？你让我夜里开车做什么？

山　本：开夜车的意思是夜里还学习，不睡觉。

大　卫：那不行，开完夜车，考试的时候，我就该睡着了。

（二）

安　娜：这个星期太紧张了！

金中一：是啊，我每天晚上都学习到一两点。

安　娜：你考得怎么样？

金中一：还不知道呢，我没去看成绩。

马　丁：我也没看呢。安娜，你看了吗？

安　娜：我看了，四门成绩都知道了。

金中一：都满意吗？

安　娜：有一门考得不太好。

金中一：怎么回事儿？

安　娜：考试前一天我感冒了，头疼，发烧，睡不着觉，没办法复习。

马　丁：一门没考好，有什么关系！

安　娜：当然有关系！成绩很重要，成绩不好，我们学校很可能不给我奖学金。

马　丁：是吗？那怎么办？

生词语

1. 学期	xuéqī	(n)	[个]	semester, school term
2. 结束	jiéshù	(v)		to conclude, come to an end

a. 这门课，下个星期就要结束了。

b. 学期考试是昨天结束的。

3. 考	kǎo	(v)	to examine, test; to take an examination

a. 今天我们考了两门，明天还要考一门。

b. 你考完了吗？考得怎么样？

4. 最后	zuìhòu	(n,adv)	last, lastly, final
5. 门	mén	(m)	(for school classes or courses)
6. 放假	fàng jià	(vo)	to have time off, take a holiday
放	fàng	(v)	to place, set
假	jià	(n)	holiday, time off

a. 放假的时候，你回日本吗？

b. 今年夏天，你们放多少天假？

7.	可怕	kěpà	(adj)	to be frightening, terrible

a. 昨天晚上又刮风，又下大雨，真可怕！

b. 我不爱看那种可怕的电影，看完了，晚上睡不着觉。

8.	考试	kǎoshì	(n,v)	examination; to take an examination
9.	马马虎虎	mǎmahūhū	(adj)	to be so-so, fair; to be sloppy

a. 做作业不能马马虎虎。

b. 我不喜欢办事马马虎虎的人。

c. 新来的那个服务员怎么样？

——还可以，马马虎虎吧。

10.	一……就……	yī...jiù...		as soon as; if x so much as ..., ...
11.	住	zhù	(v)	(used as a complement of result with certain verbs, meaning "to a point that is fixed or firm")

a. 你拿住了！这三杯可乐是给她们的。

b. 学过的汉字，有的我记得住，有的我记不住。

12.	开夜车	kāi yèchē	(vo)		to burn the midnight oil
	开	kāi	(v)		to drive (a vehicle)
	夜车	yèchē	(n)		the night train
13.	夜里	yèlǐ	(n)		at night
14.	开车	kāi chē	(vo)		to drive (a vehicle)
	开	kāi	(v)		to drive
	车	chē	(n)	[辆 liàng]	car, vehicle
15.	意思	yìsi	(n)	[个]	meaning

16.	睡觉	shuì jiào	(vo)	to sleep
	睡	shuì	(v)	to sleep
	觉	jiào	(n) [个]	a sleep

a. 每天你几点钟睡觉？几点钟起床？

b. 我爷爷每天中午都睡一会儿觉。

c. 我太累了，星期日下午睡了一个大觉。

17.	该	gāi	(o, v)	will probably (no negative form)

a. 如果我睡不好觉，第二天上课就该睡着了。

b. 如果我不帮她做饭，她就该不高兴了。

c. 我的发音不好，我一念课文，你们就该笑了。

18.	成绩	chéngji	(n)	results, achievement
19.	满意	mǎnyì	(v)	to be satisfied

a. 我们每次来这家饭馆儿吃饭，都觉得很满意。

b. 姐姐不满意自己的考试成绩。

20.	回	huí	(m)	(for actions and events, happenings) time
	怎么回事儿	zěnme huí shìr	(i.e)	What happened? What's the matter?
21.	前	qián	(n - pw)	before
22.	感冒	gǎnmào	(v, n)	to catch cold; a cold
23.	头	tóu	(n) [个]	head
24.	疼	téng	(adj)	to be painful
25.	发烧	fā shāo	(vo)	to run a fever
	发	fā	(v)	to emit
	烧	shāo	(v)	heat

a. 医生问他："发烧不发烧？"

b. 我妹妹感冒了，发了两天烧。

26. 办法	bànfǎ	(n)	[个]	means, way out (of something)
27. 关系	guānxi	(n)		relevance; relationships
28. 重要	zhòngyào	(adj)		to be important

a. 那件事重要不重要？如果不重要，就先不用办。

b. 这是一个很重要的问题。

29. 可能	kěnéng	(adv, adj, n)		possibly, to be possible, possibility

a. 妈妈买的那些东西，很可能放在楼上的房间里了。

—— 我想不可能。我刚从楼上下来，没看见那些东西。

b. 毕业以后，哥哥有可能马上找到工作吗？

—— 我想没有可能，现在找工作多么难啊！

30. 奖学金	jiǎngxuéjīn	(n)	[笔]	scholarship
31. 怎么办	zěnme bàn			What's to be done? What'll I/you/we do?

补充生词

1. 医院	yīyuàn	(n)	hospital
2. 咳嗽	késou	(v)	to cough
3. 药	yào	(n)	medicine

语法点

1. Kuài … le 快……了, yào … le 要……了, kuàiyào … le 快要……了, jiùyào … le 就要……了

“快……了”“要……了”“快要……了”“就要……了”

These expressions are used to indicate that an action or situation will occur in the immediate future.

这四种结构都可以用来表示一个动作或一种情况将会很快发生。

S + 快, etc. + V + 了

a. Xīnnián kuài dào le, wǒ dǎsuàn huí jiā qù guò xīnnián.

新年快到了，我打算回家去过新年。

It'll soon be New Year's. I'm planning to go home for New Year's.

b. Wǒ jiějie dàxué kuài yào bìyè le.

我姐姐大学快要毕业了。

My sister is just about to graduate from university.

c. Yào shàng kè le, kuài qù jiàoshì ba.

要上课了，快去教室吧。

Class is beginning. Let's hurry to the classroom.

d. Míngnián wǒ jiù yào bìyè le, bìyè yǐhòu wǒ xiǎng dào màoyì gōngsī qù gōngzuò.

明年我就要毕业了，毕业以后我想到贸易公司去工作。

I'll graduate next year. After graduating, I want to work in a trading company.

e. Wǒ péngyou xīngqīyī jiù yào lái le. Wǒ dǎsuàn dào jīchǎng qù jiē tā.

我朋友星期一就要来了。我打算到机场去接她。

My friend is arriving on Monday and I am planning to go to the airport to meet her.

NOTE that jiù yào … le can be preceded by time modifiers (examples d, e), whereas kuài … le and kuài yào … le cannot. Yào … le ordinarily is not preceded by time expressions.

注意："就要……了"的前面可以有时间词作状语（例d，e），"快……了""快要……了"不行。"要……了"前面一般也不用时间词。

2. Yī … jiù … 一……就 "as soon as", "once"

"……就……"

These adverbs precede the verb or adjective in a first and second clause respectively. The subject of each clause need not be the same.

"一"和"就"分别用在两个分句里，即前一动词（或形容词）和后一动词（或形容词）之前，表示两件事紧接着发生（如：例a、b）。或者表示只要具备前面的条件，就会出现后面的情况（结果）（如：例c、d、e）。两个分句可以主语相同，也可以不同。

a. Tā yí xià kè jiù huí jiā.

他一下课就回家。

He goes home as soon as he gets out of class.

b. Nǐ yí fùxí wán, wǒmen jiù qù kàn diànyǐngr, hǎo bu hǎo?

你一复习完，我们就去看电影，好不好？

Let's go see a film right after you've finished reviewing.

c. Wǒ yì kǎoshì jiù jǐnzhāng.

我一考试就紧张。

I get tense as soon as I take an exam.

d. Tā Hànyǔ shuō de hái kěyǐ, búguò yì xiě Hànzì jiù bù xíng le.

他汉语说得还可以，不过一写汉字就不行了。

He speaks Chinese passably, but is no good once he starts to write characters.

e. Zài sùshè lǐ, wǒ yì kāi yèchē biéde rén jiù méi bànfǎ shuì jiào le.

在宿舍里，我一开夜车别的人就没办法睡觉了。

In the dormitory, once I start burning the midnight oil no one else is able to sleep.

3. Potential complement

可能补语

De 得 "can" or bu 不 "cannot" are placed between the verb and its complement, resultative (Lesson 12) or directional (Lesson 13), to indicate an action's possibility.

"得"或"不"放在动词和补语(结果补语，十二课；趋向补语，十三课)之间，就可以构成可能补语，表示可能。

S + V + 得/不 + CR/CDI + O

a. Wǒ jì bú zhù nàge Hànzì.

我记不住那个汉字。

I can't remember that Chinese character.

b. Wǒ zhǐ xué le sān ge yuè Zhōngwén, hái kàn bu dǒng Zhōngwén xiǎoshuō.

我只学了三个月中文，还看不懂中文小说。

I've only studied Chinese now for three months so can't read Chinese novels yet.

c. Míngtiān yào kǎoshì le, nǐ shuì de zháo ma?

明天要考试了，你睡得着吗？

You're taking an exam tomorrow. Will you be able to sleep?

Shuì de zháo, wǒ bù jǐnzhāng.

睡得着，我不紧张。

Sure, I'm not nervous.

Note the affirmative/negative type question: tīng de dǒng tīng bu dǒng 听得懂听不懂 "Can you understand (by listening)?" Xué de hǎo xué bu hǎo 学得好学不好 "Can you learn it well?"

注意：正反疑问形式，如："听得懂听不懂""学得好学不好"。

d. Jīntiān xiàwǔ liù diǎn bàn, nǐ huí de lái huí bu lái?

今天下午六点半，你回得来回不来？

Will you be able to get back by 6:30 this afternoon?

e. Nǐ kàn de jiàn kàn bu jiàn shū shang de Hànzì?

你看得见看不见书上的汉字？

Can you see the Chinese characters in the book?

NOTE these characteristics of the potential complement:

注意可能补语的下列特点：

1. In most declarative situations, the negative form of the potential complement is used with greater frequency. The affirmative is more often selected for questions and answers.

   在陈述句中可能补语的否定形式用得最多。肯定形式在问句或答句中才常见。

2. In affirmative situations, the néng optative can be used, in seemingly redundant fashion, before the main verbal construction.

   在带可能补语肯定式的句子里，也可以在动词前再用上能愿动词“能”，以加强语气。

a. Jīntiān xiàwǔ sì diǎn bàn, tā yídìng néng huí de lái.

今天下午四点半，他一定能回得来。

He can surely get back by half past four this afternoon.

b. Bié jǐnzhāng, búyòng kāi yèchē yě néng fùxí de wán.

别紧张，不用开夜车也能复习得完。

Don't worry, you'll be able to finish reviewing even without working into the wee hours.

NOTES 注释

1. Pà shénme! 怕什么！ Shénme, the general "what", implies a speaker's disagreement with the situation when used after the verb. In our dialogue, it means that there is nothing to be concerned about.

   "怕什么！""什么"出现在动词后可以有另一种作用，表示说话者不同意对方说的某一观点，本课的意思是"没有什么可担心的"。

2. Nǐ ràng wǒ yèlǐ kāi chē zuò shénme? 你让我夜里开车做什么？ Zuò shénme here means "why?", the whole sentence meaning "why do you want me to drive at night?"

   "你让我夜里开车做什么？"这句话里的"做什么"相当于"为什么"。全句的意思是："为什么你让我夜里开车？"

词组和句子

1. 快要考试了，我得好好儿复习一下儿，这个星期日不去公园了。
2. 他下星期就要回国了，我们跟他一起照张相吧。
3. 春天就要来了，天气就要暖和了。
4. 我的感冒快要好了，已经不发烧了，头也不疼了。
5. 快放假了，放假以后你去哪儿？
6. 奶奶的生日快要到了，爸爸和妈妈已经订好了一个生日大蛋糕。
7. 爷爷和奶奶要来了，妈妈和姐姐正在厨房里忙着做饭呢。
8. 别说话，小弟弟要睡着了。
9. 哥哥每天一下课就去图书馆。
10. 妹妹一到学校，就拿到奖学金了。
11. 学期一结束，我们就回国。

12. 他们一到公园，就去划船了。
13. 他一着急，夜里就睡不好觉。
14. 这儿一到夏天，就常常下大雨，天气非常潮湿。
15. 大卫一开夜车，第二天就头疼，不舒服。
16. 安娜一高兴，就唱歌儿。
17. 我一听音乐，就把不高兴的事儿都忘了。
18. 你说的是什么意思？我听不懂。
19. 我现在还看不懂中文小说。
20. 这么多水果和饼干，我们一定吃不完。
21. 今天天气不好，如果去照相，我想一定照不好。
22. 听说那个电影非常好，现在去买票，一定买不着了。
23. 没有票，当然进不去。
24. 你早上六点钟起得来吗？

　　—— 起不来，我七点钟起得来。
25. 骑自行车难不难？你说我学得会学不会？

　　—— 骑自行车很容易学，你一定能学得会。
26. 这件事你记得住记不住？

　　—— 别担心，我记得住。

参考资料

拼音课文

Xuéqī kuài jiéshù le

(I)

Shānběn: Zhège xuéqī kuài jiéshù le. Hòutian kǎowán zuìhòu liǎng mén, jiù yào fàng jià le.

Dàwèi: Hòutian, kěpà de hòutian!

Shānběn: Zěnme la? Hòutian wèishénme nàme kěpà?

Dàwèi: Wǒ pà hòutian de kǎoshì.

Fāng Xiǎoyīng: Nǐ Zhōngwén xué de hěn hǎo a, pà shénme!

Dàwèi: Wǒ shuō de hái mǎmahūhū, yì xiě jiù bù xíng le, wǒ jì bu zhù nàme duō zì.

Shānběn: Bié nàme jǐnzhāng, hǎohāor fùxí, nǐ yídìng néng kǎo de hěn hǎo.

Fāng Xiǎoyīng: Kāi liǎng tiān yèchē jiù xíng le.

Dàwèi: Kāi yèchē? Nǐ ràng wǒ yèli kāi chē zuò shénme?

Shānběn: Kāi yèchē de yìsi shi yèli hái xuéxí, bú shuì jiào.

Dàwèi: Nà bù xíng, kāiwán yèchē, kǎoshì de shíhou, wǒ jiù gāi shuìzháo le.

(II)

Ānnà: Zhège xīngqī tài jǐnzhāng le!

Jīn Zhōngyī: Shì a, wǒ měi tiān wǎnshang dōu xuéxí dào yì-liǎng diǎn.

Ānnà: Nǐ kǎo de zěnmeyàng?

Jīn Zhōngyī: Hái bù zhīdào ne, wǒ méi qù kàn chéngji.

Mǎdīng: Wǒ yě méi kàn ne. Ānnà nǐ kàn le ma?

Ānnà: Wǒ kàn le, sì mén chéngji dōu zhīdao le.

Jīn Zhōngyī: Dōu mǎnyì ma?

Ānnà: Yǒu yì mén kǎo de bú tài hǎo.

Jīn Zhōngyī: Zěnme huí shìr?

Ānnà: Kǎoshì qián yì tiān wǒ gǎnmào le, tóu téng, fā shāo, shuì bu zháo jiào, méi bànfǎ fùxí.

Mǎdīng: Yì mén méi kǎohǎo, yǒu shénme guānxi!

Ānnà: Dāngrán yǒu guānxi! Chéngji hěn zhòngyào, chéngji bù hǎo, wǒmen xuéxiào hěn kěnéng bù gěi wǒ jiǎngxuéjīn.

Mǎdīng: Shì ma? Nà zěnme bàn?

英译课文

The semester is about over

(I)

Yamamoto: This semester is about over. After our last two exams day after tomorrow, we're on vacation.

David: The day after tomorrow, formidable day after tomorrow!

Yamamoto: What's the matter? What's so scary about the day after tomorrow?

David: I'm scared of the test day after tomorrow.

Fang Xiaoying: You're doing so well with Chinese what's there to be scared of?

David: I can manage with speaking but am no good with writing. I can't remember so many characters.

Yamamoto: You'll do fine, no question, if you can be less tense and review the material well.

Fang Xiaoying: Drive the midnight wagon for a couple of nights and you'll be alright.

David: Drive the midnight wagon? Why do you want me to drive a wagon in the middle of the night?

Yamamoto: "Drive the midnight wagon" means study through the night without sleeping.

David: No way. After I've driven all night, I'll probably fall asleep when I'm taking the exam.

(II)

Anna: This week has been too pressured!

Kim Chung-il: You said it. I've studied every night until 1:00 or 2:00 am.

Anna: How did you do on your exams?

Kim Chung-il: I don't know yet. I haven't checked the results.

Martin: I haven't either. Anna, have you looked at them?

Anna:	Yes. I know my grades for the four courses.
Kim Chung-il:	Are you pleased?
Anna:	I did't do so well in one of the courses.
Kim Chung-il:	What happened?
Anna:	The day before the exam I caught a cold. I had a headache, was fevered and couldn't sleep. There was no way I could review.
Martin:	What does it matter if you don't test well in one course?
Anna:	Of course it matters! Grades are important. If I don't get good grades my school may not give me my scholarship.
Martin:	Oh? Then what do you do?

课堂活动

I. yī … jiù …

一……就……

A. Students form pairs and make sentences using yī … jiù … on the basis of their card illustrations.

二人一组，根据图示，用“一……就……”造句。

一……　　　　就……

B. Prepare two sets (I and II) of cards for students, one with yī … ("as soon as") clauses and the other with the follow-on clause, … jiù ("then …"). Distribute set II cards (jiù …) to all students. The instructor then gives students an yī … clause, and those with suitable … jiù clause responses on their card will complete the sentence. For the second part of the exercise, instructor and students will reverse roles. Remember that yī … and jiù … will FOLLOW the subject.

老师准备(1)、(2)两套卡片，发给学生。进行首轮练习时，先将第(2)套卡片发给所有学生，然后由老师做"一……"的句子，让学生看看自己所拿到的卡片中的各项，如果是能够与老师的句子连起来的，就做一个"就……"的句子。进行第二轮练习时，先将第(1)套卡片发给所有学生，并由老师做"就……"的句子，让学生做能相配的"一……"的句子。(注意："一"和"就"都要用在主语之后)

Example situation:

There are five students, A through E, the jiù … clause cards they hold are

有A、B、C、D、E五个学生，所拿到的(B)组卡片上的短句分别是，

A. qù kàn diànyǐngr 去看电影

B. hěn gāoxìng 很高兴

C. kǎo bù hǎo 考不好

D. jǐnzhāng 紧张

E. qù túshūguǎn 去图书馆

The instructor's clause is Dàwèi yì kǎowán …. Thus, students A, B and E have logically connectible clauses. They should raise their hands and complete the sentence in turn.

老师做的句子是："大卫一考完……"，A、B、E三人所拿到的短句都能跟老师的句子连起来，他们三人应举手造句。

1. "一……"的句子
上课
下课
喝茶
觉得饿
考完
开夜车
喝酒
头疼
没钱
到冬天
说中文
看电视
下雨
毕业
考试
放假
高兴

2. "就……"的句子
想睡觉
去图书馆
睡不着
去食堂
去看电影
头疼
考不好
跟朋友借钱
不舒服
下雪
刮风
问问题
暖和
凉快
找工作
紧张
担心
觉得累
着急

打电话
唱歌儿
很高兴
不想吃饭

II. Potential complements

可能补语

Pairs of students ask each other questions and answer on the basis of card illustration content using potential complements (V + de wán, V + de jiàn, V + de dǒng, V + de hǎo, V + de zháo, V + de qù, V + de dào)

二人一组，按照图示，用可能补语（V + 得完／V + 得见／V + 得懂／V + 得好／V + 得着／V + 得去／V + 得到）来提问及回答。

(一) 	(二) 
(三) 	(四) 
(五) 	(六) 
(七) 	(八) 

(九)

(十)

阅读练习

新年这几天，天气有一点儿冷，可是跟北方比，还不能说“冷”，这儿的冬天跟北方的秋天差不多，气温大概是13到18度。听说北方这时候已经下雪了，非常冷，比这儿冷多了。可是，夏天这儿就没有北方那么舒服。这儿的夏天特别热，很潮湿，如果没有空调很不舒服。我想，夏天住在北方，冬天最好住在南方。

前天是新年，小马请我们几个同学到他家去过年，我们一共五个人，去以前都约好了时间，还带了糖、水果、蛋糕和一些别的东西。到小马家的时候，已经快十点了。小马的爸爸说：“你们都是小马的好同学，能来，我们就已经很高兴了，不应该再带什么东西。真是太客气了。”

小马的妈妈那天最忙了，她说：“我们北方人过年，一定要吃饺子，你们想帮我做饺子吗？”“当然想。”我们都说。他妈妈在厨房做菜，我们和小马还有小马的爸爸和妹妹都在客厅做饺子。做饺子真有意思，每个人做的都不一样。有的大，有的小；有的好看，有的不好看。大家看着，都笑了。做饺子的人多，很快就把饺子做好了。

那天的菜很多，每个菜都非常好。吃完了饭，大家又聊了很久。我们走的时候都说：“今天我们非常高兴，吃得也非常好，谢谢你们请我们来过年。”

第四单元复习

1. Verbal predicate sentences with special features (2)

   特殊的动词谓语句 (2)

   I. Pivotal sentences

      兼语句

      a. They let me go rowing together with them.

         他们让我跟他们一起去划船。

      b. She asked me to drive to the station to pick her up.

         她叫我开车去车站接她。

      c. There are many people at our house today. Dad invited his friends over to eat.

         今天我们家里人很多，爸爸请了他的朋友来吃饭。

      d. Mother won't let me walk to the park. She says it is too tiring.

         妈妈不让我走着去公园，她说那样太累了。

   II. Verbal expressions in series (2)

      连动句 (2)

      a. Mother took younger brother and younger sister to the park.

         妈妈带着弟弟和妹妹去公园了。

      b. He's busy. He stood eating a bit of food, then left.

         他很忙，站着吃了一点儿饭，就走了。

      c. I'm going by bicycle; he's going by bus.

         我骑自行车去，他坐公共汽车去。

d. Do you know how to use chopsticks to eat?

你会用筷子吃饭吗？

e. Is it all right if I use this wine glass to drink cola?

我用这个酒杯喝可乐，可以吗？

III. <u>Bǎ</u> sentences

“把”字句

a. Kim Chung-il lost the new dictionary he bought.

金中一把他新买的词典丢了。

b. I fixed your camera. Check it and you'll see you can use it now.

我把你的照相机修理好了，你看，能用了吧。

c. I should write an email to let people at home know about the exam grades.

我应该写个电邮 (diànyóu, email)，把考试成绩告诉家里。

d. Please take this letter to her.

请你把这封信给她送去。

e. I returned Kim Chung-il's umbrella to him.

我把金中一的雨伞还给他了。

f. Please put your things here.

请把您的东西放在这儿。

g. Please take the air conditioner to my house, will you?

请把空调送到我家里，好吗？

h. He let the apples sit for two weeks and they rotted bad. There's no way they can be eaten.

他把苹果放了两个星期，苹果都坏了，没办法吃了。

i. The snow was all blown away by the wind.

风把雪都刮走了。

IV. Passive sentences

被动句

a. Where have the sugar and salt been put?

糖和盐放在哪儿了？

b. I've forgotten to bring both notebook and pen. (or, Both notebook and pen were forgotten and not brought along.)

本子和笔都忘了带来了。

c. The wine has been drunk and the food all eaten.

酒喝完了，菜也都吃了。

d. What should I do? My name has been written incorrectly.

我的名字写错了，怎么办？

V. Shì … de … sentences

"是……的"句

a. Where did you find this magazine?

这本杂志你是在哪儿找到的？

b. Did you bring this bottle of soy sauce from the kitchen?

这瓶酱油，你是从厨房拿来的吗？

c. These characters were written with my pen; those characters were written with his pen.

这几个字是用我的笔写的，那几个字是用他的笔写的。

d. He got off at the third station and I got off at the fourth station. I missed the (right) station.

他是在第三站下的车，我是在第四站下的车，我坐过了站。

e. She took little brother to the park. She didn't go by herself.

她是带着小弟弟去的公园，不是一个人去的。

f. I didn't sleep last night at twelve; I slept at eleven.
昨天晚上我不是十二点睡的觉，我是十一点睡的。

2. Comparatives
比较

I. Write Bǐ
用"比"

a. He examined better in this course than that one.
他这门课考得比那门好。

b. He examined a bit better in this course than that one.
他这门课比那门考得好一点儿。

c. November is colder than October.
十一月比十月冷。

d. December is much colder than October.
十二月比十月冷得多。

e. January is much colder than October.
一月比十月冷多了。

II. With méiyǒu ... (nàme/zhème)
用"没有……(那么/这么)……"

a. Spring in the north is not as good as spring in the south.
北方的春天没有南方的春天好。

b. Yamamoto's pronunciation isn't as clear as David's.
山本的发音没有大卫的清楚。

c. He doesn't like to eat *jiaozi* as much as I do.
他没有我这么爱吃饺子。

d. She doesn't like to sing as much as Anna does.
她没有安娜那么爱唱歌儿。

3. With yǒuyìdiǎnr and yìdiǎnr

“有一点儿”和“一点儿”

a. It's a bit cold today. You should wear two layers of clothing.

今天有一点儿冷，你应该穿两件衣服。

b. It's a bit warm in the room. Is the air conditioner broken?

房间里有一点儿热，是不是空调坏了？

c. I need to buy some things. But things in nearby shops are a bit expensive, so I don't feel like going to them.

我要买一点儿东西，可是附近商店的东西有一点儿贵，我不想去。

d. Yesterday's exam was a bit hard, so none of us did too well.

昨天的考试有一点儿难，我们都考得不太好。

e. Today is a bit colder than yesterday.

今天比昨天冷一点儿。

f. Yesterday's exam was a bit harder than today's.

昨天的考试比今天的难一点儿。

g. Things in that shop are a bit cheaper than this shop.

那个商店的东西比这个商店便宜一点儿。

4. Potential complements and complements of degree

可能补语和程度补语

I. Potential complements

可能补语

V + 得 + V/adj

a. Do you understand his speech?

你听得懂他的话吗？

b. Can you see those characters clearly?

你看得清楚那些字吗？

c. Can he get back before six this afternoon?

他下午六点以前回得来吗？

V + 不 + V/adj

d. I can't understand his speech.

我听不懂他说的话。

e. I can't see those characters clearly.

我看不清楚那些字。

f. He can't get back before six o'clock.

他六点以前回不来。

g. The car is too big. It can't fit in.

汽车太大，进不去。

II. Complements of degree

程度补语

V + 得 (+ 很) + adj

a. I can see those characters very clearly.

那些字我看得很清楚。

b. He came very early.

他来得很早。

V + 得 + 不 + adj

c. He didn't read (aloud) those characters very clearly.

这些生词他念得不清楚。

d. He didn't come early. (= It wasn't early when he came.)

他来得不早。

Potential Complements and Complements of Degree Compared
可能补语和程度补语的比较

	肯定式 Affirmative	否定式 Negative	正反疑问式 Affirmative-negative type	宾语的位置 Position of the object
可能补语 Potential complement	写得好	写不好	写得好写不好	他写不好汉字。 汉字他写不好。
程度补语 Complement of degree	写得（很）好	写得不好	写得好不好	他写汉字写得不好。 汉字他写得不好。

阅读

小同常常想自己太笨了。课文不会念，作业不会做，很多事儿也不懂。怎么样才能让自己变得聪明一点儿呢？

有一天，他去找医生。他跟医生说："医生，能不能给我一点儿药吃，让我变得聪明一点儿呢？"医生想了想说："好吧！"就给了他一瓶药水儿，叫他每天喝一次。

过了一个星期，小同把药喝完了，他又来找医生，他跟医生说："医生，我已经喝了一个星期药水儿了，为什么还没有变聪明呀？"

医生就又给了他一瓶药水儿。

又过了一个星期，小同第三次来找医生，他跟医生说："我已经喝了两瓶药水儿了，怎么还没有变聪明呀？我想你给我的大概不是药水儿，可能是糖水吧。"

医生听了小同的话，高兴地说："哎呀，你变聪明了。"

生词语

1.	笨	bèn	(adj)	to be stupid, clumsy
2.	变	biàn	(v)	to change
3.	聪明	cōngming	(adj)	to be intelligent, bright
4.	聪明一点儿	cōngming yìdiǎnr	(adj)	a bit more intelligent
5.	药	yào	(n)	medicine
6.	药水儿	yàoshuǐr	(n)	liquid medicine
7.	水	shuǐ	(n)	water, liquid

第二十一课

开个联欢晚会

汉字课文

大　卫：晚会开始以前，我们应该把教室布置一下。

马　丁：对，把椅子重新摆一摆，把那张大桌子搬走。

安　娜：把录音机放在这儿比较好。

方小英：金中一，你的字写得好，你把黑板擦干净，在上边写几个字。

金中一：写什么？写"联欢晚会"还是"汉语节目表演会"？

安　娜：写"联欢晚会"吧！

马　丁：你们把节目单放到哪儿了？

山　本：节目单在我这儿。我把它挂在黑板旁边儿，好吗？

金中一：好。我把字写完了。你们看行不行？

方小英：最后那个"会"字不好看，你能不能把它改一下？

山　本：我把节目单再念一遍，你们看对不对？第一个，安娜唱中文歌；第二个，马丁弹吉他；第三个，金中一跳舞……

金中一：我一个人不能跳。

马　丁：方小英，你和金中一一起跳吧。

方小英：我不会跳韩国舞。

金中一：没关系，我教你，一学就会。

山　本：第四个节目是马丁和山本的合唱；第五个是大卫讲笑话儿。大卫，你讲什么啊？

大　卫：我讲啊，我讲"有个孩子叫大山"。

方小英：什么？"有个孩子叫大山"？

大　卫：对啊。"有个孩子叫大山。有一天，大山不想上学，就给老师打电话，说：'喂，是老师吗？大山病了，今天不能去上学了。'老师说：'请问，你是谁？'大山回答：'我，我是我爸爸。'"

安　娜：我想这个孩子不叫大山，叫大卫吧？

马　丁：对，你真聪明！

山　本：不过，你现在把故事讲了，一会儿节目开始，你怎么办呢？

大　卫：没关系，我可以再讲一个故事，叫"有个孩子叫大本"或者"有个孩子叫小丁"。

马丁和山本：好啊，你讲我们！

生词语

1.	开	kāi	(v)		to hold (a meeting, party, etc.)
2.	联欢	liánhuān	(v)		to have a get-together

a. 下星期我们要跟新同学联欢。

b. 今天下午第一班跟第二班一起开联欢晚会。

3.	晚会	wǎnhuì	(n)	[个]	evening social event (entertainment, show, etc.)
4.	布置	bùzhì	(v)		to arrange, fix up, decorate (a room, etc.)

a. 快过新年了，我们应该把客厅布置一下。

b. 老师正在给学生布置作业。

5.	椅子	yǐzi	(n)	[把，个]	chair
6.	重新	chóngxīn	(adv)		anew, again

a. 这个汉字你写得不对，请你重新写一下。

b. 他那个故事还没讲完，大家都说没意思，让他重新讲一个。

7.	摆	bǎi	(v)		to place, set
8.	搬	bān	(v)		to move (something)

a. 今天有一位老师要来听我们班的课，请你从别的教室搬一把椅子来。

b. 请你把这些东西搬开，我要过去。

9.	录音机	lùyīnjī	(n)	[个]	tape recorder
10.	黑板	hēibǎn	(n)	[块，个]	blackboard
11.	擦	cā	(v)		to erase, rub
12.	节目	jiémù	(n)	[个]	program
13.	表演	biǎoyǎn	(v)		to perform
14.	会	huì	(n)	[个]	a meeting
15.	节目单	jiémùdān	(n)	[张，个]	(printed) program
16.	它	tā	(pro)		it
17.	挂	guà	(v)		to hang
18.	改	gǎi	(v)		to change, alter; to correct

a. 这个字错了，请你把它改对。

b. 老师每天给我们改作业，一定很累。

19.	弹	tán	(v)		to play (a string instrument or piano)
20.	吉他	jítā	(n)	[把]	guitar
21.	跳舞	tiào wǔ	(vo)		to dance
	跳	tiào	(v)		to jump
	舞	wǔ	(n)	[个]	dance
22.	合唱	héchàng	(v)		sing in chorus, sing together

23. 讲	jiǎng	(v)		to tell, explain (sometimes: to say, to speak)

a. 他很会讲故事，我们让他给我们讲一个吧。

b. 老师说明天讲第二十二课。

c. 我把老师讲的都记在本子上了。

d. 谢老师讲课讲得非常清楚。

e. 这个字怎么讲，你说一说。

24. 笑话儿	xiàohuar	(n)	[个]	joke
25. 孩子	háizi	(n)	[个]	child, children
26. 上学	shàng xué	(vo)		to attend school
27. 病	bìng	(v, n)		to be ill; illness

a. 他病了，今天请假。

b. 他的病怎么样了？快好了吧？

28. 聪明	cōngming	(adj)		to be intelligent, bright
29. 故事	gùshi	(n)	[个]	story, tale
30. 或者	huòzhě	(c)		or

a. 你喝啤酒，还是喝可乐？

—— 啤酒或者可乐都行。

b. 每天早上你应该到外边去散散步或者打打网球。

语法点

1. Huòzhě
或者

<u>Huòzhě</u> 或者 is a conjunction used in choice type situations, "either, or".

"或者"是连词，表示选择。

a. Xīngqīrì shàngwǔ wǒ chángcháng qù yóuyǒng huòzhě dǎ wǎngqiú.

星期日上午我常常去游泳或者打网球。

On Saturday mornings, I often go to swim or to play tennis.

b. A: Míngtiān shéi lái bāng wǒ xiū kōngtiáo?

明天谁来帮我修空调？

Who'll come tomorrow to help me repair the air-conditioner?

B: Wǒ huòzhě wǒ gēge.

我或者我哥哥。

Either I or my brother.

c. Huòzhě nǐ qù, huòzhě tā qù dōu kěyi.

或者你去，或者他去都可以。

Either you go or he goes; it makes no difference.

NOTE that while huòzhě 或者 and háishi 还是 (Lesson 14, pp. 335–336) both are "either ... or" choice conjunctions, háishi 还是 is used in interrogative sentences while huòzhě is used in affirmative sentences.

注意："或者"和"还是"(见第14课335–336页)都是选择连词。"还是"用于疑问句，"或者"用于陈述句 。

d. Nǐ xǐhuan hē píjiǔ háishi hē kělè? Píjiǔ huòzhě kělè wǒ dōu xǐhuan.

你喜欢喝啤酒还是喝可乐？啤酒或者可乐我都喜欢。

Do you like to drink beer or cola? I like either beer or cola.

2. Hǎo ā

好啊

Hǎo ā 好啊 can be ironic, indicating a sense of dissatisfaction or indignation, lighter or heavier dependent upon the situation.

"好啊"可以是一句反话，表示不满或气愤，语气的轻重取决于上下文。

a. Hǎo ā, nǐ bǎ shuǐguǒ dōu chī le! Biéde rén hái chī shénme?

好啊，你把水果都吃了！别的人还吃什么？

Wonderful, you ate all the fruit! What are others going to eat? (For the rhetorical use of <u>hái</u> 还, see also Lesson 19, note 3).

b. Bàba shuō: "Hǎo ā, Dàshān! Nǐ bú qù shàng xué, hái gěi lǎoshī dǎ diànhuà!"

爸爸说："好啊，大山！你不去上学，还给老师打电话！"

Father said, "Terrific, Dashan, you don't go to school and then even (have the audacity to) telephone the teacher!" (meaning compounded bad behavior.)

Our lesson text sentence, "Terrific! You're making a joke about us!" has a teasing tone to it to blunt the edge of the dissatisfaction sense.
本课的意思是："真糟糕！你拿我们开玩笑"，也带有一种开玩笑的语气。

参考资料

拼音课文

Kāi ge liánhuān wǎnhuì

Dàwèi: Wǎnhuì kāishǐ yǐqián, wǒmen yīnggāi bǎ jiàoshì bùzhì yí xiàr.

Mǎdīng: Duì, bǎ yǐzi chóngxīn bǎi yi bǎi, bǎ nèi zhāng dà zhuōzi bānzǒu.

Ānnà: Bǎ lùyīnjī fàng zài zhèr bǐjiào hǎo.

Fāng Xiǎoyīng: Jīn Zhōngyī, nǐ de zì xiě de hǎo, nǐ bǎ hēibǎn cā gānjing, zài shàngbianr xiě jǐ ge zì.

Jīn Zhōngyī: Xiě shénme? Xiě "Liánhuān Wǎnhuì" háishi "Hànyǔ Jiémù Biǎoyǎn Huì"?

Ānnà: Xiě "Liánhuān Wǎnhuì" ba!

Mǎdīng: Nǐmen bǎ jiémùdān fàng zài nǎr le?

Shānběn: Jiémùdān zài wǒ zhèr. Wǒ bǎ tā guà dào hēibǎn pángbiānr hǎo ma?

Jīn Zhōngyī: Hǎo, wǒ bǎ zì xiěwán le. Nǐmen kàn xíng bu xíng?

Fāng Xiǎoyīng: Zuìhòu nèige "huì" zì bù hǎokàn, nǐ néng bu néng bǎ tā gǎi yíxiàr?

Shānběn: Wǒ bǎ jiémùdān zài niàn yí biàn, nǐmen kàn duì bu duì? Dì-yī ge, Ānnà chàng Zhōngwén gē; dì-èr ge, Mǎdīng tán jítā; dì-sān ge, Jīn Zhōngyī tiào wǔ ...

Jīn Zhōngyī: Wǒ yí ge rén bù néng tiào.

Mǎdīng: Fāng Xiǎoyīng, nǐ hé Jīn Zhōngyī yìqǐ tiào ba.

Fāng Xiǎoyīng: Wǒ bú huì tiào Hánguo wǔ.

Jīn Zhōngyī: Méi guānxi, wǒ jiāo ni, yì xué jiù huì.

Shānběn: Dì sì ge jiémù shi Mǎdīng hé Shānběn de héchàng; dì-wǔ ge shi Dàwèi jiǎng xiàohuar. Dàwèi, nǐ jiǎng shénme a?

Dàwèi: Wǒ jiǎng a, wǒ jiǎng "Yǒu ge háizi jiào Dàshān".

Fāng Xiǎoyīng: Shénme? "Yǒu ge háizi jiào Dàshān"?

Dàwèi: Duì a. "Yǒu ge háizi jiào Dàshān. Yǒu yì tiān, Dàshān bù xiǎng shàng xué, jiù gěi lǎoshī dǎ diànhuà, shuō: 'Wèi, shi lǎoshī ma? Dàshān bìng le, jīntian bù néng qù shàng xué le.' Lǎoshī shuō: 'Qǐngwèn, nǐ shi shéi?' Dàshān huídá: 'Wǒ, wǒ shi wǒ bàba.'"

Ānnà: Wǒ xiǎng zhèige háizi bú jiào Dàshān, jiào Dàwèi ba?

Mǎdīng: Duì, nǐ zhēn cōngming!

Shānběn: Búguò, nǐ xiànzài bǎ gùshi jiǎngle, yíhuìr jiémù kāishǐ, nǐ zěnme bàn ne?

Dàwèi: Méi guānxi, wǒ kěyǐ zài jiǎng yí ge gùshi, jiào "Yǒu ge háizi jiào Dàběn" huòzhě "Yǒu ge háizi jiào Xiǎodīng".

Mǎdīng hé Shānběn: Hǎo a, nǐ jiǎng wǒmen!

英译课文

Having an evening get-together

David:	We should decorate the classroom before the party.
Martin:	Yes, rearrange the chairs and move that table out.
Anna:	This is a better place to put the tape recorder.
Fang Xiaoying:	Kim Chung-il, you write well. Wipe off the blackboard and write a few characters.
Kim Chung-il:	What shall I write? Shall I write "Evening Get-together" or "Performance in Chinese"?
Anna:	Write "Evening Get-together"!
Martin:	Where did you put the program sheet?
Yamamoto:	The program is here. I'll hang it by the side of the blackboard, how's that?
Kim Chung-il:	Fine. I've finished writing the characters. Do you think they're all right?
Fang Xiaoying:	The "meeting" character at the end is not very attractive. Can you dress it up?
Yamamoto:	I'll read the program again and you see if it's right. First, Anna sings a Chinese song; second, Martin plays the guitar; third, Kim Chung-il dances ...
Kim Chung-il:	I can't dance alone.
Martin:	Fang Xiaoying, why don't you dance with Kim Chung-il.
Fang Xiaoying:	I don't know how to dance Korean dance.
Kim Chung-il:	That's all right. I'll teach you. You'll get it right away.
Yamamoto:	The fourth item is a duet by Martin and Yamamoto; fifth is David telling a joke. David, what are you going to say?
David:	I'm going to tell one, tell one called "A Kid Named Dashan".
Fang Xiaoying:	What? "A Kid Named Dashan"?

David: Yes. "There was a kid named Dashan. One day, Dashan didn't feel like going to school. So he called the teacher and said: 'Hello, is this the teacher? Dashan is sick and can't come to school today.' The teacher responded: 'Excuse me but who is this?' Dashan answered: 'I, I'm my father.'"

Anna: I don't think that the kid is named Dashan, but rather David (Dawei), no?

Martin: Right, you're on the ball.

Yamamoto: But you've told the story now. What are you going to do when the program gets going?

David: That's all right, I can tell another one, called "A Kid Named Daben (Big Yamamoto)" or "A Kid Named Xiao Ding (Little Martin)".

Martin and Yamamoto: Terrific! You're making a joke about us!

第二十二课

祝你们旅行愉快

汉字课文

安　娜：假期你们打算怎么过？是去旅行还是回国？

马　丁：当然是去旅行。

山　本：学校一放假，我们就去上海。

安　娜：还去别的地方吗？

大　卫：还去北京和西安。

安　娜：你们坐火车去还是坐飞机去？

马　丁：我们先坐飞机到上海，然后再坐火车去北京，最后去西安。

安　娜：票都买好了吗？

山　本：到上海去的飞机票已经订好了。去北京的火车票，准备在上海买。

安　娜：能买到吗？听说火车票不太好买。

大　卫：是，所以我们一到上海，就先去买票。

安　娜：你们打算去多久？

山　本：大概半个月。

安　娜：半个月不够吧？你们为什么不多玩儿一两个星期？

马　丁：我们没有那么多钱。你的行李都收拾好了吗？

安　娜：差不多了。我还想给我爸爸妈妈买一点儿东西。

山　本：你应该给你爸爸买一点儿中国茶叶。

大　卫：你可以给你妈妈买几件真丝衬衫。

安　娜：嗯，好主意！我下午就去买。

马　丁：你什么时候走？

安　娜：大后天。我先去日本看一个朋友，然后再回国。

马　丁：去日本的签证好办吗？手续麻烦不麻烦？

安　娜：不用办签证。

大　卫：把你在英国的地址给我们留下吧。

安　娜：好，我把学校和家里的地址都留下，还有电话号码。你们如果到英国去，一定要来找我啊！

马　丁：安娜，给我一张照片好吗？

安　娜：好吧，就把桌子上那张送给你吧。真可惜，这次不能跟你们一起去旅行。

山　本：没关系，以后还会有机会。

安　娜：祝你们旅行愉快！

大　卫：祝你拿到奖学金！

生词语

1.	旅行	lǚxíng	(v)		to travel
2.	愉快	yúkuài	(adj)		to be content, happy; to be pleasant (of an affair, event)
3.	假期	jiàqī	(n)		vacation
4.	打算	dǎsuan	(v, n)	[个]	to plan to; plan

a. 明天要开联欢会，你打算表演什么节目？

—— 我打算唱个中文歌儿。

b. 如果学校不给你奖学金，你打算怎么办？

c. 毕业以后，你有什么打算？

5. 火车 huǒchē (n) [列 liè] train

6. 飞机 fēijī (n) [架 jià] plane

7. 准备 zhǔnbèi (v) to prepare

a. 后天要考试了，你准备得怎么样了？

b. 放假以后，你准备到哪儿去旅行？

c. 在晚会上，他们让我唱歌儿，可是我没有准备，所以没唱。

8. 所以 suǒyǐ (c) so, therefore

9. 久 jiǔ (adj) to be long (in duration)

10. 玩 wánr (v) to play, to pass time enjoyably

11. 行李 xíngli (n) [件] luggage

12. 收拾 shōushi (v) to arrange, clear up

a. 这几天在考试，没有时间，星期日我得好好儿收拾一下儿房间。

b. 你把桌子上的书收拾一下儿，好吗？

c. 她正在收拾行李，我们去帮帮她。

13. 茶叶 cháyè (n) tea leaves

14. 真丝 zhēnsī (n) pure silk

15. 衬衫 chènshān (n) [件] shirt, blouse

16. 主意 zhúyi, zhǔyì (n) [个] idea

17. 大后天 dàhòutiān (n) the day after the day after tomorrow

18. 签证 qiānzhèng (n) visa

19. 好 hǎo (adv) to be easy, uncomplicated

20. 手续 shǒuxù (n) procedure

21. 麻烦 máfan (adj, v, n) to be troublesome, to trouble, trouble

a. 这件事太麻烦，我真不想去办。

b. 她要自己收拾行李，不想麻烦别人。

c. 对不起，麻烦你一下儿，请帮我把这件行李放在上边儿，好吗？

d. 这是他自己找来的麻烦，我们也没办法。

22. 地址	dìzhǐ	(n)	[个]	address
23. 留	liú	(v)		leave (an address, etc.), keep, remain behind, behind (liú zuòyè = to give homework)

a. 王老师说今天不留作业，明天再留。

b. 这块蛋糕留给他，我已经吃了。

c. 她的行李太多了，她说留下一件，请你回上海的时候，帮她带去。

d. 这张照片你留着吧，我还有一张。

24. 可惜	kěxī	(adj)		to be regrettable, unfortunate

a. 你昨天没看那个电影，太可惜了。

b. 我们在公园划船的照片都照坏了，真可惜。

c. 这张照片里，每个人都照得很好，可惜有点儿不清楚。

d. 这件衣服真好看，可惜有点儿大。

e. 听说那本词典不错，可惜已经卖完了。

f. 这真是一件非常可惜的事。

25. 机会	jīhui	(n)	[个]	opportunity

专有名词

1.	上海	Shànghǎi	Shanghai
2.	北京	Běijīng	Beijing, Peking
3.	西安	Xī'ān	Xi'an, Hsi-an

补充生词

1.	寒假	hánjià	(n)	winter vacation
2.	暑假	shǔjià	(n)	summer vacation
3.	护照	hùzhào	(n)	passport
4.	香港	Xiānggǎng	(n)	Hong Kong
5.	广州	Guǎngzhōu	(n)	Guangzhou, Canton

语法点

1. Hǎo 好 in an adverbial position means easy to.
   "好"也是一个副词，意思是"容易"，在句中修饰动词。

   a. Zhè shì ge xīn diànyǐng, piào hǎo mǎi ma?
   这是个新电影，票好买吗？
   This is a new film. Are tickets easy to buy?

   b. Tā shi Shànghǎirén. Tā shuō de huà bù hǎo dǒng.
   他是上海人。他说的话不好懂。
   He is a Shanghainese. It's not easy to understand what he's saying.

   c. Gāng xiàwán yǔ, zhèi tiáo lù bù hǎo zǒu, nèi tiáo lù hǎo zǒu.
   刚下完雨，这条路不好走，那条路好走。
   It's just stopped raining. It's difficult to go by this road, but that road is all right.

2. Duō wánr yì-liǎng ge xīngqī 多玩儿一两个星期 "Enjoy yourself for a week or two more". Here, duō 多 is adverbial indicating "more than originally planned, figured, etc.".
   "多"可以出现在动词前修饰动词，表示原来计划的数目有所增加。动词后要有数量词。

a. Jīntiān yǒu yìdiǎnr lěng, nǐ duō chuān yí jiàn yīfu ba.

今天有一点儿冷，你多穿一件衣服吧。

It's a bit cold today, wear one more layer of clothing.

b. Wǒ duō mǎile liǎng zhāng piào, nǐmen yào bú yào?

我多买了两张票，你们要不要？

I bought two extra tickets, do you want them?

c. Qǐng nǐ duō děng yíhuìr, tā zhèngzài dǎ diànhuà.

请你多等一会儿，她正在打电话。

Please wait a while longer, she's on the telephone.

d. Fāng Xiǎoyīng hé Ānnà yào qù nèige shāngchǎng. Wǒ xiǎng tāmen děi duō dài diǎnr qián.

方小英和安娜要去那个商场。我想她们得多带点儿钱。

Fang Xiaoying and Anna are going to that mall. I think they should take a bit more money with them.

NOTE that it is INCORRECT to say chuān duō yí jiàn yīfu 穿多一件衣服 or děng duō yìhuǐr 等多一会儿. Modifier precedes modified. Duō 多 as an adverb precedes its verb.

注意："多"必须出现在动词前，不能出现在动词后，下面的句子是错误的："穿多一件衣服""等多一会儿"。

参考资料

拼音课文

Zhù nǐmen lǚxíng yúkuài

Ānnà: Jiàqī nǐmen dǎsuan zěnme guò? Shì qù lǚxíng háishi huí guó?

Mǎdīng: Dāngrán shi qù lǚxíng.

Shānběn:	Xuéxiào yí fàng jià, wǒmen jiù qù Shànghǎi.
Ānnà:	Hái qù biéde dìfang ma?
Dàwèi:	Hái qù Běijīng hé Xī'ān.
Ānnà:	Nǐmen zuò huǒchē qù háishi zuò fēijī qù?
Mǎdīng:	Wǒmen xiān zuò fēijī dào Shànghǎi, ránhòu zài zuò huǒchē qù Běijīng, zuìhòu qù Xī'ān.
Ānnà:	Piào dōu mǎihǎo le ma?
Shānběn:	Dào Shànghǎi qù de fēijīpiào yǐjing dìnghǎo le. Qù Běijīng de huǒchēpiào, zhǔnbèi zài Shànghǎi mǎi.
Ānnà:	Néng mǎidào ma? Tīngshuō huǒchēpiào bú tài hǎo mǎi.
Dàwèi:	Shì, suǒyǐ wǒmen yí dào Shànghǎi, jiù xiān qù mǎi piào.
Ānnà:	Nǐmen dǎsuan qù duō jiǔ?
Shānběn:	Dàgài bàn ge yuè.
Ānnà:	Bàn ge yuè bú gòu ba? Nǐmen wèishénme bù duō wánr yì-liǎng ge xīngqī?
Mǎdīng:	Wǒmen méiyou nàme duō qián. Nǐ de xíngli dōu shōushi hǎo le ma?
Ānnà:	Chàbuduō le. Wǒ hái xiǎng gěi wǒ bàba māma mǎi yìdiǎnr dōngxi.
Shānběn:	Nǐ yīnggāi gěi nǐ bàba mǎi yìdiǎnr Zhōngguó cháyè.
Dàwèi:	Nǐ kěyi gěi nǐ māma mǎi jǐ jiàn zhēnsī chènshān.
Ānnà:	Ng, hǎo zhúyi! Wǒ xiàwǔ jiù qù mǎi.
Mǎdīng:	Nǐ shénme shíhou zǒu?
Ānnà:	Dàhòutiān. Wǒ xiān qù Rìběn kàn yí gè péngyou, ránhòu zài huí guó.
Mǎdīng:	Qù Rìběn de qiānzhèng hǎo bàn ma? Shǒuxù máfan bu máfan?
Ānnà:	Búyòng bàn qiānzhèng.
Dàwèi:	Bǎ nǐ zài Yīngguo de dìzhǐ gěi wǒmen liúxia ba.

Ānnà:	Hǎo, wǒ bǎ xuéxiào hé jiā li de dìzhǐ dōu liúxia, hái yǒu diànhuà hàomǎ. Nǐmen rúguǒ dào Yīngguo qu, yídìng yào lái zhǎo wǒ a!
Mǎdīng:	Ānnà, gěi wǒ yì zhāng zhàopiàn hǎo ma?
Ānnà:	Hǎo ba, jiù bǎ zhuōzi shang nèi zhāng sònggěi ni ba. Zhēn kěxī, zhèi cì bù néng gēn nǐmen yìqǐ qù lǚxíng.
Shānběn:	Méi guānxi, yǐhòu hái huì yǒu jīhuì.
Ānnà:	Zhù nǐmen lǚxíng yúkuài!
Dàwèi:	Zhù nǐ nádào jiǎngxuéjīn!

英译课文

I hope you have a good trip

Anna:	What are you going to do during the break? Are you travelling or going home?
Martin:	Definitely travelling.
Yamamoto:	As soon as the break begins, David and I are going to Shanghai.
Anna:	Are you going to other places too?
David:	We're also going to Beijing and Xi'an.
Anna:	Are you going by train or plane?
Martin:	We're going by plane first to Shanghai, then by train to Beijing and finally Xi'an.
Anna:	Have you got your tickets?
Yamamoto:	Tickets for Shanghai are already reserved. We're planning to buy the Beijing tickets in Shanghai.
Anna:	Will you be able to get them? I hear it's not too easy to get train tickets.
David:	I know, so as soon as we get to Shanghai we'll buy train tickets first thing.

Anna: How long will you be away?

Yamamoto: About half a month.

Anna: A half a month isn't enough, is it? Why don't you make it (literally, enjoy yourself for) a week or two more?

Martin: We don't have that much money. Are your bags all packed?

Anna: Almost. I still have to buy something for my father and mother.

Yamamoto: You should buy some Chinese tea for your father.

David: You can buy a few silk blouses for your mother.

Anna: Hey, good ideas! I'll get them this afternoon.

Martin: When are you going to leave?

Anna: Three days from now. I'm going to Japan to see a friend first, then going home.

Martin: How was it getting a Japanese visa? Was the procedure difficult?

Anna: I didn't have to get a visa.

David: Leave your English address for us.

Anna: All right. I'll leave both school and home addresses. And telephone numbers as well. If you go to England, you must definitely look me up!

Martin: Anna, let me have your photo.

Anna: All right, I'll give you that one on the table. I'm so sorry that I can't go with you this time.

Yamamoto: That's all right. There'll be another chance later.

Anna: I hope you have a good trip!

David: I hope you get your scholarship!

Vocabulary
词汇总表

(References are to chapter numbers.)

A

啊	ā	(part, i)		(modal particle, added to verbs, adjectives or sentences to give assurance or agreement emphasis, or stress the speaker's point of view)	6
哎呀	āiyā	(i)		yow! wow! ah!	14
爱	ài	(v)		to be fond of, like to; to love	18
八	bā	(nu)		eight	2
把	bǎ	(prep)		(the pretransitive or disposal preposition)	18
爸爸	bàba	(n)	[个 gè]	dad, papa	15

B

吧	ba	(part)		(modal particle indicating doubt or seeking confirmation)	4
摆	bǎi	(v)		to place, set	21
班	bān	(n)	[个]	section, class	2
搬	bān	(v)		to move (something)	21
半	bàn	(nu)		half	5
办	bàn	(v)		to manage, do	17
办法	bànfǎ	(n)	[个]	means, way out (of something)	20
半天	bàntiān	(n)		a long time (in the user's perception, often exaggerated)	15

帮	bāng	(v)		to help	18
杯子	bēizi	(n)	[个]	glass, cup	18
北边儿	běibianr	(n-pw)		north side	9
北方	běifāng	(n)		the north, northern part	19
本	běn	(m)		(measure word for books)	5
本子	běnzi	(n)	[个，本]	notebook	4
笔	bǐ	(n)	[支 zhī]	writing instrument	13
比	bǐ	(prep, v)		comparative preposition; to compare, match against	19
比较	bǐjiào	(adv, v)		to compare; comparatively	10
毕业	bì yè	(vo)		to graduate (from school)	15
遍	biàn	(m)		number of times	14
边儿	biānr	(n)		side	9
表演	biǎoyǎn	(v)		to perform	21
别	bié	(adv)		don't	10
别的	biéde	(pro)		other	8
别提啦	bié tí la	(i.e)		It's a long story! Indescribable! What a mixup? (Lit., "Don't even bring it up.")	17
饼干	bǐnggān	(n)	[块 kuài]	cookie, biscuit	17
病	bìng	(v, n)		to be ill; illness	21
不错	búcuò	(adj)		pretty good, not bad; correct	12
不过	búguò	(c)		but	5
不见不散	bú jiàn bú sàn			(fixed expression) "Don't leave until I get there." "Wait there till I arrive."	6
不用	búyòng	(o.v)		need not	6

不	bù	(adv)		(negates verbs, including adjectival and optative verbs)	1
布置	bùzhi	(v)		to arrange, fix up, decorate (a room, etc.)	21

C

擦	cā	(v)		to erase, rub	21
才	cái	(adv)		then, just at that time	15
菜	cài	(n)	[个]	items of food, dishes; green vegetables	14
菜单	càidān	(n)	[张 zhāng，份 fèn]	menu	14
菜名	cài míng			name of a dish, item of prepared food	14
厕所	cèsuǒ	(n)	[个]	toilet (as in all languages, roundabout terms are available for the squeamish. Xǐshǒujiān "washroom" (see below) is one.)	8
茶叶	cháyè	(n)		tea leaves	22
差不多	chàbuduō	(adj)		almost, nearly	13
长	cháng	(adj)		to be long	11
常	cháng	(adv)		often	14
尝	cháng	(v)		to taste	14
常常	chángcháng	(adv)		frequently, always (hyperbolic)	10
唱歌	chàng gēr	(vo)		to sing	13
唱	chàng	(v)		to sing	
歌儿	gēr	(n)	[个，支]	song	
潮湿	cháoshī	(adj)		to be damp (of the air and related phenomena)	19
车	chē	(n)	[辆 liàng]	vehicle (wheeled)	16
衬衫	chènshān	(n)	[件 jiàn]	shirt, blouse	22

成绩	chéngji	(n)		results, achievement	20
吃饭	chī fàn	(vo)		to eat	4
吃	chī	(v)		to eat	
饭	fàn	(n)	[顿 dùn]	cooked rice, meal	
重新	chóngxīn	(adv)		anew, again	21
出	chū	(v)		to go out of (a place), to exit	11
出发	chūfā	(v)		to set out, set off	17
厨房	chú fáng	(n)	[个，间 jiān]	kitchen	18
穿	chuān	(v)		to wear (clothing)	11
春天	chūntiān	(n)	[个]	spring	19
词典	cídiǎn	(n)	[本，部 bù]	dictionary	5
次	cì	(m)		number of times	14
聪明	cōngming	(adj)		to be intelligent, bright	21
从	cóng	(prep)		from	7
醋	cù	(n)	[瓶 píng]	vinegar	18
错	cuò	(adj)		to be wrong	7

D

打	dǎ	(v)		(in context) to send, transmit as a phone call; to hit	6
打	dǎ	(v)		to strike, hit; to play (with objects indication sports, etc.)	9
打	dǎ	(v)		to open, hold up (an umbrella or flag)	19
打算	dǎsuàn	(v, n)	[个]	to plan to; plan	22
大	dà	(adj)		to be big	8
大概	dàgài	(adv)		probably	7

大后天	dàhòutiān	(n)		the day after the day after tomorrow	22
大家	dàjiā	(pro)		everyone	13
大学	dàxué	(n)	[个]	university	15
带	dài	(v)		to bring	17
担心	dānxīn	(vo)		to be concerned, worry	14
淡	dàn	(adj)		to be not salty; be insipid; be pale or light (of color)	18
蛋糕	dàngāo	(n)	[个，块]	cake	13
当然	dāngrán	(adj, adv)		certainly, of course	8
到	dào	(v)		to arrive	6
倒	dào	(v)		to pour	18
的	de	(part)		(structural particle)	2
得	de	(part)		(structural particle, placed between verb or adjective and a complement of degree)	10
得	děi	(o.v)		must, have to	11
等	děng	(v)		to wait	4
第	dì	(pref)		(ordinal prefix)	7
递	dì	(v)		to pass to	18
弟弟	dìdi	(n)	[个]	younger brother	15
地方	dìfang	(n)	[个]	place	11
地铁	dìtiě	(n)		underground transport	16
地址	dìzhǐ	(n)	[个]	address	22
点	diǎn	(m)		hour-point on the clock, e.g., yìdiǎn 1:00	5
点	diǎn	(v)		to order	14
电车	diànchē	(n)	[辆]	electric streetcar, tram, trolley	17

电话	diànhuà	(n)	[个]	telephone	6
电视	diànshì	(n)	[个]	television	19
电影	diànyǐng	(n)	[个，部]	film, movie	4
电影院	diànyǐngyuàn	(n)	[个，家 jiā]	cinema, theater	4
订	dìng	(v)		to book, reserve (a ticket); to subscribe (to a newspaper, etc.)	6
定	dìng	(v)		to reserve, fix, sign up for	9
丢	diū	(v)		to lose	12
东边儿	dōngbianr	(n-pw)		east side	9
冬天	dōngtiān	(n)	[个]	winter	19
东西	dōngxi	(n)	[件]	thing	11
懂	dǒng	(v)		to understand	10
都	dōu	(adv)		all (sums up two or more preceding nominals)	5
度	dù	(m)		degree	19
端	duān	(v)		to carry level with both hands, out-stretched, as a tray, basin	18
对	duì	(adj)		to be correct	3
对不起	duì bu qǐ			I'm sorry, I beg your pardon	7
多	duō	(adj)		to be many	2
多	duō	(adv)		how (questioning degree)	11
多（么）	duō(me)	(adv)		how (as in "how beautiful") — to that degree	19
多少	duōshao	(pro)		how much, how many	3

E

饿	è	(v)		to be hungry	13
二	èr	(nu)		two	2

欸	ế	(i)		(surprise exclamation)	13

F

发烧	fā shāo	(vo)		to run a fever	20
发	fā	(v)		to emit	
烧	shāo	(v)		heat	
发音	fāyīn	(n)		pronunciation	18
饭店	fàndiàn	(n)	[家，个]	hotel	16
饭馆儿	fànguǎnr	(n)	[个，家]	restaurant	14
方便	fāngbiàn	(adj)		to be convenient	16
房间	fángjiān	(n)	[个]	room	13
放	fàng	(v)		to place, put	18
放假	fàng jià	(vo)		to have time off, take a holiday	20
放	fàng	(v)		to place, set	
假	jià	(n)		holiday, time off	
非常	fēicháng	(adv)		unusually	16
飞机	fēijī	(n)	[架 jià]	plane	22
分	fēn	(m)		a minute of time	5
分	fēn	(m)		cent	12
分钟	fēnzhōng	(m)		a minute of time	11
服务员	fúwùyuán	(n)	[个，位 wèi]	attendant, general term for those who wait on customers at restaurants and elsewhere in the service industry	14
附近	fùjìn	(n)		vicinity	11
复习	fùxí	(v)		to review (a lesson)	5

G

该	gāi	(o.v)		will probably (no negative form)	20

改	gǎi	(v)		to change, alter; to correct	21
干净	gānjing	(adj)		to be clean	17
干燥	gānzào	(adj)		to be dry (of the air and related phenomena)	19
感冒	gǎnmào	(v)		to catch a cold; a cold	20
刚	gāng	(adv)		just	19
高兴	gāoxìng	(adj)		to be happy, to be delighted	15
告诉	gàosu	(v)		to tell	10
哥哥	gēge	(n)	[个]	older brother	15
个	gè	(m)		(general measure word)	2
给	gěi	(prep)		to, for (instrumental function word, often untranslatable)	7
给	gěi	(v)		to give	10
跟	gēn	(prep)		together with; and (connecting nouns and nominals)	4
更	gèng	(adv)		more, -er	19
公共	gōnggòng	(adj)		public	16
公司	gōngsī	(n)	[个，家]	company	15
公园	gōngyuán	(n)	[个]	park	16
工作	gōngzuò	(v, n)		to work; work	15
够	gòu	(adj)		to be enough, adequate	18
故事	gùshi	(n)	[个]	story, tale	21
刮风	guā fēng	(vo)		to be windy	19
刮	guā	(v)		to blow	
风	fēng	(n)		wind	
挂	guà	(v)		to hang	21
拐	guǎi	(v)		to turn (a corner), make a turn	16
关系	guānxi	(n)		relevance; relationships	20

贵	guì	(adj)		to be expensive	11
国	guó	(n)		country	1
过	guò	(v)		to pass by, to go by	12
过	guò	(v)		go through the process of; to celebrate	13
过	guò	(v)		to go past, to pass	17
过	guo	(part)		(aspect particle, attached to verbs and adjectives, expresses experience = "have done X")	12

H

还	hái	(adv)		still, yet	9
还	hái	(adv)		again (future repetition of an action)	12
还是	háishi	(c)		or (used in alternative questions)	14
孩子	háizi	(n)	[个]	child, children	21
好	hǎo	(adj)		to be good	1
好	hǎo	(adv)		to be easy, uncomplicated	22
好吃	hǎochī	(adj)		to be tasty	8
好好儿	hǎohāor	(adj)		well, wholeheartedly	7
好看	hǎokàn	(adj)		to be attractive (to look at)	10
号	hào	(n)		day of the month; number (a bound word)	3
号码	hàomǎ	(n)	[个]	number	7
喝	hē	(v)		to drink	13
和	hé	(c)		and (connects NOMINALS)	3
合唱	héchàng	(n, v)		sing in chorus, sing together	21
合适	héshì	(adj)		to be fitting, appropriate	16

黑板	hēibǎn	(n)	[块，个]	blackboard	21
很	hěn	(adv)		very (somewhat lighter than the English "very")	2
后边儿	hòubianr	(n-pw)		at the back, to the rear	8
后天	hòutiān	(n)		the day after tormorrow	3
划船	huá chuán	(vo)		to row a boat	16
划	huá	(v)		to row	
船	chuán	(n)	[只，条 tiáo]	boat	
坏	huài	(adj)		to be bad, to be broken (malfunction), to go bad (as food)	19
欢迎	huānyíng	(v)		to welcome	8
还	huán	(v)		to return (goods, books, etc.)	17
换	huàn	(v)		to change, change to	16
回	huí	(v)		to return	4
回	huí	(m)		(for actions and events, happenings time)	20
怎么回事儿	zěnme huí shìr	(i.e)		What happened? What's the matter?	20
回答	huídá	(v)		to answer; reply	3
会	huì	(o.v)		to know how to	10
会	huì	(n)	[个]	a meeting	21
火车	huǒchē	(n)	[列 liè]	train	22
或者	huòzhě	(c)		or	21

J

机场	jīchǎng	(n)	[个]	airport	17
机会	jīhuì	(n)	[个]	opportunity	22
吉他	jítā	(n)	[把 bǎ]	guitar	21

几	jǐ	(pro)		how many of something (must be followed by m)	3
几	jǐ	(pro)		several	12
记	jì	(v)		to write down	14
家	jiā	(n)	[个]	home, family	4
假期	jiàqī	(n)	[个]	vacation	22
见	jiàn	(v)		to see, meet	9
件	jiàn	(m)		an item of, article of (clothing, business matter, etc.)	11
见面	jiàn miàn	(vo)		to meet	6
见	jiàn	(v)		to see	
面	miàn	(n)		the face	
讲	jiǎng	(v)		tell, explain (sometimes: to say, to speak)	21
奖学金	jiǎngxuéjīn	(n)	[笔 bǐ]	scholarship	20
酱油	jiàngyóu	(n)		soy sauce	18
教	jiāo	(v)		to teach	10
交	jiāo	(v)		to hand in, give over to	10
饺子	jiǎozi	(n)	[个]	Chinese dumplings	18
叫	jiào	(v)		to be called	2
叫	jiào	(v)		to have do (cause to do)	13
教室	jiàoshì	(n)	[个，间]	classroom	8
接	jiē	(v)		to receive	7
节	jié	(m)		a section of a whole as "a class hour"	7
节目	jiémù	(n)	[个]	program	21
节目单	jiémùdān	(n)	[张]	(printed) program	21
结束	jiéshù	(v)		to conclude, to come to an end	20

姐姐	jiějie	(n)	[个]	older sister	15
借	jiè	(v)		to borrow; to lend	17
介绍	jièshào	(v)		to introduce	8
今年	jīnnián	(v)		this year	3
今天	jīntiān	(n)		today	3
紧张	jǐnzhāng	(adj)		to be nervous, tense	10
近	jìn	(adj)		to be near, close	11
进	jìn	(v)		to enter	15
九	jiǔ	(nu)		nine	2
酒	jiǔ	(n)		wine; generic noun for wine and spirits	18
久	jiǔ	(adj)		to be long (in duration)	22
旧	jiù	(adj)		to be old (in the outdated or second-hand sense)	5
就	jiù	(adv)		(often with the equational shi, and often handled through voice emphasis in English) precisely, that's it	7
觉得	juéde	(v)		to feel, be of the opinion	8

K

开	kāi	(v)		to hold (a meeting, party, etc.)	21
开车	kāi chē	(vo)		to drive (a vehicle)	20
开	kāi	(v)		to drive	
车	chē	(n)	[辆]	car, vehicle	
开始	kāishǐ	(v)		to begin	15
开玩笑	kāi wánxiào	(vo)		to joke, to jest	14
开	kāi	(v)		to make (in limited contexts)	
玩笑	wánxiào	(n)	[个]	joke	

开夜车	kāi yèchē	(vo)		to burn the midnight oil	20
开	kāi	(v)		to drive (a vehicle)	
夜车	yèchē	(n)		the night train	
看	kàn	(v)		to look, look at, watch (film, TV), to read	4
看见	kànjian	(v)		to see	19
考	kǎo	(v)		to examine, test; to take an examination	20
考试	kǎoshì	(n,v)		examination; to take an examination	20
渴	kě	(v)		to be thirsty	17
可乐	kělè	(n)	[瓶，杯 bēi]	cola	14
可能	kěnéng	(adv, adj, n)		possibly; to be possible; possibility	20
可怕	kěpà	(adj)		to be frightening, terrible	20
可是	kěshì	(c)		but	11
可惜	kěxī	(adj)		to be regrettable, unfortunate	22
可以	kěyǐ	(o.v)		(before another verb) may, can; not bad, pretty good	8
刻	kè	(m)		a quarter of the hour	5
课	kè	(n, m)		class, lesson	5
客气	kèqi	(adj)		to act with politeness or modest restraint; to be polite	18
客厅	kètīng	(n)	[个，间]	living room, parlor	18
课文	kèwén	(n)	[课]	lesson text	5
空调	kōngtiáo	(n)	[个]	air conditioner	19
口	kǒu	(m)		(measure for number of people, as in a family)	15
快	kuài	(adj)		to be quick, fast	10

块	kuài	(m)		a piece of; dollar	12
快乐	kuàilè	(adj)		to be happy	13
筷子	kuàizi	(n)	[双 shuāng，只 zhī]	chopsticks	8

L

辣	là	(adj)		to be (spicy) hot	14
来	lái	(v)		to come	4
来	lái	(v)		(replaces another verb, creating a familiar or casual tone)	13
老师	lǎoshī	(n)	[位，个]	teacher	2
了	le	(part)		(modal particle, indicating a completed action)	6
了	le	(part)		(aspect particle, attached to V indicating a completed action)	9
累	lèi	(adj)		to be tired	16
冷	lěng	(adj)		to be cold (of weather)	19
离	lí	(prep)		(distance) from	11
里	lǐ	(n-pw)		inside	8
礼堂	lǐtáng	(n)	[个]	auditorium	8
礼物	lǐwù	(n)	[件，个]	a gift, present	13
联欢	liánhuān	(v)		to have a get-together	21
练习	liànxí	(v,n)		to practice; practice	10
凉快	liángkuai	(adj)		to be cool (of the weather)	19
两	liǎng	(nu)		two of something (must be followed by m)	2
聊天儿	liáo tiānr	(vo)		to chat, have light conversation	18
零	líng	(nu)		zero	5
零钱	língqián	(n)		small change	12

留	liú	(v)		leave (an address, etc); keep remain behind, behind (liú zuòyè = to give homework)	22
六	liù	(nu)		six	2
楼	lóu	(n)		storied building; floor (1, 2 etc.) of a building	11
楼上	lóushàng	(n)		upstairs	11
楼下	lóuxià	(n)		downstairs	11
路	lù	(n)		road	16
路	lù	(m)		route (of buses, etc.)	16
录音机	lùyīnjī	(n)	[个]	tape recorder	21
旅行	lǚxíng	(v)		to travel	22

M

妈妈	māma	(n)	[个]	mom, ma	15
麻烦	máfan	(adj, v)		to be troublesome, to trouble, trouble	22
马马虎虎	mămahūhū	(adj)		to be so-so, fair; to be sloppy	20
马上	măshàng	(adv)		immediately	4
吗	ma	(part)		(interrogative particle)	1
买	măi	(v)		to buy	5
卖	mài	(v)		to sell	11
满意	mănyì	(v)		to be satisfied	20
慢	màn	(adj)		to be slow	10
忙	máng	(adj)		to be busy	17
毛	máo	(m)		tenth of a dollar, ten cents	12
贸易	màoyì	(n)		trade	15

没	méi	(adv, v)		negative for <u>you</u> ("to have, to exist")	2
没关系	méi guānxi	(vo)		(fixed expression) that's alright, no problem	7
没问题	méi wèntí	(vo)		It's fine, no problem	6
没	méi	(v)		not any (a contraction of <u>méiyǒu</u>)	
问题	wèntí	(n)	[个]	problem	
没(有)	méi(you)	(adv)		negative of completed action	6
每	měi	(pro)		each	8
妹妹	mèimei	(n)	[个]	younger sister	15
门	mén	(m)		for school classes or courses	20
门口儿	ménkǒur	(n)		entrance	6
们	men	(n suff)		pluralizing suffix for pronouns and some personal nouns	1
迷路	mí lù	(vo)		to get lost, go astray	17
秘密	mìmì	(adj, n)	[个]	secret	13
明年	míngnián	(n)		next year	3
明天	míngtiān	(n)		tomorrow	3
名字	míngzi	(n)	[个]	name	2

N

拿	ná	(v)		to take, get hold	4
那(么)	nà, nème	(c)		then, in that case	12
那(么)	nème	(adv)		so, to that degree	15
奶奶	nǎinai	(n)	[个]	paternal grandmother	15
男	nán	(adj)		male (must be followed by another nominal)	2
难	nán	(adj)		to be difficult	9
哪儿	nǎr	(pro)		where	4

那儿	nàr	(pro)		there	6
呢	ne	(part)		(modal particle for questions in context)	3
哪	něi; nă	(pro)		which	1
那	nèi; nà	(pro)		that	2
能	néng	(o.v)		(before verb) to be able to	7
嗯	ǹg	(i)		mm, hm (indicating affimation or agreement)	12
你	nǐ	(pro)		you	1
你们	nǐmen	(pro)		you (plural)	5
年	nián	(n)		year (a bound word, i.e., it cannot be used alone)	3
年轻	niánqīng	(adj)		to be youthful	15
念	niàn	(v)		to read, read aloud	14
您	nín	(pro)		you (polite)	2
暖和	nuănhuo	(adj)		to be comfortably warm	19
女	nǚ	(adj)		female (must be followed by another nominal)	2

O

哦	ò	(i)		oh (expressing a discovery or new realization)	12

P

旁边儿	pángbiānr	(n-pw)		side, beside	9
陪	péi	(v)		to accompany, go along with, keep company	12
朋友	péngyou	(n)	[个，位]	friend	4
啤酒	píjiŭ	(n)	[瓶，杯]	beer	14

便宜	piányi	(adj)		to be inexpensive	11
票	piào	(n)	[张]	ticket	6
漂亮	piàoliang	(adj)		to be attractive, pretty	13
瓶	píng	(m)		bottle	14
平常	píngcháng	(adj, n)		ordinary, ordinarily	18
苹果	píngguǒ	(n)	[个]	apple	17

Q

七	qī	(nu)		seven	2
骑	qí	(v)		to ride astride (bicycle, horse)	16
起床	qǐ chuáng	(vo)		get out of bed, get up	17
汽车	qìchē	(n)	[辆]	car, automobile	16
气温	qìwēn	(n)		atmospheric temperature	19
签证	qiānzhèng	(n)		visa	22
钱	qián	(n)	[块，毛 máo，分 fēn，元 yuán]	money	12
前	qián	(n)		before	20
前边儿	qiánbianr	(n-pw)		at the front	8
前天	qiántiān	(n)		day before yesterday	12
切	qiē	(v)		to cut	13
青菜	qīngcài	(n)	[个]	vegetables, greens, dish without meat	14
清楚	qīngchu	(adj)		to be clear	12
请	qǐng	(v)		to invite; to request (politely)	14
请	qǐng	(v)		to request	7
请假	qǐng jià	(vo)		to request leave, ask to be absent	7
请	qǐng	(v)		to request	
假	jià	(n)		leave, time off	

请问	qǐngwèn	(v)		excuse me (in asking a question. Lit., "please may I ask")	7
秋天	qiūtiān	(n)	[个]	autumn, fall	19
去	qù	(v)		to go	4
去年	qùnián	(n)		last year	3
去世	qùshì	(v)		to pass away (death enphemism)	15

R

然后	ránhòu	(adv)		afterwards, after that	16
让	ràng	(v)		to let, to have do (in the sense of "to cause to do")	13
热	rè	(adj)		to be hot (of weather) (sometimes, as with lěng, used metaphorically)	19
人	rén	(n)	[个]	man (male or female), person, people	1
人民币	rénmínbì	(n)		RMB, the designation of China's currency	12
认识	rènshi	(v)		to recognize	8
日	rì	(n)		day (a bound word); sun	3
容易	róngyi	(adj)		to be easy	9
如果…就…	rúguǒ…jiù…			if … then …	10

S

三	sān	(nu)		three	2
散步	sàn bù	(vo)		to stroll, take a walk	6
沙拉	shālā	(n)		salad (often spoken as shālà)	18
商场	shāngchǎng	(n)	[个]	shopping center, arcade	11

商店	shāngdiàn	(n)	[个]	shop, store	11
上	shàng	(n-pw)		on top of (a bound word); last (of month, week, time, etc.)	3
上边儿	shàngbianr	(n-pw)		topside	11
上课	shàng kè	(vo)		to attend, go to (class, work)	5
上	shàng	(v)		to attend	
课	kè	(n)	[节 jié]	class	
上楼	shàng lóu	(vo)		to go upstairs, to upper floors	11
上	shàng	(v)		to go up, ascend	
楼	lóu	(n)		storied building	
上午	shàngwǔ	(n)	[个]	forenoon, AM	5
上学	shàng xué	(vo)		to attend school	21
少	shǎo	(adj)		to be few	2
谁	shéi; shuí	(pro)		who, whom	1
什么	shénme	(pro)		what	2
什么的	shénmede	(n)		and so forth, etc.	17
生词	shēngcí	(n)	[个]	vocabulary, new words	5
声调	shēngdiào	(n)	[个]	tones (of chinese)	18
生日	shēngrì	(n)	[个]	birthday	13
生日卡	shēngrìkǎ	(n)	[张，个]	birthday card	13
十	shí	(nu)		ten	2
时候	shíhou	(n)		time (NOTE its different shapes in different contexts)	3
时间	shíjiān	(n)		time	9
食堂	shítáng	(n)	[个]	canteen, dining hall	8
是	shì	(v)		(equational verb) equals, is	1
是	shì	(adj)		yes, right	12
事(儿)	shì(r)	(n)	[件，个]	business, a matter, thing to do	17

收拾	shōushi	(v)		to arrange, clear up	22
手续	shǒuxù	(n)		procedure	22
售货员	shòuhuò yuán	(n)	[个，位]	salesperson, clerk	12
书	shū	(n)	[本，部]	book	4
书店	shūdiàn	(n)	[个，家]	bookstore	5
舒服	shūfu	(adj)		to be comfortable	19
数	shǔ	(v)		to count	12
双	shuāng	(m)		a pair	11
水果	shuǐguǒ	(n)		fruit	18
睡	shuì	(v)		to sleep	17
睡觉	shuì jiào	(vo)		to sleep	20
睡	shuì	(v)		to sleep	
觉	jiào	(n)	[个]	a sleep	
说话	shuō huà	(vo)		to speak, talk	10
说	shuō	(v)		to talk	
话	huà	(n)		speech	
四	sì	(nu)		four	2
送	sòng	(v)		to present, give (a gift)	13
送	sòng	(v)		to bring (to someone)	14
宿舍	sùshè	(n)	[个，间]	dormitory, living quarters	4
随便	suíbiàn	(adj)		to be casual, informal; as one likes	13
所以	suǒyǐ	(c)		so, therefore	22

T

她	tā	(pro)		she, her	1
他	tā	(pro)		he, him	1
它	tā	(pro)		it	21

他们	tāmen	(pro)		they, them	1
太	tài	(adv)		too	9
弹	tán	(v)		to play (a string instrument or piano)	21
汤	tāng	(n)	[个]	soup	14
糖	táng	(n)		sugar, sweets, candy	18
疼	téng	(adj)		to pain, to ache, to be painful	20
体育馆	tǐyùguǎn	(n)	[个]	gymnasium	9
天	tiān	(n)		day of the week; sky, heaven	3
天气	tiānqì	(n)		weather	19
跳舞	tiào wǔ	(vo)		to dance	21
跳	tiào	(v)		to jump	
舞	wǔ	(n)	[个]	dance	
听	tīng	(v)		to listen	6
听见	tīngjian	(v)		to hear	15
听说	tīngshuō	(v)		to have heard	19
听写	tīngxiě	(v, n)		to take dictation; dictation	10
同学	tóngxué	(n)	[个，位]	classmate	2
头	tóu	(n)	[个]	head	20
图书馆	túshūguǎn	(n)	[个]	library	4

W

外边儿	wàibianr	(n-pw)		outside	8
完	wán	(v)		to finish, complete (does not take a direct object); wán le! 完了！ as used in the text is an idiomatic expression, meaning "I'm finished" or "I'm in trouble."	10

玩儿	wánr	(v)		to play, to pass time enjoyably	22
晚	wǎn	(adj)		to be late	16
晚会	wǎnhuì	(n)	[个]	evening social event (entertainment, show, etc.)	21
晚上	wǎnshang	(n)	[个]	evening	4
往	wǎng, wàng	(prep)		toward, to (in the direction of)	12
网球	wǎngqiú	(n)	[个]	tennis	9
网球场	wǎngqiúchǎng	(n)	[个]	tennis court	9
忘	wàng	(v)		to forget (since by its nature, it is action that has occurred, wàng is always followed by le, a resultative complement, or negated with méi)	18
位	wèi	(m)		polite measure word for people	7
喂	wèi	(i)		hello (telephone usage)	7
味道	wèidao	(n)		flavor, taste	18
为什么	wèishénme	(pro)		why	3
问	wèn	(v)		to ask	3
问题	wèntí	(n)	[个]	a question	3
我	wǒ	(pro)		I, me	1
我们	wǒmen	(pro)		we, us	2
五	wǔ	(nu)		five	2

X

西餐	xīcān	(n)	[顿]	Western food	14
西南	xīnán	(n-pw)		southwest	9
洗	xǐ	(v)		to wash	17
喜欢	xǐhuan	(v)		to like, enjoy	6

下	xià	(n-pw)		below (a bound word); next (of month, week, time, etc.)	3
下边儿	xiàbianr	(n-pw)		bottomside, under side	11
下车	xià chē	(vo)		to get off a vehicle	16
下	xià	(v)		to get down from	
车	chē	(n)	[辆]	a wheeled vehicle	
下课	xià kè	(vo)		to end class, finish a lesson	5
下	xià	(v)		to finish (class, work)	
课	kè	(n)	[节]	class	
下楼	xià lóu	(vo)		to go downstairs	11
下	xià	(v)		to go down	
楼	lóu	(n)	[层 céng]	storied building	
夏天	xiàtiān	(n)	[个]	summer	19
下午	xiàwǔ	(n)	[个]	afternoon, PM	5
下雪	xiàxuě	(vo)		to snow	19
下	xià	(v)		to come down, fall	
雪	xuě	(n)		snow	
下雨	xià yǔ	(vo)		to rain	19
下	xià	(v)		to come down, fall	
雨	yǔ	(n)		rain	
先	xiān	(adv)		first, beforehand	9
咸	xián	(adj)		to be salty	18
现在	xiànzài	(n)		now	3
箱子	xiāngzi	(n)	[个，只]	valise, suitcase, box	11
想	xiǎng	(o.v)		to want to, to think	6
小	xiǎo	(adj)		to be small; to be young	5
小姐	xiǎojie	(n)	[位]	miss (used for addressing service personel and younger women in general)	14
小时	xiǎoshí	(n)	[个]	hour	11

小说	xiǎoshuō	(n)	[本，部]	novel, fiction	17
笑	xiào	(v)		to laugh, smile	13
笑话儿	xiàohuar	(n)	[个]	joke	21
(一)些	(yì)xiē	(m)		several; some (compare jǐ-, which is specifically "a few", less than ten. Xiē can be more, but less than the majority, "a portion.")	17
鞋	xié	(n)	[双，只]	shoes	11
写字	xiě zì	(vo)		to write	10
写	xiě	(v)		to write	
字	zì	(n)	[个]	graph, character	
谢谢	xièxie	(v)		thanks	7
新	xīn	(adj)		to be new	5
新年	xīnnián	(n)		the new year; New Year's	18
信	xìn	(n)	[封 fēng]	letter	15
星期	xīngqī	(n)	[个]	week	3
星期日	xīngqīrì	(n)	[个]	Sunday	3
行	xíng	(adj)		(here:) to be capable often as here, used ironically	12
行李	xíngli	(n)	[件]	luggage	22
姓	xìng	(v, n)	[个]	to be surnamed	2
修理	xiūlǐ	(v)		to repair	19
休息	xiūxi	(v)		to rest	10
学	xué	(v)		to study	3
学期	xuéqī	(n)	[个]	semester, school term	20
学生	xuésheng	(n)	[个]	student	2
学习	xuéxí	(v)		to study	7

学校	xuéxiào	(n)	[个]	school	6

Y

盐	yán	(n)		salt	18
要	yào	(o.v)		should, be supposed to	10
要	yào	(v)		to ask for	14
爷爷	yéye	(n)	[个]	paternal grandfather	15
也	yě	(adv)		also, too	1
夜里	yèli	(n)		at night	20
一	yī	(nu)		one	2
衣服	yīfu	(n)	[件]	clothing	11
一…就…	yī … jiù …			as soon as; if X so much as …, …	20
医生	yīshēng	(n)	[个，位]	doctor	15
一定	yídìng	(adv)		definitely; to be definite, certain	9
一共	yígòng	(adv)		altogether, in all	14
一下儿	yí xiàr	(nu, m)		one time, once (as a counter following many verbs, it takes the edge off what might be taken as an order otherwise)	7
一样	yíyàng	(adj)		to be the same	15
以后	yǐhòu	(n)		after, later, afterwards	6
已经	yǐjīng	(adv)		already	12
以前	yǐqián	(n)		before	17
以为	yǐwéi	(v)		to assume, take (incorrectly) that	15
椅子	yǐzi	(n)	[把，个]	chair	21
(一)点儿	(yì)diǎnr	(m)		a little, some	11

一会儿	yíhuìr; yì huǐr	(n)		a while, a moment	9
一起	yìqǐ	(adv, n)		together	3
意思	yìsi	(n)	[个]	meaning	20
一直	yìzhí	(adv)		directly, straight on	16
阴天	yīntiān	(n)	[个]	cloudy day, overcast day	19
音乐	yīnyuè	(n)	[种 zhǒng]	music	6
饮料	yǐnliào	(n)	[瓶，杯]	beverages, drinks	14
应该	yīnggāi	(o.v)		should, ought to	14
用	yòng	(v)		to use, to spend	13
游泳	yóuyǒng	(v)		to swim	9
游泳池	yóuyǒngchí	(n)	[个]	swimming pool	9
有	yǒu	(v)		to have, to exist	2
有的	yǒude	(pro)		some	3
有（一）点儿	yǒu(yì)diǎnr	(adv)		slight, somewhat, a bit	18
有意思	yǒuyìsi	(vo)		to be interesting	6
右	yòu	(n-pw)		right	12
又	yòu	(adv)		once again (repetition which has taken place)	14
右边儿	yòubianr	(n-pw)		right side, to the right	8
又…又…	yòu … yòu …			both … and …	10
愉快	yúkuài	(adj)		to be content, happy; to be pleasant (of an affair, event)	22
雨伞	yǔsǎn	(n)	[把]	umbrella	19
预报	yùbào	(n, v)		forecast	19
预习	yùxí	(v)		to prepare for a lesson	3

元	yuán	(m)		dollar. <u>Kuài</u> above is not the normal written form; <u>yuán</u> is. Both are spoken.	12
远	yuǎn	(adj)		to be far, distant	11
约	yuē	(v)		to set (a time), to make an appointment	6
月	yuè	(n)	[个]	month (a bound word); moon	3

Z

杂志	zázhì	(n)	[本]	magazine	17
在	zài	(v, prep)		to be in, on, at	4
再	zài	(adv)		then (opens a second clause, the action of which is done only when the action of the first clause has taken place), again, once more	6
在	zài	(adv)		before verb or verb phrase, indicated that the action is in progress	15
再见	zàijiàn	(v)		goodbye	7
早	zǎo	(adj)		to be early	16
早饭	zǎofàn	(n)	[顿]	breakfast	17
早上	zǎoshang	(n)	[个]	morning	16
这么	zème; zhème	(pro)		to this degree, so	19
怎么	zěnme	(pro)		how, in what way	10
怎么办	zěnme bàn			What's to be done? What'll I/you/we do?	20
怎么啦	zěnme la	(i.e)		What's up? Is there something wrong? Have you got a problem with that?	8

怎么样	zěnme yàng	(pro)	How is it? How goes it? How about it?	6
站	zhàn	(v)	to stand	15
站	zhàn	(n, m) [个]	station, stop	16
张	zhāng	(m)	a sheet of (for flat surfaced object, including paper, tables and tortillas)	6
长	zhǎng	(v)	to grow	15
着	zháo	(v)	(a verbal complement of result, indicating the successful attaining of the action)	17
着急	zháo jí	(vo)	to be anxious, nervous	16
找	zhǎo	(v)	to look for	6
找	zhǎo	(v)	to give change; to look for	12
照片	zhàopiàn	(n) [张]	photograph	15
照相	zhào xiàng	(vo)	to take pictures, photograph	18
照相机	zhàoxiàngjī	(n) [个]	camera	18
着	zhe	(part)	(continuous aspect verbal suffix)	15
这	zhèi; zhè	(pro)	this	2
真	zhēn	(adv)	to be real, genuine	9
真的	zhēnde	(adj)	really	14
真丝	zhēnsī	(n)	pure silk	22
正在	zhèngzài	(adv)	in the process of (same as zài above, except that zhèngzài is used for immediate ongoing actions)	15
这儿	zhèr	(pro)	here	4
支	zhī	(m)	measure for slender objects, e.g., pens, chopsticks	13

知道	zhīdao	(v)		to know	9
直接	zhíjiē	(adj)		to be direct	17
只	zhǐ	(adv)		only (usually followed by a quantified noun that *is not* the subject)	12
纸	zhǐ	(n)	[张]	paper	12
钟	zhōng	(n)		in time expressions follows words such as diǎn to indicate time "of the clock"; a clock	6
中部	zhōngbù	(n)		the central part	19
中餐	zhōngcān	(n)	[顿]	Chinese food	14
中间(儿)	zhōngjiān(r)	(n-pw)		in the middle, at the center	8
钟头	zhōngtóu	(n)	[个]	hour	17
中午	zhōngwǔ	(n)		noon	5
中学	zhōngxué	(n)	[个]	middle school, high school	15
种	zhǒng	(m)	[个]	kind, sort	12
重要	zhòngyào	(adj)		to be important	20
主意	zhúyi	(n)	[个]	idea	22
祝	zhù	(v)		to wish, offer wishes	13
住	zhù	(v)		to reside, live	16
住	zhù	(v)		(used as a complement of result with certain verbs, meaning "to a point that is fixed or firm")	20
准备	zhǔnbèi	(v)		to prepare	22
桌子	zhuōzi	(n)	[张，个]	table, desk	15
自己	zìjǐ	(pro)		oneself	13
自行车	zìxíngchē	(n)	[辆]	bicycle	16
总是	zǒngshi	(adv)		always	19

总站	zǒngzhàn	(n)	[个]	terminus, last stop	16
走	zǒu	(v)		to walk	11
走	zǒu	(v)		to go away, to leave; to walk	18
最	zuì	(adv)		most	5
最后	zuìhòu	(adv, n)		last, lastly, final	20
最近	zuìjìn	(n)		recently	17
昨天	zuótiān	(n)		yesterday	3
左	zuǒ	(n-pw)		left	16
左边儿	zuǒbianr	(n-pw)		left side, to the left	8
做	zuò	(v)		to do	4
坐	zuò	(v)		to sit	13
作业	zuòyè	(n)		homework	4

专有名词 Proper Nouns

安娜	Ānnà		Anna	2
北京	Běijīng		Beijing	22
大卫	Dàwèi		David	1
德国	Déguó		Germany	7
方小英	Fāng Xiǎoyīng		Fang Xiaoying	1
韩国	Hánguó		Korea (Southern)	1
汉语	Hànyǔ		the Han Language, Chinese	5
《汉语小词典》	*Hànyǔ Xiǎo Cídiǎn*	[本]	*A Concise Chinese Dictionary*	5
汉字	Hànzì	[个]	Chinese characters	10
家常豆腐	jiāchángdòufu		homestyle bean curd	14
假日饭店	Jiàrì Fàndiàn		Holiday Inn	16

金中一	Jīn Zhōngyī	Kim Chung-il	1
辣子鸡丁儿	làzijīdīngr	diced chicken with chili peppers	14
马丁	Mădīng	Martin	8
美国	Měiguó	America	1
南湖公园	Nánhú Gōngyuán	Southlake Park	16
日本	Rìběn	Japan	1
山本	Shānběn	Yamamoto	1
上海	Shànghăi	Shanghai	22
糖醋鱼	tángcùyú	sweet and sour fish	14
天星电影院	Tiānxīng Diànyĭngyuàn	Star Theater	4
王	Wáng	(a surname)	10
西安	Xī'ān	Xi'an	22
谢	Xiè	(a surname)	10
《新英汉词典》	*Xin Yīng Hàn Cídiăn* [本]	*A New English-Chinese Dictionary*	12
英国	Yīngguó	England	1
张	Zhāng	(a surname)	2
中国	Zhōngguó	China	1
中文	Zhōngwén	Chinese (usually, but not always, refers to the written language)	8

Grammar Notes — Index
语法点索引

(References in parentheses are to chapter and section numbers. Following them are page numbers.)